STUDY GUIDE

FOR

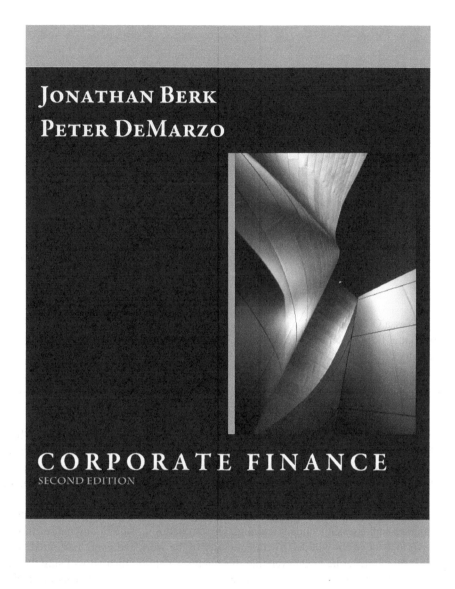

JONATHAN BERK
PETER DEMARZO

CORPORATE FINANCE
SECOND EDITION

MARK SIMONSON

Arizona State University

Pearson Prentice Hall

Boston San Francisco New York
London Toronto Sydney Tokyo Singapore Madrid
Mexico City Munich Paris Cape Town Hong Kong Montreal

Acquisitions Editor: Tessa O'Brien
Executive Developmental Editor: Rebecca Ferris-Caruso
Production Editor: Alison Eusden
Manufacturing Buyer: Linda Cox

Pearson Prentice Hall™ is a trademark of Pearson Education, Inc.

Prentice Hall
is an imprint of

www.pearsonhighered.com

1 2 3 4 5 6 BRR 13 12 11 10

ISBN-13: 978-0-13-610395-0
ISBN-10: 0-13-610395-2

Contents

Contents

Preface

This study guide for the Second Edition of *Corporate Finance* by Jonathan Berk and Peter DeMarzo is designed to help students prepare for exams by ensuring that they grasp all the major ideas in the chapters as well as the general problem-solving methodology.

The study guide's focus is on: 1) providing a comprehensive chapter synopsis, 2) presenting a description of key terms that should be understood for exams, 3) providing answers to the Concept Check questions in the textbook, and 4) providing a general methodology for solving the different types of problems that may be asked on a typical exam along with detailed, step-by-step solutions. There are also further practice problems as well, but remember that the textbook has several good problems that can be used to get further practice solving problems.

Each chapter contains five sections.

- The "Chapter Synopsis" provides a two to three page overview of the chapter's discussion. Readers can reinforce their general understanding of the vast majority of the chapter's 30 pages or so in a few pages.

- The "Selected Concepts and Key Terms" section provides a description of the important Key Terms identified by the authors in the text.

- The "Concept Check Questions and Answers" section lists the Concept Check questions along with a brief answer drawn from the discussion in the textbook.

- The "Examples with Step-by-Step Solutions" section discusses a general methodology that can be used to solve problems based on the chapter's content and provides some relatively complex examples with detailed, step-by-step solutions. Emphasis is on providing a problem-solving framework and walking through the thought process used to solve the problems rather than just showing the final solution.

- The "Questions and Problems" section provides further example question and problems with solutions.

Used in conjunction with the textbook, course lectures, and other course assignments and case studies, I hope that this study guide will help the reader gain an in-depth understanding of the theory and practice of corporate finance.

Mark Simonson
W. P. Carey School of Business
Arizona State University

CHAPTER 1

The Corporation

Chapter Synopsis

1.1 The Four Types of Firms

A **sole proprietorship** is a business owned by one person who has unlimited liability for the debt and other liabilities incurred by the firm. The business itself pays no income taxes; instead, the owner is responsible for paying tax on the firm's profits. An estimated 72% of businesses in the United States are organized as sole proprietorships, but they account for only 5% of business revenue.

A **partnership** is a business with at least two owners who have unlimited liability for the debt and other liabilities of the firm. Similar to sole proprietorships, the partners are responsible for paying taxes on the profits the firm generates, but the partnership pays no business taxes. An estimated 5% of businesses in the United States are partnerships, and they account for about 8% of revenue.

A **limited partnership** is a partnership with two kinds of owners: general partners, who are responsible for overseeing the firm's activities and have unlimited liability; and limited partners, who have limited liability but cannot legally be involved in making managerial decisions for the business.

A **limited liability company** (LLC) is a firm with one or more owners in which there is limited liability for the owner(s). LLCs are typically taxed like a sole proprietorship or partnership. Only about 2% of all business are LLCs, and they account for just 3% of revenue.

A **corporation** is a legal entity separate from its owners, whose liability is limited to the amount they have invested in the firm. Corporations make up 20% of all U.S. businesses and account for 85% of revenue. Ownership in a corporation is divided into shares of stock and owners are called stockholders or shareholders. A corporation is generally more complicated to form, and its governance is dictated by its corporate charter and laws in the state in which it is incorporated. A corporation meeting certain restrictions, such has having fewer than 75 stockholders, can elect to be treated as an S-corporation and be taxed like a sole proprietorship or partnership. Otherwise, the corporation must pay corporate taxes on profits every year and is referred to as a C-corporation. If a C-corporation elects to pay dividends from its after-tax net income, the stockholders receiving the dividends are generally taxed on the dividends received, which results in double taxation.

1.2 Ownership Versus Control of Corporations

Shareholders exercise control over the firm's operations by voting for the **board of directors** who are responsible for overseeing the firm's operation. The board delegates most daily decision making authority to the firm's management, which is headed by the chief executive officer (CEO).

Within the corporation, financial managers are responsible for three main tasks: making investment decisions, making financing decisions, and managing the firm's cash flows.

In theory, the goal of a firm should be determined by the firm's owners. A sole proprietorship has a single owner who runs the firm, so the goals of a sole proprietorship are the same as the owner's goals. But in organizational forms with multiple owners, the appropriate goal of the firm—and thus of its managers—is not as clear.

Since corporations frequently have thousands of shareholders, ownership and control of the firm are separated. Potentially, most of the stock is owned by a widely diffused group of stockholders who aren't on the board of directors or management team, but the board of directors and senior managers have direct control of the corporation. The separation of ownership and control in this context is generally referred to as an **agency** (or **principal-agent**) **problem:** The board and managers are agents of the principals (the stockholders), and there is a problem if the two have different interests. The stockholders can try and reduce any agency problems by ensuring that managers' compensation is tied to firm performance and that underperforming managers are fired. They can also mount a hostile takeover (or threaten a hostile takeover) by acquiring a controlling interest in the firm's stock and replacing the existing board.

1.3 The Stock Market

Since stock in a corporation can be widely held and has limited liability, it is often listed on a **stock exchange** and traded in the public **stock market** so the firm is a **public corporation.** Publicly traded stock often has a high level of **liquidity,** which refers to the ability to sell shares close to the price you can contemporaneously buy them for.

When a corporation itself issues new shares of stock and sells them to investors, it does so in the **primary market.** After this initial transaction between the corporation and investors, the shares continue to trade in a **secondary market** between investors without the involvement of the corporation.

The New York Stock Exchange (NYSE) is a physical exchange in which **market makers** known as **specialists** match buyers and sellers by posting prices at which they are willing to buy shares (the **bid price**) and prices at which they will sell shares (the **ask price**). In general, the lower the **bid-ask spread**, the greater the liquidity of a given stock. While the bid-ask spread is a **transaction cost** to traders, it is a source of profit for the market makers.

The Nasdaq is a non-physical stock exchange in which multiple market makers are able to post bid and ask prices on a computer network.

Selected Concepts and Key Terms

Sole Proprietorship

A business owned by one person who has unlimited liability for the debt and other liabilities incurred by the firm. The business itself pays no income taxes; instead, the owner is responsible for paying tax on the firm's profits.

Partnership

A business with at least two owners who have unlimited liability for the debt and other liabilities of the firm. It is similar to a sole proprietorship in that the partners are responsible for paying taxes on the profits the firm generates but the partnership pays no business taxes.

Limited Partnership

A partnership with two kinds of owners: **general partners** who are responsible for overseeing the firm's activities and have unlimited liability; and **limited partners** who have limited liability but cannot legally be involved in making managerial decision for the business.

Limited Liability Company

A firm with one or more owners in which there is limited liability to the owner(s) that is typically taxed like a sole proprietorship or partnership.

Corporation

A legal entity separate from its owners, who have limited liability. Ownership in a corporation is divided into shares of stock and owners are called stockholders. A corporation meeting certain restrictions, such has having fewer than 75 stockholders, can elect to be treated as an **S-corporation** and be taxed like sole proprietorship or partnership. Otherwise the corporation must pay corporate taxes on profits every year and is referred to as a **C-corporation**. If a C-corporation elects to pay dividends from its after-tax net income, the stockholders receiving the dividends are generally taxed on the dividend, which results in double taxation.

Chief Financial Officer (CFO)

The most senior financial manager in a corporation who often reports directly to the CEO.

Agency Problem or Principal-Agent Problem

A problem that may arise in a corporation because of the separation of ownership and control: Managers may have little incentive to work in the interests of the shareholders when this means working against their own self-interest.

Primary Market

The stock market in which a corporation itself issues new shares of stock and sells them directly to investors.

Secondary Market

After the initial transaction between the corporation and investors in the primary market, the shares continue to trade in the secondary market between investors without the involvement of the corporation.

Liquidity

The ability to sell shares close to the price you can contemporaneously buy them for. **Market makers** match buyers and sellers by posting prices at which they are willing to buy shares (the **bid price**) and prices at which they will sell shares (the **ask price**). In general, the lower the **bid-ask spread,** the greater the liquidity of a given stock. While the bid-ask spread is a **transaction cost** to traders, it is a source of profit for the market makers.

Concept Check Questions and Answers

1.1.1. What is a limited liability company (LLC)? How does it differ from a limited partnership?

A limited liability company (LLC) is a limited partnership without a general partner. All the owners have limited liability, but they can also run the business. A limited partnership, in contrast, has two kinds of owners: general partners and limited partners. General partners run the business and are personally liable for the firm's debt obligations. Limited partners cannot run the business, and their liability is limited to their investment in the limited partnership.

1.1.2. What are the advantages and disadvantages of organizing a business as a corporation?

A corporation has the following advantages: 1) Stockholders have limited liability; 2) it is easy to transfer ownership; 3) the corporation has unlimited life; and 4) outside funding is only limited by the corporation's future business prospects. The disadvantage of a corporation is double taxation: The corporation pays tax on its profits, and when the profits are distributed to the shareholders, the shareholders pay their own personal income tax on this income.

1.2.1. What are the three main tasks of a financial manager?

Financial managers are responsible for three main tasks: making investment decisions, making financing decisions, and managing the firm's cash flows.

1.2.2. What is a principal-agent problem that may exist in a corporation?

The principal-agent problem arises from the separation of ownership and control in a corporation. Managers may pursue their own self-interest instead of working for the interests of the shareholders.

1.2.3. How may a corporate bankruptcy filing affect the ownership of a corporation?

In bankruptcy, management is given the opportunity to reorganize the firm and renegotiate with debt holders. If this process fails, control of the corporation generally passes from equity holders to debt holders. In most cases, the end result is often a change in ownership of the corporation.

1.3.1. What is the New York Stock Exchange (NYSE)?

The NYSE is the largest stock exchange in the world. Billions of dollars of stocks are exchanged every day on the NYSE. The NYSE is a physical place located in New York City. On the floor of the NYSE, market makers, known as specialists, match buyers and sellers.

1.3.2. What advantage does a stock market provide to corporate investors?

The advantage a stock market provides to corporate investors is liquidity. Investors in a public company can easily and quickly turn their investments into cash by simply selling their shares on one of the organized stock markets.

CHAPTER 2

Introduction to Financial Statement Analysis

Chapter Synopsis

2.1 Firms' Disclosure of Financial Information

U.S. companies with publicly traded securities are required to file financial statements with the Securities and Exchange Commission (SEC) in accordance with the 1933 and 1934 Securities Acts. In addition to the annual filings (form 10-K) and quarterly filings (form 10-Q) to the SEC, firms must also include financial statements in the annual report provided for shareholders. The statements must conform to Generally Accepted Accounting Principals (GAAP) and be audited by an independent third-party accounting firm. Investors, financial analysts, managers, and other interested parties such as creditors rely on financial statements to obtain reliable information about a corporation.

The production of financial statements to satisfy SEC requirements is called financial reporting. Firms may also produce different financial statements for the Internal Revenue Service in what is known as tax reporting. For financial reporting, every public company is required to produce four financial statements: the balance sheet, the income statement, the statement of cash flows, and the statement of stockholders' equity.

2.2 The Balance Sheet

The **balance sheet,** or **Statement of Financial Position,** lists the firm's assets and liabilities at a point in time and is divided into two parts (or sides): **assets** and **liabilities and stockholders' equity.** Assets are broken into two categories:

- **Current assets** include cash and assets that can be converted into cash within one year, such as marketable securities, accounts receivable, and inventory.

- **Long-term** (or **fixed**) **assets** include property, plant, and equipment, such as real estate, buildings, or machinery. D**epreciation** is deducted from the value of long-term assets every year. Depreciation is not an actual cash expense but reduces an asset's **book value,** which equals the price paid for the assets minus accumulated depreciation from prior years.

Total assets = total current assets + book value of long-term assets. The liabilities and stockholders' equity side of the balance sheet shows the firm's obligations to creditors as well as stockholders' equity; it includes:

- **Current liabilities** are obligations that will be paid within one year, such as accounts payable, notes payable, and deferred expenses. **Net working capital** is the difference between current assets and current liabilities.

- **Long-term liabilities** include loans longer than one year and capital leases that obligate a firm to make payments to use a long-term asset.

- **Stockholders' equity**, also known as **book value of equity** or **net worth**, is defined as the difference between total assets and total liabilities in the balance sheet identity:

The Balance Sheet Identity

Assets = Liabilities + Stockholders' Equity

The book value of equity is distinct from the **market value of equity**, or stock **market capitalization,** which equals the current stock price times the number of shares outstanding. The market value of equity is generally different because the book value of assets does not perfectly match the market value of the assets and because many of the firm's intangible assets are not captured on the balance sheet at all, such as its ability to manufacture a proprietary software product.

2.3 Balance Sheet Analysis

Useful measures based on balance sheet information include:

$$\text{Market-to-Book Ratio} = \frac{\text{Market Value of Equity}}{\text{Book Value of Equity}}$$

$$\text{Debt-Equity Ratio} = \frac{\text{Total Debt}}{\text{Total Equity}}$$

$$\text{Enterprise Value} = \text{Market Value of Equity} + \text{Debt} - \text{Cash}$$

Variations in the **market-to-book** ratio reflect differences in firm characteristics, such as the industry in which it operates, as well as its growth prospects and the value added by management. The **debt-equity** ratio is commonly used to assess a firm's **leverage,** or the extent to which it relies on debt as a source of financing. As discussed later in the text, a firm's debt-equity ratio has important consequences for the risk and return of its stock, as well the probability of it encountering financial distress. The **enterprise value** of a firm can be used to assess the value of the firm's assets, unencumbered by debt and separate from any cash and marketable securities.

2.4 The Income Statement

The income statement reports a firm's revenues and expenses over a period of time and has the following general form.

    Sales revenue
-   Cost of goods sold (COGS)
=   Gross profit
-   Selling, general and administrative costs (SG&A)
-   Research and development (R&D)
=   Earnings before interest, taxes, depreciation and amortization (EBITDA)
-   Depreciation and amortization
=   Earnings before interest and taxes (EBIT)
-   Interest expense
=   Earnings before taxes (EBT)
-   Taxes
=   Net income

Earnings per share (EPS), which equals (net income) ÷ (shares outstanding), can be measured based on the current amount of shares outstanding or on a fully diluted basis, in which the denominator includes the number of shares that would be issued if all employee stock options were exercised and convertible bonds were converted to stock.

2.5 Income Statement Analysis

Useful ratios based on income statement information include:

$$\text{Net Profit Margin} = \frac{\text{Net Income}}{\text{Sales}}$$

$$\text{Return on Equity (ROE)} = \frac{\text{Net Income}}{\text{Book Value of Equity}}$$

$$\text{Price-to-Earnings (P/E) Ratio} = \frac{\text{Market Capitalization}}{\text{Net Income}} = \frac{\text{Stock Price}}{\text{Earnings per Share}}$$

Profitability ratios, such as the net profit margin and ROE, are an indication of a firm's efficiency and its pricing strategy. Valuation ratios, such as the P/E ratio and the market-to-book ratio, tend to be high for **growth stocks,** which are expected to have high earnings growth, and to be low for **value stocks**, which have low growth prospects.

The determinants of a firm's ROE can be analyzed using a tool called the **DuPont Identity,** named for the company that popularized its use. The DuPont Identity expresses the ROE in terms of the firm's profitability, asset efficiency, and leverage.

$$\text{ROE} = \underbrace{\left(\frac{\text{Net Income}}{\text{Sales}}\right)}_{\text{Net Profit Margin}} \times \underbrace{\left(\frac{\text{Sales}}{\text{Total Assets}}\right)}_{\text{Asset Turnover}} \times \underbrace{\left(\frac{\text{Total Assets}}{\text{Book Value of Equity}}\right)}_{\text{Equity Multiplier}}$$

The first term in the DuPont Identity is the firm's net profit margin, which measures its overall profitability. The second term is the firm's **asset turnover,** which measures how efficiently the firm is utilizing its assets to generate sales. The final term is a measure of leverage called the **equity multiplier,** which indicates the value of assets held per dollar of shareholder equity. The equity multiplier will be higher the greater the firm's reliance on debt financing.

Analysts use a number of ratios to gauge the market value of the firm. The most common is the firm's price-earnings ratio (P/E).

$$P/E \text{ Ratio} = \frac{\text{Market Capitalization}}{\text{Net Income}} = \frac{\text{Share Price}}{\text{Earnings per Share}}$$

The P/E ratio is used to assess whether a stock is over- or undervalued based on the idea that the value of a stock should be proportional to the level of earnings it can generate for its shareholders. P/E ratios tend to be higher for firms with high growth rates.

2.6 The Statement of Cash Flows

The statement of cash flows reclassifies information reported on the balance sheet and income statement and specifies the impact each of three activities has on the firm's cash:

- Cash from **operating activities** = net income + depreciation – changes in net working capital

- Cash from **investment activities** = capital spending – proceeds from sales of long-term assets

- Cash from **financing activities** = new debt + new stock – dividends – stock repurchased

The bottom line of the statement reports the change in the firm's cash over the period, based on the totals from these three activities.

2.7 Other Financial Statement Information

Complete financial reporting statements also include the following.

- The **management discussion and analysis** is a preface to the statements in which management discusses recent events and discloses significant developments.

- The **statement of stockholders' equity** breaks down the stockholders' equity on the balance sheet into the amount that came from issuing new shares versus retained earnings.

- The **notes to the financial statements** discuss details such as stock-based compensation plans for employees and the firm's different types of outstanding debt and leases.

Selected Concepts and Key Terms

Financial Statements

Every public company is required to produce four financial statements: the balance sheet, the income statement, the statement of cash flows, and the statement of stockholders' equity. These financial statements provide investors and creditors with an overview of the firm's financial performance.

Balance Sheet (also called the Statement of Financial Position)

The balance sheet lists the firm's assets and liabilities at a given point in time. It is divided into two parts ("sides"): the assets on the left side and the liabilities and stockholders' equity on the right. The assets list the cash, inventory, property, plant and equipment, and other investments the company has made; the liabilities show the firm's obligations to creditors. Stockholders' equity, the difference between the firm's assets and liabilities, is an accounting measure of the firm's net worth. The two sides of the balance sheet must balance according to the **balance sheet identity**: assets = liabilities + stockholder's equity.

Income Statement (also called the Statement of Financial Performance)

The income statement lists the firm's revenues and expenses over a period of time. The last line of the income statement shows the firm's net income, which is a measure of its after-tax profitability during the period.

Statement of Cash Flows

The statement of cash flows measures the change in cash over a period of time. It is divided into three sections: operating activities, investment activities, and financing activities. The first section, operating activities, adjusts net income by adding back all non-cash entries related to the firm's operating activities. The next section, investment activities, lists the net cash used for investment. The third section, financing activities, shows the flow of cash between the firm and its investors.

Book Value

The book value of a long-term asset is equal to its acquisition cost less accumulated depreciation. Depreciation is not an actual cash expense; it is a way of recognizing that buildings and equipment wear out and thus become less valuable as they get older. For example, net property, plant, and equipment is equal to the total book value of a firm's long-term assets after subtracting the total depreciation from previous years. The **book value of equity**, also known as **stockholders' equity** or **net worth**, is defined as the difference between total assets and total liabilities in the balance sheet identity.

Short-term Debt

Debt that will be repaid within one year.

Market Capitalization

Also known as the total market value of equity, it equals the market price per share times the number of shares. The market capitalization does not depend on the historical cost of the firm's assets; instead, it depends on what investors expect those assets to produce in the future. The book value of equity should not be confused with the market value of equity: The market value of equity may be different because the book value of assets does not perfectly match the market value of the assets and because many of the firm's intangible assets are not captured on the balance sheet.

Enterprise Value

The enterprise value of a firm assesses the value of the underlying business assets, unencumbered by debt and separate from any cash and marketable securities. It can be expressed as:

$$\text{Enterprise Value} = \text{Market Value of Equity} + \text{Debt} - \text{Cash}$$

Asset Turnover

A measure of how efficiently the firm is utilizing its assets to generate sales, which is calculated as Sales/Total Assets.

Equity Multiplier

A measure of leverage that indicates the value of assets held per dollar of shareholder equity; it is calculated as Total Assets/Book Value of Equity. The equity multiplier will be higher the greater the firm's reliance on debt financing.

DuPont Identity

A measurement that summarizes the determinants of a firm's ROE and is calculated as

$$ROE = \underbrace{\left(\frac{\text{Net Income}}{\text{Sales}} \right)}_{\text{Net Profit Margin}} \times \underbrace{\left(\frac{\text{Sales}}{\text{Total Assets}} \right)}_{\text{Asset Turnover}} \times \underbrace{\left(\frac{\text{Total Assets}}{\text{Book Value of Equity}} \right)}_{\text{Equity Multiplier}}.$$

EBIT Margin

A measure of profitability calculated as EBIT/Sales.

Gross Margin

A measure of profitability calculated as Gross Profit/Sales.

Intangible Assets

The balance sheet item that equals the difference between the price paid for the company and the book value assigned to its tangible assets.

Impairment Charge

A reduction in the amount listed on the balance sheet that reflects the change in value of previously acquired intangible assets.

Inventory Days

A measure of how long inventory is held and is calculated as Inventory/Average Daily Cost of Sales.

Sarbanes-Oxley Act (SOX)

Legislation enacted in 2002 that contains provisions intended to improve the accuracy of information given to both boards and shareholders. SOX attempted to achieve this goal in three ways: (1) by overhauling incentives and the independence in the auditing process; (2) by stiffening penalties for providing false information; and (3) by forcing companies to validate their internal financial control processes.

Concept Check Questions and Answers

2.1.1. What are the four financial statements that all public companies must produce?

All public companies must produce four financial statements: the balance sheet, the income statement, the statement of cash flows, and the statement of stockholders' equity.

2.1.2. What is the role of an auditor?

An auditor is a neutral third party hired by the corporation to check the annual financial statements, ensure that they are prepared according to the generally accepted accounting principals (GAAP), and verify that the information is reliable.

2.2.1. What is the balance sheet identity?

Assets = Liabilities + Stockholders' Equity

2.2.2. The book value of a company's assets usually does not equal the market value of those assets. What are some reasons for this difference?

The value of many of the assets listed on the balance sheet is based on their historical cost rather than their true value today. Furthermore, many of the firm's valuable assets, such as the firm's reputation in the marketplace, are not captured on the balance sheet.

2.3.1. What is the difference between a firm's book debt-equity ratio and its market debt-equity ratio?

The book debt-equity ratio uses the values of debt and equity from the balance sheet, while the market debt-equity ratio uses the market values of debt and equity.

2.3.2. What is a firm's enterprise value?

The enterprise value of a firm assesses the value of the underlying business assets, unencumbered by debt and separate from any cash and marketable securities.

It can be expressed as: Enterprise Value = Market Value of Equity + Debt − Cash

2.4.1. What it is the difference between a firm's gross profit and its net income?

Gross profit equals sales minus cost of goods sold, while net income equals sales minus all income statement expenses.

2.4.2. What is diluted earnings per share?

The diluted earnings per share shows the earnings per share the company would have if all the stock options were exercised and all the convertible securities were converted into common shares. The diluted EPS must be lower than the basic EPS.

2.5.1. What is the DuPont Identity?

The DuPont Identity is a measurement that summarizes the determinants of a firm's ROE and is calculated as

$$\text{ROE} = \underbrace{\left(\frac{\text{Net Income}}{\text{Sales}} \right)}_{\text{Net Profit Margin}} \times \underbrace{\left(\frac{\text{Sales}}{\text{Total Assets}} \right)}_{\text{Asset Turnover}} \times \underbrace{\left(\frac{\text{Total Assets}}{\text{Book Value of Equity}} \right)}_{\text{Equity Multiplier}}.$$

2.5.2. How do you use the price-earnings (P/E) ratio to gauge the market value of a firm?

The P/E ratio is the ratio of the stock price to the firm's earnings per share. It is used to assess whether a stock is over- or undervalued based on the idea that the value of a stock should be proportional to the level of earnings it can generate for its shareholders. P/E ratios tend to be higher for firms with high growth rates.

2.6.1. Why does a firm's net income not correspond to cash generated?

There are two reasons that net income does not correspond to cash earned. First, there are non-cash expenses on the income statement, such as depreciation and amortization.

Second, certain uses of cash, such as purchasing a building, are not reported on the income statement.

2.6.2. What are the components of the statement of cash flows?

The statement of cash flows is divided into three sections: operating activities, investment activities, and financing activities.

2.7.1. Where do off-balance sheet transactions appear in a firm's financial statements?

Management is required to disclose any off-balance sheet transactions on the management discussion and analysis (MD&A). Even though off-balance sheet transactions do not appear on the balance sheet, they can have a material impact on the firm's future performance.

2.7.2. What information do the notes to financial statements provide?

The notes to financial statements provide additional information that is very important in fully interpreting the firm's financial statements. For example, the notes show accounting assumptions that were used in preparing the statements. Details of acquisitions, spin-offs, leases, taxes, and risk management activities are also given.

2.8.1. Describe the transactions Enron used to increase its reported earnings.

Enron sold assets at inflated prices to other firms, together with the promise to buy back those assets at even higher future prices. Thus, Enron received cash today in exchange for a promise to pay more cash in the future. But Enron recorded the incoming cash as revenue, and then hid the promises to buy back the assets in a variety of ways.

2.8.2. What is the Sarbanes-Oxley Act?

In 2002, Congress passed the Sarbanes-Oxley Act, which requires, among other things, that CEOs and CFOs certify the accuracy and appropriateness of their firm's financial statements and increases the penalties against them if their financial statements later prove to be fraudulent.

Examples with Step-by-Step Solutions

Solving Problems

Problems using the concepts in this chapter generally involve understanding the basic format used in simple financial statements. For example, you should be able to identify which statements would be affected by specific events and what effect the events would have on variables such as earnings per share and book value of equity. You may also have to calculate ratios based on the financial statement information.

Examples

1. Your firm is considering purchasing a machine for $2.5 million, which would be depreciable straight line over 5 years. The machine will allow you to sell products that increase sales by $5 million per year. The cost of goods sold would increase by 50% of sales, but other costs would not change. If the firm has 1 million shares outstanding and pays 35% in taxes, what affect would this project have on earnings per share in each of the next 5 years?

   Step 1. Determine what financial statements would be affected and what statement(s) need to be forecasted to answer the question.

The question asks for the effect on earnings per share, which depends on net income, so the incremental income statements must be forecasted each year.

Step 2. Forecast the income statements for years 1 through 5 using the fact that depreciation would be $2.5 million / 5 = $500,000 million per year.

	1	2	3	4	5
Sales revenue	5,000,000	5,000,000	5,000,000	5,000,000	5,000,000
- Cost of goods sold	2,500,000	2,500,000	2,500,000	2,500,000	2,500,000
= Gross profit	2,500,000	2,500,000	2,500,000	2,500,000	2,500,000
- Depreciation	500,000	500,000	500,000	500,000	500,000
= EBT	2,000,000	2,000,000	2,000,000	2,000,000	2,000,000
- Taxes	700,000	700,000	700,000	700,000	700,000
= Net income	1,300,000	1,300,000	1,300,000	1,300,000	1,300,000

Step 3. Calculate EPS by dividing net income by 1 million shares.

	1	2	3	4	5
Net income	1,300,000	1,300,000	1,300,000	1,300,000	1,300,000
Number of shares	1,000,000	1,000,000	1,000,000	1,000,000	1,000,000
Earnings per share	$1.30	$1.30	$1.30	$1.30	$1.30

So, earnings per share would increase by $1.30 each year.

2. **Your firm is considering purchasing the machine in problem 1 for $2.5 million, which would be depreciable straight line over 5 years. To finance the purchase, you will issue $2.5 in new common stock. Working capital would not change. If your firm pays no dividends, what affect will the project have on the book value of equity in each of the next 5 years?**

Step 1. Determine what financial statements would be affected and what statement(s) need to be forecasted to answer the question.

The book value of equity is on the balance sheet, so that must be forecasted. In addition, retained earnings need to be determined, so the income statements must also be forecasted—which is already done in the solution to problem 1.

Step 2. Forecast the balance sheets using the fact that retained earnings will be $1,300,000 each year because no net income is paid as dividends.

Cash	0	1,300,000	2,600,000	3,900,000	5,200,000	6,500,000
Total current assets	0	1,300,000	2,600,000	3,900,000	5,200,000	6,500,000
Long-term assets	2,500,000	2,500,000	2,500,000	2,500,000	2,500,000	2,500,000
Less: Accumulated depr.	0	500,000	1,000,000	1,500,000	2,000,000	2,500,000
Net Long-term assets	2,500,000	2,000,000	1,500,000	1,000,000	500,000	0
Total Assets	2,500,000	3,300,000	4,100,000	4,900,000	5,700,000	6,500,000
Liabilities and Equity						
Current liabilities	0	0	0	0	0	0
Long-term liabilities	0	0	0	0	0	0
Total Liabilities	0	0	0	0	0	0
Book value of equity	2,500,000	3,300,000	4,100,000	4,900,000	5,700,000	6,500,000
Total Liabilities and Equity	2,500,000	3,300,000	4,100,000	4,900,000	5,700,000	6,500,000

At time 0, book value of equity will increase by $2.5 million, the amount of the new stock issued.

Beginning in year 1, book value of equity will increase each year by $800,000.

3. **Your firm is considering purchasing the machine in problem 1 for $2.5 million, which would be depreciable straight line over 5 years. To finance the purchase, you will issue $2.5 in new stock. Working capital would not change. How would the purchase of the machine affect how much cash the firm has in years 1–5?**

   Step 1. Determine what financial statements would be affected and what statement(s) need to be forecasted to answer the question.

   The statement of cash flows can be forecasted to determine the change in cash. [Note that you could also just use the information on the income statements and balance sheets to measure the same change.]

   Step 2. Forecast the statement of cash flows.

Depreciation	500,000	500,000	500,000	500,000	500,000
Cash from operating activities	1,800,000	1,800,000	1,800,000	1,800,000	1,800,000
Investment activities					
Capital expenditures	-2,500,000	0	0	0	0
Cash from investing activities	-2,500,000	0	0	0	0
Financing activities					
Dividends paid	0	0	0	0	0
Sale or purchase of stock	2500000	0	0	0	0
Increase in borrowing	0	0	0	0	0
Cash from financing activities	2500000	0	0	0	0
Change in Cash	1,800,000	1,800,000	1,800,000	1,800,000	1,800,000

Thus, cash increases by $1.8 million each year.

Questions and Problems

1. On October 2nd of 2005, Starbucks had a book value of equity of $2 billion, 768 million shares outstanding, and a market price of $30 per share. Starbucks also had cash of $207 million, and total debt of $1.4 billion.
   [A] What was Starbucks' market capitalization? What was Starbucks' market-to-book ratio?
   [B] What was Starbucks' book debt-equity ratio? What was its market debt-equity ratio?
   [C] What was Starbucks' enterprise value?

2. Suppose your firm receives a $10 million order on the last day of the accounting period. You fill the order with $5 million worth of inventory. The customer picks up the products the same day, pays $1 million now, and will pay the remaining balance in 30 days. Ignoring tax consequences how does the transaction affect net working capital in that accounting period?

3. Suppose a firm's tax rate is 40%.
   [A] What effect would a $100 million operating expense have on this year's Net Income? What effect would it have on next year's Net Income?
   [B] What effect would a $100 million capital expense have on Net Income in future years if the capital is depreciated straight line over 5 years?

4. Your firm is considering purchasing a machine for $3 million, which would be depreciable straight line over 3 years. The machine will allow you to sell products that increase sales by $10 million per year and the cost of goods sold would increase by 50% of sales but not change any other costs. If the firm has 1 million shares outstanding and pays 35% in taxes, what affect would this project have on earnings per share in each of the next 3 years?

5. Your firm is considering purchasing the machine in problem 4 for $3 million, which would be depreciable straight line over 3 years. To finance the purchase, you will issue $3 in new stock. Working capital would not change. If your firm pays no dividends, what affect will the project have on the book value of equity in each of the next 3 years?

Solutions to Questions and Problems

1. [A] Market Capitalization = 768 million × $30 = $23 billion

$$\text{Market-to-book ratio} = \frac{\$23\,\text{billion}}{\$2\,\text{billion}} = 11.5$$

   [B] Book debt-equity ratio = $\frac{1.4}{2}$ = 0.70

   Market debt-equity ratio = $\frac{1.4}{23}$ = 0.06

   [C] Enterprise value = Market Value of Equity + Debt − Cash = 23 + 1.4 − .207
   = $24.193 billion

2. Since inventory decreased by $5 million and accounts receivable increased by $9 million:

Δ net working capital = Δ current assets − Δ current liabilities = (−$5 + $9) − 0 = $4 million .

3. [A] A $100 million operating expense would be immediately expensed, increasing operating expenses by $100 million. This would lead to a reduction in taxes of 40% × $100 million = $40 million. Thus, earnings would decline by 100 − 40 = $60 million. There would be no effect on next year's earnings.

[B] Depreciation of $20 million would appear each year as an operating expense. Thus, net income would change each of the next 5 years by – $20(0.40)= – $8 million

4. Earnings per share will increase by $2.60 in each of the next three years.

		1	2	3
	Sales revenue	10,000,000	10,000,000	10,000,000
-	Cost of goods sold	5,000,000	5,000,000	5,000,000
=	Gross profit	5,000,000	5,000,000	5,000,000
-	Depreciation	1,000,000	1,000,000	1,000,000
=	EBT	4,000,000	4,000,000	4,000,000
-	Taxes	1,400,000	1,400,000	1,400,000
=	Net income	2,600,000	2,600,000	2,600,000
	Number of shares	1,000,000	1,000,000	1,000,000
	Earnings per share	$2.60	$2.60	$2.60

5. Book value of equity will increase from $3 million at date 0, to $3.9 million at the end of year 3.

	0	1	2	3
Assets				
Cash	0	1,300,000	2,600,000	3,900,000
Total current assets	0	1,300,000	2,600,000	3,900,000
Long-term assets	3,000,000	3,000,000	3,000,000	3,000,000
Less: Accumulated depr.	0	1,000,000	2,000,000	3,000,000
Net Long-term assets	3,000,000	2,000,000	1,000,000	0
Total Assets	3,000,000	3,300,000	3,600,000	3,900,000
Liabilities and Equity				
Current liabilities	0	0	0	0
Long-term liabilities	0	0	0	0
Total Liabilities	0	0	0	0
Book value of equity	3,000,000	3,300,000	3,600,000	3,900,000
Total Liabilities and Equity	3,000,000	3,300,000	3,600,000	3,900,000

CHAPTER 3

Arbitrage and Financial Decision Making

Chapter Synopsis

3.1 Valuing Decisions

When considering an investment opportunity, a financial manager must systematically compare the costs and benefits associated with the project in order to determine whether it is worthwhile. Determining the cash value today of the costs and benefits is one way to make such a comparison.

In a **competitive market,** a good can be bought and sold at the same price, so the market price can be used to determine the cash value today of the good. Because competitive markets exist for many assets, such as commodities and financial securities, they can be used to determine cash values and evaluate decisions in many situations. For example, if gold trades at $250/ounce in a competitive market, then 20 ounces of gold have a cash value today of $5000. A buyer wouldn't need to pay more, and a seller wouldn't need to accept less, so individual preferences are not relevant.

If a manager can observe competitive market prices, he may be able to use them to determine the current cash value of different costs and benefits so they can be compared. For example, if someone offers to trade the manager 20 ounces of gold for 10 ounces of platinum, which trades at $550 per ounce in a competitive market, he should reject the trade. The benefit (the cash value today of the gold, $5000) is smaller than the cost (the cash value today of the platinum, $5500).

By evaluating cost and benefits using competitive market prices, we can determine whether a decision will make the firm and its investors wealthier. This point is one of the central and most powerful ideas in finance, which we call the Valuation Principle:

> The value of an asset to the firm or its investors is determined by its competitive market price. The benefits and costs of a decision should be evaluated using these

market prices, and when the value of the benefits exceeds the value of the costs, the decision will increase the market value of the firm.

The Valuation Principle provides the basis for decision making throughout this text.

3.2 Interest Rates and the Time Value of Money

Many financial problems require the valuation of cash flows occurring at different times. However, money received in the future is worth less than money received today because the money received today can be invested to grow to have a larger value in the future. Thus, money has **time value,** and it is only possible to compare cash flows occurring at different times by bringing them to the same point in time.

For example, suppose that there is an annual **risk-free rate**, r_f, of 7% at which you can borrow or lend without risk. If you have the opportunity to lend $100,000 dollars to receive $105,000 in one year, you should not accept this opportunity. The benefit (the cash value today of the $105,000 in 1 year = $105,000 / (1.07) = $98,131) is smaller than the cost (the cash value today of the $100,000, which is just $100,000). You would be better off investing the $100,000 at the risk-free rate and receiving $107,000 in one year.

3.3 Present Value and the NPV Decision Rule

When the value of a cost or benefit is computed in terms of cash today, it is referred to as the **present value** (PV). The **net present value** (NPV) of a project or investment is the difference between the present value of its benefits and the present value of its costs:

$$\text{Net Present Value (NPV)} = \text{PV(Benefits)} - \text{PV(Costs)}$$

Because the NPV represents a project in terms of cash today, it simplifies decision making and leads to the **net present value rule**:

> When making an investment decision, take the alternative with the highest NPV. Choosing this alternative is equivalent to receiving its NPV in cash today.

Regardless of individual preferences for cash today versus cash in the future, everyone should always maximize NPV first. Investors can then borrow or lend to shift cash flows through time to achieve their preferred pattern of cash flows.

3.4 Arbitrage and the Law of One Price

In a competitive market, the price of a good cannot trade in two different markets at different prices. Such a price discrepancy represents an **arbitrage opportunity** because you can make a riskless profit without making an investment by buying in the low price market and selling in the high price market. Because an arbitrage opportunity has a positive NPV, whenever an arbitrage opportunity appears in financial markets, investors will quickly take advantage of it. The presence of such arbitrage activity leads to the **Law of One Price**:

> If equivalent goods or securities trade simultaneously in different competitive markets, then they will trade for the same price in both markets.

A competitive market in which there are no arbitrage opportunities can be referred to as a **normal market.**

3.5 No-Arbitrage and Security Prices

The Law of One Price has implications for valuing securities, such as a bond. (A bond is a security issued by governments and corporations to raise money from investors today in exchange for future payments.)

For example, suppose you can either (1) buy a riskless bond paying $1000 in one year, or (2) invest money in a riskless bank account that pays 5%. It would require a $1000 / (1.05) = $952.38 investment in the bank account to generate $952.38(1.05) = $1000 in one year. Thus, the price of the bond must be $952.38 or an arbitrage opportunity would exist:

- When the bond is priced below $952.38, the arbitrage strategy involves buying the bond and borrowing $952.38 from the bank. You will owe the bank $1000 in one year, but you can use the bond's payment to pay that back. Your profit today = $952.38 – P > 0.

- When the bond is priced above $952.38, the arbitrage strategy involves selling the bond and investing $952.38 of the proceeds in the bank account. [Note that if you do not own the bond you can **short sell** the bond by borrowing it from your broker and selling it with the promise to replace it in the future.] You will still receive $1000 (from the bank now instead of from the bond) in one year. Your profit today = P – $952.38 > 0.

Thus, the existence of investors trying to exploit such opportunities leads to the existence of the **no-arbitrage price,** $952.38.

When securities trade at no-arbitrage prices, then investing in securities is a zero NPV investment. Thus, in normal markets, trading securities neither creates nor destroys value. Instead, value is created by the real investment projects made by firms, such as developing new products, opening new stores, or creating more efficient production methods. It follows that the firm's investment decision can be separated from its financing choice. This concept is referred to as the **separation principle.**

The Law of One Price has implications for packages of securities as well. Consider two securities, A and B. Suppose a third security, C, has the same cash flows as A and B combined. Because security C is equivalent to the portfolio of A and B, by the Law of One Price, they must have the same price; otherwise, an obvious arbitrage opportunity would exist. This relationship is known as **Value Additivity**:

$$Price(C) = Price(A) + Price(B).$$

Value additivity has an important consequence for the value of an entire firm. Since the cash flows of the firm are equal to the total cash flows of all projects and investments within the firm, the value of the firm equals the sum of the values of all of its projects and other assets. Thus, to maximize the value of the firm, managers should make decisions that maximize the NPV of each project, which represents the project's contribution to the firm's total value.

Appendix: The Price of Risk and Arbitrage with Transaction Costs

Thus far we have considered only cash flows that have no risk. However, in many settings, cash flows are risky. Intuitively, investors will pay less to receive a risky cash flow in the future than they would to receive a certain cash flow because they don't like risk. The notion that investors prefer to have a safe income rather than a risky one of the same average amount is called **risk aversion.**

Because investors care about risk, we cannot use the risk-free interest rate to compute the present value of a risky future cash flow. The increase in the discount rate over the risk-free rate that investors use to value risky cash flows is called the **risk premium.** *When a cash flow is risky, to compute its present value you must discount the expected cash flow at a rate equal to the risk-free interest rate plus an appropriate risk premium.*

The risk of a security cannot be evaluated in isolation. Even when a security's returns are quite variable, if the returns vary in a way that offsets other risks investors are holding, the security may reduce rather than increase investors' risk. As a result, risk can only be assessed relative to the other risks that investors face, so *the risk of a security must be evaluated in relation to the fluctuations of other investments in the economy. A security's risk premium will be higher the more its returns tend to vary with the overall economy and the market index. If the security's returns vary in the opposite direction of the market index, it offers insurance and will have a lower or even a negative risk premium.*

In most markets, you must pay **transaction costs** to trade securities. First, you must pay your broker a commission on the trade. Second, because you will generally pay a slightly higher price when you buy a security (the ask price) than you receive when you sell (the bid price), you will also pay the bid-ask spread. *Thus, when there are transaction costs, arbitrage keeps prices of equivalent goods and securities close to each other. However, prices can deviate, but not by more than the transaction costs of the arbitrage.*

Selected Concepts and Key Terms

Competitive Market

A market in which goods can be bought and sold at the same price. Because competitive markets exist for most commodities and financial assets, we can use them to determine cash values and evaluate decisions in many situations.

Time Value of Money

The idea that it is only possible to compare cash flows occurring at different times by bringing them to the same point in time. When the expected rate of return on invested cash is positive, cash received in the future is worth less than cash received today because less cash can be invested today to equal the future amount. Thus, the **present value** of a future cash flow is less than the amount received in the future, and the **future value** of a cash flow invested in a previous period is worth more than the amount invested in the past.

Risk-Free Interest Rate

The interest rate at which you can borrow or lend without risk. $(1 + r_f)$ is the **interest rate factor** for risk-free cash flows; it defines the exchange rate across time.

Net Present Value (NPV)

The difference between the present value of an investment's benefits and the present value of its costs. The NPV of a project represents its value in terms of cash today.

NPV Decision Rule

Select all projects that have a positive NPV. When choosing among mutually exclusive alternatives, take the alternative with the highest NPV. Choosing this alternative is equivalent to receiving its NPV in cash today.

Arbitrage

The practice of buying and selling equivalent goods in different markets to take advantage of a price difference. A situation in which it is possible to make a profit without taking any risk or making any investment is an **arbitrage opportunity.**

Normal Market

A competitive market in which there are no arbitrage opportunities. The term *efficient market* is also sometimes used to describe a market that, along with other properties, is without arbitrage opportunities.

Law of One Price

If equivalent goods or securities trade simultaneously in different competitive markets, then they will trade for the same price in both markets.

Separation Principle

The idea that a firm's investment decision can be separated from its financing choice. This follows from the idea that, in normal markets, trading securities neither creates nor destroys value. Instead, value is created by the real investment projects made by firms, such as developing new products, opening new stores, or creating more efficient production methods.

Concept Check Questions and Answers

3.1.1. In order to compare the costs and benefits of a decision, what must we determine?

In order to compare the costs and benefits, we need to evaluate them in the same terms—cash today.

3.1.2. If crude oil trades in a competitive market, would an oil refiner that has a use for the oil value it differently than another investor?

No, if crude oil trades in a competitive market, the value of crude oil depends only on the current market price. The personal opinion of an oil refiner or any investor does not alter the value of the decision today.

3.2.1. How do you compare costs at different points in time?

We can compare costs at different points in time by converting the costs in the future to dollars today using the interest rate.

3.2.2. If interest rates rise, what happens to the value *today* of a promise of money in one year?

When interest rates rise, the value of money today to be received in one year is lower. In other words, the higher the discount rate, the lower the value of money today.

3.3.1. What is the NPV decision rule?

The NPV decision rule states that when choosing among alternatives, we should take the alternative with the highest NPV. Choosing this alternative is equivalent to receiving its NPV in cash today.

3.3.2. Why doesn't the NPV decision rule depend on the investor's preferences?

Regardless of our preferences for cash today versus cash in the future, we should always maximize NPV first. We can then borrow or lend to shift cash flows through time and find our most preferred pattern of cash flows.

3.4.1. If the Law of One Price were violated, how could investors profit?

If the Law of One Price were violated, investors can profit by arbitrage. They buy goods or securities at a lower price in one market and simultaneously resell the goods or securities at a higher price in a different market to take advantage of a price difference.

3.4.2. When investors exploit an arbitrage opportunity, how do their actions affect prices?

Investors exploit an arbitrage opportunity when taking advantage of price differences in two separate markets. In doing so, investors will buy in the market where it is cheap and simultaneously sell in the market where it is expensive. As more and more investors compete, the price will rise with increased buy orders in one market and fall with increased sell orders in the other. Arbitrage activities will continue until the prices in the two markets are equal.

3.5.1. If a firm makes an investment that has a positive NPV, how does the value of the firm change?

If a firm makes an investment that has a positive NPV, the value of the firm will increase by the NPV amount today.

3.5.2. What is the separation principle?

The separation principle states that security transactions in a normal market neither create nor destroy value on their own. Therefore, we can evaluate the NPV of an investment decision separately from any security transactions the firm is considering. That is, we can separate the firm's investment decision from its financing choice.

3.5.3. In addition to trading opportunities, what else do liquid markets provide?

Competitive markets depend upon liquidity because liquid markets allow market prices to be determined. When markets become illiquid, it may not be possible to trade at the posted price. As a consequence, we can no longer rely on market prices as a measure of value.

3.A.1 Why does the expected return of a risky security generally differ from the risk-free interest rate? What determines the size of its risk premium?

The expected return of a risky security generally differs from the risk-free interest rate because the expected return includes a risk premium. The higher the variability of returns, the higher the risk premium demanded by investors.

3.A.2. Explain why the risk of a security should not be evaluated in isolation.

The risk of a security must be evaluated in relation to the fluctuations of other investments in the economy. A security's risk premium will be higher the more its returns tend to vary with the overall economy and the market index.

3.A.3. In the presence of transactions costs, why might different investors disagree about the value of an investment opportunity?

In the presence of transaction costs, different investors might disagree about the value of an investment opportunity because investors with high transaction costs will value the investment opportunity less.

3.A.4. By how much could this value differ?

When there are transaction costs, arbitrage keeps prices of equivalent securities close to each other. Prices can deviate, but not by more than the transaction costs of the arbitrag

Examples with Step-by-Step Solutions

Solving Problems

Problems using the ideas in this chapter generally involve:

- Finding the NPV of an investment (or comparing different investment alternatives) by calculating the benefits minus the costs using either competitive market prices, the risk-free rate, or currency exchange rates; or

- Determining no arbitrage prices based on current market prices.

Below are examples of finding the net present value of an investment by calculating the benefits minus the costs using the risk-free rate, finding the net present value of an investment by calculating the benefits minus the costs using competitive market prices, and determining a no-arbitrage price based on current market prices.

Examples

1. You are going to retire in one year, and your defined benefit retirement plan will pay you $3 million on the date you retire. If you work another year, you will get one more year's salary of $100,000 (paid one year from today). Your firm has offered to pay you an early retirement package of $2.9 million if you quit today. The risk-free interest rate is 5%, and there are no income tax effects. Ignoring the fact that one option involves having to show up at work one more year:
   [A]   Which option should you take if you compare them based on dollars today?
   [B]   Which option should you take if you compare them based on dollars in one year?
   [C]   What is the lowest retirement value today that would make you indifferent between the two options?

Step 1. Determine the value of each option in today's dollars. Since there are no cash outflows, the NPV is just the present value of the cash inflows.

Present value of retiring today = $2,900,000

$$\text{Present value of retiring in one year} = \frac{\$3,000,000 + \$100,000}{1.05} = \$2,952,381$$

Thus, you should keep working.

Step 2. Determine the value of each option in next year's dollars.

Future value of retiring today = $2,900,000(1.05) = $3,045,000

Future value of retiring in one year = $3,000,000 + $200,000 = $3,200,000

Thus, you should keep working.

The two approaches, whether comparing the options based on present values or future values, will always provide the same answer.

Step 3. Determine the lowest retirement package today that would make you indifferent between the two options.

You would accept the present value of retiring in one year, $2,952,381. This is equivalent to having $3,200,000 in one year since $2,952,381(1.05) = $3,200,000. In other words, you can take the $2,952,381 payment and invest it at the risk-free rate and end up with $3,200,000.

2. Suppose your employer offers you a choice between a $20,000 bonus and 30 ounces of gold. Whichever one you choose will be awarded today. Gold is trading today at $500 per ounce. Ignoring income tax implications:
   [A] Which form of the bonuses should you choose?
   [B] What do you tell your broker, who advises you to take the gold because he predicts that the price of gold is going to double in value this year?

Step 1. Determine the value of each option.

Value of bonus = $20,000

$$\text{Value of the gold} = 30\left(\frac{\$500}{1\ \text{ounce of gold}}\right) = \$15,000 < \$20,000 \text{ cash bonus.}$$

So, you should take the cash bonus.

Step 2. Address the concern that gold is a good investment.

The reason you can compare the two options above is because gold trades in a competitive market and you can buy it and sell it for the same price. Thus, you would be better of taking the bonus and buying 30 ounces of gold for $15,000; you would still have $5,000 left over.

3. A hedge fund has a portfolio consisting of 1 million shares of Microsoft, which trades at $30 per share, and 1 million shares of Intel, which trades at $20. A stockholder in the hedge fund, which has 500,000 shares outstanding, has offered to sell you 1,000 shares for $75 per share. Does this represent an arbitrage opportunity? If so, how can you exploit it?

Step 1. Determine the no-arbitrage price.

Because the hedge fund is equivalent to a portfolio of Microsoft and Intel, by the Law of One Price, they must have the same price, so:

Value(hedge fund) = Value(Microsoft stock) + Value(Intel Stock)

$$= \$30(1\ \text{million}) + \$20(1\ \text{million}) = \$50\ \text{million.}$$

So, the Value(hedge fund) per share $= \dfrac{\$50,000,000}{500,000} = \$100 > \$75 \Rightarrow$ an arbitrage opportunity.

Step 2. Determine how you would exploit it.

Since you can buy it at a lower price than the components are worth, you should buy the hedge fund shares and sell the components. You can short sell the stocks by borrowing them from your broker and selling them with the promise to replace them in the future.

To take advantage of the situation, you should buy the 1,000 shares for $75(1,000) = $75,000.

Next, short sell $\left(\dfrac{\$30(1,000,000)}{\$30(1,000,000)+\$20(1,000,000)}\right)(\$75,000) = \$45,000$ in Microsoft, and short sell $75,000 – $45,000 = $30,000 of Intel. This amounts to short selling $\dfrac{\$45,000}{\$30} = 1,500$ shares of Microsoft and $\dfrac{\$30,000}{\$20} = 1,500$ shares of Intel. The NPV of the transactions is $25,000.

Questions and Problems

1. Suppose a Treasury bill with a risk-free cash flow of $10,000 in one year trades for $9,615 today. If there are no arbitrage opportunities, what is the current risk-free interest rate?

2. You have an investment opportunity in Italy. It requires an investment of $1 million today and will produce a cash flow of 1 million euros in one year with no risk. Suppose the risk-free interest rate in the United States is 4%, the risk-free interest rate in Italy is 5%, and the current competitive exchange rate is € 1.2 per $1. What is the NPV of this investment? Is it a good opportunity?

3. Suppose the risk-free interest rate is 5.5%.
   [A]   Having $100,000 today is equivalent to having what amount in one year?
   [B]   Having $100,000 in one year is equivalent to having what amount today?

4. Your firm has identified three potential investment projects. All of the projects would use the same a tract of land, so you can only select one of them. All of the projects would generate risk-free cash flows and the risk-free rate is 5%.

   ▨   Project 1 costs $1 and pays $1 million in 1 year

   ▨   Project 2 costs $10 million and pays $12 million in 1 year

   ▨   Project 3 has a cash inflow of $10 million today but a cash outflow of $11 million in 1 year

   What should the firm do?

5. Your employer has notified you that in 1 year you will be lose your job that pays $200,000 per year when you reach mandatory retirement age. They have offered you the choice of leaving today and keeping your company car, a 2005 Mercedes SLK with a Kelley blue book market value of $40,000. If you stay, you don't keep the car. You believe that the most you could make elsewhere is $100,000 next year if you quit and forego your current salary. The risk-free rate is 6%. Ignoring taxes, and assuming that you are paid your salary at the end of the year, what should you do?

Solutions to Questions and Problems

1. The PV of the security's cash flow is ($10,000) / (1 + r), where r is the one-year risk-free interest rate. If there are no arbitrage opportunities, this PV equals the security's price of $9,615 today. Therefore,

$$\$9,615 = \frac{\$10,000}{(1+r)} \Rightarrow (1+r) = \frac{\$10,000}{\$9,615} = 1.04 \Rightarrow r = .04, \text{ or } 4\%.$$

2. Cost = $1 million today

   Benefit = €1 million in one year

$$PV = \left(\frac{€1 \text{ million in one year}}{1.05} \right) = €0.9524 \text{ million today}$$

$$= €0.95 \text{ million today} \times \left(\frac{€1.2}{\$ \text{ today}} \right) = \$1.142857 \text{ million today}$$

$$\Rightarrow NPV = \$1.142857 - \$1 \text{ million } = \$142,857$$

   The NPV is positive, so it is a good investment opportunity.

3. [A]   Having $100,000 today is equivalent to having $100,000 \times 1.055 = \$105,500$ in 1 year.

   [B]   Having $100,000 in one year is equivalent to having $100,000 / 1.055 = \$94,787$ today.

4. Projects 2 and 3 are equally as valuable—select either one.

$$NPV_1 = -\$1 + \frac{\$1,000,000}{1.05} = \$952,381$$

$$NPV_2 = -\$10,000,000 + \frac{\$12,000,000}{1.05} = \$1,428,571.$$

$$NPV_3 = \$10,000,000 + \frac{-\$9,000,000}{1.05} = \$1,428,571$$

5. NPV of staying $= \dfrac{\$200,000}{1.06} = \$186,679$

   NPV of leaving $= \dfrac{\$100,000}{1.06} + 40,000 = \$134,340$

So, you should stay one more year.

CHAPTER 4

The Time Value of Money

Chapter Synopsis

Many financial problems require the valuation of cash flows occurring at different times. However, money received in the future is worth less than money received today because the money received today can be invested to grow to have a larger value in the future. Thus, money has **time value,** and it is only possible to compare cash flows occurring at different times by valuing them at the same point in time.

4.1 The Timeline

The first step in most problems is to put the cash flows involved on a timeline in which each point is a specific date, such as this representation of a $10,000 loan made by a bank to a borrower who promises to pay $6,000 to the bank in each of the next two years:

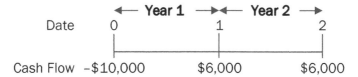

The space between date 0 and date 1 represents the time period between these dates. Date 0 is the beginning of the first year, and date 1 is the end of the first year. Similarly, date 1 is the beginning of the second year, and date 2 is the end of the second year. The signs of the cash flows are important: in the diagram, –$10,000 represents a cash outflow, and $6,000 represents a cash inflow.

4.2 The Three Rules of Time Value

To correctly account for the time value of money, three general rules must be followed:

(1) It is only possible to compare or combine values at the same point in time;

(2) To move a cash flow forward in time, you must compound it; and

(3) To move a cash flow backward in time, you must discount it.

For example, valuation problems often require the determination of the **future value** (FV) of a series of cash flows at a given interest rate, such as in a retirement savings planning application. Invested cash that is earning a positive rate of interest grows at an increasing rate over time in a process called **compounding** in which interest earned in the later periods accrues on both the original value of the cash and the interest earned in the prior periods. The general expressions for the FV of a lump sum, C, invested at rate r for n periods is as follows.

Future Value of a Cash Flow

$$FV_n = C(1+r)^n$$

Other problems seek to determine the **present value** (PV) of a series of future cash flows, such as in the valuation today of a bond that promises to make a series of payments in the future. The process of determining the present value of future cash flows is referred to as **discounting**, and the result is a discounted cash flow value. The general expression for the PV of a lump sum is as follows.

Present Value of a Cash Flow

$$PV = \frac{C_n}{(1+r)^n}$$

4.3 Valuing a Stream of Cash Flows

Applications often involve accurately considering a stream of cash flows occurring at different points in time over N periods:

The PV of such a stream can be found by using:

Present Value of a Cash Flow Stream

$$PV = \frac{C_1}{(1+r)^1} + \frac{C_2}{(1+r)^2} + \cdots + \frac{C_N}{(1+r)^N} = \sum_{n=0}^{N} \frac{C_n}{(1+r)^n}$$

While this equation can generally be used to calculate the present value of future cash flows, there are often certain types of cash flow streams, such as annuities and perpetuities discussed below, that make the calculation less tedious.

4.4 Calculating the Net Present Value

An investment decision can be represented on a timeline as a stream of cash flows. The Net Present Value (NPV) of the project is thus the present value of the stream of cash flows of the opportunity:

NPV = PV(benefits) – PV(costs).

4.5 Perpetuities, Annuities, and Other Special Cases

A **perpetuity** is a stream of equal cash flows that occurs at regular intervals and lasts forever. For example, suppose you could invest $100 in a bank account paying 5% interest per year forever, and you want to create a perpetuity by taking $5 out each year. At the end of one year, you will have $105 in the bank, and you can withdraw the $5 interest and reinvest the $100 for a second year. Again you will have $105 after one year, and you can withdraw $5 and reinvest $100 for another year as depicted in the diagram:

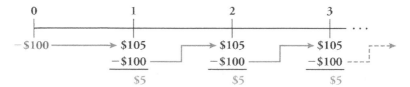

Thus, the PV of the $5 perpetuity with $r = 5\%$ must be $100 = $5 / .05 = C/r$—the cost of replicating the cash flow stream. Thus, the present value of receiving C in perpetuity is:

Present Value of a Perpetuity

$$PV(C \text{ in perpetuity}) = \frac{C}{r}$$

An **annuity** is a stream of equal cash flows paid each period for N periods. Examples of annuities are home mortgage loans and corporate bonds. To determine the PV of an annuity suppose once again that you invest $100 in a bank account paying 5% interest. At the end of one year, you will have $105 in the bank. Using the same strategy as for a perpetuity, suppose you withdraw the $5 interest and reinvest the $100 for a second year. Once again you will have $105 after two years, and you can repeat the process, withdrawing $5 and reinvesting $100 every year for 20 years to close the account and withdraw the principal:

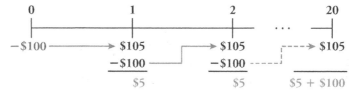

You have created a 20-year, $5 annuity. The value must be the NPV of the cash flows associated with creating it: the initial amount required to fund the annuity minus the PV of the return of the initial amount in N years, or $100 - $100 / (1.05)^{20} = $62.31. In general, the PV of an N-year annuity paying C per period with the first payment one period from date 0 is as follows.

Present Value of an Annuity

$$PV(\text{annuity of } C \text{ for } N \text{ periods}) = C \times \frac{1}{r}\left(1 - \frac{1}{(1+r)^N}\right)$$

Based on these equations, the future value of an annuity can now be calculated as:

Future Value of an Annuity

$$FV(\text{annuity of } C \text{ for } N \text{ periods}) = C \times \frac{1}{r}\left(1 - \frac{1}{(1+r)^N}\right)(1+r)^N = C \times \frac{1}{r}\left((1+r)^N - 1\right)$$

A **growing perpetuity** is a cash flow stream that occurs at regular intervals and grows at a constant rate forever. For example, suppose you invest $100 in a bank account that pays 5% interest. At the end of the first year, you will have $105 in the bank. If you withdraw $3, you will have $102 to reinvest. This amount will then grow to in the following year to $102(1.05) = $107.10 and you can withdraw $3.06 leaving the balance at $104.04.

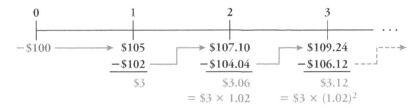

You have created a 2% growing perpetuity with a first payment of $3 so the value must equal the cost to create it, $100 = $3/(.05 − .02)= C/(r − g). In general, the PV of a perpetuity growing at g percent that pays C one period from date 0 is as follows.

Present Value of a Growing Perpetuity

$$PV(\text{perpetuity growing at } g)=\frac{C_1}{r-g}$$

Finally, a **growing annuity** is a stream of N growing cash flows paid at regular intervals, where $N<\infty$. Assuming that the first cash flow, C, is paid at the end of the first period, the present value of an N-period growing annuity is:

Present Value of a Growing Annuity

$$PV(\text{annuity growing at } g)=C\times\left(\frac{1}{r-g}\right)\left(1-\left(\frac{1+g}{1+r}\right)^N\right)$$

4.6 Solving Problems with a Spreadsheet Program

Microsoft Excel has time value of money functions based on the variables defined above. In the program: N = NPER, r = RATE, PV = PV, C = PMT, and FV = FV. You must input four of these variables and then Excel finds the fifth (one can be zero). For example, if you invest $20,000 at 8% for 15 years, how much will you have in 15 years?

The Excel function is = FV(RATE,NPER,PMT,PV)=FV(0.08,15,0,-20000) and the resulting FV equals $63,443.

	NPER	RATE	PV	PMT	FV	Excel Formula
Given	15	8.00%	− 20,000	0		
Solve for FV					63,443	= FV(0.08,15,0,− 20000)

You can also use a financial calculator to do the same calculations. The calculators work in much the same way as the annuity spreadsheet. You enter any four of the five variables, and the calculator calculates the fifth variable.

4.7 Solving for Variables Other Than Present Value or Future Value

Any of the equations above (the future value of a lump sum, the present value of a lump sum, the present value of a perpetuity, the present value of an annuity, the future value of an annuity, the present value of a growing annuity, and the present value of a growing perpetuity) can be solved for any of the variables as long as the remaining variables in the equation are known. For example, the rate of return that makes the net present value of a stream of cash flows equal to zero, the **internal rate of return** (IRR), can be found using the present value of an annuity equation if the present value of the annuity payments (PV), the number of payments (N), and the periodic level cash flow (C) are all known.

Selected Concepts and Key Terms

Time Value of Money

The idea that it is only possible to compare cash flows occurring at different times by bringing them to the same point in time. When the expected rate of return on invested cash is positive, cash received in the future is worth less than cash received today because less cash can be invested today to equal the future amount. Thus, the present value of a future cash flow is less than the amount received in the future, and the future value of a cash flow invested in a previous period is worth more than the amount invested in the past.

Compounding

The process of moving cash forward in time over more than one time period. When cash is invested over multiple periods in the future, interest earned in the later periods grows at an increasing rate because it accrues on both the original value of the cash and the interest earned in the prior periods.

Discounting

The process of moving cash backwards in time. When interest rates are positive, the present value received is less than the value of the future cash flow. The process of calculating such present values is commonly referred to as discounting.

Perpetuity

A stream of cash flows that is received over equal, periodic intervals that lasts forever. A perpetuity can have level cash flows or it can have cash flows that grow at a constant rate, which is referred to as a **growing perpetuity.**

Annuity

A stream of cash flows that is received over equal, periodic intervals that ends at some future time period. An annuity generally has level cash flows, but it can also be a **growing annuity** and have cash flows that grow at a constant rate.

Internal Rate of Return

The rate of return that makes the net present value of a stream of cash flows equal to zero. The internal rate of return (IRR) is a popular measure used to evaluate the desirability of an investment based on its projected cash flows.

Concept Check Questions and Answers

4.1.1. What are the key elements of a timeline?

A timeline is a linear representation of the timing of the cash flows. Date 0 represents the present. Date 1 is one period (a month or a year) later; that is, it represents the end of the first period. The cash flow shown below date 1 is the payment you will receive at the end of the first period. You continue until all the cash flows and their timing are shown on the timeline.

4.1.2. How can you distinguish cash inflows from outflows on a timeline?

To differentiate between the two types of cash flows, we assign a positive sign to cash inflows and a negative sign to cash outflows.

4.2.1. Can you compare or combine cash flows at different times?

No, you cannot compare or combine cash flows at different times. A dollar today and dollar in one year are not equivalent.

4.2.2. What is compound interest?

Compound interest is the effect of earning "interest on interest." For compound interest, you can earn interest on the original investment and the interest reinvested from prior periods.

4.2.3. How do you move a cash flow backward and forward in time?

To move a cash flow forward in time, you must compound it. To move a cash flow back in time, you must discount it.

4.3.1. How do you calculate the present value of a cash flow stream?

The present value of cash flow stream is the sum of the present values of each cash flow.

4.3.2. How do you calculate the future value of a cash flow stream?

The future value of a cash flow stream is the sum of the future values of each cash flow.

4.4.1. How do you calculate the net present value of a cash flow stream?

The net present value of a cash flow stream is the present value of all the benefits minus the present value of all the costs. The benefits are the cash inflows and the costs are the cash outflows.

4.4.2. What benefit does a firm receive when it accepts a project with a positive NPV?

When a firm accepts a project with a positive NPV, the value of the firm will increase by the NPV today.

4.5.1. How do you calculate the present value of a

a. Perpetuity?

The present value of a perpetuity is the annual cash flow divided by the appropriate discount rate.

b. Annuity?

The present value of an annuity of C for n periods with interest rate r is:

$$\text{PV(annuity of } C \text{ for } N \text{ periods)} = C \times \frac{1}{r}\left(1 - \frac{1}{(1+r)^N}\right).$$

c. Growing perpetuity?

The present value of a growing perpetuity is:

$$\text{PV(perpetuity growing at } g) = \frac{C_1}{r-g}.$$

d.   Growing annuity?

$$\text{PV(annuity growing at } g)=C \times \left(\frac{1}{r-g}\right)\left(1-\left(\frac{1+g}{1+r}\right)^N\right)$$

4.5.2. How are the formulas for the present value of a perpetuity, annuity, growing perpetuity, and growing annuity related?

The formula for the present value of growing annuity is a general solution. From this formula, we can deduce the formulas for the present value of a perpetuity, annuity, and growing perpetuity.

4.6.1. What tools can you use to simplify the calculation of present values?

Two shortcuts you can use to simplify the calculation of present values are the use of spreadsheets and financial calculators.

4.6.2. What is the process for using the annuity spreadsheet?

Spreadsheet programs such as Excel have a set of functions that performs the calculations that finance professionals do most often. In Excel, the functions are NPER, RATE, PV, PMT, and FV.

4.7.1. How do you solve for the periodic payment of an annuity?

The cash flow of an annuity (or the loan payment) in terms of the amount borrowed *P*, interest rate *r*, and number of payments *n*, can be computed as:

$$C = \frac{P}{\dfrac{1}{r}\left[1-\dfrac{1}{(1+r)^n}\right]}.$$

4.7.2. What is the internal rate of return, and how do you calculate it?

The internal rate of return (IRR) is the interest rate that sets the net present value of the cash flows equal to zero. You can guess the IRR and manually calculate its value. An easier solution is to use a spreadsheet or calculator to automate the guessing process.

4.7.3. How do you solve for the number of periods to pay off an annuity?

To solve for the number of periods to payoff an annuity, you use the trial and error method, guessing, and manually calculate the value of *N*. Alternatively, you can use an annuity spreadsheet to solve for *N*.

Examples with Step-by-Step Solutions

Solving Problems

Problems using the concepts in this chapter can be solved by first determining the timeline of the known and unknown cash flows and then determining which valuation equation is necessary. Some problems will involve using two or more of the equations and two or more steps. You just need to make sure that each equation you are solving has only one unknown variable: PV, FV, *C*, *r*, *N*, or *g*. The examples below demonstrate the general procedure for solving these types of problems.

Examples

1. **You would like to endow a scholarship. In-state tuition is currently $10,000, and the rate will grow by 3% per year. How much would it cost today to endow a scholarship that pays full tuition once every year forever starting 10 years from now? Assume a 5% annual percentage rate (APR) rate of return on your investment to fund the scholarship.**

Step 1. Put the cash flows that are known and unknown on a timeline.

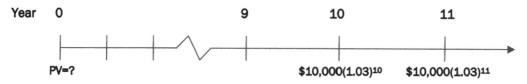

Step 2. Determine the type or types of valuation problems involved.

This problem involves the following additional steps 3 and 4:

[3]   finding the present value in year 9 of the known tuition payments in years 10 to infinity, and

[4]   finding the present value at time 0 of the time 9 value found in step 3.

Step 3. Find the present value in year 9 of the known tuition payments in years 10 to infinity.

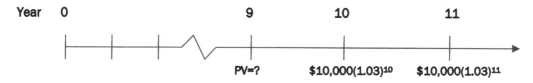

Using the present value of a growing perpetuity with $C = \$10,000(1.03)^{10}$, $r = .05$, and $g = .03$:

$$PV_9 = \frac{C}{r-g}\left[\frac{10,000(1.03)^{10}}{.05-.03}\right] = \left[\frac{13,439}{.05-.03}\right] = \$671,958$$

Step 4. Find the present value of at time 0 of the time 9 value found in step 3.

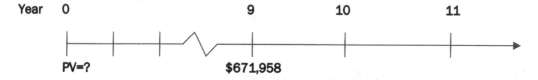

Using the present value of a lump sum equation with FV = $671,958, $r = .05$, and $N = 9$:

$$PV_0 = \frac{\$671,958}{(1.05)^9} = \$433,150$$

You would need to make invest $433,150 into the account today.

2. **You have determined that you will need $50,000 per year for four years to send your daughter to college. You have already saved $10,000 and placed the money in an account that you expect will yield a monthly compounded 12% APR (1% per month). Money for the first of the four payments will be removed from the account exactly 15 years from now and the last withdrawal will be made 18 years from now. You have decided to save more by**

making monthly payments into the same account yielding an expected 12% APR (1% per month) over the next 14 years beginning next month. You will take the money out of the 12% account and place it in a 6% APR account in 14 years and take the cash out as needed. How large must these monthly payments be?

Step 1. Put the cash flows that are known and unknown on a timeline.

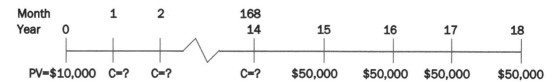

Step 2. Determine the type or types of valuation problems involved. This problem can be solved using the following additional steps 3–5:

[3]   Find the present value in year 14 of the known $50,000 payments in years 15–18,
[4]   Find the future value of the $10,000 you have today at time 14 years, and
[5]   Find the unknown monthly annuity payment that has the future value at time 14 equal to the value found in step 3 minus the value found in step 4.

Step 3. Find the present value of the known $50,000 payments. Since it is only possible to compare values at the same point in time, the first step in a problem like this is to find the value of the known cash flows at one point in time. The most straightforward time to value the cash flows is time 14 because then you can use the present value of an annuity equation, which assumes that the first cash flow occurs one period after it is being valued, time 15.

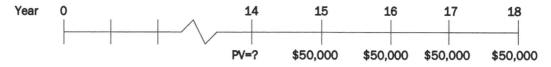

Using the present value of an annuity equation with $N = 4$, $r = 0.06$, and $C = \$50,000$:

$$PV = \$50,000\left(\frac{1}{.06}\right)\left[1 - \frac{1}{.06(1.06)^4}\right] = \$173,255$$

Step 4. Find the future value of the $10,000 you have today at time 14 years.

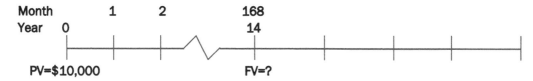

Using the future value of a lump sum equation with $N = 12 \times 14 = 168$, $r = 0.01$, and PV = $10,000:

$$FV = 10,000(1.01)^{168} = \$53,210$$

Step 5. Find the unknown monthly annuity payment that has the future value at time 14 equal to the amount found in part a minus the amount found in part b.

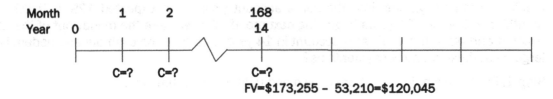

Using the future value of an annuity equation with $N = 12 \times 14 = 168$, $r = 0.01$, and FV = $120,045:

$$FV = 120{,}045 = C\left[\frac{1}{.01} - \frac{1}{.01(1.01)^{168}}\right](1.01)^{168} \Rightarrow C = \$278.$$

You would need to make monthly payments of $278 into the account.

3. **Some Republicans would like to give those contributing to Social Security the option of investing in their own personal accounts and in assets riskier than Treasury Bonds. Assume that the average worker will contribute $5,000 into his or her retirement account next year, and can choose option 1 and invest in T-bonds, which have a 4% expected return, or option 2 and invest in a stock index fund that has a 12% expected return. In both options at the date of retirement, the money will be placed in an account with an expected return of 3% APR (0.25% per month). Assume that the amount workers contribute will grow by 3% per year, and the average worker is 35 years from retirement age. If the money is withdrawn from the account beginning the month after retirement, and the average worker is expected to live for 20 years after retirment, what size monthly payment would the average worker be able to withdraw in both of the options?**

Step 1. Put the cash flows that are known and unknown on a timeline.

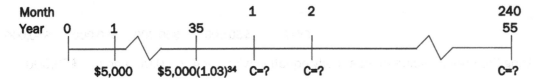

Step 2. Determine the type or types of valuation problems involved.

This problem involves the following additional steps 3–4:

[3]   finding the future value of the known growing annuity of payments that will have accumulated in 35 years, and

[4]   finding the unknown monthly annuity payment that has that present value.

Step 3. Find the future value of the growing annuity of payments.

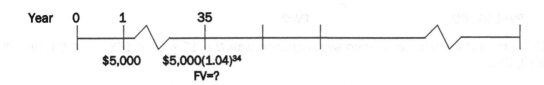

The future value of a growing annuity can be found using the present value of a growing annuity equation and the future value of a lump sum equation as follows:

The present value of the payments at time $0 = PV_0 = \left(\dfrac{C}{r-g}\right)\left[1-\left(\dfrac{1+g}{1+r}\right)^N\right]$,

so the future value at time $35 = FV_{35} = PV_0(1+r)^{35}$, or

$$FV_{35} = \left(\dfrac{C}{r-g}\right)\left[1-\left(\dfrac{1+g}{1+r}\right)^N\right](1+r)^{35}.$$

For both of the options, C = \$5,000, g = 3%, and N = 35. For the T-bond option, r = 4%, and for the stock index fund option, r = 12%.

$$FV_{35}^{\text{T-bond}} = \left[\left(\dfrac{5{,}000}{.04-.03}\right)\left[1-\left(\dfrac{1.03}{1.04}\right)^{35}\right]\right](1.04)^{35} = \$566{,}113$$

$$FV_{35}^{\text{Stock}} = \left[\left(\dfrac{5{,}000}{.12-.03}\right)\left[1-\left(\dfrac{1.03}{1.12}\right)^{35}\right]\right](1.12)^{35} = \$2{,}776{,}986$$

Step 4. Find the 240 month annuity payment that has that present value.

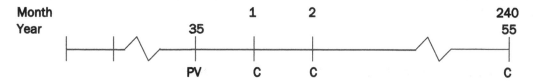

Using the present value of an annuity equation with PV = FV_{35} from step 3, N = 12 x 20 = 240,

r = .03 / 12 = 0.0025, and solving for C, you have:

$$FV_{35}^{\text{T-bond}} = PV = \$566{,}113 = C\left[\dfrac{1}{.0025}-\dfrac{1}{.0025(1.0025)^{240}}\right] \Rightarrow C = \$3{,}140$$

$$FV_{35}^{\text{Stock}} = PV = \$2{,}776{,}986 = C\left[\dfrac{1}{.0025}-\dfrac{1}{.0025(1.0025)^{240}}\right] \Rightarrow C = \$15{,}401$$

Under the 4% T-bond plan, workers could withdraw \$3,140 per month, and under the 12% Stock Index plan, workers could withdraw \$15,401 per month.

Questions and Problems

1. The historical average return on U.S. T-bills is 3.8% per year, while the average return for small company stocks is 16.9% per year. Assuming these rates occur annually in the future, how much more cash would you have in 20 years by investing \$50,000 in small company stocks rather than T-bills?

2. Your daughter is currently 8 years old. You anticipate that she will be going to college in 10 years. You would like to have \$100,000 in a savings account at that time. If the account

promises to pay a fixed interest rate of 3% per year, how much money do you need to put into the account today to ensure that you will have $100,000 in ten years?

3. You have determined that you will need $3,000,000 when you retire in 40 years. You plan to set aside a series of payments each year in an account yielding 12% per year to reach this goal. You will put the first payment in the account one year from today, and the payments will grow with your income by 3% per year. Calculate your first annual payment into this account. Calculate the last payment.

4. Like in problem 3, you have determined that you will need $3,000,000 when you retire in 40 years, and you plan to set aside a series of payments each year in an account yielding 12% per year to reach this goal. You will put in the first payment in the account one year from today and the payments will grow with your income by 3% per year. Assuming that the money is placed in a 6% APR account throughout your retirement period, and you plan to withdraw $25,000 per month, approximately how many years will the money last you?

5. You are offering the employees in your small firm a so-called defined benefit pension plan. Beginning exactly 21 years from today you will pay out the first annual payment of a guaranteed 30-year stream of annual payments. The first payment will be $100,000 for 10 employees, or $1 million. The payment stream will grow by 3% per year each year to match expected inflation. You have already started investing in the pension account, which has a balance of $113,971.84 today. You expect that the account will always yield 13% APR, and you will always leave the money in the account, only withdrawing the money as needed by the plan. To supplement the plan, you will make 20 even, annual payments over the next 20 years, beginning one year from today. How big must the annual payment that you will contribute be?

Solutions to Questions and Problems

1. This problem requires using the FV of a lump sum equation:

$$FV_{20} = \$50,000(1.038)^{20} = \$105,418.56$$
$$FV_{20} = \$50,000(1.169)^{20} = \$1,135,691.11$$

2. This problem requires using the PV of a single cash flow equation:

$$PV_0 = \frac{FV_{10}}{(1+r)^{10}} = \frac{100,000}{(1.03)^{10}} = \$74,409.39$$

3. Set $3,000,000 equal to the present value a growing annuity equation and solve for the first payment, C_1.

$$FV_{40} = \left[\frac{C}{.12-.03} \right] \left[1 - \left(\frac{1.03}{1.12} \right)^{40} \right] (1.12)^{40} = 3,000,000$$

$$= C \left[11.1111 \right] \left[.96494 \right] 93.05$$

$$= C(997.643) \Rightarrow C = \$3,007$$

Thus, the first payment is $3,007 and the last payment is ($3,007)(1.03)^{39} = $9,523.

4. You need to solve the following present value of an annuity equation for N.

$$\$3,000,000 = \$25,000 \left(\frac{1}{.005} \right) \left(1 - \frac{1}{.005(1.005)^N} \right) \Rightarrow N = 184 \text{ months, or 15 years and 4 months.}$$

5. You must contribute $99,648:

$$PV_{20} = \left[\frac{1,000,000}{.13 - .03} \right] \left[1 - \left(\frac{1.03}{1.13} \right)^{30} \right] = \$9,379,469$$

$$PV_0 = \frac{\$9,379,469}{(1.13)^{20}} - \$113,971.84 = \$813,972 - 113,971.84 = \$700,000$$

$$\$700,000 = C \left[\frac{1}{.13} - \frac{1}{.13(1.13)^{20}} \right] \Rightarrow C = \$99,648$$

CHAPTER 5

Interest Rates

Chapter Synopsis

5.1 Interest Rate Quotes and Adjustments

Interest rates can compound more than once per year, such as monthly or semiannually. An **annual percentage rate** (APR) equals the periodic interest rate, r, times the number of compounding periods per year, k. Because it does not include the effect of compounding, an APR understates the amount of interest that will be received if interest compounds more than once per year.

To compute the actual amount of interest earned in one year, an APR can be converted to an **effective annual rate** (EAR), which includes the effect of compounding and provides a measure of the amount of interest that will actually be earned over a year:

Converting an APR to an EAR

$$EAR = \left(1 + \frac{APR}{k}\right)^k - 1$$

The more compounding periods, the greater the EAR. For example, suppose a bank offers a certificate of deposit with an interest rate of "6% APR with monthly compounding." In this case, you will earn 6% / 12 = 0.5% every month. To determine the value of $100 invested for one year, you can either compound over 12 months at the monthly rate of 0.5% or you can compound over one year at the EAR = $(1 + {}^{.06}\!/_{12})^{12} - 1 = 6.17\%$:

$$FV_1 = \$100(1.005)^{12} = \$100(1.0617) = \$106.17.$$

Many loans, such as home mortgages and car loans, have monthly payments and are quoted in terms of an APR with monthly compounding. These types of loans are typically **amortizing loans** in which each month's payment includes the interest that accrues that month along with some part of the loan's balance. Each monthly payment is the same, and the loan is fully repaid with the final payment. Since the loan balance declines over time, the interest portion of the payment declines over time while the principal repayment portion increases. The number of compounding periods is generally equal to the number of payments per year by convention.

For example, suppose you are offered a $30,000 car loan at "6.75% APR for 60 months." You can find the monthly payment using the PV of an annuity equation:

$$\$30,000 = C\frac{1}{.005625}\left[1 - \frac{1}{(1.005625)^{60}}\right] \Rightarrow C = \$590.50$$

In the first month, interest equals $30,000(0.005625) = $168.75 and the loan's balance is reduced by $590.50 – 168.75 = $421.75 to $29,578.25. In the second month, interest equals $29,578.25(0.005625) = $166.38 and the loan's balance is reduced by $590.50 – 166.38 = $424.12 to $29,154.13. This process continues until the beginning of the 60th month when the loan balance will be $578.20, so interest equals $587.20(0.005625) = $3.30 and the loan's balance is reduced by $590.50 – 3.30 = $587.20 to $0. A tabular depiction of this process is called an **amortization table.**

5.2 Application: Discount Rates and Loans

To calculate a loan payment, you first equate the outstanding loan balance with the present value of the loan payments using the discount rate from the quoted interest rate of the loan and then solve for the loan payment. Many loans, such as mortgages and car loans, have monthly payments and are quoted in terms of an APR with monthly compounding. These types of loans are amortizing loans, which means that each month you pay interest on the loan plus some part of the loan balance. Each monthly payment is the same, and the loan is fully repaid with the final payment.

Typical terms for a new car loan might be "6.75% APR for 60 months." This quote means that the loan will be repaid with 60 equal monthly payments, computed using a 6.75% APR with monthly compounding. The payment, C, is set so that the present value of the cash flows, evaluated using the loan interest rate, equals the original principal amount of $30,000. So, using the annuity formula to compute the present value of the loan payments, the payment C must satisfy

$$C \times \frac{1}{0.005625}\left(1 - \frac{1}{(1+0.005625)^{60}}\right) = 30,000$$

$$\text{and therefore, } C = \frac{30,000}{\frac{1}{0.005625}\left(1 - \frac{1}{(1+0.005625)^{60}}\right)} = \$590.50$$

Alternatively, we can solve for the payment C using the annuity spreadsheet:

	NPER	RATE	PV	PMT	FV	Excel Formula
Given	60	0.5625%	30,000		0	
Solve for PMT				−590.50		=PMT(0.005625,60,30000,0)

5.3 The Determinants of Interest Rates

Nominal interest rates, which indicate the actual rate at which interest will accrue, are typically stated in loan agreements and quoted in financial markets. If prices in the economy are also growing due to inflation, the nominal interest rate does not represent the increase in purchasing power that will result from investing at this rate. The rate of growth of purchasing power, after adjusting for inflation, is determined by the **real interest rate,** r_r. If r is the nominal interest rate and i is the rate of inflation, the real rate can be calculated as follows.

The Real Interest Rate

$$r_r = \frac{r-i}{1+i}$$

Interest rates affect firms' incentives to raise capital and invest as well as individuals' propensities to save. For example, an increase in interest rates will generally decrease an investment's NPV and reduce the number of positive-NPV investments available to firms. The U.S. Federal Reserve as well as central banks in other countries use this idea to try and influence economic activity. Central banks can lower interest rates to stimulate investment if the economy is slowing and raise interest rates to reduce investment if the economy is perceived to be growing too fast ,which may lead to an increase in the inflation rate.

Interest rates generally depend on the horizon, or term, of the investment or loan. The relation between an investment's term and its interest rate is called the **term structure of interest rates,** and it can be plotted on a graph called the **yield curve.** Common equations used for computing present values, such as the annuity and perpetuity formulas, are based on discounting all of the cash flows at the same rate. In situations in which cash flows need to be discounted at different rates depending on when they occur, the following equation can be used:

$$\text{PV} = \frac{C_1}{1+r_1} + \frac{C_2}{1+r_2} \cdots \frac{C_N}{1+r_N} = \sum_{n=0}^{N} \frac{C_n}{\left(1+r_n\right)^n}$$

The Federal Reserve determines short-term interest rates through its influence on the **federal funds rate**, which is the rate at which banks can borrow cash reserves over one night. All other interest rates on the yield curve are set in the market and are adjusted until the supply of lending matches the demand for borrowing at each loan term. Expectations of future interest rate changes have a major effect on investors' willingness to lend or borrow for longer terms and, therefore, on the shape of the yield curve. An increasing yield curve, with long-term rates higher than short-term rates, generally indicates that interest rates are expected to rise in the future. A decreasing (inverted) yield curve, with long-term rates lower than short-term rates, generally signals an expected decline in future interest rates. Because interest rates tend to drop in response to an economic slowdown, an inverted yield curve is often interpreted as a negative economic forecast.

5.4 Risk and Taxes

U.S. Treasury securities are widely regarded as risk-free because there is virtually no chance the U.S. government will fail to pay the interest or default on these bonds; thus, the rate on Treasury securities is often referred to as the **risk-free rate.** All other borrowers are generally assumed to have some risk of default. For these loans, the stated interest rate is the maximum amount that investors will receive. Investors may receive less if the company is unable to fully repay the loan. To compensate for the risk that they will receive less if the firm defaults, investors demand a higher interest rate than the rate on U.S. Treasuries. The difference between the interest rate of the loan and the Treasury rate is called the **credit spread.**

If the cash flows from an investment are taxed, the net cash flow that the investor will receive will be reduced by the amount of the taxes paid. In general, if the interest rate is r and the tax rate is τ, then for each \$1 invested you will earn interest equal to r and owe tax of $\tau \times r$ on the interest. Thus, the equivalent **after-tax interest rate** is $r(1 - \tau)$. For example, if an investment pays 8% interest for one year, and you invest $100 at the start of the year, you will earn 8% × $100 = $8 in interest at year-end. If you must pay taxes at 40% on this interest, you will owe 40% × $8 = $3.20. Thus you will receive only $8 − $3.20 = $4.80 after paying taxes. This amount is equivalent to earning 4.80% interest and not paying any taxes, so the after-tax interest rate is $r(1 - \tau) = 8\%(1 - .40) = 4.80\%$.

5.5 The Opportunity Cost of Capital

The discount rate used to evaluate cash flows is the **cost of capital**, or **opportunity cost of capital,** which is the best available expected return offered in the market on an investment of comparable risk and term to the cash flow being discounted. The cost of capital is the return the investor forgoes when making a new investment. For a risk-free project, it will typically correspond to the interest rate on U.S. Treasury securities with a similar term. For risky projects, it will include a **risk premium.**

Selected Concepts and Key Terms

Amortizing Loan

A loan in which each month you pay interest on the loan plus some part of the loan principal, or amount borrowed. Each monthly payment is the same, and the loan is fully repaid with the final payment. Since the loan balance declines over time, the interest portion of the payment declines over time while the principal repayment portion increases.

Annual Percentage Rate (APR)

The periodic interest rate, r, times the number of compounding periods per year, k. Because it does not include the effect of compounding, the APR quote is less than the actual amount of interest that will be received if $k > 1$.

Opportunity Cost of Capital

The best available expected return offered in the market on an investment of comparable risk and term to the cash flow being discounted. The cost of capital is the return the investor forgoes when the making a new investment. For a risk-free project, it will typically correspond to the interest rate on U.S. Treasury securities with a similar term. For risky projects, it will include a risk premium.

Credit Spread

The difference between the interest rate of the loan and the risk-free Treasury security rate.

Effective Annual Rate (EAR)

The amount of interest that will be earned over a year. The more compounding periods, the greater the EAR for a given APR.

Nominal Interest Rate

The actual rate at which money will grow. Nominal rates are typically stated in loan agreements and quoted in financial markets. If prices in the economy are also growing due to inflation, the nominal interest rate does not represent the increase in purchasing power that will result from investing at the nominal rate.

Real Interest Rate

The rate of growth of purchasing power after adjusting for inflation.

Term Structure

The relation between an investment's term and its interest rate is called the term structure of interest rates, and it can be plotted on a graph called the yield curve.

Concept Check Questions and Answers

5.1.1. What is the difference between an EAR and an APR quote?

An annual percentage rate is the rate that interest earns in one year before the effect of compounding. An effective annual rate is the rate that the amount of interest actually earns at the end of one year. Because the APR does not include the effect of compounding, it is typically less than the EAR.

5.1.2. Why can't the APR be used as a discount rate?

Because the APR does not reflect the true amount you will earn one year, the APR itself cannot be used as a discount rate.

5.2.1. How can you compute the outstanding balance on a loan?

The outstanding balance can be computed by constructing an amortization table or by finding the present value of the remaining payments.

5.2.2. What is an amortizing loan?

It is a loan in which each month you pay interest on the loan plus some part of the loan principal, or amount borrowed. Each monthly payment is the same, and the loan is fully repaid with the final payment. Since the loan balance declines over time, the interest portion of the payment declines over time while the principal repayment portion increases.

5.3.1. What is the difference between a nominal and real interest rate?

The nominal interest rate is the rate quoted by banks and other financial institutions, whereas the real interest rate is the rate of growth of purchasing power, after adjusting for inflation. The real interest rate is approximately equal to the nominal rate less the rate of inflation.

5.3.2. How do investors' expectations of future short-term interest rates affect the shape of the current yield curve?

The shape of the yield curve tends to vary with investors' expectations of future economic growth and interest rates. It tends to be inverted prior to recessions and to be steep coming out of a recession.

5.4.1. Why do corporations pay higher interest rates on their loans than the U.S. government?

Corporations pay higher interest rates on their loans than the U.S. government does because all corporations have some risk of default, while there is virtually no chance the U.S. government will fail to pay the interest or default on the loans.

5.4.2. How do taxes affect the interest earned on an investment? What about the interest paid on a loan?

The interest the investor earned on an investment is taxable and will be reduced by the amount of the tax payments. In some cases, since the interest on loans is tax deductible, the cost of paying interest on the loan is offset by the benefit of the tax deduction.

5.5.1. What is the opportunity cost of capital?

The opportunity cost of capital is the best available return offered in the market on an investment of comparable risk and term to the cash flow being discounted.

5.5.2. Why do different interest rates exist, even in a competitive market?

The interest rates we observe in the market will vary based on quoting conventions, the term of investment, and risk. The actual return kept by an investor will also depend on how the interest is taxed.

Examples with Step-by-Step Solutions

Solving Problems

Problems using the concepts in this chapter often involve solving problems using the valuation equations in Chapter 4. It is helpful to represent the cash flows involved on a timeline, and it is important to use the correct periodic interest rate. For instance, in example 1 below, the loan involves monthly payments at a 6% APR with monthly compounding, so the correct rate to use is the monthly rate = 6% / 12 = 0.5%. Other problems may involve finding real cash flows. To do this, it is generally necessary to calculate and use real interest rates using the relation between nominal rates, real rates and inflation. Example 2 below provides such an example. Finally, problems may involve understanding the mechanics of an amortizing loan, as in example 3 below.

Examples

1. **You want to buy a vacation house in Hood River, Oregon, by borrowing $400,000.**
   - **[A]** **If you obtain a 30-year loan at 6% APR with monthly compounding, what is your monthly payment? How much goes to interest and how much to principal over the loan's life?**
   - **[B]** **If you obtain a 15-year loan at 6% APR with monthly compounding, what is your monthly payment? How much goes to interest and how much to principal over the loan's life?**

Step 1: Put the known and unknown cash flows on a timeline.

The 30-year Loan.

The 15-year Loan.

Step 2: Since this problem involves the present value of an annuity in which C is unknown, set the PV of annuity equation equal to $400,000 with $r = 0.05$ and $N = 360$ months for part [A] and 180 months for part [B]. Solve for C to get each loan's payment.

$$[A]\,\$400,000 = C\left[\frac{1}{.005} - \frac{1}{.005(1.005)^{360}}\right] \Rightarrow C = \$2,398.20$$

$$[B]\,\$400,000 = C\left[\frac{1}{.005} - \frac{1}{.005(1.005)^{180}}\right] \Rightarrow C = \$3,375.43$$

Step 3. Once the payment is calculated, you can calculate the total interest paid as the total payments made minus the $400,000 principal that was paid.

[A] Total = 360(2,398.20) = 863,353

$\qquad$ − Principal = 400,000

$\qquad$ = Interest = 463,353

[B] Total = 180(3,375.48) = 607,577

$\qquad$ − Principal = 400,000

$\qquad$ = Interest = 207,577

Thus, the payment and interest paid is $2,398 and $463,353 for the 30-year loan and $3,375 and $207,577 for the 15-year loan.

2. You plan on drawing on retirement income exactly 30 years from today. You have liquidated $1 million worth of investments and are going to move to Spain, taking whatever cash is left after funding your retirement account. You want the retirement account to pay exactly $10,000 per month in today's (real) dollars for 20 years. You are going to place enough into an account yielding a nominal 12% APR, or 1% per month. At retirement, you will place the accumulated money into an account yielding a nominal 6% APR, which compounds monthly at 0.5%, and remove cash from this account according to the payment schedule. You expect that inflation will be 0.25% per month. What payment to the 12% account is required to fund the retirement plan?

Step 1. Put the cash flows that are known and unknown on a timeline.

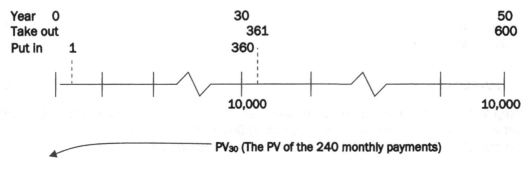

PV₃₀ (The PV of the 240 monthly payments)

PV₀ (The PV of the month 360 value)

Step 2. Determine the type or types of valuation problems involved.

This problem can be solved using the following additional steps 3–6:

[3] find the real monthly interest rates in the first 30 years and last 20 years,
[4] find the present value in real terms in year 30 of the $10,000 payments in months 361–600,
[5] find the present value of the year 30 value found in step 4,
[6] subtract the value in step 5 from the $1 million.

Step 3. The real rates are:

$$r_{real}^{Years\ 30\text{-}50} = \frac{r-i}{1+i} = \frac{.005-.0025}{1+.025} \Rightarrow r_{real} \approx 0.0025 = 0.25\% \text{ per month.}$$

$$r_{real}^{Years\ 1\text{-}30} = \frac{r-i}{1+i} = \frac{.01-.0025}{1+.025} \Rightarrow r_{real} \approx 0.75\% \text{ per month.}$$

Step 4. Using the present value of an annuity equation:

$$PV_{30} = 10,000 \left[\frac{1}{.0025} - \frac{1}{.0025(1.0025)^{240}} \right] = \$1,803,109 \text{ in real dollars.}$$

Step 5. Using the PV of a single cash flow equation:

$$PV = \frac{1,803,109}{(1.0075)^{360}} = \$122,406.$$

Step 6. Make a conclusion.

You can take $1,000,000 - $122,406 = $877,594 with you and put the rest in the account.

3. **The Boston Beer Company is shopping for a new bottling machine. The machine has a manufacturer's suggested retail price of $350,000.**
   [A] **Dealer A offers to sell them the machine for $290,000 with a 6% APR monthly amortizing 10-year loan. Dealer B will charge the full $350,000 but offers them 0% APR monthly payment loan with financing over 10 years. Which of these two options is a better deal?**
   [B] **If they decide to buy the machine from dealer A, how much of the first two payments goes to paying down the $290,000 principal? How much is interest?**

[C] **If they decide to buy the machine from dealer A and sell it in three years, how much must they sell it for in order to pay back the remaining balance of the loan? (Ignore tax effects.)**

Step 1. To answer part [A], you need to determine which payment option has the lowest present value.

Since both options have the same term and monthly payments, this is the same as finding which option has the lowest payment.

Using the PV of an annuity equation:

$$\$290,000 = C\left[\frac{1}{.005} - \frac{1}{.005(1.005)^{120}}\right] \Rightarrow C = \$3,219.59 \text{ is the payment for dealer A.}$$

$$\frac{\$350,000}{120} = \$2,916.67 \text{ is the payment for dealer B.}$$

Also, note that the present value of dealer B's payments at 6% APR is $262,714 which is less than the present value of dealer A's payments at 6% APR, $290,000.

Thus, you should select dealer B.

Step 2. To answer part [B] of the problem, you can construct the first two months of an amortization table with a payment of $3,219.59, an original balance of $290,000, and a periodic (monthly) interest rate of 6% / 12 = 0.50%:

Month	Principal	Interest=0.005 x Principal	Payment	Ending Balance
1	290,000.00	1,450.00	3,219.59	288,230.41
2	288,230.41	1,441.15	3,219.59	286,451.97

Now, calculate the principal repaid = 290,000 – 286,451.97 = $3,548.03.

After two months, the total principal repaid is $3,548.03 and the total interest paid is 2(3,219.59) – $3,548.03 = 1,450.00 + 1,441.15 = $2,891.15.

Step 3. To answer part [C] you could construct an amortization table, but without the aid of a spreadsheet this would be too time-consuming. Thus, you can solve for the present value of the remaining payments, which must be the remaining balance of the loan.

Using the present value of an annuity equation with C = $3,219.59, r = 6%/12 = 0.5%, and N = 120 – 36 = 84:

$$PV = \frac{3,219.59}{0.005}\left(1 - \frac{1}{(1.005)^{84}}\right) = \$220,390.73.$$

Thus, they must sell it for at least $220,390.73 or else they will have to pay off some of the balance with cash from a different source.

Questions and Problems

1. You won $1 in million the Lottery. The prize is paid out in equal, semi-annual payments over 50 years with the first payment immediately. GenexCapital.com has offered to buy the ticket for $250,000 in cash today. In the contract, they claim to be using an 8% APR with semi-annual compounding. Are they? (Ignore taxes)

2. You have a $50,000 balance on your credit card, and you have set your Wells Fargo checking account bill pay for monthly payments of $1,000. The interest rate is 18% APR with monthly

compounding. How many years until you have paid it off? How long would it take if your balance was $70,000?

3. You are considering paying for a 2006 Mercedes SLK 350 with an MSRP of $50,000 using a 5-year loan. Based on the MSRP, the dealer's finance manager has quoted you a zero down, 4.8% APR (compounded monthly) loan with a payment of $966.64 and your first payment is due one month from today.
   [A]   Is the rate you would be paying really 4.8% APR?
   [B]   For every $500 that you get the dealer to lower the price of the car at a 4.8% APR, how much does your monthly payment decrease?
   [C]   Based on a price of $45,000, how much would your down payment need to be to make your payments equal $700 per month at 4.8% APR?

4. You have decided to refinance your mortgage. You plan to borrow whatever is outstanding on your current mortgage. The current monthly payment is $5,200, and there are exactly 27 years left on the loan. You have just made your 36th monthly payment and the mortgage interest rate is 6% APR. How much do you owe on the mortgage today?

5. You have just sold your house for $2,000,000. Your mortgage was originally a 30-year mortgage with monthly payments, and an initial balance of $400,000. The mortgage is exactly 10 years old, and you have just made a monthly payment. If the fixed interest rate on the mortgage is 3.6% (APR), how much will you have from the sale once you pay off the mortgage?

Solutions to Questions and Problems

1. If they are paying 8% APR (4% per six months), then the PV of the annuity payments at this rate must be $250,000.

$$PV = \$10,000 \left[\frac{1}{.04} - \frac{1}{.04(1.04)^{99}} \right] + 10,000 = \$254,852 > \$250,00.$$

Since they are paying less than $250,000, they are using a bit higher rate.

The actual rate is: $\$10,000 \left[\dfrac{1}{r} - \dfrac{1}{r(1+r)^{99}} \right] + 10,000 = \$250,000 \Rightarrow APR \approx 8.175\%$.

2. This is a present value of an annuity problem in which you must solve for N.

$$\$1,000 \left[\frac{1}{.015} - \frac{1}{.015(1.015)^N} \right] = \$50,000$$

⇒ T = 93.11 months, or about 7 years and 10 months.

For the $70,000 balance, note that if you paid $1,000 in perpetuity:

$$\left(\frac{\$1,000}{.015} \right) = \$66,667, \text{ so you could never pay it off, since } \$70,000 > \$66,667.$$

3. [A]   The actual payment at 4.8% APR would be:

$$50,000 = C\left[\frac{1}{.004} - \frac{1}{.004(1.004)^{60}}\right] \Rightarrow C = \$938.99.$$

So the actual rate is higher. The implied rate in the payment can be found as follows:

$$50,000 = 966.64\left[\frac{1}{r} - \frac{1}{r(1+r)^{60}}\right] \Rightarrow r = 0.5\%, \text{ or } 6\% \text{ APR.}$$

[B] $\$500 = C\left(\frac{1}{.004} - \frac{1}{.004(1.004)^{60}}\right) \Rightarrow C = \$9.39.$

So, for every $500 reduction, the payment would decrease by $9.39.

[C] $\$45,000 = 700\left(\frac{1}{.004} - \frac{1}{.004(1.004)^{60}}\right) + \text{Down Payment}$

$\Rightarrow \text{Down Payment} = \$45,000 - \$37,274 = \$7,726$

4. To find out what is owed, compute the PV of the remaining payments:

$$PV = \frac{5,200}{0.005}\left(1 - \frac{1}{(1.005)^{324}}\right) = \$833,352.89.$$

5. First compute the original loan payment:

$$C = \frac{400,000 \times 0.003}{\left(1 - \frac{1}{(1.003)^{360}}\right)} = \$1,818.58.$$

Now compute the PV of continuing to make these payments.

Using the formula for the PV of an annuity:

$$PV = 1,818.58\left(\frac{1}{0.003} - \frac{1}{(1.003)^{240}}\right) = \$310,809.15.$$

So you would get to keep $2,000,000 – $310,809.15 = $1,689,190.85.

CHAPTER 6

Investment Decision Rules

Chapter Synopsis

6.1 NPV and Stand-Alone Projects

The net present value (NPV) of a project is the difference between the present value of its benefits and the present value of its costs. Since a project's NPV represents its value in terms of cash today, the **NPV investment rule,** which states that all positive NPV projects should be accepted, is consistent with maximizing the value of the firm.

The internal rate of return (IRR) is the rate of return that makes the net present value of a stream sof cash flows equal to zero. Thus, accepting projects with an IRR above the required return, or cost of capital, is generally equivalent to accepting projects with a positive NPV. The difference between the cost of capital and the IRR can be thought of as the maximum amount of estimation error in the cost of capital estimate that can exist without altering the original decision.

6.2 The Internal Rate of return

The **IRR investment rule** advises taking investment opportunities in which the IRR exceeds the opportunity cost of capital. The IRR rule will give the same answer as the NPV rule in many, but not all, applications. The following are cases in which the IRR rule may fail to reliably provide the correct decision.

- When the initial cash flow is positive and all later cash flows are negative, the IRR rule will provide the opposite decision provided by the NPV rule.

- In some cases, such as when there is no required investment for a project, the IRR does not exist.

- There may be multiple IRRs when the sign of the project's cash flows changes more than once, so the IRR rule cannot be relied upon.

While these are limitations to the usefulness of the IRR rule, the IRR itself remains a useful tool. Not only does the IRR measure the sensitivity of the NPV to estimation error in the cost of capital, but it also measures the average return of the investment.

6.3 The Payback Rule

The **payback investment rule** is based on the idea that an opportunity that pays back its initial investment quickly is a good idea. To apply the payback rule, you first calculate the amount of time it takes to pay back the initial investment, called the **payback period.** If the payback period is less than a pre-specified length of time, you accept the project. The payback rule is not a reliable method of determining if projects will increase the value of the firm since it does not consider the timing of a project's cash flows or cost of capital.

6.4 Choosing Between Projects

Sometimes a firm must choose among **mutually exclusive projects** in which only one of two or more projects being considered can be selected. In this case, the NPV rule advises picking the project with the highest NPV and provides the best answer.

Picking one project over another simply because it has a larger IRR can lead to errors.

■   Because the IRR measures only the return of the investment opportunity, it does not depend on the scale of the investment opportunity. Hence the IRR rule cannot be used to compare projects of different scales because larger scale projects may be more valuable.

■   Investment opportunities with the same NPV can have different IRRs because the IRR depends on the timing of the cash flows even when a change in timing does not affect the NPV. By altering the timing of the cash flows, it is possible to change the ranking of the IRRs of two mutually exclusive projects without changing either project's NPV.

The **incremental IRR investment rule** applies the IRR rule to the difference between the cash flows of the two mutually exclusive alternatives. For example, assume you are comparing two mutually exclusive opportunities, A and B, and the IRRs of both opportunities exceed the cost of capital. If you subtract the cash flows of opportunity B from the cash flows of opportunity A, then you should take opportunity A if the incremental IRR exceeds the cost of capital. Otherwise, you should take opportunity B. Although the incremental IRR rule often provides a reliable method for choosing among mutually exclusive projects, it can be difficult to apply correctly, and it is much simpler to just use the NPV rule.

6.5 Project Selection with Resource Constraints

Sometimes there is a fixed supply of capital, or other resources, so that all possible opportunities cannot be undertaken. The **profitability index** can be used to identify the optimal combination of projects to undertake in such situations, where:

$$\text{Profitability Index} = \frac{\text{NPV}}{\text{Resource Consumed}}$$

Projects should be selected in order of profitability index ranking starting with the project with the highest index and moving down the ranking until the resource is consumed. While this procedure generally leads to the most valuable combination of projects, the only guaranteed way to find the best combination of projects is to search through all of them. Linear programming techniques have been developed to solve this kind of problem.

Selected Concepts and Key Terms

Net Present Value (NPV) Investment Rule

Select all projects that have a positive net present value (NPV), where NPV is the difference between the present value of an investment's benefits and the present value of its costs. A project's NPV represents its value in terms of cash today. Choosing this alternative is equivalent to receiving its NPV in cash today, so positive NPV projects should be accepted. When choosing among mutually exclusive alternatives, the alternative with the highest NPV should be selected.

NPV profile

A graph of a project's NPV over a range of discount rates.

Internal Rate of Return (IRR) Investment Rule

Take investment opportunities in which the IRR exceeds the opportunity cost of capital. The **internal rate of return** (IRR) is the rate of return that makes the net present value of a stream of cash flows equal to zero. The IRR investment rule will give the same answer as the NPV rule in many, but not all, applications.

Mutually Exclusive Projects

A situation where only one of two or more projects being considered can be selected. In this case, the NPV rule provides the best answer: Pick the project with the highest NPV. Picking one project over another simply because it has a larger IRR can lead to errors.

Incremental IRR

The **incremental IRR investment rule** applies the IRR rule to the difference between the cash flows of the two mutually exclusive alternatives. Although the incremental IRR rule often provides a reliable method for choosing among mutually exclusive projects, it can be difficult to apply correctly, and it is much simpler to just use the NPV rule.

Profitability Index

The NPV of a project divided by the amount of a resource (such as capital) consumed. When there is a limited resource (such as capital), projects should be selected in order of profitability index ranking starting with the project with the highest index and moving down the ranking until the resource is consumed.

Payback Investment Rule

If the payback period is less than a pre-specified length of time, you accept the project. The **payback period** is the amount of time it takes to pay back the initial investment. The payback rule is not a reliable method of determining if projects will increase the value of the firm since it does not consider the timing of a project's cash flows or cost of capital.

Concept Check Questions and Answers

6.1.1. Explain the NPV rule for stand-alone projects.

The NPV rule for stand-alone projects states that when choosing among alternatives, we should take the project with the highest positive NPV.

6.1.2. What does the difference between the cost of capital and the IRR indicate?

In general, the difference between the cost of capital and the IRR is the maximum amount of estimation error in the cost of capital estimate that can exist without altering the original decision.

6.2.1. Under what conditions do the IRR rule and the NPV rule coincide for a stand-alone project?

The IRR rule is only guaranteed to work for a stand-alone project if all of the project's negative cash flows precede its positive cash flows. If this is not the case, the IRR rule can lead to incorrect decisions.

6.2.2. If the IRR rule and the NPV rule lead to different decisions for a stand-alone project, which should you follow? Why?

When investment rules conflict, you should follow the NPV rule because following the alternative rules means you are not taking a positive NPV project, and thus, you are not maximizing wealth. In these cases, the alternative rules lead to bad decisions.

6.3.1. Can the payback rule reject projects that have positive NPV? Can it accept projects that have negative NPV?

Yes, because the payback rule does not take into consideration the required rate of return and the exact timing of the cash flows.

6.3.2. If the payback rule does not give the same answer as the NPV rule, which rule should you follow? Why?

The NPV rule because it correctly accounts for the required rate of return and the exact timing of the cash flows while the payback rule does not.

6.4.1. For mutually exclusive projects, explain why picking one project over another because it has a larger IRR can lead to mistakes.

For mutually exclusive projects, picking one project over another because it has a larger IRR can lead to mistakes. Problems arise when projects have differences in scale (require different initial investments) and when they have different cash flow patterns.

6.4.2. What is the incremental IRR rule and what are its shortcomings?

The incremental IRR rule applies to the difference between the cash flows of two mutually exclusive projects. Suppose you compare two mutually exclusive projects, A and B, and the IRR of both projects exceeds the cost of capital. If you subtract the cash flows of project B from the cash flows of project A, then you should choose project A if the incremental IRR exceeds the cost of capital. Otherwise, choose project B.

6.5.1. Explain why ranking projects according to their NPV might not be optimal when you evaluate projects with different resource requirements.

When there is a fixed supply of the resource so that you cannot undertake all the mutually exclusive projects, choosing the highest NPV project may not lead to the best decision. The project that has the highest NPV may use up the entire resource. Therefore, it would be a mistake to take it. A combination of other projects may produce a combined NPV that exceeds the NPV of the best single project.

6.5.2. How can the profitability index be used to identify attractive projects when there are resource constraints?

Practitioners often use the profitability index to identify the optimal combination of projects to undertake because the profitability index measures the value created in terms of NPV per unit of resources consumed. After computing the profitability index, practitioners rank projects from the highest index down until the resource is used up.

Examples with Step-by-Step Solutions

Solving Problems

Problems using the concepts in this chapter generally involve determining the NPV or IRR for a simple project. The ability to evaluate mutually exclusive projects using the NPV rule may be asked as well. Finally, there may be applications involving selecting projects in the presence of a limited amount of capital (or some other resource) using the profitability index. The examples below demonstrate these three types of problems.

Examples

1. **Microsoft is considering moving 1,000 employees from a help-desk call center in Seattle to Bombay. The total after-tax cost of a Seattle worker is $50,000 per year and the total after-tax cost of a Bombay worker is $30,000 per year. The move would require paying an upfront severance package worth $40,000 after taxes per former Seattle employee. Assume for this analysis that the cost savings would last forever and that Microsoft's cost of capital is 20%.**
   [A]   Should the project be accepted based on the NPV rule?
   [B]   What is the IRR of the project?
   [C]   Can the IRR be relied on in this application?

   Step 1. Put the cash flows on a time line.

   The time 0 cost is $40,000(1,000) = $40 million. The annual savings is $50,000(1,000) = $50 million, and the new annual cost is$30,000(1,000) = $30 million, so the annual net incremental cash flow is $20 million.

Year	0	1	8	9	10
	-$40 million	$20 million	$20 million	$20 million	$20 million

   Step 2. Determine the NPV. Since the cash flows after time 0 are a perpetuity:

   $$\text{NPV} = \sum_{n=0}^{N}\frac{C_n}{(1+r)^n} = \sum_{n=0}^{\infty}\frac{C_n}{(1.2)^n} = C_0 + \frac{C}{r} = -40,000,000 + \frac{20,000,000}{.2} = \$60 \text{ million}$$

   Since the NPV > 0, the project should be accepted.

   Step 3. Determine the IRR by setting the NPV equal to zero and solving for the rate.

   $$\text{NPV} = 0 \Rightarrow \sum_{n=0}^{\infty}\frac{C_n}{(1+\text{IRR})^n} = -40,000,000 + \frac{20,000,000}{\text{IRR}} = 0 \Rightarrow \text{IRR} = \frac{20,000,000}{40,000,000} = 50\%$$

Since the IRR > 20%, the IRR rule says to accept the project as well.

Step 4. Determine if the IRR rule can be relied on.

The IRR rule can be relied on here because the cash flow at time 0 is negative and all future cash flows are positive. Also, the decision being made involves a stand-alone project, not mutually exclusive projects, in which case the IRR could not be relied in.

2. **Pulte Homes purchased 100 acres in suburban Los Angeles. They are considering the following development options:**

	NPV in millions	Acres used
Housing development A	$30	100
Housing development B	$24.5	70
Drug store	$3	3
Strip mall	$3.5	7
Golf course	$8	20

Which project(s) should the firm choose?

Step 1. Since the amount of land is a limited resource, calculate the profitability indices for each project relative to how much land they use.

$$\text{Profitabiliy Index} = \frac{\text{NPV}}{\text{Land Used}}$$

	Profitability Index	Acres used
Housing development A	.30	100
Housing development B	.35	70
Drug store	1.00	3
Strip mall	.50	7
Golf course	.40	20

Step 2. Rank the projects based on how much land they use:

	Rank	Acres used
Drug store	1	3
Strip mall	2	7
Golf course	3	20
Housing development B	4	70
Housing development A	5	100

Step 3. Select the projects in descending order of profitability index until all the land is used.

Select the drug store, strip mall, golf course, and housing development A.

3. **You are deciding between two mutually exclusive investment opportunities. They both require the same initial investment of $10 million. Project X generates $5 million per year (starting at the end of the first year) in perpetuity. Project Y generates $4 million at the end of the first year and will grow at 5% per year for every year after that. The cost of capital is 10%.**
   [A] Which investment has the higher IRR?
   [B] What project should be chosen?
   [C] In this case, when does picking the higher IRR give the correct answer as to which investment is the best opportunity?

Step 1. Put the cash flows of each project on a time line.

Project X

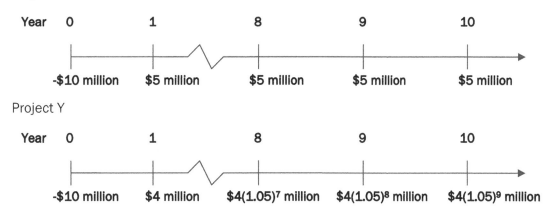

Project Y

| Year | 0 | 1 | 8 | 9 | 10 |

-\$10 million   \$4 million $4(1.05)^7$ million $4(1.05)^8$ million $4(1.05)^9$ million

Step 2. Calculate the IRR of each project.

Project X is a perpetuity and project Y is a growing perpetuity, so set the NPV of those valuation equations equal to zero.

$$NPV_A = 0 = -10,000,000 + \left(\frac{5,000,000}{IRR} \right) \Rightarrow IRR = \frac{5,000,000}{10,000,000} = 50\%$$

$$NPV_B = 0 = -10,000,000 + \left(\frac{4,000,000}{IRR - .05} \right) \Rightarrow IRR = \frac{4,000,000}{10,000,000} + .05 = 45\%$$

Step 3. Since the projects are mutually exclusive, the NPV must be calculated to determine which investment is better.

$$NPV_A = -10,000,000 + \left(\frac{5,000,000}{.10} \right) \Rightarrow NPV = \$40 \text{ million}$$

$$NPV_B = -10,000,000 + \left(\frac{4,000,000}{.10 - .05} \right) \Rightarrow NPV = \$70 \text{ million}$$

Since the NPV of Project Y is much higher, it is the best project. In this case relying on the IRR rule would lead to the wrong conclusion since Project X has a higher IRR.

Questions and Problems

1. You own a gold mining company and are considering opening a new mine. The mine is expected to generate $10 million for the next 21 years. After 21 years, the gold is expected to be depleted, but the site can be sold for an expected $20 million. If the cost of capital is 8%, what is the most you should invest to open the mining operation at time 0?

2. You are considering opening a new hotel. The hotel will cost $150 million upfront and will be built immediately. It is expected to produce profits of $20 million every year forever. Calculate the NPV of this investment opportunity if your cost of capital is 10%. Should you make the investment? Calculate the IRR and use it to determine the maximum deviation allowable in the cost of capital estimate to leave the decision unchanged.

3. The Professional Golf Association (PGA) is considering developing a new PGA-branded golf ball. Development will take 3 years at a cost of $250,000 per year. Once in production, the ball is expected to make $250,000 per year for 5 years at which time new technology will make it obsolete. The cost of capital is 10%. Calculate the NPV of this investment opportunity. Should the PGA make the investment?

4. You are considering making a movie. The movie is expected to cost $100 million upfront and take a year to make. After that, it is expected to make $85 million in the first year it is released and $5 million for the following 20 years. What is the payback period of this investment? If you require a payback period of two years, will you make the movie? Does the NPV rule agree with the payback rule if the cost of capital is 10%?

5. Your corporation has $1 million to spend on capital investments this year and is evaluating four investments. The following table summarizes NPV and cost of these investments.

	NPV	Cost
1	$400,000	$400,000
2	$300,000	$200,000
3	$650,000	$400,000
4	$150,000	$600,000

Which project(s) should the firm choose?

Solutions to Questions and Problems

1. Using X as the initial investment:

$$NPV = X + \frac{10}{.08}\left(1 - \frac{1}{(1.08)^{21}}\right) + \frac{20}{(1.08)^{21}} = X + 100 + 4 = 0 \Rightarrow X = -\$104 \text{ million.}$$

Thus, the most you should invest is $104 million.

2. $NPV = -150 + \frac{20}{.10} = -150 + 200 = \$50 \text{ million, so you should accept the project.}$

The IRR can be found by setting the NPV = 0:

$$NPV = -150 + \frac{20}{IRR} = 0 \Rightarrow IRR = \frac{20}{150} = 13.3\%.$$

So the cost of capital can be underestimated by 3.3% without changing the decision.

3. $NPV = \frac{-250,000}{.10}\left(1 - \frac{1}{(1.10)^3}\right) + \left(\frac{1}{(1.10)^3}\right)\frac{250,000}{.10}\left(1 - \frac{1}{(1.10)^5}\right)$

   $= -621,713 + 712,019 = 90,036 > 0.$

NPV > 0, so the company should take the project.

4. It will take 4 years to pay back the initial investment, so the payback period is 4 years. You will <u>not</u> make the movie.

$$NPV = -100 + \frac{85}{(1.10)^2} + \frac{5}{.10}\left(1 - \frac{1}{(1.10)^{20}}\right)\frac{1}{(1+r)^2}$$

   $= -100 + 70.2 + 42.6 = \$12.8 \text{ million} > 0.$

So the NPV does not agree with the payback rule in this case.

5.

	Profitability Index	Cost
1	1.000	$400,000
2	1.500	$200,000
3	1.625	$400,000
4	0.250	$600,000

Select the projects in descending order of profitability index until all the money is used. They should select 3, 2, and 1.

CHAPTER 7

Fundamentals of Capital Budgeting

Chapter Synopsis

7.1 Forecasting Earnings

A firm's **capital budget** lists all of the projects that a firm plans to undertake during the next period. The selection of projects that should be included in the capital budget is called the **capital budgeting** decision. To evaluate a project, the project's future free cash flows must first be estimated. Some aspects of a project will affect the firm's revenues, while others will affect its costs.

The first step is generally to generate revenue and cost estimates and forecast expected incremental income statements for the project. For example, in the HomeNet project example in this chapter, the following income statements were forecasted in Spreadsheet 7.1:

TABLE 7.1 SPREADSHEET   **HomeNet's Incremental Earnings Forecast**

Year	0	1	2	3	4	5
Incremental Earnings Forecast ($000s)						
1 Sales	—	26,000	26,000	26,000	26,000	—
2 Cost of Goods Sold	—	(11,000)	(11,000)	(11,000)	(11,000)	—
3 Gross Profit	—	15,000	15,000	15,000	15,000	—
4 Selling, General, and Administrative	—	(2,800)	(2,800)	(2,800)	(2,800)	—
5 Research and Development	(15,000)	—	—	—	—	—
6 Depreciation	—	(1,500)	(1,500)	(1,500)	(1,500)	(1,500)
7 EBIT	(15,000)	10,700	10,700	10,700	10,700	(1,500)
8 Income Tax at 40%	6,000	(4,280)	(4,280)	(4,280)	(4,280)	600
9 Unlevered Net Income	(9,000)	6,420	6,420	6,420	6,420	(900)

▪ **Capital Expenditures and Depreciation.** Investments in plant, property, and equipment are not directly listed as expenses when calculating earnings. Instead, the firm deducts a fraction of the cost of these items each year as depreciation. Several different methods are used to compute depreciation. The simplest method is straight-line depreciation, in which the asset's cost is divided equally over its life.

- **Interest Expenses.** When evaluating a capital budgeting decision, interest expense is generally not included in the income statement. The effects of using debt financing, such as incurring interest expense, is accounted for in the appropriate discount rate used to evaluate this project, the weighted average cost of capital, which is discussed in detail later in the text. Thus, the net income computed in Spreadsheet 7.1 is referred to as the **unlevered net income** of the project, indicating that it does not include any interest expenses associated with using debt financing.

- **Taxes.** The correct tax rate to use is the firm's marginal corporate tax rate, which is the tax rate it will pay on an incremental dollar of pre-tax income.

Project externalities are indirect effects of the project that may increase or decrease the cash flow of other business activities of the firm.

- The **opportunity cost** of using a resource is the value it could have provided in its best alternative use. Because this value is lost when the resource is used by another project, the opportunity cost should be included as an incremental cost of the project.

- A **sunk cost** is any cost that has been paid (such as past research and development expenses) or will be paid regardless of the decision whether to proceed with the project. Therefore, it is not incremental with respect to the current decision and should not be included in the analysis.

- When sales of a new product displace sales of an existing product, the situation is often referred to as **cannibalization.**

- **Overhead expenses** are associated with activities that are not directly attributable to a single business activity but instead affect many different areas of the corporation. To the extent that these overhead costs are fixed and will be incurred in any case, they are not incremental to the project and should not be included.

7.2 Determining Free Cash Flow and NPV

The incremental effect of a project on the firm's available cash is the project's **free cash flow** (FCF). It can be calculated as:

Free Cash Flow (FCF) = $EBIT \times (1 - \tau)$ + Depreciation − Capital Expenditures − ΔNWC

- Since depreciation is not a cash expense (it is a method used for accounting and tax purposes to allocate the original purchase cost of the asset over its life), it should be added back to the unlevered net income. Depreciation does have an effect on FCF—it reduces taxes be Depreciation $\times (1 - \tau)$, the **depreciation tax shield.**

- **Capital expenditures** are cash payments made to acquire fixed assets.

- **Net working capital** is the difference between current assets and current liabilities. The main components of net working capital are cash, inventory, accounts receivable, and accounts payable.

Net Working Capital (NWC) = Current Assets − Current Liabilities

$$\approx \text{Cash} + \text{Inventory} + \text{Accounts Receivable} - \text{Accounts Payable}$$

Most projects will require the firm to invest in net working capital—often at a project's inception (time 0). The annual investment required investment is as follows.

$$\Delta NWC_t = NWC_t - NWC_{t-1}$$

While it is generally assumed that cash flows occur at annual intervals beginning in one year, in reality, cash flows will typically be spread throughout the year. Cash flows can also be forecasted on a quarterly, monthly, or even continuous basis when greater accuracy is required.

Because depreciation contributes positively to the firm's cash flow through the depreciation tax shield, the most accelerated method of depreciation that is allowable for tax purposes increases the value of a project. In the United States, the most accelerated depreciation method allowed by the IRS is Modified Accelerated Cost Recovery System (MACRS) depreciation. With MACRS depreciation, assets are categorized according to their asset class, and a corresponding MACRS depreciation tables assigns a fraction of the purchase price that the firm can depreciate each year.

For the HomeNet project considered in the chapter, FCFs were forecasted in Spreadsheet 7.3.

TABLE 7.3 SPREADSHEET — Calculation of HomeNet's Free Cash Flow (Including Cannibalization and Lost Rent)

Year	0	1	2	3	4	5
Incremental Earnings Forecast ($000s)						
1 Sales	—	23,500	23,500	23,500	23,500	—
2 Cost of Goods Sold	—	(9,500)	(9,500)	(9,500)	(9,500)	—
3 Gross Profit	—	14,000	14,000	14,000	14,000	—
4 Selling, General, and Administrative	—	(3,000)	(3,000)	(3,000)	(3,000)	—
5 Research and Development	(15,000)	—	—	—	—	—
6 Depreciation	—	(1,500)	(1,500)	(1,500)	(1,500)	(1,500)
7 EBIT	(15,000)	9,500	9,500	9,500	9,500	(1,500)
8 Income Tax at 40%	6,000	(3,800)	(3,800)	(3,800)	(3,800)	600
9 Unlevered Net Income	(9,000)	5,700	5,700	5,700	5,700	(900)
Free Cash Flow ($000s)						
10 Plus: Depreciation	—	1,500	1,500	1,500	1,500	1,500
11 Less: Capital Expenditures	(7,500)	—	—	—	—	—
12 Less: Increases in NWC	—	(2,100)	—	—	—	2,100
13 Free Cash Flow	(16,500)	5,100	7,200	7,200	7,200	2,700

Once the FCFs over the life of a project have been determined, the NPV can be calculated as:

$$NPV = FCF_0 + \frac{FCF_1}{(1+r)^1} + \frac{FCF_2}{(1+r)^2} + \cdots + \frac{FCF_T}{(1+r)^T} = \sum_{t=0}^{T} \frac{FCF_t}{(1+r)^t}.$$

For the HomeNet example in the chapter, the NPV was found to be positive; it was calculated in Spreadsheet 7.5.

TABLE 7.5 SPREADSHEET	Computing HomeNet's NPV						
Year	**0**	**1**	**2**	**3**	**4**	**5**
Net Present Value ($000s)							
1 Free Cash Flow		(16,500)	5,100	7,200	7,200	7,200	2,700
2 Project Cost of Capital	12%						
3 Discount Factor		1.000	0.893	0.797	0.712	0.636	0.567
4 PV of Free Cash Flow		(16,500)	4,554	5,740	5,125	4,576	1.532
5 NPV		5,027					

7.3 Choosing Among Alternatives

In many situations, you must compare mutually exclusive alternatives, each of which has consequences for the firm's cash flows. In such cases, you can make the best decision by first computing the free cash flow associated with each alternative and then choosing the alternative with the highest NPV.

7.4 Further Adjustments to Free Cash Flow

A number of complications can arise when estimating a project's free cash flow, such as non-cash charges, alternative depreciation methods, liquidation or continuation values, and tax loss carryforwards.

Other non-cash items that appear as part of incremental earnings should not be included in the project's free cash flow. The firm should include only actual cash revenues or expenses. For example, the firm adds back any amortization of intangible assets (such as patents) to unlevered net income when calculating free cash flow.

Because depreciation contributes positively to the firm's cash flow through the depreciation tax shield, it is in the firm's best interest to use the most accelerated method of depreciation that is allowable for tax purposes. By doing so, the firm will accelerate its tax savings and increase its present value. In the United States, the most accelerated depreciation method allowed by the IRS is MACRS (Modified Accelerated Cost Recovery System) depreciation. With MACRS depreciation, the firm first categorizes assets according to their recovery period. Based on the recovery period, MACRS depreciation tables assign a fraction of the purchase price that the firm can recover each year.

Assets that are no longer needed often have a resale value or some salvage value if the parts are sold for scrap. When an asset is liquidated, any gain on sale is taxed. The gain on sale is the difference between the sale price and the book value of the asset. The book value is equal to the asset's original cost less the amount it has already been depreciated for tax purposes. You must adjust the project's free cash flow to account for the after-tax cash flow that would result from an asset sale as:

After-Tax Cash Flow from Asset Sale = Sale Price − (t_c x Gain on Sale).

Sometimes the firm explicitly forecasts free cash flow over a shorter horizon than the full horizon of the project or investment. This is necessarily true for investments with an indefinite life, such as an expansion of the firm. In this case, we estimate the value of the remaining free cash flow beyond the forecast horizon by including an additional, one-time cash flow at the end of the forecast horizon called the **terminal** or **continuation value** of the project. This amount represents the market value (as of the last forecast period) of the free cash flow from the project at all future dates. For example, when analyzing investments with long lives, it is common to explicitly calculate free cash flow over a short horizon, and then assume that cash flows grow at some constant rate beyond the forecast horizon.

Since 1997, companies can utilize **tax loss carrybacks** from the last two years to offset taxable income in the current year. They can also utilize **tax loss carryforwards** and use losses in the current year to reduce taxable income for up to 20 years in the future.

7.5 Analyzing the Project

Sensitivity analysis shows how the NPV varies when changing one variable. **Scenario** analysis considers the effect on the NPV of changing multiple project variables together. As part of a project analysis it is useful to perform **break-even analysis** by studying how far a variable can be changed until the project's NPV is 0.

Selected Concepts and Key Terms

Capital Budgeting, Capital Budget

The capital budget lists all of the projects that a firm plans to undertake during the next period. The selection of projects that should be included in the capital budget is called the capital budgeting decision.

Unlevered Net Income

When evaluating a capital budgeting decision, interest expense is generally not included in the income statement, and the effects of using debt financing, such as incurring interest expense, is accounted for in the appropriate discount rate used to evaluate this project, the weighted average cost of capital, discussed in detail later. Thus, the net income does not include interest expense, and it is referred to as the unlevered net income.

Marginal Corporate Tax Rate

The tax rate a firm will pay on the next incremental dollar of pre-tax income.

Cannibalization

When sales of a new product displace sales of an existing product.

Opportunity Cost

The value an asset could provide in its best alternative use. Because this value is lost when the resource is used by another project, it should be included as an incremental cost of the project.

Sunk Cost

Any unrecoverable cost for which the firm is already liable. Sunk costs have been or will be paid regardless of the decision whether to proceed with the project, and therefore they should not be included in the analysis of the project.

Free Cash Flow

The periodic incremental effect of a project on the firm's available cash. It can generally be calculated as operating cash flow minus capital spending minus the increase in net working capital.

Trade Credit

The difference between accounts receivable and accounts payable; it is the net amount of the firm's capital that is used as a result of credit transactions.

Depreciation Tax Shield

The tax savings that results from the ability to deduct depreciation. It generally equals depreciation expense × tax rate.

Modified Accelerated Cost Recovery System (MACRS) Depreciation

The most accelerated depreciation method allowed by the Internal Revenue Service. Assets are categorized according to their asset class and a corresponding MACRS depreciation tables assigns a fraction of the purchase price that the firm can depreciate each year.

Terminal Value, Continuation Value

The present value (as of the last forecast period) of the free cash flow from the project at all future dates after the last forecast period.

Break-Even Analysis

Studying how far a variable can be changed until the project's NPV is 0.

Sensitivity Analysis

An analysis of how the NPV of a project varies when changing one variable.

Scenario Analysis

An analysis of how the NPV of a project varies when changing multiple project variables together.

Concept Check Questions and Answers

7.1.1. How do we forecast unlevered net income?

Interest and other financing-related expenses are excluded from the forecasted income statements to determine a project's unlevered net income.

7.1.2. Should we include sunk costs in the cash flows of a project? Why or why not?

We should not include sunk costs in the cash flows of a project because sunk costs must be paid regardless of whether or not the firm decides to proceed with the project. Sunk costs are not incremental with respect to the current decision.

7.1.3. Explain why you must include the opportunity cost of using a resource as an incremental cost of a project.

We must include the opportunity cost of using a resource as an incremental cost of a project because that resource can be used in the next-best alternative way. It is a mistake to assume that the resource is free.

7.2.1. What adjustments must you make to a project's unlevered net income to determine its free cash flows?

You must add depreciation back (because it is a non-cash expense) and subtract capital spending and the change in working capital.

7.2.2. What is the depreciation tax shield?

The depreciation tax shield is the reduction in tax expense from the ability to deduct depreciation expense before determining taxable income.

7.3.1. How do you choose between mutually exclusive capital budgeting decisions?

You can make the best decision by first computing the free cash flows and NPVs of each alternative and then choosing the alternative with the highest NPV.

7.3.2. When choosing between alternatives, what cash flows can be ignored?

Components of free cash flow that are the same in each alternative can be ignored.

7.4.1. Explain why it is advantageous for a firm to use the most accelerated depreciation schedule possible for tax purposes.

Because depreciation contributes positively to the firm's cash flow through the depreciation tax shield, it is in the firm's best interest to use the most accelerated method of depreciation that is allowable for tax purposes. By doing so, the firm will accelerate its tax savings and increase its present value.

7.4.2. What is the continuation or terminal value of a project?

The continuation or terminal value of a project is the estimated value of the remaining free cash flow beyond the forecast horizon of the project. This amount represents the market value (as of the last forecast period) of the free cash flow from the project at all future dates.

7.5.1. What is sensitivity analysis?

Sensitivity analysis breaks the NPV calculation into its component assumptions and shows how the NPV varies as the underlying assumptions change. In this way, sensitivity analysis allows us to explore the impact of errors in NPV estimates for the project.

7.5.2. How does scenario analysis differ from sensitivity analysis?

Sensitivity analysis changes one parameter at a time. Scenario analysis changes the effect on NPV of changing multiple project parameters simultaneously.

Examples with Step-by-Step Solutions

Solving Problems

Problems using the concepts in this chapter generally involve finding the NPV of potential projects given a cost of capital. The NPV is the present value of a project's free cash flow from time 0 to the end of the project. This requires forecasting income statements over the life of the project, calculating free cash flow = EBIT(1 – t) + depreciation – capital expenditures – the increase in net working capital each year, and calculating the NPV. You may also need to determine a project's IRR, which is the discount rate that makes the NPV of the project's FCFs equal to $0.

Examples

1. Your firm owns a Volkswagen dealership, and you are considering entering into a 5-year agreement to also sell Audi A4s. The cars would cost $26,000, and you believe that you can sell 50 Audis per year at an average price of $30,000. You would have to hire 2 new sales people that you would pay $30,000 per year each plus 5% of the revenue they each generate. Audi would require that you invest $200,000 (depreciable straight line over 5 years) in Audi-related signs, equipment, and furniture to place in your dealership. You would also be required to invest in 20 cars to keep in inventory over the life of the project. After 5 years, you can recover any investment in working capital, and the unneeded equipment would have a market value of $50,000. Your firm requires a 12% return on all new investments, and the tax rate is 40%. Should you accept the project? Show your work and justify your answer.

Step 1. Determine how you should make the decision.

The project's NPV will indicate whether the project will add value to your firm, so the NPV should be calculated.

Step 2. Determine the income statements for years 1 through 5 of the project.

Since there is straight line depreciation on the $200,000 investment in capital assets, annual depreciation is $200,000 / 5 = $40,000.

Each year will be the same.

Sales	1,500,000
Cost of goods sold	1,300,000
Gross profit	200,000
Selling, general & admin. costs	
Salary	60,000
Commission	75,000
EBITDA	65,000
Depreciation	40,000
EBIT	25,000
–Tax @ 40%	10,000
Net Income	$15,000

Step 3. Determine the Free Cash Flows for years 0 through 5.

Operating cash flow equals net income + depreciation each year, which is $15,000 + $40,000 = $55,000.

Capital spending is $200,000 at time 0.

At the end of year 5, the equipment can be sold for $50,000, resulting in an after-tax cash flow = sale price $- \tau \times$ (sale price – book value) = $50,000 – 0.40($50,000 – 0) = $30,000.

The time 0 investment in working capital is 20 cars at $26,000, or $520,000.

At the end of the project, the investment in working capital could be recovered. The year 5 income statement's cost of goods sold would be overstated by $520,000, since you effectively bought 20 of the cars you sold in year 5 at time 0, so the decrease in working capital is a $520,000 cash inflow.

	0	1	2	3	4	5
Operating cash flow	–	55,000	55,000	55,000	55,000	55,000
– Capital expenditures	200,000	0	0	0	0	-30,000
– Increases in working capital	520,000	0	0	0	0	-520,000
Free Cash Flow	-720,000	55,000	55,000	55,000	55,000	605,000

Step 4. Calculate the project's NPV.

$$NPV = -720,000 + \frac{55,000}{(1.12)} + \frac{55,000}{(1.12)^2} + \frac{55,000}{(1.12)^3} + \frac{55,000}{(1.12)^4}$$
$$+ \frac{55,000+30,000+520,000}{(1.12)^5} = -\$209,653 < 0$$

Since the NPV is less than zero, the project cannot be justified given the forecasts. In other words, the project costs $720,000 and is only worth about $510,347 (720,000 – 209,653). This implies that the IRR is less than 12% and can be calculated to be about 3%.

2. **Calaveras Vineyards, a highly profitable wine producer, is considering the purchase of 10,000 French oak barrels at a cost of $900 each, or $9 million for all of them. The barrels would be considered a capital expense and would be depreciated straight line over 5 years. After 4 years, the barrels will be useless for making fine wine, but they expect to be able to sell them for $3 million to Gallo. The increase in the quality of its zinfandel line of wines due to the use of the new French oak barrels is expected to increase revenue by $7 million in years 3 and 4. The barrels would have no influence on COGS, SG&A, other operating expenses, or working capital. The tax rate is 40%, and the required return is 15%.**
   [A]   According to the NPV rule, is the purchase of the barrels a good idea?
   [B]   According to the IRR rule, is the purchase of the barrels a good idea?

Step 1. In order to calculate the NPV and IRR, the FCFs over the life of the project (years 0 through 4) need to be calculated. Thus, the each year's income statement must be determined.

Step 2. Determine the income statements from years 1 through 4 for the project.

	1	2	3	4
Sales	0	0	7,000,000	7,000,000
– Cost of goods sold	0	0	0	0
– Selling, general & admin. costs	0	0	0	0
EBITDA	0	0	7,000,000	7,000,000
– Depreciation	1,800,000	1,800,000	1,800,000	1,800,000
EBIT	-1,800,000	-1,800,000	5,200,000	5,200,000
– Tax	-720,000	-720,000	2,080,000	2,080,000
Net income	-1,080,000	-1,080,000	3,120,000	3,120,000

Step 3. Determine operating cash flow in years 1 through 4.

	1	2	3	4
Net income	-1,080,000	-1,080,000	3,120,000	3,120,000
+ Depreciation	1,800,000	1,800,000	1,800,000	1,800,000
= Operating cash flow	720,000	720,000	4,920,000	4,920,000

Step 4. Determine the Free Cash Flows for years 0 through 4.

	0	1	2	3	4
Operating cash flow	0	720,000	720,000	4,920,000	4,920,000
– Capital expenditures	9,000,000	0	0	0	2,520,000
– Increase in working capital	0	0	0	0	0
Free Cash Flow	–9,000,000	720,00	720,00	4,920,00	7,440,000

Since the book value of the barrels is $1.8 million after 5 years, the after-tax cash flow from selling the barrels in year 5 is = sale price $- \tau \times$ (sale price – book value) = $3 million – 0.40($3 million – 1.8 million) = $2.52 million.

Step 5. Calculate the project's NPV.

$$NPV = -9,000,000 + \frac{720,000}{(1.15)} + \frac{720,000}{(1.15)^2} + \frac{4,920,000}{(1.15)^3} + \frac{7,440,000}{(1.15)^4} = -\$340,666 < 0$$

Since the NPV is less than zero, the project cannot be justified given the forecasts. However it is pretty close, the project costs $9,000,000 and is worth about $8,660,000 and there may be other strategic issues (such as an increase in the perceived value of the brand due to the quality increase from the zinfandel) that are not included in this scenario.

Step 6. Calculate the project's IRR.

$$NPV = -9,000,000 + \frac{720,000}{(1+IRR)} + \frac{720,000}{(1+IRR)^2} + \frac{4,920,000}{(1+IRR)^3} + \frac{7,440,000}{(1+IRR)^4} = 0 \Rightarrow IRR = 13.7\%$$

The IRR is less than 15%, so the project cannot be justified based on the forecasts.

Note that the determination of IRR requires iteration, i.e., trying various IRRs until the NPV=$0. This process is best performed using the IRR function in a spreadsheet as shown below.

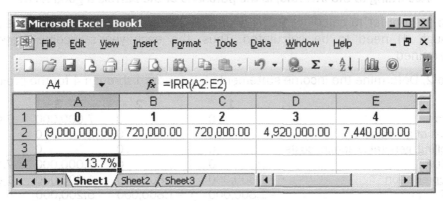

3. Your firm has a vacant warehouse in Louisiana that has a market value of $15 million and a book value of $0. You are considering entering into a 10-year contract to become the exclusive Coca-Cola bottler for your region. You would need to purchase $10 million worth of equipment, which you would depreciate straight line over 5 years; after 10 years, the equipment would have a market value of $2 million. You would also need to invest $2 million in working capital, which you can recover at the end of the project. You would sell $5 million worth of Coke products each year. Total costs (excluding taxes and depreciation) would be 60% of sales per year. You anticipate that the value of the warehouse will increase by about 2% per year and be worth $18 million in 10 years. The tax rate is 40% and the firm's cost of

capital is 12%. Does the project satisfy your investment criteria? Show your work and justify your answer.

Step 1. Determine how you should make the decision.

The project's NPV will indicate whether the project will add value to your firm, so the NPV should be calculated.

Step 2. Determine the income statements from years 1 through 10 for the project along with the operating cash flows.

	1-5	6-10
Sales	5,000,000	5,000,000
Cost of goods sold + SG&A	3,000,000	3,000,000
EBITDA	2,000,000	2,000,000
Depreciation	2,000,000	0
EBIT	0	2,000,000
- Tax @ 40%	0	800,000
Net Income	0	1,200,000
+ Depreciation	2,000,000	0
= Operating cash flow	2,000,000	1,200,000

Note that depreciation =$10,000,000/5 = $2,000,000 for years 1–5 and $0 in years 6–10.

Step 3. Calculate the Free Cash Flows.

Free Cash Flows for years 0 through 10 are:

	0	1-5	6-9	10
Operating cash flow	0	2,000,000	1,200,000	1,200,000
- Capital expenditures	19,000,000	0	0	-12,000,000
- Increase in working capital	2,000,000	0	0	-2,000,000
Free Cash Flow	-21,000,000	2,000,000	1,200,000	15,200,000

Time 0 capital spending includes the $10 million of equipment that would need to be purchased. There is also an opportunity cost associated with using the warehouse. The after-tax cash flow = sale price $- \tau \times$ (sale price – book value) = $15 million – 0.40($15 million – 0) = $9 million. Thus, capital spending is $19 million.

NWC will increase by $2 million at time 0, and it will decrease by $2 million in year 10.

Step 4. Calculate the NPV.

$$NPV = -21,000,000 + 2,000,000 \left[\frac{1}{.12} - \frac{1}{.12(1.12)^5} \right] + \frac{1,200,000 \left[\frac{1}{.12} - \frac{1}{.12(1.12)^4} \right]}{1.12^5} + \frac{15,200,000}{1.12^{10}}$$

$$= -\$6,828,286 < 0$$

Since the NPV is above zero, the project cannot be justified given the forecasts, and it should be rejected.

Questions and Problems

1. Your large, highly profitable golf course management firm owns 200 acres in Surprise, Arizona. The land is surrounded by a housing development and is zoned exclusively for a golf course. The non-depreciable land has increased in value over the year since you bought it from $10 million to $35 million, and someone has offered to buy it for this price. Your original plan was to develop the land over the next 3 years by spending $20 million per year in pre-tax development costs. You would also have to spend $30 million in capital equipment today, and this would be depreciated straight line over 3 years. Based on the performance of the other courses you own, you expect annual revenue from the course to be $40 million when it opens 3 years from today and that all operating costs (excluding tax and depreciation) will amount to 50% of revenue. From then on, you expect that the free cash flow the course generates will grow by 3% forever. The tax rate is 40%, and you require a 15% return.

2. You are considering the purchase of super-automatic espresso machines to replace the existing manually operated machines in your chain of 1,000 coffee shops around the country. Each machine has a cost of $10,000, and you would have to buy 1,000. You could then sell the 1,000 existing La Marzocco machines in the stores now for $2,000 each. The old machines have zero book values. The new machines would have no effect on revenues, but you could save an estimated $3,000 per store per year in labor and training costs since operating a super-automatic espresso machine is easier. The new machines would have a 10-year depreciable life and be worthless after 10 years. You require a 15% return on all investments and are taxed at 40%. Does the project satisfy your investment criteria? Show your work and justify your answer.

3. You are considering the purchase of 1,000 Coke machines in the greater Chicago area. The machines cost $2,500 each and are depreciable straight-line over 5 years. Sales are expected to be 3,000 bottles per machine in the first year at a selling price of $1 per bottle. Sales revenue is expected to be constant every year thereafter. The cost of each bottle is $0.30. Operating expenses include stocking and maintenance and are expected to amount to $1,000 per year per machine. You would have to stock each machine with 200 bottles at the beginning of the project. After 5 years, you plan to sell the machines for $1,000 each and recover any investment in working capital. The tax rate is 40%. The firm uses all equity financing, and stockholders require a 15% return. Determine whether the project is a good idea. Does the project have an IRR above or below 15%?

4. Your firm manufactures custom-labeled, purified bottled water. Your plant generates $10 million in annual sales and runs at full capacity. You currently have four full-time employees who are paid $50,000 each per year and are responsible for removing the bottles from the manufacturing line and packaging them in boxes for delivery. You are considering replacing these four employees with a packaging machine that will do their same jobs. The machine costs $900,000 and would be depreciable straight line over 4 years. The purchase price includes a full warranty that guarantees to keep the machine in working order for 6 years. After 6 years, you would sell the machine back for $100,000. You require a 15% return on investments and the tax rate is 40%. Should you buy the machine?

5. 3com is considering producing a new handheld, wireless internet device. Management spent $3 million last year on test marketing and has developed a set of forecasts. Total cash costs (COGS, SG&A, etc...) of the device will be $30 each, and they will sell them all for $100 each. They can produce 50,000 each year for the next five years, and they expect to sell them all each year. They would have to construct a manufacturing plant, which would cost $10 million to be constructed immediately and be depreciable over 10 years using straight-line depreciation. They would have to invest $2 million in inventory beginning today, and this

amount would not change over the life of the project. In 5 years, they will quit, dispose of the plant for $1 million, and recover working capital. The tax rate is 40%, the firm uses stock financing, and stockholders require a 15% return. Should 3com accept the project? Show any needed calculations and justify the answer.

Solutions to Questions and Problems

1. The project's NPV will indicate whether the project is worth more than the value of just selling the land, so it should be calculated.

   Determine the income statements from years 1 through 4 for the project along with the operating cash flows.

	1-3	**4**
Sales	0	40,000,000
Cost of goods sold + SG&A	20,000,000	20,000,000
EBITDA	−20,000,000	20,000,000
Depreciation	10,000,000	0
EBIT	−30,000,000	20,000,000
– Tax @ 40%	−12,000,000	8,000,000
Net Income	−18,000,000	12,000,000
+ Depreciation	10,000,000	0
= Operating cash flow	-8,000,000	12,000,000

   Depreciation =$30,000,000 / 3 = $10,000,000 for years 1–3 and $0 in year 4 and on.

   Calculate the Free Cash Flows for years 0–4:

	0	**1-3**	**4**
Operating cash flow	–	−8,000,000	12,000,000
– Capital expenditures	30,000,000	0	0
– Increases in working capital	0	0	0
Free Cash Flow	−30,000,000	−8,000,000	12,000,000

   Calculate the NPV.

   $$NPV = -30 + \frac{-8}{1.15} + \frac{-8}{1.15^2} + \frac{-8}{1.15^3} + \frac{\left(\frac{12}{.15-.03}\right)}{1.15^3} = \$17.5 \text{ million}$$

   You would generate 35 – (35 – 10).4 = $25 million > $17.5 million by selling the land, so you should sell.

2. The project's NPV or IRR will indicate whether the project will add value to your firm, so at least the NPV should be calculated.

   Determine the income statements from years 1 through 10 for the project.

   Each year will be the same.

Sales	0
Cost of goods sold	0
Gross profit	0
Selling, general & admin. costs	−3,000,000
EBITDA	3,000,000
Depreciation	1,000,000
EBIT	2,000,000
−Tax @ 40%	800,000
Net Income	$1,200,000

Since there is straight line depreciation on the $10 million investment in capital assets, annual depreciation is $10 millon/10 = $1 million.

The Free Cash Flows for years 0 through 10 are:

Year	0	1-10
Operating cash flow	–	2,200,000
Capital expenditures	−8,800,000	0
Increases in working capital	0	0
Free Cash Flow	−8,800,000	2,200,000

Operating cash flow equals net income + depreciation each year, which is $1,200,000 + $100,000 = $2,200,000.

Capital spending on the new machines is 1,000($10,000) = $10 million at time 0. You can also sell the old machines for $2,000 each resulting in an after-tax cash flow = sale price − $\tau \times$ (sale price − book value) = $2,000 − 0.40($2,000 − 0) = $1,200 each or $1,200(1,000) = $1.2 million for all of them. Thus, capital spending is $8.8 million.

Calculate the project's NPV.

$$NPV = -8,800,000 + 2,200,000 \left[\frac{1}{.15} - \frac{1}{.15(1.15)^{10}} \right] = 2,241,291 > 0$$

Since the NPV is above zero, the project can be justified given the forecasts. This implies that the IRR is above 15%, and can be calculated to be about 21%.

3. If the NPV is greater than 0, the project is acceptable. Once the NPV is calculated, it can be determined if the IRR is above or below 15%.

Determine the income statements from years 1 through 5 for the project (each year is the same) and calculate operating cash flow each year.

Sales	3,000,000
Cost of goods sold	900,000
Gross profit	2,100,000
Selling, general & admin. Costs	1,000,000
EBITDA	1,100,000
Depreciation	500,000
EBIT	600,000
− Tax @ 40%	240,000
Net Income	360,000
+ Depreciation	500,000
= Operating cash flow	860,000

Sales = 3,000(1,000)$1 = $3 million.

Cost of goods sold is 0.30($1)/$1 = 30% of sales each year.

SG&A is $1,000 per machine, or 1,000($1,000) = $1,000,000 for all of them.

Depreciation = $2,500(1,000)/5 = $500,000 each year.

Free Cash Flows for years 0 through 5.

Year	0	1-4	5
Operating cash flow	–	860,000	860,000
– Capital expenditures	2,500,000	0	-600,000
– Increases in working capital	60,000	0	-60,000
Free Cash Flow	-2,560,000	860,000	1,520,000

The after-tax cash flow = sale price – $\tau \times$ (sale price – book value) = $1 million – 0.40($1 million – 0) = $600,000.

Now, the NPV can be calculated.

$$NPV = -2{,}560{,}000 + 860{,}000 \left[\frac{1}{.15} - \frac{1}{.15(1.15)^4} \right] + \frac{1{,}520{,}000}{1.15^5} = 650{,}990 > 0$$

Since the NPV is above zero, the project can be justified given the forecasts. This implies that the IRR is above 15%, and it can be calculated to be about 24%.

4. The project's NPV will indicate whether the project will add value to your firm, so the NPV should be calculated.

Determine the income statements in years 1 through 6 for the project along with the operating cash flows.

	1-4	5-6
Sales	0	0
Cost of goods sold + SG&A	-200,000	-200,000
EBITDA	-200,000	200,000
Depreciation	225,000	0
EBIT	-25,000	200,000
– Tax @ 40%	-10,000	80,000
Net Income	-15,000	120,000
+ Depreciation	225,000	0
= Operating cash flow	210,000	120,000

Depreciation =$900,000 / 4 = $225,000 for years 1–4 and $0 in years 5–6.

Free Cash Flows for years 0 through 6 are:

	0	1-4	5	6
Operating cash flow	–	210,000	120,000	120,000
– Capital expenditures	900,000	0	0	-60,000
– Increases in working capital	0	0	0	0
Free Cash Flow	-900,000	210,000	120,000	180,000

The after-tax cash flow in year 6 from selling the machine = sale price − $\tau \times$ (sale price − book value) = \$100,000 − 0.40(\$100,000 − 0) = \$60,000.

Calculate the NPV.

$$NPV = -900,000 + \frac{210,000}{(1.15)} + \frac{210,000}{(1.15)^2} + \frac{210,000}{(1.15)^3} + \frac{210,000}{(1.15)^4} + \frac{120,000}{(1.15)^5} + \frac{120,000 + 60,000}{(1.15)^6}$$

= −\$162,974, so the firm is worth more with the employees given these assumptions.

5. If the NPV is greater than 0, the project is acceptable.

   Determine the income statements and operating cash flow in years 1 through 5.

Sales	5,000,000
Cost of goods sold	1,500,000
Gross profit	3,500,000
Selling, general & admin. Costs	0
EBITDA	3,500,000
Depreciation	1,000,000
EBIT	2,500,000
− Tax @ 40%	1,000,000
Net Income	1,500,000
+ Depreciation	1,000,000
= Operating cash flow	2,500,000

Free Cash Flows for years 0 through 5 are:

Year	0	1-4	5
Operating cash flow	–	2,500,000	2,500,000
− Capital expenditures	10,000,000	0	−2,600,000
− Increases in working capital	2,000,000	0	−2,000,000
Free Cash Flow	−12,000,000	2,500,000	7,100,000

The after-tax cash flow = sale price − $\tau \times$ (sale price − book value) = \$1 million − 0.40(\$1 million − \$5 million) = \$2.6 million.

Now, the NPV can be calculated.

$$NPV = -12,000,000 + 2,500,000 \left[\frac{1}{.15} - \frac{1}{.15(1.15)^4} \right] + \frac{7,100,000}{1.15^5} = -\$1,332,599 < 0$$

Since the NPV is below zero, the project cannot be justified given the forecasts. This implies that the IRR is below 15%, and it can be calculated to be about 11%.

CHAPTER 8

Valuing Bonds

Chapter Synopsis

8.1 Bond Cash Flows, Prices, and Yields

A bond is a security sold at **face value** (FV), usually $1,000, to investors by governments and corporations. Bonds generally obligate the borrower to make a promised future repayment of face value at the **maturity date** along with interest payments called **coupon payments** that are typically paid semiannually. The amount of each coupon payment is determined by the **coupon rate** of the bond. By convention, the coupon rate is expressed as an APR, so the amount of each coupon payment is:

$$CPN = \frac{\text{Coupon Rate} \times \text{Face value}}{\text{Number of Coupon Payments Per Year}}$$

For example, a "10-year, $1,000 face value bond with a 10% semiannual coupon rate" will pay coupon payments of $1000 \times 0.10/2 = $50 every six months and repay the face value, or **principal**, in 10 years. The terms of the bond are described as part of the bond certificate, which indicates the amounts and dates of all payments to be made.

A **zero-coupon bond**'s only payment is the face value of the bond on the maturity date—it does not make coupon payments. Treasury bills, which are U.S. government bonds with a maturity of up to one year, are zero-coupon bonds and can be valued easily using the present value of a cash flow equation. For example, a one-year, risk-free, zero-coupon bond with a $1,000 face value with a required return of 3.5% is worth:

$$PV = \frac{\$1,000}{1.035} = \$966.18.$$

Zero-coupon bonds always trade at a **discount** (a price lower than the face value) and are sometimes referred to as **pure discount bonds**.

The **yield to maturity** (YTM) of a bond is the discount rate that sets the present value of the promised bond payments equal to the current market price of the bond. For the zero-coupon bond above, the YTM is the return an investor will earn from holding the bond to maturity and can be calculated as:

$$\$966.18 = \frac{\$1,000}{1 + YTM} = \$966.18 \Rightarrow YTM = \frac{\$1,000}{\$966.18} - 1 = 0.035 = 3.5\%.$$

In general, the YTM for a zero coupon bond can be calculated as:

$$P = \frac{FV}{(1 + YTM)^n} \Rightarrow YTM = \left(\frac{FV}{P}\right)^{\frac{1}{n}} - 1.$$

The yield to maturity of an *n*-year, zero-coupon, risk-free bond is generally referred to as the **risk-free interest rate**, or the **spot rate**. The risk-free yield curve, which plots interest rate for risk-free bonds with different maturities, is often constructed using yields of zero coupon Treasury securities, which are generally considered to be risk free.

U.S. **Treasury notes**, which have original maturities from one to ten years, and **Treasury bonds**, which have original maturities of more than ten years, as well as most **corporate bonds** make semiannual coupon payments. The price of a coupon-paying bond with a required return of y can be calculated as:

$$P_0 = \frac{CPN}{1 + y} + \frac{CPN}{(1 + y)^2} + \frac{CPN}{(1 + y)^3} + \cdots + \frac{CPN + FV}{(1 + y)^N} = CPN \times \frac{1}{y}\left(1 - \frac{1}{(1 + y)^N}\right) + \frac{FV}{(1 + y)^N}.$$

Unlike zero-coupon bonds, the yield to maturity for coupon-paying bonds cannot be solved directly with a simple equation. Instead, the calculation requires iteration—guessing until the discount rate that sets the present value of the promised bond payments equal to the current market price of the bond is found. Excel and financial calculators can be used to perform this iteration quickly.

8.2 Dynamic Behavior of Bond Prices

Coupon bonds may trade at:

- **par** (when their price is equal to their face value),
- a **discount** (when their price is less than their face value), or
- a **premium** (when their price is greater than their face value).

Bonds trading at a discount generate a return from both receiving the coupons and from receiving a face value that exceeds the price paid for the bond. As a result, the yield to maturity of discount bonds exceeds the coupon rate. Conversely, the YTM on bonds selling at a premium is lower than the coupon rate because the face value received is less than the price paid for the bond. A bond selling at par has a YTM equal to its coupon rate.

Between coupon payments, the prices of all bonds rise at a rate equal to the semiannual yield to maturity. Also, as shown in Figure 8.1 below:

- As each coupon is paid, the price of a bond drops by the amount of the coupon.
- When the bond is trading at a premium, the price drop when a coupon is paid will be larger than the price increase between coupons, so the bond's premium will tend to decline as time passes.

■ If bond is trading at a discount, the price increase between coupons will exceed the drop when a coupon is paid, so the bond's price will rise, and its discount will decline as time passes.

■ When the bond matures, the price of the bond equals the bond's face value.

Bond prices are subject to the effects of both the passage of time and changes in interest rates. While, as shown in Figure 8.1 below, bond prices converge to the bond's face value due to the time effect, they also move up and down due to unpredictable changes in bond yields. A higher yield to maturity means a higher discount rate for a bond's remaining cash flows, reducing their present value and thus the bond's price. Therefore, there is an inverse relation between bond prices and yields: as the discount rate increases, a bond's price falls, and as the discount rate falls, a bond's price increases.

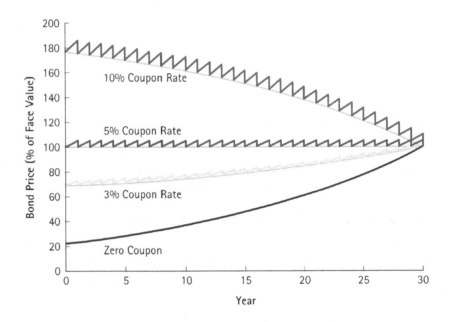

Figure 8.1

The graph illustrates the effects of the passage of time on bond prices per $100 face value when the yield of a bond remains constant at 5%.

The sensitivity of a bond's price to changes in interest rates depends on the timing of its cash flows.

■ Shorter maturity bonds are less sensitive to changes in interest rates because the present value of a cash flow that will be received in the near future is less dramatically affected by interest rates than a cash flow in the distant future.

■ Bonds with higher coupon rates are less sensitive to interest rate changes than otherwise identical bonds with lower coupon rates because they pay a higher proportion of their cash flows sooner.

The sensitivity of a bond's price to changes in interest rate can be measured by its **duration,** which is discussed later in the text.

8.3 The Yield Curve and Bond Arbitrage

It is possible to replicate the cash flows of a risk-free coupon bond using zero-coupon bonds. For example, a three-year, $1,000 bond can be replicated with 1-year, 2-year, and 3-year zero coupon bonds. By the Law of One Price, the three-year coupon bond must trade for the price it costs to replicate the payoffs using the zero-coupon bonds. If the price of the coupon bond were higher, you could earn an arbitrage profit by selling the coupon bond and buying the zero-coupon bond portfolio. If the price of the coupon bond were lower, you could earn an arbitrage profit by buying the coupon bond and short selling the zero-coupon bonds. The no-arbitrage price of a risk-free coupon bond can also be found by discounting its cash flows using the risk-free zero-coupon yields using:

$$P_0 = \frac{CPN}{1 + YTM_1} + \frac{CPN}{(1 + YTM_2)^2} + \frac{CPN}{(1 + YTM_3)^3} + \cdots + \frac{CPN + FV}{(1 + YTM_N)^N}.$$

where YTM_n is the yield to maturity of a zero-coupon bond that matures at the same time as the nth coupon payment. Thus, the information in the zero-coupon yield curve is sufficient to price all other risk-free bonds.

8.4 Corporate Bonds

Corporate bonds have **credit risk,** which is the risk that the borrower will default and not pay all specified payments. As a result, investors pay less for bonds with credit risk than they would for an otherwise identical default-free bond. Because the YTM for a bond is calculated using the promised cash flows, the yields of bonds with credit risk will be higher than that of otherwise identical default-free bonds. However, the YTM of a bond with default risk is always higher than the expected return of investing in the bond because it is calculated using the promised cash flows rather than the expected cash flows.

Bond rating agencies, such as Standard & Poor's and Moody's, evaluate the creditworthiness of bonds and publish bond ratings. The ratings encourage widespread investor participation and bond market liquidity. In descending order of credit quality, ratings by the two firms are as follows.

Standard & Poor's	Moody's	
AAA	Aaa	
AA	Aa	Investment grade
A	A	
BBB	Baa	
BB	Ba	
B	B	Junk bonds
CCC	Caa	

Bonds in the top four categories are often referred to as **investment-grade bonds** and have very low default risk. Bonds in the bottom categories are often called **junk bonds** or **high-yield bonds** because their likelihood of default is relatively high.

Selected Concepts and Key Terms

Corporate Bonds

Bonds issued by corporations. They typically have $1,000 face values and pay semiannual coupon payments.

Coupon Bonds

The promised interest payments of a bond. The bond certificate typically specifies that the coupons will be paid semiannually until the maturity date of the bond.

Coupons, Coupon rate

The interest payments on a bond that are usually paid semiannually. The amount of each coupon payment is determined by the **coupon rate** of the bond. By convention, the coupon rate is expressed as an APR, so the amount of each coupon payment equals [coupon rate × face value] ÷2.

Credit Risk, Credit Spread

Bonds that are not risk free, such as corporate bonds, have **credit risk,** which is the risk that the borrower will default and not make all specified payments. As a result, investors pay less for bonds with credit risk than they would for an otherwise identical default-free bond. Because the YTM for a bond is calculated using the promised cash flows, the yield of bonds reflect a **credit spread** and thus will be higher than that of otherwise identical default-free bonds.

Discount Bond

A bond with a price lower than the face value. For example, zero-coupon bonds are **pure discount bonds.**

High-Yield Bonds, Junk Bonds

Bonds rated below BBB by Standard & Poor's or below Baa by Moody's that have relatively high default risk and relatively high yields.

Investment-Grade Bonds

Bonds rated BBB and above by Standard & Poor's or Baa and above by Moody's that have low default risk.

Maturity Date

The date that a bond repays its face value.

On-the-Run Bond

The most recently issued Treasury bonds for a given maturity.

Premium

The term used for bonds selling at a price greater than their face value.

Face Value (FV)

The amount that a bond pays at its maturity data, typically $1,000. Also referred to as the **principal** or **par value.**

Spot Interest Rates

The yield to maturity of an *n*-year, zero-coupon, risk-free bond.

Treasury Bills, Notes, and Bonds

Securities issued by the U.S. Treasury. Treasury bills have original maturities less than one year and are zero-coupon bonds that are sold at a discount. Treasury notes, which have original maturities from one to ten years, and Treasury bonds, which have original maturities of more than ten years, typically make semiannual coupon payments.

Yield to Maturity (YTM)

The discount rate that sets the present value of the promised bond payments equal to the current market price of the bond. The YTM is the return an investor will earn from holding the bond to maturity

Zero-Coupon Bond

A bond in which the only payment is the face value of the bond on the maturity date—it does not make coupon payments. Treasury bills, which are U.S. government bonds with a maturity of up to one year, are zero-coupon bonds.

Concept Check Questions and Answers

8.1.1. What is the relationship between a bond's price and its yield to maturity?

The yield to maturity of a bond (or the IRR of a bond) is the discount rate that sets the present value of the promised bond payments equal to the current market price of the bond. Thus, the bond price is negatively related to its yield to maturity. When interest rate and bond's yield to maturity rise, the bond price will fall (and vice versa).

8.1.2. The risk-free interest rate for a maturity of *n*-years can be determined from the yield of what type of bond?

The risk-free interest rate for a maturity of *n*-years can be determined from the yield of a default free zero-coupon bond with the same maturity. Because a default-free, zero-coupon bond that matures on date *n* provides a risk-free return over the same period, the Law of One Price guarantees that the risk-free interest rate equals the yield to maturity on such a bond.

8.2.1. If a bond's yield to maturity does not change, how does its cash price change between coupon payments?

Between coupon payments, the prices of all bonds rise at a rate equal to the yield to maturity as the remaining cash flows of the bonds become closer. But as each coupon is paid, the price of a bond drops by the amount of the coupon.

8.2.2. What risk does an investor in a default-free bond face if he or she plans to sell the bond prior to maturity?

An investor in a default-free bond will face the interest rate risk if she plans to sell the bond prior to maturity. If she chooses to sell and the bond's yield to maturity has decreased, then she will receive a high price and earn a high return. If the yield to maturity has increased and the bond price is low at the time of sale, she will earn a low return.

8.2.3. How does a bond's coupon rate affect its duration—the bond price's sensitivity to interest rate changes?

The higher the coupon rate, all else equal, the lower the duration.

8.3.1. How do you calculate the price of a coupon bond from the prices of zero-coupon bonds?

Because we can replicate a coupon-paying bond using a portfolio of zero-coupon bonds, the price of a coupon-paying bond can be determined based on the zero-coupon yield curve using the Law of One Price. In other words, the information in the zero-coupon yield curve is sufficient to price all other risk-free bonds.

8.3.2. How do you calculate the price of a coupon bond from the yields of zero-coupon bonds?

Since zero-coupon bond yields represent competitive market interest rate for a risk-free investment with a term equal to the term of the zero-coupon bond, the price of a coupon bond must equal the present value of its coupon payments and face value discounted at these the zero-coupon bond yields.

8.3.3. Explain why two coupon bonds with the same maturity may each have a different yield to maturity.

The coupon bonds with the same maturity can have different yields depending on their coupon rates. The yield to maturity of a coupon bond is a weighted average of the yields on the zero-coupon bonds. As the coupon increases, earlier cash flows become relatively more important than later cash flows in the calculation of the present value.

8.4.1. There are two reasons the yield of a defaultable bond exceeds the yield of an otherwise identical default-free bond. What are they?

Because the yield must be higher to compensate for the risk of not receiving the required cash flows and to compensate for the fact that the expected cash flow is lower than the required cash flows

8.4.2. What is a bond rating?

A bond rating is a classification provided by several companies that assess the creditworthiness of bonds and make this information available to investors. By consulting these ratings, investors can assess the creditworthiness of a particular bond issue. The ratings therefore encourage widespread investor participation and relatively liquid markets. The two best-known bond-rating companies are Standard & Poor's and Moody's.

Examples with Step-by-Step Solutions

Solving Problems

Problems using the concepts in this chapter generally involve determining the value of a bond. This requires understanding the cash flows associated with bonds and bond terminology, such coupon rate, face value, maturity, and yield to maturity. The valuation of a bond generally involves utilizing the present value of an annuity equation and the present value of a cash flow equation. The yield to maturity can be found by setting the price equal to the present value of the bond's cash flows and solving for the discount rate that equates these two values.

Examples

1. You have an opportunity to buy several B-rated bonds for $841. B-rated bonds currently yield 12% APR, and these bonds have a coupon rate of 10%. The bonds have a face value of $1,000, mature in exactly six years, and the next semiannual coupon payment will occur in exactly 6 months.
   [A]   What is the value of one bond?
   [B]   Is the bond's yield to maturity at a price of $841 equal to, above, or below 12% APR?
   [C]   If you bought some of these bonds and held them until maturity, what would your annual return be?

Step 1. Determine the bond's cash flows. The bond pays semi-annual coupon payments of 0.10($1,000)/2=$50 and pays $1,000 in 6 years.

Step 2. Calculate the value of the bond.

Since similar bonds yield 12% APR, the semi-annual rate of 12%/2=6% should be used to value this bond.

The next coupon is 6 months from today and the face value is repaid exactly 6 years from today. So, using the PV of an annuity equation and the PV of a single cash flow equation:

$$P_0 = 50\left[\frac{1}{.06} - \frac{1}{.06(1.06)^{12}}\right] + \frac{1,000}{(1.06)^{12}} = \$419.19 + 496.97 = \$916.16.$$

Thus, you should buy as many bonds as you can at a price of $841 because they are selling below the market value. Even if you don't want to hold them until maturity, you can expect to sell them for $916.16.

Step 3. Determine if the bond's yield to maturity at a price of $844 is equal to, above, or below 12% APR.

This part does not require any calculations. Since the YTM would be 12% if the value that was found in step 2 was $841, it does not equal 12%. Since the price found in step 2 is greater than $841, the only way to lower the value from $916.16 is to raise the discount rate above 12%, so the YTM must be higher than 12%.

Step 4. Your return is the yield to maturity.

The YTM is the rate that makes the bond's value equal to $841, so

$$P_0 = \$841 = 50\left[\frac{1}{\frac{YTM}{2}} - \frac{1}{\frac{YTM}{2}(1+\frac{YTM}{2})^{12}}\right] + \frac{1,000}{(1+\frac{YTM}{2})^{12}}.$$

Without a financial calculator or spreadsheet, this problem requires iteration—guessing until the equation is correct. From step 3, we know that the YTM must be higher than 12% APR, or 6% per 6 months. So try 7%:

$$P_0 = \$841 = 50 \left[\frac{1}{\frac{YTM}{2}} - \frac{1}{\frac{YTM}{2}(1+\frac{YTM}{2})^{12}} \right] + \frac{1,000}{(1+\frac{YTM}{2})^{12}} \Rightarrow \frac{YTM}{2} = 0.07 \Rightarrow YTM = 14\%.$$

So your return would be the annual YTM, 14% APR.

2. **It is March 16, 2009. Assume that a BBB-rated, 6% semiannual coupon, $1,000 face value bond matures on March 15, 2039. The 30-year Treasury-bond yield is 6.5%.**
   [A]   **If BBB-rated currently have a 4.5% credit spread, how much should you pay for the bond?**
   [B]   **What would the value of the bond be if yields do not change in four months? What would the clean price be at this time?**

Step 1. Put the cash flows on a time line. The bond pays semi-annual coupon payments of 0.06($1,000)/2=$30 and pays $1,000 in 30 years.

Year	2009		2010					2039
Month	March	Sept.	March					March
Payment		1	2					60

$30 $30   [$1,000 + $30]

Step 2. Determine the discount rate.

The risk-free rate on bonds with the same term is 6.5%, and the credit spread is 4.5%, so the market rate on this bond is 6.5% + 4.5% = 11%. So, the semi-annual rate of 11%/2=5.5% should be used to value this bond.

Step 3. Determine the value today.

Since the bond paid a coupon yesterday, the next coupon is 6 months from today and the face value is repaid exactly 30 years from today. So using the PV of an annuity equation and the PV of a single cash flow equation:

$$\text{Value} = \frac{\text{Coupon}}{2} \left[\frac{1}{\left(\frac{r}{2}\right)} - \frac{1}{\left(\frac{r}{2}\right)\left(1+\frac{r}{2}\right)^{2M}} \right] + \frac{\text{Face Value}}{(1+\frac{r}{2})^{2M}}$$

$$= 30 \left[\frac{1}{.055} - \frac{1}{.055(1.055)^{60}} \right] + \frac{1,000}{(1.055)^{60}} = 523.49 + 40.26 = \$563.75.$$

Step 4. Determine the cash value in four months.

The value in four months is the value on the date that the next coupon is paid discounted back two months. Since the EAR = (1 + .055)^2 – 1 = 11.30%, the two-month discount rate is (1.113)$^{2/12}$ – 1 = 1.80%.

So

$$\text{Value} = \frac{\left\{\frac{\text{Coupon}}{2}\left[\frac{1}{\left(\frac{r}{2}\right)} - \frac{1}{\left(\frac{r}{2}\right)\left(1+\frac{r}{2}\right)^{2M}}\right] + 30 + \frac{\text{Face Value}}{(1+\frac{r}{2})^{2M}}\right\}}{1+r_{2\ \text{months}}}$$

$$= \frac{\left\{30\left[\frac{1}{.055} - \frac{1}{.055(1.055)^{59}}\right] + 30 + \frac{1,000}{(1.055)^{59}}\right\}}{1.018} = \$584.24.$$

To verify that this is correct, calculate the holding period return that this implies:

$$\text{Return} = \frac{584.24 - 563.75}{563.75} = 0.036,\ \text{which is the four-month return implied in a 11.3\%:}$$

$$\text{EAR} = (1.113)^{\frac{4}{12}} - 1 = 0.036.$$

Step 5. Determine the clean price.

This is the value (or cash price or dirty price) that was found in step 4, less the accrued interest. The accrued interest is (4/6) × $30 = $20, so the clean price is $564.24.

3. **The following table summarizes prices of zero-coupon U.S. Treasury securities per $100 of face value.**

Maturity in Years	Price
1.	98.04
2.	93.35
3.	86.38
4.	79.21

[A] **Plot the zero-coupon yield curve based on these bonds.**
[B] **Describe the shape of the yield curve.**
[C] **What is the value of a four-year 7% annual coupon Treasury bond with a face value of $1,000 that pays its first coupon in one year?**

Step 1. First, the yield to maturity of each bond must be calculated.

Using the equation $P_0 = \frac{\$100}{(1+\text{IRR})^N}$ and solving for IRR:

$$98.04 = \frac{100}{(1+\text{IRR})^1} \Rightarrow \text{IRR} = \frac{100}{98.04} - 1 = 2.0\%$$

$$93.35 = \frac{100}{(1+\text{IRR})^2} \Rightarrow \text{IRR} = \left(\frac{100}{93.35}\right)^{1/2} - 1 = 3.5\%$$

$$86.38 = \frac{100}{(1+\text{IRR})^3} \Rightarrow \text{IRR} = \left(\frac{100}{86.38}\right)^{1/3} - 1 = 5.0\%$$

$$79.21 = \frac{100}{(1+\text{IRR})^3} \Rightarrow \text{IRR} = \left(\frac{100}{79.21}\right)^{1/4} - 1 = 6.0\%$$

Step 2. Now, the zero-coupon Treasury yield curve can be drawn.

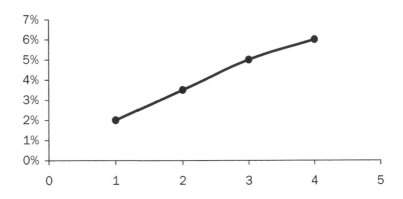

The yield curve is upward sloping. A yield curve with a positive slope is sometimes referred to as a normal yield curve.

Step 3. By the Law of One Price, the 4-year coupon bond must trade for the price it costs to replicate the payoffs using the zero-coupon bonds. The no-arbitrage price can be found by discounting its cash flows using the risk-free zero-coupon yields.

The annual coupon payment is 0.07($1,000) = $70, so

$$P_0 = \frac{70}{1.02} + \frac{70}{(1.035)^2} + \frac{70}{(1.05)^3} + \frac{70+1{,}000}{(1.06)^4}$$

$$= 68.63 + 65.35 + 60.47 + 847.54 = \$1{,}041.99.$$

Questions and Problems

1. Several major companies like Citigroup, Disney, and AT&T have issued Century Bonds. These bonds pay regular semiannual coupons, but do not mature until 100 years after they are issued. Some critics have stated that they are extremely risky because you can't predict what will happen to the companies in 100 years. Assume that such bonds were just issued with a $1,000 par value and an 8% semiannual coupon rate.
   [A] If current market rates are 8%, what is the present value of the principal repayment at maturity?
   [B] What is the total value today of the final 40 years (years 61–100) of payments, including coupons and principal?

2. Below is a quote from finance.yahoo.com for a Northrop Grumman bond. Assume it is March 2, 2006 and the $1,000 face value bond just paid a coupon payment yesterday.

Price	81.95
Coupon (%)	7.750
Maturity Date	1-March-2016
Debt Rating	BBB

Coupon Payment Frequency	Semiannual
First Coupon Date	1-Sept-1996
Type	Corporate
Industry	Industrial

[A]   What is the value of the bond if your required return is 6% APR?

[B]   If the bond were a zero-coupon bond and its only payment was the return of face value at maturity, what would the yield-to-maturity be at the price quoted?

[C]   Assume the bond was originally issued for a price of $1,000. In one sentence, explain something specifically could have happened in the economy or to the firm that could have made the bond sell for its current price.

[D]   The day before the bond matures and pays its last coupon payment, what will its value be?

3. Suppose that Ford has a B-rated bond with exactly 30 years until maturity, a face value of $1,000, and a semiannual coupon rate of 6%. The yield to maturity on B-rated bonds today is 10%.

[A]   What was the price of this bond today?

[B]   Assuming the yield to maturity remains constant, what is the price of the bond immediately before and after it makes its next coupon payment?

4. Suppose a ten-year, $1000 bond with a 9% coupon rate and semiannual coupons is trading for a price of $1,156.

[A]   What is the bond's yield to maturity (expressed as an APR with semiannual compounding)?

[B]   If the bond's yield to maturity changes to 12% APR, what will the bond's price be?

5. The following table summarizes the yields to maturity on several one-year, zero-coupon bonds:

Bond	% Yield
Treasury	4.1
AA corporate	4.8
BBB corporate	6.2
CCC corporate	10.5

[A]   What is the value of a one-year, $1,000 face value, zero-coupon corporate bond with a CCC rating?

[B]   What is the credit spread on AA-rated corporate bonds?

[C]   What is the credit spread on B-rated corporate bonds?

Solutions to Questions and Problems

1. [A] $\dfrac{1,000}{(1.04)^{200}}=\$0.39$

   [B] $\dfrac{40\left[\dfrac{1}{.04}-\dfrac{1}{.04(1.04)^{80}}\right]}{(1.04)^{120}}+0.39=\dfrac{956.61}{110.66}=\$8.64+.39=\$9.03$

2. [A] $P_0=38.75\left[\dfrac{1}{.03}-\dfrac{1}{.03(1.03)^{20}}\right]+\dfrac{1,000}{(1.03)^{20}}=576.50+553.68=\$1,130.18$

   [B] $819.50=\dfrac{1,000}{(1+r)^{20}}\Rightarrow(1+r)^{20}=1.22\Rightarrow1+r=(1.22)^{\frac{1}{20}}=1.01\Rightarrow r=1\%$

   So the YTM APR = 2(1%) = 2%.

   [C] Either the firm's default risk increased leading to a higher credit spread or rates in the economy increased leading to an increase in the risk-free interest rates.

   [D] $1,000 + 38.75 = $1,038.75.

3. [A] $P=\$30\left[\dfrac{1}{.05}-\dfrac{1}{1.05(1.05)^{60}}\right]+\dfrac{1,000}{(1.05)^{60}}=567.88+53.54=\$621.42$

   [B] Before the next coupon payment, the price of the bond is

   $P=\$30\left[\dfrac{1}{.05}-\dfrac{1}{1.05(1.05)^{59}}\right]+\dfrac{1,000}{(1.05)^{59}}+30=566.27+56.21+30=\$652.48$

   After the next coupon payment, the price of the bond will be

   $P=\$30\left[\dfrac{1}{.05}-\dfrac{1}{1.05(1.05)^{59}}\right]+\dfrac{1,000}{(1.05)^{59}}=566.27+56.21=\$622.48$

4. [A] $P_0=45\left[\dfrac{1}{\frac{.12}{2}}-\dfrac{1}{\frac{.12}{2}(1+\frac{.12}{2})^{20}}\right]+\dfrac{1,000}{(1+\frac{.12}{2})^{20}}\Rightarrow P=\$827.95$

   [B] $P_0=\$45\left[\dfrac{1}{\frac{.12}{2}}-\dfrac{1}{\frac{.12}{2}(1+\frac{.12}{2})^{20}}\right]+\dfrac{1,000}{(1+\frac{.12}{2})^{20}}\Rightarrow P=\$827.95$

5. [A] The price of this bond will be $\qquad P=\dfrac{1,000}{1.105}=\$904.98$

   [B] The credit spread on AA-rated corporate bonds is 0.048 – 0.041 = 0.7%

   [C] The credit spread on BBB-rated corporate bonds is 0.062 – 0.041 = 2.1%

CHAPTER 9

Valuing Stocks

Chapter Synopsis

9.1 The Dividend-Discount Model

A stock generates cash flow by either paying dividends or by being sold at a gain. An investor considering holding the stock for one year would be willing to pay:

$$P_0 = \frac{Div_1 + P_1}{1 + r_E}.$$

where Div_1 is the dividend paid in one year, P_1 is the stock price in one year, and r_E is the **equity cost of capital**, which is the expected rate of return available in the market on other investments with equivalent risk to the firm's shares. If the price was lower, it would be a positive-NPV investment and investors would buy it, driving up the stock's price. If the price was greater than this amount, investors would sell, and the price would fall.

Based on the one-year valuation equation, the equity cost of capital can be written as:

$$r_E = \frac{Div_1 + P_1}{P_0} - 1 = \underbrace{\overbrace{\frac{Div_1}{P_0}}^{\text{Dividend Yield}} + \overbrace{\frac{P_1 - P_0}{P_0}}^{\text{Capital Gain Rate}}}_{\text{Total Return}}.$$

The stock's **dividend yield** is the percentage return the investor expects to earn from the dividend paid by the stock. The **capital gain rate** is the return the investor will earn based on the sale price minus the purchase price for the stock. The sum of the dividend yield and the capital gain rate is the total return of the stock.

All investors (with the same beliefs) will attach the same value to a stock, independent of their investment horizons because they can sell the stock at any date for the present value of the remaining dividends. Thus, how long they intend to hold the stock, and whether they collect their return in the form of dividends or capital gains, is irrelevant. Thus, the value of a stock is:

$$P_0 = \frac{Div_1}{1+r_E} + \frac{Div_2}{(1+r_E)^2} + \frac{Div_3}{(1+r_E)^3} + \cdots + \frac{Div_N + P_N}{(1+r_E)^N} = \sum_{n=1}^{\infty} \frac{Div_N}{(1+r_E)^N},$$

which is referred to as the **dividend-discount model**.

9.2 Applying the Dividend-Discount Model

The simplest forecast for the firm's future dividends is that they will grow at a constant rate, g, forever:

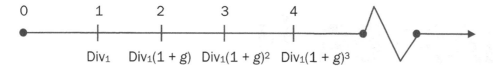

Because the expected dividends are a growing perpetuity, the value of this dividend stream can be determined as:

$$P_0 = \frac{Div_1}{r_E - g}, \text{ and } r_E \text{ can be written as } r_E = \frac{Div_1}{P_0} + g.$$

The dividend growth rate can be estimated by using the expected earnings growth rate if a firm is expected to pay out a constant fraction of earnings in the future.

Firms that have non-constant dividend growth currently may be expected to eventually have constant growth and can be valued using the constant long-term growth dividend-discount model:

$$P_0 = \frac{Div_1}{1+r_E} + \frac{Div_2}{(1+r_E)^2} + \frac{Div_3}{(1+r_E)^3} + \cdots + \frac{Div_N}{(1+r_E)^N} + \frac{\left(\dfrac{Div_{N+1}}{r_E - g}\right)}{(1+r_E)^N}.$$

Due to the high degree of uncertainty associated with forecasting of a firm's future dividends, the dividend discount model has limitations and is best applied to firms that have predictable dividend growth rates, such as public utility companies.

9.3 Total Payout and Free Cash Flow Valuation Models

The **discounted free cash flow model** determines a firm's **enterprise value**, which is the total value of the firm to all investors, including both equity and debt holders. Enterprise value can be defined as:

Enterprise Value = Market Value of Equity + Total Debt − Excess Cash.

A firm's enterprise value can be estimated as the present value of the free cash flows (FCFs) that the firm has available to pay all investors. FCF is usually calculated as:

Free Cash Flow $= EBIT \times (1 - \tau) + $ Depreciation $-$ Capital Expenditures $-$ Increase in NWC.

Enterprise value, V_0, can thus be expressed as:

$$V_0 = \text{PV(FCFs)} = \frac{FCF_1}{1 + r_{wacc}} + \frac{FCF_2}{\left(1 + r_{wacc}\right)^2} + \frac{FCF_3}{\left(1 + r_{wacc}\right)^3} + \ldots + \frac{FCF_N}{\left(1 + r_{wacc}\right)^N} + \frac{V_N}{\left(1 + r_{wacc}\right)^N}$$

where V_N (the terminal value) is often estimated as a growing perpetuity, $\left[\dfrac{FCF_N(1+g)}{\left(r_{wacc} - g\right)}\right]$.

The share price can then be calculated as:

$$P_0 = \frac{\text{Market Value of Equity}}{\text{Shares Outstanding}} = \frac{V_0 - \text{Total Debt} + \text{Excess cash}}{\text{Shares Outstanding}}$$

Since this method discounts the free cash flow that will be paid to both debt and equity holders, the discount rate is the firm's **weighted average cost of capital** (WACC or r_{wacc}). For now, the WACC can be interpreted as the expected return the firm must pay to investors to compensate them for the risk of holding the firm's debt and equity together. Using and estimating the WACC is discussed in detail in parts IV and V of the text.

Firms can pay cash to shareholders by repurchasing shares instead of paying dividends. The **total payout model** discounts the total payouts that the firm makes to shareholders, which equals the total amount spent on both dividends and share repurchases, and then divides by the current number of shares outstanding to determine the share price. While this method is more reliable when the firm's future share repurchases can be forecasted, this is often difficult to do.

9.4 Valuation Based on Comparable Firms

Stocks can also be valued by using valuation multiples of comparable firms. For example, by observing the price-earnings (P/E) ratio of firm C, which is in the same industry as the firm being valued, firm X, firm X's stock price can be estimated as:

$$\frac{\text{Price}_C}{\text{EPS}_C} \times \text{EPS}_X = \text{Price}_X.$$

Other valuation multiples use enterprise value in the numerator and EBIT, EBITDA (earnings before interest, taxes, depreciation, and amortization), and free cash flow in the denominator. Most practitioners rely on enterprise value to EBITDA multiples.

Many other valuation multiples are possible. For firms with substantial tangible assets, the ratio of price-to-book value of equity per share is sometimes used. Some multiples are specific to an industry; for example, in the cable TV industry it is useful to consider the multiple of enterprise value to number of subscribers.

If comparables firms were identical, the multiple used was always proportionately related to value; if comparable firms were always valued correctly, the comparable multiples approach would be accurate and reliable. However, this is not generally the case. Most importantly, firms are not identical, and the usefulness of a valuation multiple depends on the nature of the differences between firms and the sensitivity of the multiples to these differences. The differences in multiples for a sample of firms generally reflect differences in expected future growth rates and risk.

Furthermore, the comparable firm multiples approach does not take into account the important differences among firms. The fact that a firm has an exceptional management team, has developed an efficient manufacturing process, or has just secured a patent on a new technology is ignored when a valuation multiple is used. Discounted cash flow methods have the advantage that they allow specific information about the firm's cost of capital or future growth to be incorporated. Thus, because the true driver of value for any firm is its ability to generate cash flows for its investors, the discounted cash flow methods have the potential to be more accurate than the use of valuation multiples.

9.5 Information, Competition, and Stock Prices

For a publicly traded firm, the stock price generally is thought to reflect the information of all investors regarding the true value of the shares. Therefore, a valuation model can be applied to learn something about the firm's future cash flows or cost of capital based on its current stock price. Only if you happen to have superior information that other investors lack regarding the firm's cash flows and cost of capital would it may make sense to second-guess the stock price.

The idea that competition among investors works to eliminate all positive-NPV trading opportunities is referred to as the **efficient markets hypothesis.** It implies that securities will be fairly priced given all information that is available to investors. There are two types of information.

■ **Public, easy to interpret information.** Competition between investors should cause stock prices to react nearly instantaneously to information that is available to all investors, such as news reports, financials statements, and corporate press releases. A few investors might be able to trade a small quantity of shares before the price fully adjusts. Most investors, however, will find that the stock price already reflects the new information before they are able to trade on it. It is generally believed that the efficient markets hypothesis holds very well with respect to this type of information.

■ **Private, difficult to interpret information.** When private (non-public or difficult to determine) information is known by a single or small number of investors, it may be profitable to trade on the information. In this case, the efficient markets hypothesis does not hold. However, as these informed traders begin to trade, they will tend to move prices, so over time prices will begin to reflect their information as well. If the profit opportunities from having this type of information are large, other individuals will attempt to gain the expertise and devote the resources needed to acquire it. As more individuals become better informed, competition to exploit this information will increase. Thus, in the long run, we should expect that the degree of inefficiency in the market will be limited by the costs of obtaining the information.

If stocks are fairly valued as the efficient market hypothesis suggests, then the value of a firm is determined by the cash flows that it can pay to its investors. Therefore managers should do the following.

■ **Focus on NPV and free cash flow** and make investments that increase the NPV of the firm using the capital budgeting methods outlined in Chapter 7.

■ **Avoid accounting illusions.** The NPV of its FCFs, not the accounting consequences of a decision, determines the value of the firm, so accounting measures should not drive decision making.

■ **Use financial transactions to finance valuable investments.** Since buying or selling a security is a zero-NPV transaction, it is not a source of value for the firm. Financial policy should therefore be driven by the firm's real investment needs.

Selected Concepts and Key Terms

Capital Gain

The difference between the sale price and purchase price of the stock. The capital gain divided by the beginning of period stock price is the **capital gain rate.**

Constant Dividend Growth Model

A model in which the value of firm's stock equals the dividend paid in one year divided by the equity cost of capital minus the dividend growth rate. It is an application of the present value of a perpetuity equation.

Discounted Free Cash Flow Model

A model in which the value of a firm's debt and equity equals the present value of the future free cash flows (FCFs) it will generate. Annual FCF can generally be calculated as operating cash flow minus capital spending minus the increase in net working capital.

Dividend Yield

The percentage return earned from the dividend paid by the stock. It equals the dividends paid over a period divided by the stock price at the beginning of the period.

Dividend-Discount Model

A model in which the value of a firm's stock equals the present value of the future dividends it pays. All investors (with the same beliefs) will attach the same value to the stock, independent of their investment horizons because they can sell the stock at any date for the present value of the remaining dividends. Thus, how long they intend to hold the stock, and whether they collect their return in the form of dividends or capital gains, is irrelevant.

Efficient Markets Hypothesis

The idea that competition among investors works to eliminate all positive-NPV trading opportunities. It implies that securities will be fairly priced given all information that is available to investors.

Enterprise Value

The value of the firm's underlying business. It is generally calculated as the market value of equity plus the value of long-term debt minus excess cash.

Equity Cost of Capital

The expected return of other securities available in the market with equivalent risk to the firm's equity.

Comparable Firm Valuation Method

A method of estimating the value of the firm based on the value of comparable firms that are expected to generate similar cash flows in the future and have the same level of risk.

Total Payout Model

A model in which the value of a firm's stock equals the present value of the total payouts that the firm makes to shareholders, including the total amount spent on both dividends and share repurchases.

Valuation Multiple

A ratio of value to another variable. Firm valuation multiples generally use equity value or enterprise value in the numerator and net income, EBIT, EBITDA, or free cash flow in the denominator. While the most common valuation multiple is the price-earnings (P/E) ratio, most practitioners rely on enterprise value to EBITDA multiples.

Weighted Average Cost of Capital

The cost of capital that reflects the risk of the overall business, which is the combined risk of the firm's equity and debt. Using and estimating the WACC is discussed in detail in parts IV and V of the text.

Concept Check Questions and Answers

9.1.1. How do you calculate the total return of a stock?

The total return is the expected return that the investor will earn for a one-year investment in the stock and is computed as the sum of the dividend yield and the capital gain rate.

9.1.2. What discount rate do you use to discount the future cash flows of a stock?

The discount rate used to discount the future cash flows of a stock must be the equity cost of capital for the stock, which is the expected return of other investments available in the market with equivalent risk to the firm's shares.

9.1.3. Why will a short-term and long-term investor with the same beliefs be willing to pay the same price for a stock?

Because the value of the stock at any point in time is equal to the present value of the future dividends from that point on. Thus, the value of the stock to an investor who plans to hold on to the stock indefinitely, an investor who will collect dividends for N years and then sell the stock, or to a series of investors who hold the stock for shorter periods and then resell it are all the same. Thus, all investors (with the same beliefs) will attach the same value to the stock, independent of their investment horizons. How long they intend to hold the stock and whether they collect their return in the form of dividends or capital gains is irrelevant.

9.2.1. In what three ways can a firm increase its future dividend per share?

Since the dividend each year is the firm's earnings per share (EPS) multiplied by its dividend payout ratio, the firm can increase its dividend in three ways: (1) by increasing its earnings (net income); (2) by increasing its dividend payout rate; or (3) by decreasing its shares outstanding.

9.2.2. Under what circumstances can a firm increase its share price by cutting its dividend and investing more?

Cutting the firm's dividend to increase investment will raise the stock price if, and only if, the new investments have a positive NPV.

9.3.1. How does the growth rate used in the total payout model differ from the growth rate used in the dividend-discount model?

In the total payout model, we use the growth rate of earnings, rather than earnings per share, when forecasting the growth of the firm's total payouts.

9.3.2. What is the enterprise value of the firm?

It is the value of the firm's underlying business. It is generally calculated as the market value of equity plus the value of long-term debt minus excess cash.

9.3.3. How can you estimate a firm's stock price based on its projected free cash flows?

A firm's enterprise value (V_0) can be estimated as the present value of the free cash flows that the firm has available to pay all investors. Then, the equity value can be determined as:

$$P_0 = \frac{V_0 - \text{Total Debt} + \text{Excess cash}}{\text{Shares Outstanding}} = \frac{\text{Market Value of Equity}}{\text{Shares Outstanding}}.$$

9.4.1. What are some common valuation multiples?

Valuation multiples commonly used to value stocks include the price-earnings ratio, the ratio of enterprise value to EBIT, the ratio of enterprise value to EBITDA, the ratio of enterprise value to free cash flow, the ratio of enterprise value to sales, and the ratio of stock price to book value of equity per share.

9.4.2. What implicit assumptions are made when valuing a firm using multiples based on comparable firms?

Using valuation multiples based on comparable firms assumes that comparable firms have the same risk and future growth as the firm being valued.

9.5.1. State the efficient market hypothesis.

The efficient markets hypothesis states that competition eliminates all positive-NPV trades, which is equivalent to stating that securities with equivalent risk have the same expected returns.

9.5.2. What are the implications of the efficient market hypothesis for corporate managers?

To raise the stock price in an efficient market, corporate managers should 1) focus on NPV and free cash flow from the firm's investments; 2) avoid accounting illusion; and 3) use financial transactions to support investments.

Examples with Step-by-Step Solutions

Solving Problems

Problems using the concepts in this chapter generally involve valuing stocks using the dividend discount model. The most difficult part of applying the model is correctly incorporating the present value of a perpetuity calculation that is typically part of the calculation. The examples below show how this is done. Other problems involve using the discounted free cash flow model, which applies the same model to free cash flows and determines enterprise value, not equity value. Problems may also involve applying an estimate of firm value based on comparable firm valuation multiples, such as price-to-earnings ratios, price-to-book ratios, enterprise value-to-sales ratios, and enterprise value-to-EBITDA ratios.

Examples

1. **Ford stock is trading at $8.20. The firm paid dividends of $0.40 per share last year.**
   [A]   Assuming you expect that Ford's dividends will grow by 3% per year in the future and you require a 12% APR return, do you think that Ford is overvalued based on the dividend discount model? (Assume the next annual dividend is in one year.)
   [B]   If the market does require a 12% return, what rate of dividend growth would justify the current price based on the dividend discount model?
   [C]   If dividends do grow at 3%, what return will you get at the current market price based on the dividend discount model?

Step 1. Put the future dividends on a time line.

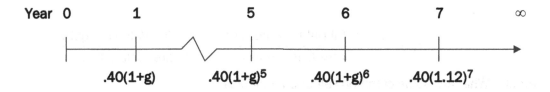

Step 2. To determine if Ford is overvalued, the value must be calculated.

The cash flow stream is a growing perpetuity with $r = 12\%$ and $g = 3\%$, so

$$P = \frac{D_{\text{Last Year}}(1+g)}{r-g} = \frac{0.40(1.03)}{.12 - .03} = \$4.58.$$

Thus, based on these assumptions, it is overvalued at $8.20.

Step 3. Now, set the present value of the dividends equal to the current price, $8.20, and solve for the constant growth rate assuming that $r = 12\%$.

$$P = \frac{D_{\text{Last Year}}(1+g)}{r-g} = 8.20 = \frac{0.40(1+g)}{.12-g} \Rightarrow .12 - g(8.20) = .40 + .40g \Rightarrow .12 - g = .0488 + .0488g$$
$$\Rightarrow 1.0488g = .0712 \Rightarrow g = 6.8\%$$

Thus, if the dividends grow at exactly 6.8% every year, and you pay $8.20 for the stock today, your annually compounded rate of return will be 12%.

Step 4. Finally, set the present value of the dividends equal to the current price, $8.20, and solve for the discount rate assuming that $g = 3\%$.

$$P = \frac{D_{\text{Last Year}}(1+g)}{r-g} = 8.20 = \frac{0.40(1.03)}{r-.03} \Rightarrow r - .03 = .05 \Rightarrow r = 8\%.$$

Thus, if the dividends grow at exactly 3% every year, and you pay $8.20 for the stock today, your annually compounded rate of return will be 8%.

2. Your broker is recommending a stock that is expected to pay its first dividend of $1.20 per share in exactly 1 year. **The annual dividend is expected to be $1.44 the second year and $4.32 in the third year. In the fourth year, the dividend is expected to grow at 5% from then on.**
   [A]   If you require a 20% return, how much would you pay for a share of the stock?
   [B]   Given the information in the problem, if you could buy the stock for $17, would you expect a higher or lower return than 20%?

[C] **If your expectations are correct, how much will the stock be worth in exactly two years (after the second dividend is paid)?**

Step 1. Put the dividends on a timeline.

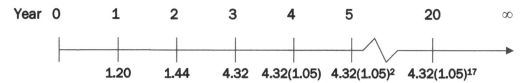

Step 2. The present value of the dividends can be calculated several ways:

One method is to find the present value of the first 3 years' dividends and then add on the time 3 terminal value, the present value of the dividends in years 4 through infinity valued at time 3.

$$P_0 = \frac{1.2}{1.2} + \frac{1.44}{1.2^2} + \frac{4.32}{1.2^3} + \frac{\left(\frac{4.32(1.05)}{.20 - .05}\right)}{1.2^3} = 1 + 1 + 2.50 + 17.50 = \$22$$

Another method is to find the present value of the first 2 years' dividends and then add on the time 2 terminal value, the present value of the dividends in years 3 through infinity valued at time 2.

$$P_0 = \frac{1.2}{1.2} + \frac{1.44}{1.2^2} + \frac{\left(\frac{4.32}{.20 - .05}\right)}{1.2^2} = 1 + 1 + 20 = \$22$$

In any case, the stock is worth $22 given these assumptions, and you shouldn't pay more than that price.

Step 3. Determine if a $17 price would provide a higher return.

This requires no calculations. If a price of $22 provides a 20% return, given the forecasted dividends, then a lower price would provide a higher return. Finding the exact return requires solving the equation:

$$17 = \frac{1.2}{1 + r} + \frac{1.44}{(1 + r)^2} + \frac{\left(\frac{4.32}{r - .05}\right)}{(1 + r)^2} \Rightarrow r = 23.7\%.$$

Step 4. Determine the time line in two years.

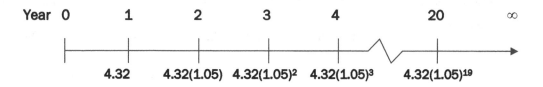

Step 5. Once again, the present value of the dividends can be calculated several ways:

One method is to find the present value of the first years' dividend and then add on the present value of the dividends in years 2 through infinity valued at time 1.

$$P_0 = \frac{4.32}{1.2} + \frac{\left(\dfrac{4.32(1.05)}{.20 - .05}\right)}{1.2} = 3.60 + 25.20 = \$28.80$$

Another method is to find the present value of the dividends in years 1 through infinity valued at time 0.

$$P_0 = \left(\frac{4.32}{.20 - .05}\right) = \$28.80$$

Finally, you can verify that buying at $22, receiving the year 1 dividend and reinvesting it at 20%, and receiving the year two dividend and selling at $28.80 in two years represents a 20% annual return:

$$\text{Return} = \left(\frac{[28.80 + 1.20(1.20) + 1.44] - 22}{22}\right) = 0.44,$$

So, the annual return is $(1.44)^{1/2} - 1 = 0.20$, or 20%.

3. **Last year, Microsoft had $44 billion in sales, $17 billion in free cash flow (FCF), and a stock market capitalization of $260 billion. The firm has no debt and $30 billion of excess cash.**

   [A] **Is Microsoft overvalued based on the discounted free cash flow model if you expect FCF to grow by 5% per year forever and require a 15% return?**

   [B] **Is Microsoft overvalued based on the enterprise value to sales ratio if comparable firms in the industry have an average enterprise value to sales ratio of 3.4?**

Step 1. The discounted free cash flow model finds:

Enterprise value = market value of equity + total debt − excess cash

⇒ market value of equity = enterprise value − total debt + excess cash.

To determine the whether the equity value is above or below $260 billion based on the discounted free cash flow model, use the present value of a growing perpetuity equation to find the present value of the FCFs and add excess cash to find enterprise value:

$$\text{Value} = \left(\frac{\$17}{.12 - .05}\right) = \$243\,\text{billion}$$

and add the value of the excess cash

$$\$243 + \$30 = \$273\,\text{billion} > \$260\,\text{billion}.$$

So based on your assumptions, the stock does not seem to be overvalued.

Step 2. Next, calculate the implied value based on an enterprise value to sales ratio of 3.4.

$$\frac{\text{Enterprise Value}}{\text{Sales}} \times \text{Sales} = \text{Enterprise Value} = \text{Market Value of Equity} + \text{Total Debt} - \text{Excess Cash}$$

$$= 3.4 \times \$44 = \$150\,\text{billion} = \text{Market Value of Equity} + 0 - 30$$

$$\Rightarrow \text{Market Value of Equity} = \$180\,\text{billion}$$

So based on the comparison firms, the stock is overvalued by 44%.

Questions and Problems

1. General Electric stock is priced at $25 per share. The firm is expected to pay an annual dividend of $0.50 per share in one year. Analysts were predicting a five-year growth rate in earnings of 8% per year. If the market expects GE to keep its retention ratio (the fraction of earning paid out as dividends) constant, and this growth rate continues in perpetuity, what is the market's required return for an investment in GE stock?

2. Exxon-Mobil Corporation will pay an annual dividend of $1.35 one year from now. Analysts expect this dividend to grow at 20% per year each year until five years from now. After year 5, the growth will level off to 3% per year. According to the dividend discount model, what is the value of a share of Exxon-Mobil stock if the firm's required return is 8%?

3. Suppose Oracle pays no dividends but spent $2 billion on share repurchases last year. If Oracle's equity cost of capital is 15%, and if the amount spent on repurchases is expected to grow by 5% per year, estimate Oracle's market capitalization. If they have 2 billion shares outstanding, what stock value per share?

4. Gap had EPS of $1.08 last year and a book value of equity of $6 per share. Firms in the clothing retail industry have an average price-to-earnings ratio of 22 and an average market-to-book ratio of 2.3. Is Gap, currently trading at $16 per share, overvalued based on:
   [A]   The industry-average P/E multiple?
   [B]   The industry-average price-to-book multiple?

5. Boeing's share price is $75. Its dividend is going to be $1.20 next year, and you expect the firm to raise this dividend by 5% per year in perpetuity.
   [A]   If Boeing's equity cost of capital is 7%, what share price would you expect based on your estimate of the dividend growth rate?
   [B]   Given Boeing's current share price and equity cost of capital, what would you conclude about your assessment of Boeing's future dividend growth?

Solutions to Questions and Problems

1. The net present value of an investment in GE is:

$$NPV = -25 + \frac{0.50}{r - 0.08} = 0$$

Solving for r gives:

$$NPV = -25 + \frac{0.50}{r - 0.08} = 0 \Rightarrow r - .08 = \frac{0.50}{25} \Rightarrow r = 0.02 + 0.08 = .10$$

So, the implied market return is 10%.

2. The value of the first 5 dividend payments is:

$$PV_{1-5} = \frac{1.35}{(0.08 - 0.20)}\left(1 - \left(\frac{1.20}{1.08}\right)^5\right) = (-11.25) \times (-.6935) = \$7.80$$

The value on date 5 of the rest of the dividend payments is:

$$PV_5 = \frac{1.35(1.20)^4\, 1.02}{0.08 - 0.02} = 47.59$$

Discounting this value to the present gives

$$PV_0 = \frac{47.59}{(1.08)^5} = \$32.39.$$

So the value of Exxon-Mobil is: $P = PV_{1-5} + PV_0 = 7.80 + 32.39 = \$40.18$

3. Total payout next year = 2 billion × 1.05 = $2.10 billion

   Equity Value = 2.10/(15% – 5%) = $21 billion

   Share price = 21/2 = $10.50.

4. [A] $\dfrac{P}{EPS} \times EPS = P = 22 \times 1.08 = \$23.76 > \$16$

   So, Gap is undervalued based on a comparable price-to-earnings ratio valuation.

   [B] $\dfrac{P}{\text{Book Value per Share}} \times \text{Book Value per Share} = P = 6 \times 2.3 = \$13.80 < \$16$

   So, Gap is overvalued based on a comparable market-to-book ratio valuation.

5. [A] $P = 1.20 / (.07 - .05) = \$60$

   [B]   Based on the market price, your growth forecast may be too high.

   A growth rate consistent with market price is $g = r_E$ – div yield = 7% – 1.20/75 = 5.4%.

CHAPTER 10

Capital Markets and the Pricing of Risk

Chapter Synopsis

10.1 A First Look at Risk and Return

Historically there has been a large difference in the returns and variability from investing in different types of investments. Figure 10.1 below shows the value of $100 in 2004 if it were invested in different portfolios of assets at the beginning of 1926.

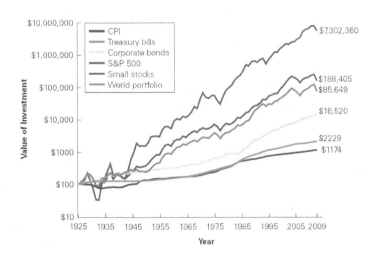

Figure 10.1

The value of $100 Invested at the end of 1925 in U.S. Large Stocks (S&P 500), Small Stocks, World Stocks, Corporate Bonds, and Treasury Bills. Also shown is the change in the consumer price index.

10.2 Common Measures of Risk and Return

When the return on an investment is uncertain and its possible returns can be specified, its future returns can be represented by a **probability distribution**, which shows the probability that each possible return will occur.

Given the probability distribution of returns:

■ The expected return, $E(R)$, is the mean return,

$$E[R] = \sum_R p_r \times R$$

which is the sum of the probability that each return will occur, p_r, times the return, R, for all possible returns.

■ The most common measures of risk of a probability distribution are the **variance**, $VAR(R)$, and **standard deviation**, $SD(R)$:

$$VAR(R) = E(R - E[R])^2 = \sum_R p_R \times (R - E[R])^2, \text{ and } SD(R) = \sqrt{SD(R)}.$$

10.3 Historical Returns of Stocks and Bonds

The **realized return** is the sum of the dividend yield and the capital gain rate of return over a time period. If you assume that all dividends are immediately reinvested and used to purchase additional shares of the same security, and the stock pays dividends at the end of each quarter, then the total annual return is:

$$R_{annual} = (1 + R_{Q1})(1 + R_{Q2})(1 + R_{Q3})(1 + R_{Q4}) - 1$$

Once realized annual returns have been computed, the **average annual return** of an investment during a period is the average of the realized returns for each year:

$$\overline{R} = \frac{1}{T}(R_1 + R_2 + \cdots + R_T) = \left(\frac{1}{T}\right)\sum_{t=1}^{T} R_t.$$

The standard deviation of the probability distribution can be estimated as:

$$VAR(R) = \left(\frac{1}{T-1}\right)\sum_{t=1}^{T}(R_t - \overline{R})^2.$$

Because a security's historical average return is only an estimate of its true return, the standard error of the estimate can be used to measure the amount estimation error. If the distribution of a stock's return is identical each year, and each year's return is independent of prior years' returns, then the standard error of the estimate of the expected return is:

$$SD(\text{Average if Independent, Identical Risks}) = \frac{SD(\text{Individual Risk})}{\sqrt{\text{Number of Observations}}}.$$

In a large sample, the average return will be within two standard errors of the true expected return approximately 95% of the time, so the standard error can be used to determine a reasonable range for the true expected value. For example, a **95% confidence interval** for the expected return is equal to the historical average return ± (2 × the standard error).

10.4 The Historical Trade-off between Risk and Return

Between 1926 and 2009, the average return and standard deviation for the large portfolios in Figure 10.1 are shown in the following table.

Investment	Average Return	Standard Deviation
Small stocks	20.9%	41.5%
S&P 500	11.6%	20.6%
Corporate bonds	6.6%	7.0%
Treasury bills	3.9%	3.1%

The statistics show that there is a positive relation between risk (as measured by standard deviation) and average return for portfolios of assets. However, this is not true for individual stocks. When the same statistics are calculated for stocks comprising the S&P 500 from 1926–2004, you find that:

■ There is not a clear positive relation between a stock's average return and its volatility;

■ Larger stocks tend to have lower overall volatility, but even the largest stocks are typically more risky than a portfolio of large stocks;

■ All stocks seem to have higher risk and lower returns than would be predicted based on extrapolation of data for large portfolios.

Thus, while volatility (standard deviation) seems be a reasonable measure of risk when evaluating a large portfolio, it is not adequate to explain the returns of individual securities, since there is no clear relation between volatility and return for individual stocks.

10.5 Common Versus Independent Risk

The averaging out of independent risks in a large portfolio is called **diversification**. The principle of diversification is used routinely in the insurance industry. For example, the theft insurance industry relies on the fact that the number of claims is relatively predictable in a large portfolio. Since thefts in different houses are not related to each other, the risk of theft is uncorrelated and independent across homes. There are thus two kinds of risk:

■ **Independent risk** is risk that is uncorrelated and independent for all risky assets; it can be eliminated in a diversified portfolio. For example, if theft insurance policy risks are independent, the number of claims is predictable for a large insurance company in a given period and thus the number of claims expected in not very risky.

■ **Common risk** is risk that affects the value of all risky assets, and it cannot be eliminated in a diversified portfolio. For example, common risk cannot be eliminated for a large portfolio of earthquake insurance policies in the same geographic region, and so the number of claims expected is very risky, even for a large insurance company.

10.6 Diversification in Stock Portfolios

Given the fact that the value of most stocks is affected by common risks, there are two kinds of risk from investing in a stock.

■ **Idiosyncratic risk** is variation in a stock's return due to firm-specific news. This type of risk is also called **firm-specific, unsystematic, unique,** or **diversifiable risk.**

■ **Systematic risk,** or **undiversifiable risk,** refers to the risk that market-wide news will simultaneously affect the value of all assets.

Diversification eliminates idiosyncratic risk but does not eliminate systematic risk. Because investors can eliminate idiosyncratic risk, they should not require a risk premium for bearing it. Because investors cannot eliminate systematic risk, they must be compensated for taking on that risk. As a consequence, the risk premium for an asset depends on the amount of its systematic risk, rather than its total risk (standard deviation).

10.7 Measuring Systematic Risk

When evaluating the risk of an investment, an investor with a diversified portfolio will only care about its systematic risk, which cannot be eliminated through diversification. In exchange for bearing systematic risk, investors want to be compensated by earning a higher return. So determining investors' expected return requires both measuring the investment's systematic risk and determining the risk premium required to compensate for that amount of systematic risk.

Measuring systematic risk requires locating a portfolio that contains only systematic risk. Changes in the market value of this portfolio will correspond to systematic shocks to the economy. Such a portfolio is called an **efficient portfolio**. Because diversification improves with the number of stocks held in a portfolio, an efficient portfolio should be a large portfolio containing many different stocks. Thus, it is reasonable to consider a portfolio that contains all shares of all stocks and securities in the market, which is called the **market portfolio**. It is standard to use the S&P 500 portfolio as a proxy for the unobservable market portfolio of all risky assets.

The systematic risk of a security's return is most often measured by its beta. The **beta** (β) of a security is the sensitivity of the security's return to the return of the overall market; it measures the expected percent change in the excess return of a security for a 1% change in the excess return of the market portfolio.

10.8 Beta and the Cost of Capital

A firm's cost of capital for a project is the expected return that its investors could earn on other securities with the same risk and maturity. Because the risk that determines expected returns is systematic risk, which is measured by beta, the cost of capital for a project is the expected return available on securities with the same beta. A common assumption is to assume that the project has the same risk as the firm, or other firms with similar assets.

The **market risk premium** investors can earn by holding the market portfolio (or a stock with a beta of 1) is the difference between the market portfolio's expected return and the risk-free interest rate, so they earn the market return. For investments with a beta different than 1, the expected return, r_I, is given by the **Capital Asset Pricing Model** (CAPM) equation:

$$r_I = \text{Risk-Free Interest Rate} + \text{Risk Premium} = r_f + \beta_I \times (E[R_{Mkt}] - r_f).$$

Selected Concepts and Key Terms

Excess Return

The difference between the average return for the investment and the average return for Treasury bills, which are generally considered a risk-free investment.

Common Risk

Risk that affects the value of all risky assets; it cannot be eliminated in a diversified portfolio.

Independent Risk

Risk that is uncorrelated and independent for all risky assets; it can be eliminated in a diversified portfolio.

Diversification

The averaging out of independent risks in a large portfolio.

Firm-Specific, Idiosyncratic, Unsystematic, Unique, or Diversifiable Risk

Risk arising from investing in a risky asset that is due to potential firm-specific news and events.

Systematic, Undiversifiable, or Market Risk

The risk that market-wide news and events will simultaneously affect the value of all assets.

Efficient Portfolio

A portfolio of risky assets that contains only systematic risk. Changes in the value of this portfolio correspond to systematic shocks to the economy.

Market Portfolio

A portfolio that contains all risky assets in the market. It is standard to use the S&P 500 portfolio as a proxy for the unobservable market portfolio of all risky assets.

Beta (β)

The sensitivity of a security's return to the return of the overall market; it measures the expected percent change in the excess return of a security for a 1% change in the excess return of the market portfolio.

Concept Check Questions and Answers

10.1.1. From 1926 to 2009, which of the following investments had the highest return: Standard & Poor's 500, small stocks, world portfolio, corporate bonds, or Treasury bills?

From 1926 to 2009, the small stock portfolio (the smallest 10% of all stocks traded on the NYSE) had the highest rate of return.

10.1.2. From 1926 to 2009, which investment grew in value in every year? Which investment had the greatest variability?

From 1926 to 2009, the investment in three-month Treasury Bills made modest gains every year and the investment in the small stock portfolio experienced the largest fluctuations in its value.

10.2.1. How do we calculate the expected return of a stock?

The expected return of a stock is calculated as a weighted average of the possible returns, where the weights correspond to the probabilities.

10.2.2. What are the two most common measures of risk, and how are they related to each other?

The two most common measures used to measure the risk of a probability distribution are the variance and standard deviation. The variance is the expected squared deviation from the mean, and the standard deviation is the aware root of the variance.

10.3.1. How do we estimate the average annual return of an investment?

The average annual return of an investment during some historical period is simply the average of the realized returns for each year.

10.3.2. We have 83 years of data on the S&P 500 returns, yet we cannot estimate the expected return of the S&P 500 very accurately. Why?

We cannot estimate the expected return of the S&P 500 very accurately because the standard error of the estimate of the expected return is large. Furthermore, if we believe the distribution of the S&P 500 returns may have charged over time, and we can only use more recent data to estimate the expected return, then the estimate will be even less accurate.

10.4.1. What is the excess return?

The excess return is the difference between the average return for the investment and the average return for Treasury Bills, a risk free investment.

10.4.2. Do expected returns of well-diversified large portfolios of stocks appear to increase with volatility?

Yes, there is a positive relation between the standard deviation of the portfolios and their historical returns.

10.4.3. Do expected returns for individual stocks appear to increase with volatility?

No, there is no clear relationship between the volatility and return of individual stocks. While the smallest stocks have a slightly higher average return, many stocks have higher volatility and lower average returns than other stocks. And all stocks seem to have higher risk and lower returns than would be predicted based on extrapolation of data for large portfolios.

10.5.1. What is the difference between common risk and independent risk?

Common risk is the risk that is perfectly correlated across assets. On the other hand, independent risk is the risk that is uncorrelated and independent across assets.

10.5.2. Under what circumstances will risk be diversified in a large portfolio of insurance contracts?

Diversification is the average from independent risks in a large portfolio. When risks are independent, insurance companies routinely use diversification to reduce risk for a large portfolio of insurance contracts.

10.6.1. Explain why the risk premium of diversifiable risk is zero.

The risk premium for diversification risk is zero because this risk can be eliminated in a large portfolio. Investors are not compensated for holding firm-specific (unsystematic) risk.

10.6.2. Why is the risk premium of a security determined only by its systematic risk?

Because investors cannot eliminate systematic risk, they must be compensated for holding that risk. As a consequence, the risk premium for a security depends on the amount of its systematic risk rather than its total risk.

10.7.1. What is the market portfolio?

The market portfolio contains all shares of all stocks and securities in the market.

10.7.2. Define the beta of a security.

The beta is the expected percentage change in the excess return of a security for a 1% change in the excess return of the market portfolio.

10.8.1. How can you use a security's beta to estimate its cost of capital?

The cost of capital can be estimated by determining the expected return using the Capital Asset Pricing Model (CAPM) equation:

$$E[R] = \text{Risk-Free Interest Rate} + \text{Risk Premium} = r_f + \beta \times (E[R_{Mkt}] - r_f)$$

10.8.2. If a risky investment has a beta of zero, what should its cost of capital be according to the CAPM? How can you justify this?

It should equal the risk-free rate because it has no systematic risk.

Examples with Step-by-Step Solutions

Solving Problems

Problems using the concepts in this chapter may involve calculating the mean and standard deviation from a probability distribution. They may require calculating the realized return over a time period, the mean and standard deviation from historical returns, and comparing risk-return trade-offs. You also may need to consider the effect of diversification on the risk of a portfolio. Finally, problems may require using the Capital Asset Pricing Model to estimate a stock's expected return.

Examples

1. **You are considering investing in Cisco and Yahoo, which have never paid dividends and had the following end of year stock prices (adjusted for splits):**

	Cisco	Yahoo
12/31/1996	$7.07	$0.71
12/31/1997	9.29	4.33
12/31/1998	23.20	29.62
12/31/1999	53.56	108.17
12/31/2000	38.25	15.03
12/31/2001	18.11	8.87
12/31/2002	13.10	8.18
12/31/2003	24.23	22.51
12/31/2004	19.32	37.68
12/31/2005	17.12	39.18

Determine the risk-return trade-off based on the means and standard deviations of historical returns and graph the results. What is a better stock to buy?

Step 1. In order to calculate the means and standard deviations of historical returns, the annual returns must be determined.

The annual return $= \dfrac{P_{t+1} - P_1}{P_1}$, for example $\dfrac{P_{1997}^{Cisco} - P_{1996}^{Cisco}}{P_{1996}^{Cisco}} = \dfrac{9.29 - 7.07}{7.07} = 0.314 = 31.4\%$

The returns for 1997-2005 are as shown.

	Cisco	Yahoo
1997	0.314	5.099
1998	1.497	5.841
1999	1.309	2.652
2000	-0.286	-0.861
2001	-0.527	-0.410
2002	-0.277	-0.078
2003	0.850	1.752
2004	-0.203	0.674
2005	0.114	0.040

Step 2. Next, the mean returns can be calculated.

$$R_{Cisco}^{Mean} = \frac{1}{T}\sum_{t=1}^{T} R_t = \frac{0.314 + 1.497 + 1.309 + -0.286 + -0.527 + -0.277 + 0.850 + -0.203 + -0.114}{9} = 28.5\%$$

$$R_{Yahoo}^{Mean} = \frac{1}{T}\sum_{t=1}^{T} R_t = \frac{5.099 + 5.841 + 2.652 + -0.861 + -0.410 + -0.078 + 1.752 + 0.674 + 0.040}{9} = 163\%$$

Step 3. Now, the standard deviations can be calculated.

$$SD(R_{Cisco}) = \sqrt{VAR(R_{Cisco})} = \sqrt{\frac{1}{T-1}\sum_{t=1}^{T}(R_t - \overline{R})^2} =$$

$$= \sqrt{\frac{\begin{array}{l}(0.314-0.285)^2 + (1.497-0.285)^2 + (1.309-0.285)^2 + (-0.286-0.285)^2 + (-0.527-0.285)^2 \\ +(-0.277-0.285)^2 + (0.850-0.285)^2 + (-0.203-0.285)^2 + (-0.114-0.285)^2\end{array}}{8}}$$

$$= 0.753 = 75.3\%$$

$$SD(R_{Yahoo}) = \sqrt{VAR(R_{Yahoo})} = \sqrt{\frac{1}{T-1}\sum_{t=1}^{T}(R_t - \overline{R})^2}$$

$$= \sqrt{\frac{\begin{array}{l}(5.099-1.634)^2 + (5.841-1.634)^2 + (2.652-1.634)^2 + (-0.861-1.634)^2 + (-0.410-1.634)^2 \\ +(-0.078-1.634)^2 + (1.752-1.634)^2 + (0.674-1.634)^2 + (0.040-1.634)^2\end{array}}{8}}$$

$$= 2.438 = 244\%$$

Step 4. Graph the results.

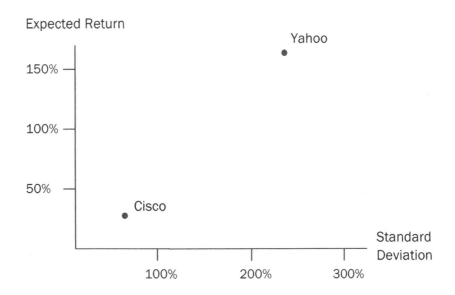

Step 5. Interpret the results.

It is not possible to conclude that either stock is a better choice. Yahoo is has a much higher expected return, but it also has a much higher standard deviation; Cisco has a lower expected return, but a lower standard deviation. Some investors may prefer Cisco and some may prefer Yahoo.

2. **The stock prices and dividends for General Electric (GE) for a 1-year period are below.**

Date	Price	Dividend
06/15/06	32.22	0.25
03/15/06	33.45	0.25
12/15/05	31.34	0.22
09/15/05	30.22	0.22
06/16/05	30.44	

What was the annual return on GE in this period?

Step 1. The quarterly returns must first be computed.

The quarterly return is calculated as:

$$= \frac{P_{t+1} + \text{Div}_{t+1} - P_t}{P_t},$$

for example,
$$\frac{P_{6/15/2006} + \text{Div}_{6/15/2006} - P_{3/15/2006}}{P_{3/15/2006}}$$
$$= \frac{32.22 + 0.25 - 33.45}{33.25} = -0.029 = -2.9\%.$$

For all four quarters, the returns are:

Date	Price	Dividend	Return
06/15/06	32.22	0.25	-0.029
03/15/06	33.45	0.25	0.075
12/15/05	31.34	0.22	0.044
09/15/05	30.22	0.22	0.000
06/16/05	30.44		

Step 2. Calculate the annual return.

$$R_{annual} = (1 + R_{Q1})(1 + R_{Q2})(1 + R_{Q3})(1 + R_{Q4}) - 1$$

$$= (1.000)(1.044)(1.075)(0.971) - 1 = 1.090 - 1 = 0.090, \text{ or } 9.0\%$$

3. **You are considering investing in 10 stocks in two different industries (all 10 stocks you chose will be in the same industry).**

   ■ **The first industry is biotechnology. You believe that the returns of all biotech stocks are totally independent because they are all developing different drugs with different probabilities of having those drugs approved. Each year you believe there is a 50% chance a stock will have a 30% return and a 50% chance a stock will have a -10% return.**

   ■ **The other industry is firms offering S&P 500 exchange-traded funds (ETFs). Since these funds all seek to track the performance of the same index, you believe that the returns on these ETFs are perfectly correlated. Each year you believe there is a 50% chance a fund will have a 25% return and a 50% chance a fund will have a -5% return.**

Which strategy is better?

Step 1. Determine what you should base your decision on.

To see if one strategy is better, you must calculate the expected return and risk (standard deviation) of each 10-stock portfolio. If one strategy has a higher expected return *and* a lower standard deviation, then it would always be preferred by a risk-averse investor. If neither satisfies these criteria, then different investors must select their preferred portfolio based on their preferences.

Step 2. Calculate expected returns of each investment.

$$E[R_{Biotech}] = \sum_R p_r \times R = .5(.3) + .5(-.1) = .10 = 10\%$$

$$E[R_{ETF}] = \sum_R p_r \times R = .5(.25) + .5(-.05) = .10 = 10\%$$

Step 3. Calculate the expected return on a 10-stock portfolio of each investment.

$$E[R_{Biotech}] = \frac{1}{T}\sum_{t=1}^{T} R_t = \frac{.10+.10+.10+.10+.10+.10+.10+.10+.10+.10}{10} = 10\%$$

$$E[R_{ETF}] = \frac{1}{T}\sum_{t=1}^{T} R_t = \frac{.10+.10+.10+.10+.10+.10+.10+.10+.10+.10}{10} = 10\%$$

Step 4. Calculate the standard deviation of each investment.

$$\sqrt{VAR(R_{Biotech})} = \sqrt{\sum_R p_R \times (R - E[R])^2} = \sqrt{.5(.3-.1)^2 + .5(-.1-.1)^2} = 20\%$$

$$\sqrt{VAR(R_{ETF})} = \sqrt{\sum_R p_R \times (R - E[R])^2} = \sqrt{.5(.25-.1)^2 + .5(-.05-.1)^2} = 15\%$$

Step 5. Calculate the standard deviation of a 10-stock portfolio of each investment.

Biotech stocks move independently. Hence the standard deviation of the portfolio is:

$$SD(\text{Portfolio of 10 biotech stocks}) = \frac{SD(\text{Individual Risk})}{\sqrt{\text{Number of Observations}}} = \frac{0.20}{\sqrt{10}} = 6.3\%.$$

Because all ETF stocks in the portfolio move together, there is no diversification benefit. So the standard deviation of the portfolio is the same as the standard deviation of one ETF, 15%.

Step 6. Make a conclusion.

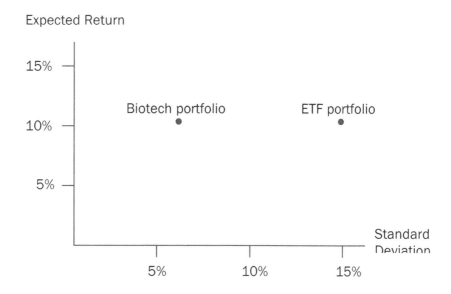

Since the biotech stock portfolio has a lower standard deviation, and both options offer a 10% return, the biotech stock portfolio is preferred to the ETF portfolio.

Questions and Problems

1. Consider the following probability distributions:

   Asset A

Return	-30%	0%	20%	40%
Probability	0.20	0.40	0.20	0.20

   Asset B

Return	-30%	0%	20%	40%
Probability	0.20	0.40	0.20	0.20

   Which asset is the best investment for a risk-averse investor?

2. [A]   During the Depression era from 1929 to 1932, which investment made money in every year, and which investment had the worst performance?

   [B]   During the 1926–2009 period, which investment had the highest return, and which investment had the worst performance?

   [C]   During the 1926–2009 period, which investment had the highest standard deviation, and which investment had the lowest standard deviation?

3. Is it true that expected returns on individual stocks increase proportionately with standard deviation? Explain.

4. Which of the following risks of a stock are likely to be firm-specific, diversifiable risks, and which are likely to be systematic risks? Which risks will affect the risk premium that investors will demand?

   [A]   One of the firm's largest factories may be destroyed by fire.

   [B]   Interest rates may rise in the economy.

   [C]   The housing market may crash, leading to negative economic growth for several years.

   [D]   The firm's major drug may be found to cause cancer and never be approved.

5. Suppose the market risk premium is 6% and the risk-free interest rate is 4%. Calculate the expected return of investing in the following stocks:

	Boston Edison	Priceline
Standard Deviation	33%	76%
Beta	0.34	2.50

Solutions to Questions and Problems

1. Expected returns:

$$E[R_A] = \sum_R p_r \times R = .20(-.30) + .40(0) + .20(.20) + .20(.40) = 6\%$$

$$E[R_B] = \sum_R p_r \times R = .20(-.20) + .10(0) + .40(.10) + .30(.20) = 6\%$$

Standard Deviations:

$$\sqrt{VAR(R_A)} \;=\; \sqrt{\sum_R (R-E[R])^2}$$

$$=\sqrt{.2(-.3-.06)^2+.4(0-.06)^2+.2(.2-.06)^2+.2(.3-.06)^2} \;=\; \sqrt{0.042}=.205=20.5\%$$

$$\sqrt{VAR(R_B)} \;=\; \sqrt{\sum_R (R-E[R])^2}$$

$$=\sqrt{.2(-.2-.06)^2+.1(0-.06)^2+.4(.1-.06)^2+.3(.2-.06)^2} \;=\; \sqrt{0.020}=.143=14.3\%$$

So B is preferable. It has the same expected return as A, but has lower risk.

2. [A]   From the graph in Figure 10.1, Treasury bills were the only asset class to have a positive return in this period. Small stocks had the worst performance in this period, losing most of their value.

   [B]   Small stocks had the highest average annual return (20.9%), and Treasury bills had the lowest average annual return (3.9%).

   [C]   Small stocks had the highest standard deviation (41.5%), and Treasury bills had the lowest standard deviation (3.1%).

3. No, there is no clear relation between standard deviation and return for individual stocks. While the smallest stocks have a slightly higher average return, many stocks have higher volatility and lower average returns than other stocks. All stocks seem to have higher risk and lower returns than we would have predicted from a simple extrapolation of our data from large portfolios. Thus, while volatility seems to be a reasonable measure of risk when evaluating a large portfolio, it is inadequate to explain the returns of individual securities.

4. Because interest rates and the health of the economy affect all stocks, risks (B) and (C) are systematic risks. These risks are not diversified in a large portfolio, and they will affect the risk premium that investors require to invest in stocks. Firms with cash flows that are related to the health of the economy must offer larger risk premiums.

   Risks (A) and (D) are firm-specific risks, and so are diversifiable. While these risks should be considered when estimating the firm's future cash flows, they will not affect the risk premium that investors will require and, therefore, will not affect the firm's cost of capital.

5. Boston Edison

   $$E[R]=4+0.34(6)=6.0\%$$

   Priceline

   $$E[R]=4+2.50(6)=19\%$$

CHAPTER 11

Optimal Portfolio Choice and the Capital Asset Pricing Model

Chapter Synopsis

11.1 The Expected Return of a Portfolio

The expected return on an n-asset portfolio is simply the weighted-average of the expected returns of the portfolio's components:

$$R_P = x_1 R_1 + x_2 R_2 + \cdots + x_n R_n = \sum_{i=1}^{n} x_i R_i \Rightarrow E[R_P] = \sum_{i=1}^{n} x_i E[R_i].$$

where x_i is the value of asset i divided by the portfolio's total value.

11.2 The Volatility of a Two-Stock Portfolio

The standard deviation of an n-asset portfolio is generally less than the weighted-average of the standard deviations of the portfolio's components. When two or more stocks are combined in a portfolio, some of their risk will generally be eliminated through diversification. The amount of risk that will remain depends on the degree to which the stocks share systematic risk. Thus the risk of a portfolio depends on more than the risk and return of the component stocks, and the degree to which the stocks' returns move together is important; their **covariance** or **correlation** must be considered:

▪ Covariance is the expected product of the deviation of each return from its mean, which can be measured from historical data as:

$$\text{Cov}(R_i, R_j) = \frac{1}{T - 1} \sum_{t=1}^{T} (R_{i,t} - \bar{R}_i)(R_{j,t} - \bar{R}_j).$$

▪ Correlation is the covariance of the returns divided by the standard deviation of each return:

$$\text{Corr}(R_i, R_j) = \frac{\text{Cov}(R_i, R_j)}{\text{SD}(R_i) \times \text{SD}(R_j)}.$$

Correlation is generally easier to interpret because it always lies between −1 and 1. The closer the correlation is to 1, the more the returns tend to move together. Assets with zero correlation move independently; assets with −1.0 correlation, move in opposite directions.

The variance of a two-asset portfolio can now be calculated as:

$$\text{Var}(R_P) = x_1^2 \text{Var}(R_1) + x_2^2 \text{Var}(R_2) + 2x_1 x_2 \text{Cov}(R_1, R_2), \text{ or}$$
$$= x_1^2 \text{Var}(R_1) + x_2^2 \text{Var}(R_2) + 2x_1 x_2 \text{Cor}(R_1, R_2)\text{SD}(R_1)\text{SD}(R_2).$$

As can be seen from the equation, only when the correlation between the two stocks is exactly 1.0 is the Var(P) equal to the weighted average of the stocks' variances—otherwise it is less. The portfolio's standard deviation equals $\sqrt{\text{Var}(P)}$ and is often referred to as **volatility**.

11.3 The Volatility of a Large Portfolio

The variance of an equally-weighted n-asset portfolio is:

$$\text{Var}(R_P) = \frac{1}{n}(Average \text{ asset variance}) + \left(1 - \frac{1}{n}\right)(Average \text{ covariance between assets}).$$

Thus, as the number of stocks, n, grows large, the variance of the portfolio is determined primarily by the average covariance among the stocks (because $1 - \frac{1}{n} \rightarrow 1$) while the average variance becomes unimportant (because $\frac{1}{n} \rightarrow 0$). Therefore, the risk of a stock in a diversified portfolio depends on its contribution to the portfolio's average covariance.

11.4 Risk Versus Return: Choosing an Efficient Portfolio

The set of efficient portfolios, which offer investors the highest possible expected return for a given level of risk, is called the **efficient frontier**. Investors must choose among the efficient portfolios based on their own preferences for return versus risk.

A positive investment in a security is referred to as a **long position**. It is also possible to invest a negative amount in a stock, called a **short position**, by engaging in a **short sale**, a transaction in which you sell a stock that you do not own and then buy that stock back in the future at hopefully a lower price. When investors can use short sales in their portfolios, the portfolio weights on those stocks are negative, and the set of possible portfolios is extended.

11.5 Risk-Free Saving and Borrowing

Portfolios can be formed by combining borrowing and lending at the risk-free rate and by investing in a portfolio of risky assets. The expected return for this type of portfolio is the weighted average of the expected returns of the risk-free asset and the risky portfolio, or:

$$E[R_{xP}] = (1 - x)r_f + xE[R_P] = r_f + x(E[R_P] - r_f)$$

Since the standard deviation of the risk-free investment is zero, the covariance between the risk-free investment and the portfolio is also zero, and the standard deviation for this type of portfolio equals simply $x\text{SD}(R_P)$ since $\text{Var}(r_f)$ and $\text{Cov}(r_f, R_P)$ are zero:

$$\text{SD}[R_{xP}] = \sqrt{(1-x)^2 \text{Var}(r_f) + x^2 \text{Var}(R_P) + 2(1-x)(x)\text{Cov}(r_f, R_P)} = x\text{SD}(R_P).$$

On a graph, the risk–return combinations of the risk-free investment and a risky portfolio lie on a straight line connecting the two investments. As the fraction x invested in the risk portfolio increases from 0% to 100%, you move along the line from 100% in the risk-free investment, to 100% in the risky portfolio. If you increase x beyond 100%, you reach points beyond the risky portfolio in the graph. In this case, you are borrowing at the risk-free rate and buying stocks on **margin.**

To earn the highest possible expected return for any level of volatility, you must find the portfolio that generates the steepest possible line when combined with the risk-free investment. The slope of the line through a given portfolio P is often referred to as the **Sharpe ratio** of the portfolio:

$$\text{Sharpe Ratio} = \frac{\text{Portfolio Excess Return}}{\text{Portfolio Volatility}} = \frac{E[R_P] - r_f}{\text{SD}(R_P)}.$$

The portfolio with the highest Sharpe ratio is called the **tangent portfolio.** You can draw a straight line from the risk-free rate through the tangent portfolio that is tangent to the efficient frontier of portfolios.

When the risk-free asset is included, all efficient portfolios are combinations of the risk-free investment and the tangent portfolio—no other portfolio that consists of only risky assets is efficient. Therefore, the optimal portfolio of risky investments no longer depends on how conservative or aggressive the investor is. All investors will choose to hold the same portfolio of risky assets, the tangent portfolio, combined with borrowing or lending at the risk-free rate.

11.6 The Efficient Portfolio and Required Returns

The beta of an investment with a portfolio is defined as:

$$\beta_i^P \equiv \frac{\text{Cov}(R_i, R_P)}{\text{Var}(R_P)} = \frac{\text{SD}(R_i) \times \cancel{\text{SD}(R_P)} \times \text{Corr}(R_i, R_P)}{\text{SD}(R_P) \times \cancel{\text{SD}(R_P)}} = \frac{\text{SD}(R_i) \times \text{Corr}(R_i, R_P)}{\text{SD}(R_P)}.$$

Beta measures the sensitivity of the investment's return to fluctuations in the portfolio's return. Buying shares of security i improves the performance of a portfolio if its expected return exceeds the required return:

$$\text{Required Return} \equiv r_i = r_f + \beta_i^P (E[R_P] - r_f).$$

A portfolio is efficient when $E[R_i] = r_i$ for all securities and the following relation holds:

$$E[R_i] = r_i \equiv r_f + \beta_i^{\text{efficient portfolio}} (E[R_{\text{efficient portfolio}}] - r_f).$$

If investors hold portfolio P, this equation yields the return that investors will require to add the asset to their portfolio—i.e. the investment's **cost of capital.** Buying shares of a security improves the performance of a portfolio if its expected return exceeds the required return based on its beta with the portfolio.

11.7 The Capital Asset Pricing Model

The **Capital Asset Pricing Model** (CAPM) makes three assumptions.

- Investors can trade all securities at competitive market prices without incurring taxes or transactions costs, and can borrow and lend at the same risk-free interest rate.

- Investors hold only efficient portfolios of traded securities—portfolios that yield the maximum expected return for a given level of volatility.

- Investors have homogeneous expectations regarding the volatilities, correlations, and expected returns of securities.

It follows that each investor will identify the same efficient portfolio of risky securities, which is the portfolio that has the highest Sharpe ratio in the economy. Because every security is owned by someone, the holdings of all investors' portfolios must equal the portfolio of all risky securities available in the market, which is known as the **market portfolio.**

Thus, when the CAPM assumptions hold, choosing an optimal portfolio is relatively straightforward for individual investors—they just choose to hold the same portfolio of risky assets, the market portfolio, combined with borrowing or lending at the risk-free rate.

The **capital market line** (CML) is the set of portfolios with the highest possible expected return for a given level of standard deviation, or volatility. Under the CAPM assumptions, on a graph in which expected return is on the y-axis and standard deviation is on the x-axis, the CML is the line through the risk-free security and the market portfolio.

11.8 Determining the Risk Premium

When the CAPM holds, a security's expected return is given by:

$$E[R_i] = r_i = r_f + \beta_i^{Mkt}(E[R_{Mkt}] - r_f).$$

Thus, there is a linear relation between a stock's beta and its expected return. On a graph in which expected return is on the y-axis and beta is on the x-axis, the line that goes through the risk-free investment (with a beta of 0) and the market (with a beta of 1) is called the **security market line** (SML).

The security market line applies to portfolios as well. For example, the market portfolio is on the SML and, according to the CAPM, other portfolios such as mutual funds must also be on the SML, or else they are mispriced. Therefore, the expected return of a portfolio should correspond to the portfolio's beta, which equals the weighted average of the betas of the securities in the portfolio:

$$\beta_P = \sum_i x_i \frac{Cov(R_i, R_{Mkt})}{Var(R_{Mkt})} = \sum_i x_i \beta_i.$$

While the CAPM is based on rather strong assumptions, financial economists find the intuition underlying the model compelling, so it is still the most commonly used to measure systematic risk. It is also the most popular method used by financial managers to estimate their firm's equity cost of capital.

Appendix: The CAPM with Differing Interest Rates

In this chapter, we assume that investors face the same risk-free interest rate whether they are saving or borrowing. However, in practice, investors generally receive a lower rate when they save than they must pay when they borrow. Thus, if borrowing and lending rates differ, investors with different preferences will choose different portfolios of risky securities. So, the first conclusion of the CAPM—that the market portfolio is the unique efficient portfolio of risky investments—is no longer valid.

The more important conclusion of the CAPM for corporate finance is the security market line, which is still valid when interest rates differ. This is because a combination of portfolios on the efficient frontier of risky investments is also on the efficient frontier of risky investments. Because all investors hold portfolios on the efficient frontier, and because all investors collectively hold the market portfolio, the market portfolio must lie on the frontier. As a result, the market portfolio will be tangent for some risk-free interest rate between the efficient portfolios based on different borrowing and lending rates.

Selected Concepts and Key Terms

Correlation

The covariance of two assets' returns divided by the product of the standard deviations of the assets' returns. Correlation is generally easier to interpret than covariance because it always lies between –1 and 1. The closer the correlation is to 1, the more the returns tend to move together. Assets with zero correlation move independently; assets with –1 correlation, move in opposite directions.

Covariance

The expected product of the deviation of each return from its mean, which can be measured from historical data as:

$$\text{Cov}(R_i, R_j) = \frac{1}{T-1} \sum_{t=1}^{T}(R_{i,t} - \bar{R}_i)(R_{j,t} - \bar{R}_j).$$

Efficient Portfolio, Efficient Frontier

An **efficient portfolio** offers investors the highest possible expected return for a given level of risk. The set of efficient portfolios for different levels of risk is called the **efficient frontier**. As investors add stocks to a portfolio, the efficient portfolio generally improves. Since efficient portfolios cannot be easily ranked, investors must choose based on their own preferences for return versus risk.

Capital Market Line (CML).

The set of portfolios with the highest possible expected return for a level of standard deviation, or volatility. Under the CAPM assumptions, on a graph in which expected return is on the y-axis and standard deviation is on the x-axis, the CML is the line through the risk-free security and the market portfolio.

Security Market Line (SML)

The line that goes through the risk-free investment (with a beta of 0) and the market (with a beta of 1). It is the equation implied by the Capital Asset Pricing Model, and shows the linear relation between the expected return and systematic risk, as measured by beta.

Sharpe Ratio

The ratio of a portfolio's excess return (or expected excess return) to the portfolio's standard deviation, or volatility. The Sharpe ratio was first introduced by William Sharpe as a measure to compare the performance of mutual funds. See William Sharpe, "Mutual Fund Performance," *Journal of Business* (January 1966): 119–138.

Short Position

A transaction in which you sell a stock that you do not own and then buy that stock back in the future at hopefully a lower price. When investors can use short sales in their portfolios, the portfolio weights on those stocks is negative, and the set of possible portfolios is extended.

Tangent Portfolio

The portfolio with the highest Sharpe ratio. Because the tangent portfolio has the highest Sharpe ratio of any portfolio, the tangent portfolio provides the biggest reward per unit of volatility of any portfolio available.

Volatility

A term often used to refer to an asset's or portfolio's standard deviation.

Concept Check Questions and Answers

11.1.1. What is a portfolio weight?

Portfolio weights represent the fraction of the total investment in the portfolio of each individual investment in the portfolio.

11.1.2. How do we calculate the return on a portfolio?

The return on the portfolio is the weighted average of the returns on the investments in the portfolio, where the weights correspond to portfolio weights.

11.2.1. What does the correlation measure?

Correlation measures how returns move in relation to each other. It is between +1 (returns always move together) and –1 (returns always move oppositely).

11.2.2. How does the correlation between the stocks in a portfolio affect the portfolio's volatility?

The lower the correlation between stocks, the lower the portfolio's volatility.

11.3.1. How does the volatility of an equally weighted portfolio change as more stocks are added to it?

The variance of an equally-weighted portfolio equals:

$$Var(R_p) = \frac{1}{n}(\text{Average Variance of the Individual Stocks})$$

$$+ \left(1 - \frac{1}{n}\right)(\text{Average Covariance between the Stocks}).$$

As the number of stocks grows large, the variance of the portfolio is determined primarily by the average covariance among the stocks.

11.3.2. How does the volatility of a portfolio compare with the weighted average volatility of the stocks within it?

The weighted average volatility of the stocks within a portfolio is greater than the volatility of the portfolio, unless the stocks are perfectly correlated.

11.4.1. How does the correlation between two stocks affect the risk and return of portfolios that combine them?

Correlation between two stocks has no effect on the expected return of the portfolios combining them; however, the volatility of the portfolios will differ depending on the correlation. In particular, the lower the correlation, the lower the volatility of the portfolios.

11.4.2. What is the efficient frontier?

Efficient portfolios offer investors the highest possible expected return for a given level of risk. The set of efficient portfolios is called the efficient frontier.

11.4.3. How does the efficient frontier change when we use more stocks to construct portfolios?

As investors add stocks to a portfolio, the efficient frontier improves.

11.5.1. What do we know about the Sharpe ratio of the efficient portfolio?

The Sharpe ratio of a portfolio is the portfolio excess return divided by the portfolio volatility. The Sharpe ratio measures the ratio of reward-to-volatility provided by a portfolio. The efficient portfolio is the portfolio with the highest Sharpe ratio in the economy.

11.5.2. If investors are holding optimal portfolios, how will the portfolios of a conservative and an aggressive investor differ?

Both will own portfolios that combine investing in the same efficient portfolio and borrowing or lending at the risk-free rate. Aggressive investors will invest a greater portion of their portfolio in the efficient portfolio.

11.6.1. When will a new investment improve the Sharpe ratio of a portfolio?

Increasing the amount invested in an investment will increase the Sharpe ratio of portfolio P if its expected return $E[Ri]$ exceeds its required return given portfolio P, defined as:

$$r_i \equiv r_f + \beta_i^P \times (E[R_P] - r_f).$$

11.6.2. An investment's cost of capital is determined by its beta with what portfolio?

The efficient portfolio, which is the portfolio with the highest Sharpe ratio of any portfolio in the economy.

11.7.1. Explain why the market portfolio is efficient according to the CAPM.

Since every investor is holding the tangent portfolio, the combined portfolio of risky securities of all investors must also equal the tangent portfolio. Furthermore, because every security is owned by someone, the sum of all investors' portfolios must equal the portfolio of all risky securities available in the market. Therefore, the efficient tangent portfolio of risky securities (the portfolio that all investors hold) must equal the market portfolio.

11.7.2. What is the capital market line (CML)?

The set of portfolios with the highest possible expected return for a level of standard deviation, or volatility. Under the CAPM assumptions, on a graph in which expected return is on the *y*-axis and standard deviation is on the *x*-axis, the CML is the line through the risk-free security and the market portfolio.

11.8.1. What is the security market line (SML)?

The line that goes through the risk-free investment (with a beta of 0) and the market (with a beta of 1). It is the equation implied by the Capital Asset Pricing Model and shows the linear relation between the expected return and systematic risk, as measured by beta.

11.8.2. According to the CAPM, how can we determine a stock's expected return?

When the CAPM holds, a security's expected return is given by:

$$E[R_i] = r_i = r_f + \beta_i^{Mkt}(E[R_{Mkt}] - r_f).$$

Examples with Step-by-Step Solutions

Solving Problems

Problems using the concepts in this chapter may require calculating the expected return on a portfolio, or the variance, standard deviation, correlation, or covariance of a two-asset portfolio. You should also be able to make conclusions regarding the standard deviation of a large portfolio, given the average variance and correlation (or covariance) of the assets in that portfolio. You also may need to determine the expected return and standard deviation of a portfolio that includes investing in a risk-free asset or a risky portfolio. Finally, you may need to calculate the beta of an asset relative to an efficient portfolio, and determine if adding the asset to your holdings would improve your portfolio.

Examples

1. You are considering investing in Cisco and Yahoo which have never paid dividends and had the following actual end-of-year stock prices (adjusted for splits):

	Cisco	Yahoo
12/31/1996	$7.07	$0.71
12/31/1997	9.29	4.33
12/31/1998	23.20	29.62
12/31/1999	53.56	108.17
12/31/2000	38.25	15.03
12/31/2001	18.11	8.87
12/31/2002	13.10	8.18
12/31/2003	24.23	22.51
12/31/2004	19.32	37.68
12/31/2005	17.12	39.18

Calculate the expected return and variance of an equally weighted portfolio, and graph the efficient frontier, assuming these are the only assets you can invest in.

Step 1. Determine the annual return on each stock.

The annual return $= \dfrac{P_{t+1} - P_t}{P_t}$, for example $\dfrac{P_{1997}^{Cisco} - P_{1996}^{Cisco}}{P_{1996}^{Cisco}} = \dfrac{9.29 - 7.07}{7.07} = 0.314 = 31.4\%$

The returns for 1997–2005 are:

	Cisco	Yahoo
1997	0.314	5.099
1998	1.497	5.841
1999	1.309	2.652
2000	-0.286	-0.861
2001	-0.527	-0.410
2002	-0.277	-0.078
2003	0.850	1.752
2004	-0.203	0.674
2005	0.114	0.040

Step 2. Calculate the expected return on each stock.

$$R_{Cisco}^{Mean} = \frac{1}{T}\sum_{t=1}^{T}R_t = \frac{\substack{0.314 + 1.497 + 1.309 + -0.286 + -0.527 + -0.277 \\ +0.850 + -0.203 + -0.114}}{9}$$
$$= 28.5\%$$

$$R_{Yahoo}^{Mean} = \frac{1}{T}\sum_{t=1}^{T}R_t = \frac{\substack{5.099 + 5.841 + 2.652 + -0.861 + -0.410 + -0.078 \\ +1.752 + 0.674 + 0.040}}{9}$$
$$= 163\%$$

Step 3. Calculate the standard deviations of each stock.

$$SD(R_{Cisco}) = \sqrt{VAR(R_{Cisco})} = \sqrt{\frac{1}{T-1}\sum_{t=1}^{T}(R_t - \overline{R})^2} =$$

$$= \sqrt{\frac{\substack{(0.314 - 0.285)^2 + (1.497 - 0.285)^2 + (1.309 - 0.285)^2 + (-0.286 - 0.285)^2 \\ +(-0.527 - 0.285)^2 + (-0.277 - 0.285)^2 + (0.850 - 0.285)^2 \\ +(-0.203 - 0.285)^2 + (-0.114 - 0.285)^2}}{8}}$$
$$= 0.753 = 75.3\%$$

$$SD(R_{Yahoo}) = \sqrt{VAR(R_{Yahoo})} = \sqrt{\frac{1}{T-1}\sum_{t=1}^{T}(R_t - \overline{R})^2}$$

$$= \sqrt{\frac{\substack{(5.099 - 1.634)^2 + (5.841 - 1.634)^2 + (2.652 - 1.634)^2 + (-0.861 - 1.634)^2 \\ +(-0.410 - 1.634)^2 + (-0.078 - 1.634)^2 + (1.752 - 1.634)^2 \\ +(0.674 - 1.634)^2 + (0.040 - 1.634)^2}}{8}}$$
$$= 2.438 = 244\%$$

Step 4. Calculate the expected return on the portfolio.

$$E[R_p] = \sum_{i=1}^{n} x_i E[R_i] = 0.5(0.285) + 0.5(1.63) = 0.958 = 95.8\%$$

Step 5. In order to calculate the portfolio standard deviation, the covariance needs to be calculated.

$$Cov(R_{Cisco}, R_{Yahoo}) = \frac{1}{T-1} \sum_{t=1}^{T} (R_{i,t} - \overline{R}_i)(R_{j,t} - \overline{R}_j)$$

$$= \frac{\begin{aligned} &(0.314-0.285)(5.099-1.634)+(1.497-0.285)(5.841-1.634)+(1.309-0.285)(2.652-1.634) \\ &+(-0.286-0.285)(-0.861-1.634)+(-0.527-0.285)(-0.410-1.634)+(-0.277-0.285)(-0.078-1.634) \\ &+(0.850-0.285)(1.752-1.634)+(-0.203-0.285)(0.674-1.634)+(-0.114-0.285)(0.040-1.634) \end{aligned}}{8}$$

$$= 1.43$$

So, the correlation is: $Corr(R_{Cisco}, R_{Yahoo}) = \dfrac{Cov(R_{Cisco}, R_{Yahoo})}{SD(R_{Cisco}) \times SD(R_{Yahoo})} = \dfrac{1.43}{0.75 \times 2.44} = 0.78$

Step 6. Calculate the portfolio's variance and standard deviation.

$$Var(R_p) = x_1^2 Var(R_1) + x_2^2 Var(R_2) + 2x_1 x_2 Cov(R_1, R_2)$$
$$= .5^2.753^2 + .5^2 2.44^2 + 2(.5)(.5)(1.43)$$
$$= .143 + 1.486 + .715 = 2.343$$
$$SD(R_p) = \sqrt{2.343} = 1.153 = 153\%$$

Step 7. Graph the results.

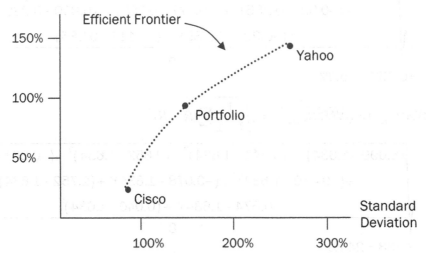

2. You are considering investing in 10 stocks in two different industries (all 10 stocks you chose will be in the same industry).

- The first industry is biotechnology. The historical average return on the stocks you are considering is 10%, and the historical average standard deviation is 30%. The stocks have an average correlation of 0.15.

- The other industry is S&P 500 exchange-traded funds (ETFs). The historical average return on the ETFs you are considering is 10%, and the historical average standard deviation is 20%. The ETFs have an average correlation of 0.99.

Which strategy is better?

Step 1. Determine what you should base your decision on.

Both strategies have an expected return of 10%. So the portfolio with the lowest standard deviation would be preferred by a risk-averse investor.

Step 2. Calculate the standard deviation of each portfolio using the variance of an n-asset portfolio equation.

$$Var(R_{Biotech}) = \frac{1}{n}(\text{Average Var}(R_i)) + (1 - \frac{1}{n})(\text{Average Cov}(R_i, R_j))$$

$$= \frac{1}{10}(.30^2) + (1 - \frac{1}{10})(0.15 \times 0.3 \times 0.30)$$

$$= 0.021, \text{ and } SD(R_{Biotech}) = .145 = 14.5\%$$

$$Var(R_{ETF}) = \frac{1}{n}(\text{Average Var}(R_i)) + (1 - \frac{1}{n})(\text{Average Cov}(R_i, R_j))$$

$$= \frac{1}{10}(.20^2) + (1 - \frac{1}{10})(0.99 \times 0.20 \times 0.20)$$

$$= 0.075, \text{ and } SD(R_{ETF}) = .275 = 27.5\%$$

Step 3. Make a conclusion.

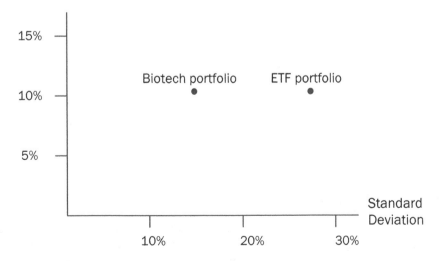

Since the biotech stock portfolio has a lower standard deviation, and both options offer a 10% return, the biotech stock portfolio is preferred to the ETF portfolio.

3. **You have decided to invest $1 million in the equally weighted portfolio of Cisco and Yahoo in problem 1 above.**

	Expected Return	Standard Deviation
Cisco	28.5%	75.3%
Yahoo	163%	244%
Equally-weighted portfolio	95.8%	118%

In addition you are going to borrow $500,000 from your margin account and invest it in the portfolio as well. If the borrowing rate is 6%, what is the expected return and standard deviation of your portfolio? Graph your results.

Step 1. Determine the expected return on the portfolio.

Since $x = \dfrac{\$1,000,000 + \$500,000}{\$1,00,000} = 1.5,$

$E[R_{xP}] = r_f + x(E[R_P] - r_f) = .06 + 1.5(.958 - .06) = 137\%$

Step 2. Determine the standard deviation of the portfolio.

$SD[R_{xP}] = xSD(R_P) = 1.5(118\%) = 177\%$

Step 3. Graph the results

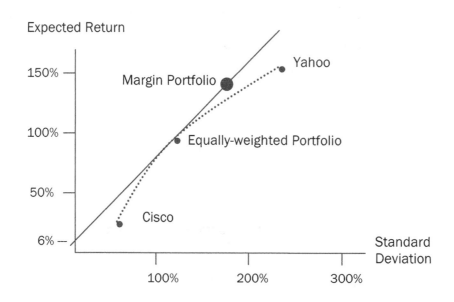

Questions and Problems

1. Your TIAA-CREF retirement account contains stock index mutual funds, corporate bond mutual funds, and government bond mutual funds. It has an expected return of 12% and a standard deviation of 18%. You are considering adding a gold exchange traded fund (ETF), which has an 8% expected return, a standard deviation of 25%, and a correlation with your

current retirement holdings of –0.44. If the risk-free rate is 5%, will adding some of the gold ETF improve your portfolio?

2. Your retirement account offers the option of investing in Treasury bills which yield 5% and *one* of the following three diversified mutual funds:

	Expected Return	**Standard Deviation**
Fidelity Magellan	16%	32%
Vanguard S&P 500 Index	14%	25%
Barclay Total Market	12%	16%

Which mutual fund should you choose?

3. The following table provides statistics for Microsoft and Anheuser-Busch between 1996 and 2004.

	Microsoft	**Anheuser-Busch**
Standard deviation	42%	18%
Correlation with Microsoft	1.00	–0.07
Correlation with Anheuser-Busch	–0.07	1.00

What is the standard deviation of an equally weighted portfolio of these two stocks?

4. The following table provides correlations for Dell and Anheuser-Busch between 1996 and 2004.

	Dell	**Anheuser-Busch**
Correlation with Dell	1.0	0.10
Correlation with Anheuser-Busch	0.10	1.0

If all 7,000 stocks in the US stock market had the same correlation, and the average stock had a standard deviation of 50%, what would be the variance of a:

[A] 2-stock equally weighted portfolio?
[B] 20-stock equally weighted portfolio?
[C] 7,000-stock equally weighted portfolio?

5. You have $100,000 in cash and are considering investing in a portfolio with an expected return of 15%, and a standard deviation of 20%.
[A] If you invest $50,000 in the portfolio and $50,000 in T-bills which yield 5%, what is the expected return and volatility (standard deviation) of your investment?
[B] If you invest $150,000 in the portfolio by borrowing $50,000 at 5%, what is the expected return and volatility (standard deviation) of your investment?

Solutions to Questions and Problems

1. The beta of the gold ETF with the portfolio is:

$$\beta_i^P = \frac{SD(R_i) \times Corr(R_i,R_j)}{SD(R_P)} = \frac{0.25 \times -0.44}{0.18} = -0.611.$$

Beta indicates the sensitivity of the investment's return to fluctuations in the portfolio's return. Buying shares of security *i* improves the performance of a portfolio if its expected return exceeds the required return, which equals:

$$r_i = r_f + \beta_i^P (E[R_P] - r_f) = 0.05 + -0.611(0.12 - 0.05) = 0.007 = 0.7\%.$$

The gold ETF has an expected return of 8% that exceeds the required return of 0.7%. Therefore, you can improve the performance of your current portfolio by investing in the gold fund.

2. To earn the highest possible expected return for any level of volatility, you must find the portfolio that generates the steepest possible line when combined with the risk-free investment. The slope of the line through a given portfolio P is often referred to as the Sharpe ratio of the portfolio.

$$\text{Sharpe Ratio} = \frac{\text{Portfolio Excess Return}}{\text{Portfolio Volatility}} = \frac{E[R_P] - r_f}{SD(R_P)}$$

$$SR^{Fidelity} = \frac{0.16 - 0.05}{0.32} = 0.344$$

$$SR^{Vanguard} = \frac{0.14 - 0.05}{0.25} = 0.360$$

$$SR^{Barclay} = \frac{0.12 - 0.05}{0.16} = 0.438$$

So the Barclay Total Market fund is the best option.

3. $Var(R_P) = x_1^2 Var(R_1) + x_2^2 Var(R_2) + 2x_1 x_2 Cov(R_1, R_2)$

$\quad\quad = .5^2 .42^2 + .5^2 18^2 + 2(.5)(.5)(-.07)(.42)(.18)$

$\quad\quad = 0.050$

$SD(R_P) = \sqrt{0.050} = .223 = 22.3\%$

4. [A] $\quad Var(R_P^{2 \text{ stock}}) = \frac{1}{n}(\text{Average } Var(R_i)) + (1 - \frac{1}{n})(\text{Average } Cov(R_i, R_j))$

$\quad\quad\quad\quad = \frac{1}{2}(.50^2) + (1 - \frac{1}{2})(0.10 \times 0.50 \times 0.50)$

$\quad\quad\quad\quad = 0.138$, and $SD(R) = .371 = 37.1\%$

[B] $\quad Var(R_P^{20 \text{ stock}}) = \frac{1}{n}(\text{Average } Var(R_i)) + (1 - \frac{1}{n})(\text{Average } Cov(R_i, R_j))$

$\quad\quad\quad\quad = \frac{1}{20}(.50^2) + (1 - \frac{1}{20})(0.10 \times 0.50 \times 0.50)$

$\quad\quad\quad\quad = 0.036$, and $SD(R) = .190 = 19.0\%$

[C] $\quad Var(R_P^{7,000 \text{ stock}}) = \frac{1}{n}(\text{Average } Var(R_i)) + (1 - \frac{1}{n})(\text{Average } Cov(R_i, R_j))$

$\quad\quad\quad\quad = \frac{1}{7,000}(.50^2) + (1 - \frac{1}{7,000})(0.10 \times 0.50 \times 0.50)$

$\quad\quad\quad\quad = 0.025$, and $SD(R) = .158 = 15.8\%$

5. [A] $\quad E[R_{xP}] = r_f + x(E[R_P] - r_f) = .05 + 0.5(.15 - .05) = 10\%$

$\quad\quad SD[R_{xP}] = xSD(R_P) = .5(20\%) = 10\%$

[B] $\quad E[R_{xP}] = r_f + x(E[R_P] - r_f) = .05 + 1.5(.15 - .05) = 20\%$

$\quad\quad SD[R_{xP}] = xSD(R_P) = 1.5(20\%) = 30\% \text{ s}$

CHAPTER 12

Estimating the Cost of Capital

Chapter Synopsis

12.1 The Equity Cost of Capital

The Capital Asset Pricing Model (CAPM) provides a practical way to determine the cost of equity capital. This estimate is provided by the Security Market Line equation of the CAPM, which states that, given the beta of the investment opportunity:

$$r_i = r_f + \underbrace{\beta_i \; (E[R_{Mkt}] - r_f)}_{\text{Risk premium for security } i} \; .$$

12.2 The Market Portfolio

It is not possible to observe the actual market portfolio which contains all risky assets, so an index of stocks is commonly used as a **market proxy**. Since the market portfolio is defined as the total supply of risky assets, the proportions of each asset should correspond to the proportion of the total market that each security represents. Thus, in the market portfolio of stocks, each security *i* should be proportional to its market capitalization, which is the total market value of its outstanding shares = price per share × number of shares. Such a portfolio is called a **value-weighted portfolio**.

Market indices measure the value of a portfolio of securities; popular indices include:

- The **S&P 500**, a value-weighted portfolio of 500 of the largest U.S. stocks, is the standard **market proxy** portfolio used to represent the market when using the CAPM in practice. Even though the S&P 500 includes only 500 of the more than 7,000 individual U.S. stocks, it represents more than 70% of the U.S. stock market capitalization.

- The **Wilshire 5,000** is a value-weighted index of all U.S. stocks listed on the major stock exchanges. While more representative of the overall market than the S&P 500, the correlation between the two indices' daily returns has exceeded 98% over the last 20 years.

▪ The **Dow Jones Industrial Average** (DJIA) is a portfolio of 30 large industrial stocks and is likely the most familiar stock index in the U.S. The DJIA is a price-weighted portfolio, which holds an equal split-adjusted number of shares of each stock, independent of their size. Thus, the index's small number of stocks and weighting scheme makes it a poor proxy for the CAPM market portfolio.

Many mutual fund companies offer **index funds** that invest in the portfolios that comprise indices such as these. There are also **exchange-traded funds** (ETFs), securities that trade on an exchange that are entirely invested in a portfolio of stocks that represent portfolios such as market indices like the S&P 500. For example, Standard and Poor's Depository Receipts (SPDRs, nicknamed "spiders") trade on the American Stock Exchange (symbol SPY) and represent ownership in the S&P 500. By investing in an index or an exchange-traded fund, an individual investor with only a small amount to invest can easily achieve the benefits of broad diversification.

The most popular approach to estimating the market risk premium, $E[R_{Mkt}] - r_f$, is to use the historical average excess return of the market over the risk-free interest rate. With this approach, it is important to use historical returns over the same time horizon as that used for the risk-free interest rate.

12.3 Beta Estimation

While the beta depends on the unobservable correlations and volatilities of the security's returns, and market's returns in the future, it is common practice to estimate beta based on the historical correlation and volatilities. This approach makes sense if a stock's beta remains relatively stable over time.

Many data sources provide estimates of beta based on historical data. Typically, these data sources estimate correlations and volatilities from two to five years of weekly or monthly returns, and use the S&P 500 as the market portfolio.

The slope coefficient in a **linear regression**, the statistical technique that identifies the best-fitting line through a set of points, is mathematically the same as the CAPM beta. Using linear regression, the following equation can be estimated:

$$(R_i - r_f) = \alpha_i + \beta_i(R_{Mkt} - r_f) + \varepsilon_i \,.$$

Given historical data for r_f, R_i, and R_{Mkt}, statistical packages for linear regression (available in most spreadsheet programs) can estimate β_i. The constant term α_i is the distance the stock's average return is above or below the SML. If alpha (α_i) is positive, the stock has performed better than predicted by the CAPM—its historical return is above the security market line. If alpha is negative, the stock's historical return is below the SML. Thus α_i is often used as a risk-adjusted performance measure for historical returns.

12.4 The Debt Cost of Capital

The yield to maturity of a bond is the IRR an investor will earn from holding the bond to maturity and receiving its promised payments. Therefore, if there is little risk that the firm will default, we can use the bond's yield to maturity as an estimate of investors' expected return. If there is a significant risk that the firm will default on its obligation, the yield to maturity of the firm's debt, which is its promised return, will overstate investors' expected return. Suppose a bond will default with probability p, in which case bond holders will receive only $(1+yL)$, where L represents the expected loss per $1 of debt in the event of default. Then the expected return of the bond is:

$$r_d = (1-p)y + p(y-L) = y - p \times L$$
$$= \text{Yield to Maturity} - \text{Prob(default)} \times \text{Expected Loss Rate.}$$

Alternatively, you can estimate the debt cost of capital using the CAPM. In principle it would be possible to estimate debt betas using their historical returns in the same way that we estimated equity betas. However, because bank loans and many corporate bonds are traded infrequently, if at all, as a practical matter we can rarely obtain reliable data for the returns of individual debt securities.

12.5 A Project's Cost of Capital

The most common method for estimating a project's beta is to identify comparable firms in the same line of business as the project we are considering undertaking. Then, if we can estimate the cost of capital of the assets of comparable firms, we can use that estimate as a proxy for the project's cost of capital.

The simplest setting is one in which we can find an all-equity financed firm in a single line of business that is comparable to the project. Because the firm is all equity, holding the firm's stock is equivalent to owning the portfolio of its underlying assets. Thus, if the firm's average investment has similar market risk to our project, then we can use the comparable firm's equity beta and cost of capital as estimates for beta and the cost of capital of the project.

If the comparable firm has debt, the returns of the firm's equity alone are not representative of the underlying assets; in fact, because of the firm's leverage, the equity will often be much riskier. Thus, the beta of the levered firm's equity will not be a good estimate of the beta of its assets and of our project. We can undo the effect of leverage and recreate a claim on the firm's assets by holding both its debt and equity simultaneously.

The firm's **asset cost of capital** or **unlevered cost of capital,** which is the expected return required by the firm's investors to hold the firm's underlying assets, is the weighted average of the firm's equity and debt costs of capital:

Asset or Unlevered Cost of Capital

$$r_U = \frac{E}{E+D} r_E + \frac{D}{E+D} r_D.$$

Because the beta of a portfolio is the weighted-average of the betas of the securities in the portfolio, we have a similar expression for the firm's **asset** or **unlevered beta,** which we can use to estimate the beta of our project:

Asset or Unlevered Beta

$$\beta_U = \frac{E}{E+D} \beta_E + \frac{D}{E+D} \beta_D.$$

12.6 Project Risk Characteristics and Financing

Firm asset betas reflect the market risk of the *average* project in a firm. However, individual projects may be more or less sensitive to market risk, so financial managers should evaluate projects based on asset betas of firms that concentrate in a similar line of business. Thus, for multi-divisional firms, identifying a set of "pure play" comparables for each division is helpful in estimating appropriate divisional costs of capital.

Another factor that can affect the market risk of a project is its degree of operating leverage, which is the relative proportion of fixed versus variable costs. Holding the cyclicality of the project's revenues fixed, a higher proportion of fixed costs will increase the sensitivity of the project's cash flows to market risk, and raise the project's beta. Thus, we should assign projects with an above-average proportion of fixed costs, and thus greater-than-average operating leverage, a higher cost of capital.

12.7 Final Thoughts on Using the CAPM

Since the assumptions of the CAPM are not completely realistic, you might be wondering: How reliable, and thus worthwhile, are the results that we can obtain following this approach? Even if the CAPM model is not perfectly accurate, it gets managers to think about risk in the correct way. Managers of widely held corporations should not worry about diversifiable risk, which shareholders can easily eliminate in their own portfolios. They should focus on, and be prepared to compensate investors for, the market risk in the decisions that they make.

Appendix: Practical Considerations When Forecasting Beta

Several practical considerations arise when estimating betas, including:

1. **The time horizon used.** For stocks, common practice is to use at least two years of weekly return data or five years of monthly return data.

2. **The index used as the market portfolio.** The S&P 500 is commonly used as the market proxy. Other proxies, such as the NYSE Composite Index, the Wilshire 5000 index of all U.S. stocks, or an even broader market index that includes both equities and fixed-income securities, are sometimes used as well. When evaluating international stocks, it is common practice to use a country or international market index.

3. **The method used to extrapolate from past betas to future betas.** The estimated beta for a firm will tend to vary over time. Since much of this variation is likely due to estimation error, you should be suspicious of estimates that are extreme relative to historical or industry norms. Also, evidence suggests that betas tend to regress toward the average beta of 1.0 over time. Thus, many practitioners use **adjusted betas**, which are calculated as a weighted average of the estimated beta and 1.0, with the estimated beta often given a weight of 2/3 and 1.0 given a weight of 1/3.

4. **The treatment of outliers in the data.** Beta estimates obtained from linear regression can be very sensitive to outliers. Thus, some practitioners advocate ignoring certain return observations with an unusually large magnitude. For example, data from 1998–2001 may be ignored to avoid distortions related to the technology, media, and telecommunications speculative bubble. On the other hand, including data from recessionary periods may be helpful in evaluating the stock's likely sensitivity to future downturns.

● ## Selected Concepts and Key Terms

Alpha

The difference between a security's expected return, and its CAPM required return, from the security market line. According to the CAPM, all stocks and securities should be on the security market line and have an alpha of zero. If some securities have a nonzero alpha, the market portfolio is not efficient, and its performance can be improved by buying securities with positive alphas and selling those with negative alphas.

Exchange Traded Fund

Securities that trade on an exchange that are entirely invested in a portfolio of stocks that represent portfolios such as market indices like the S&P 500.

Market Portfolio, Market Proxy

The portfolio in the Capital Asset Pricing Model that contains all risky assets. Because the true market portfolio is unobservable, the **S&P 500**, a value-weighted portfolio of 500 of the largest U.S. stocks, is the standard **market proxy** portfolio used to represent the market when using the CAPM in practice.

Operating Leverage

The relative proportion of fixed versus variable costs. Holding the cyclicality of the project's revenues fixed, a higher proportion of fixed costs, and thus higher operating leverage, will increase the sensitivity of the project's cash flows to market risk, and raise the project's beta.

● ## Concept Check Questions and Answers

12.1.1. According to the CAPM, we can determine the cost of capital of an investment by comparing it to what portfolio?

The market portfolio. Under the CAPM, the market portfolio is a well-diversified, efficient portfolio representing the non-diversifiable risk in the economy. Investments therefore have similar risk if they have the same sensitivity to market risk, as measured by their beta with the market portfolio.

12.1.2. What inputs do we need to estimate a firm's equity cost of capital using the CAPM?

Beta, the current risk-free rate, and the market risk premium, $E[R_{Mkt}] - r_f$.

12.2.1. How do you determine the weight of a stock in the market portfolio?

In a value-weighted portfolio, like the market portfolio, each security is held in proportion to its market capitalization. The weight of each stock is determined as the fraction of money invested in that stock corresponding to its share of the total market value of all securities in the portfolio.

12.2.2. What is a market proxy?

A portfolio used to represent the market when using the CAPM in practice.

12.2.3. How can you estimate the market risk premium?

The most popular approach to estimating the market risk premium, $E[R_{Mkt}] - r_f$, is to use the historical average excess return of the market over the risk-free interest rate.

12.3.1. How can you estimate a stock's beta from historical returns?

Given historical data for r_f, R_i, and R_{Mkt}, statistical packages for linear regression (available in most spreadsheet programs) can estimate β_i by estimating the following equation:

$$(R_i - r_f) = \alpha_i + \beta_i(R_{Mkt} - r_f) + \varepsilon_i.$$

It is common to use at least two years of weekly return data or five years of monthly data to estimate beta. We generally do not use daily returns due to the concern that short-term factors might influence returns that are not representative of the longer term risks affecting the stock.

12.3.2. How do we define a stock's alpha, and what is its interpretation?

The alpha of a stock is the difference between a stock's expected return and its required return according to the security market line. If alpha is positive, the stock has performed better than predicted by the CAPM—its historical return is above the security market line. If alpha is negative, the stock's historical return is below the SML. Thus alpha is often used as a risk-adjusted performance measure for historical returns.

12.4.1. Why does the yield to maturity of a firm's debt generally overestimate its debt cost of capital?

The yield to maturity of a bond is the IRR an investor will earn from holding the bond to maturity and receiving its promised payments. Therefore, if there is little risk the firm will default, we can use the bond's yield to maturity as an estimate of investors' expected return. If there is a significant risk that the firm will default on its obligation, the yield to maturity of the firm's debt, which is its promised return, will overstate investors' expected return.

12.4.2. Describe two methods that can be used to estimate a firm's debt cost of capital.

(1) By estimating the yield-to-maturity on a firm's bonds. (2) By using the CAPM. In principle it would be possible to estimate debt betas using their historical returns in the same way that we estimated equity betas. However, because bank loans and many corporate bonds are traded infrequently, if at all, as a practical matter we can rarely obtain reliable data for the returns of individual debt securities.

12.5.1. What data can we use to estimate the beta of a project?

Since firm asset betas reflect the market risk of the average project in a firm, individual projects may be more or less sensitive to market risk, so financial managers should evaluate projects based on asset betas of firms that concentrate in a similar line of business. Thus, for multi-divisional firms, identifying a set of "pure play" comparables for each division is helpful in estimating appropriate divisional costs of capital.

12.5.2. Why does the equity beta of a levered firm differ from the beta of its assets?

If the comparable firm has debt, the returns of the firm's equity alone are not representative of the underlying assets; in fact, because of the firm's leverage, the equity will often be much riskier. Thus, the beta of levered firm's equity will not be a good estimate of the beta of its assets, and of our project.

12.6.1. Why might projects within the same firm have different costs of capital?

Individual projects may be more or less sensitive to market risk so financial managers should evaluate projects based on the asset betas of firms that concentrate in a similar line of business. Thus, for multi-divisional firms, identifying a set of "pure play" comparables for each division is helpful in estimating appropriate divisional costs of capital.

12.6.2. Under what conditions can we evaluate a project using the firm's weighted average cost of capital?

A firm's beta reflects the market risk of the average project in a firm. So, if the firm operates in one line of business, or all of the lines of business have the same amount of market risk, then the firm's weighted-average cost of capital can be used to evaluate any project.

12.7.1. Which errors in the capital budgeting process are likely to be more important than discrepancies in the cost of capital estimate?

The revenue and other cash flow projections we must make when valuing a stock or an investment in a new product are likely to be far more speculative than any we have made in estimating the cost of capital.

12.7.2. Even if the CAPM is not perfect, why might we continue to use it in corporate finance?

Even if the CAPM model is not perfectly accurate, it gets managers to think about risk in the correct way. Managers of widely held corporations should not worry about diversifiable risk, which shareholders can easily eliminate in their own portfolios. They should focus on, and be prepared to compensate investors for, the market risk in the decisions that they make.

Examples with Step-by-Step Solutions

Solving Problems

Problems using the concepts in this chapter may involve estimating a firm's equity cost of capital using the capital asset pricing model (CAPM). Problems may also require the determination of a project weighted-average cost of capital, and may require using comparable firms that operate in a specific industry to estimate the beta risk of the industry. The examples below illustrate these concepts.

Examples

1. Intel uses 15% as its cost of capital when evaluating investment projects. The company currently has no long-term debt. Based on current market data below and a stock market risk premium of 6.1% over 30-year T-bonds, is their WACC equal to 15%? If it is not, how may using 15% affect them?

15.00	Open:	15.34	Mkt Cap:	83.77B	P/E:	19.08	Dividend:	0.14
	High:	15.60	52Wk High:	25.29	F P/E:	-	Yield:	3.73
-0.60 (-3.85%)	Low:	15.00	52Wk Low:	12.05	Beta:	1.26	Shares:	5.58B
Apr 20 - Close	Vol:	66.49M	Avg Vol:	73.03M	EPS:	0.79	Inst. Own:	64%

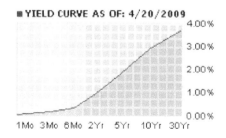

■ YIELD CURVE AS OF: 4/20/2009

Step 1. Since they have no long-term debt, their equity cost of capital, r_E, is their WACC. So you must just determine r_E.

From the information provided, the parameters of the CAPM can be determined:

$r_f = 3.5\%$, the 30-year T-bond yield in the graph.

$\beta = 1.26$ from the quote provided

$(E[r_{mkt}] - r_f) = 6.1\%$ from the problem

Next the CAPM expected return can be determined:

$r_E = r_f + \beta(E[r_{mkt}] - r_f) = .035 + 1.26(.061) = .112 = 11.2\%$

Step 2. Determine how using 15% instead of 11.2% would alter the investments they choose to accept.

Since they are using a higher discount rate, projects that would provide a return between 11.2% and 15% would be rejected because they have a negative NPV. Thus, they would likely invest in fewer projects and potentially forgo valuable investment opportunities.

2. **Your firm is considering building a casino, and you are trying to determine the cost of capital in the industry. You have collected the following information on firms in the casino industry.**

Company	Beta	Stock Price	Number of Shares	Debt
MGM Mirage	1.10	$72.67	143 million	$5.6 billion
Mandalay Resort Group	0.95	$70.43	65 million	$3.0 billion
Caesars Entertainment	1.20	$19.88	304 million	$4.6 billion

The risk-free rate is 5%, and the historical market risk premium, $(E[R_{Mkt}] - r_f)$, is 6%.

[A]   What is the equity cost of capital for an unlevered firm in the industry?
[B]   What is the equity cost of capital for a firm in the industry with a debt-to-equity ratio of 1?

Step 1. Measure the unlevered betas.

The unlevered beta, β_U, measures the market risk of the firm without leverage, which is equivalent to the beta of the firm's assets. The unlevered asset beta therefore measures the market risk of the firm's business activities, ignoring any additional risk due to leverage, and can be estimated using:

$$\beta_{assets} = \beta_{unlevered} = \beta_{equity} \frac{E}{E + D}.$$

E, the market value of equity, can be calculated as stock price × number of shares.

Company	Stock Price	Number of Shares	E
MGM Mirage	$72.67	143 million	$10.4 billion
Mandalay Resort Group	$70.43	65 million	$4.6 billion
Caesars Entertainment	$19.88	304 million	$6.0 billion

Now, unlevered betas can be calculated:

$$\beta^{MGM}_{Assets} = \frac{10.4}{10.4 + 5.6}1.10 = 0.72,$$

$$\beta^{Mandalay}_{Assets} = \frac{4.6}{4.6 + 3.0}0.95 = 0.58,$$

$$\beta^{Caesars}_{Assets} = \frac{6.0}{6.0 + 4.6}1.2 = 0.68 .$$

Step 3. Calculate the unlevered equity cost of capital based on the average unlevered betas of the comparable firms. A common method is to use the average of the unlevered betas of the comparison firms.

The average unlevered beta is $\dfrac{0.72 + 0.58 + 0.68}{3} = 0.66.$

The equity cost of capital can be determined from the CAPM:

$$E[R] = r_f + \beta^{Mkt}_i(E[R_{Mkt}] - r_f) = 0.05 + 0.66(0.06) = 9.0\%.$$

Step 4. Calculate the levered beta when D/E = 1.0.

When a firm changes its capital structure without changing its investments, its unlevered beta will remain unaltered. However, its equity beta will change to reflect the effect of the capital structure change on its risk, and the levered equity beta can be calculated as:

$$\beta_{Equity} = \left(1 + \frac{D}{E}\right)\beta_{Assets} = \left(1 + \frac{1}{1}\right)0.66 = 1.32.$$

Step 5. Calculate the levered equity cost of capital based on the average unlevered beta of the comparable firms levered to reflect a D/E ratio of 1.0.

The equity cost of capital can now be determined from the CAPM:

$$E[R] = r_f + \beta^{Mkt}_i(E[R_{Mkt}] - r_f) = 0.05 + 1.32(0.06) = 12.9\%$$

3. **Nordstrom is spinning off its casual clothing segment and you are trying to determine the value of the spun-off entity. You estimate that the division's free cash flow in the coming year to be $100 million, and you expect the free cash flows will grow by 3% per year in subsequent years. Because the spin-off isn't publicly traded yet, you do not have an accurate assessment of the division's equity beta. However, you do have beta data for Gap, Inc., a firm it closely resembles. Gap has an equity beta of 1.1, a debt beta of 0, and a debt-equity ratio of 0.20.**

   Nordstrom has a beta of 2.2, a debt-equity ratio of 1.0 (the spun-off firm will maintain this leverage ratio), and has been told by its investment bankers that the debt cost of capital will be 6%. The corporate tax rate is 40%, the risk-free rate is 5%, and the historical market risk premium, $(E[R_{Mkt}] - r_f)$, is 6%.

   [A] Estimate the division's WACC.
   [B] Estimate the spun-off unit's share value based on the 100 million shares that will be outstanding after the spinoff.

Step 1. Unlever the Gap beta.

The unlevered beta, β_U, measures the market risk of the firm without leverage, which is equivalent to the beta of the firm's assets. The unlevered asset beta therefore measures the market risk of the firm's business activities, ignoring any additional risk due to leverage, and can be estimated using:

$$\beta_{assets} = \beta_{unlevered} = \beta_{equity} \frac{E}{E + D}$$

$$\beta_{assets} = \left(\frac{E}{E + D}\right)\beta_{equity} = \left(\frac{1}{1 + 0.2}\right)1.1 = 0.92$$

Step 2. Relever the beta to reflect the division's debt-equity ratio of 1.0.

$$\beta_{equity} = \beta_{assets}\left(1 + \frac{D}{E}\right) = 0.92\left(1 + \frac{1}{1}\right) = 1.84$$

Step 3. Calculate the levered cost of equity.

$$E[r] = r_f + \beta(E[R_{Mkt}] - r_f) = 0.05 + 1.84(0.06) = 0.16.0\%$$

Step 4. Calculate the WACC.

$$WACC = \frac{D}{D+E}r_D(1-t) + \frac{E}{D+E}r_E = \frac{1}{1+1}0.06(1 - 0.4) + \frac{1}{1+1}0.16 = 0.018 + 0.08 = 0.098$$

Step 5. The value of the division can be determined.

The value of the levered firm using the WACC method is:

$$V_0^{Levered\ Firm} = \sum_{t=1}^{\infty} \frac{FCF_t}{r_{WACC} - g} = \frac{\$100 \text{ million}}{0.098 - 0.03} = \$1.471 \text{ billion}.$$

The WACC method values the division as a whole, so the equity value is:

E = V − D = $1.471 billion − 0.50($1.471) = $735 million,

and the per share value is $735 million/100 million = $7.35.

Questions and Problems

1. The following information is what your firm, which has a beta of 1.4, relies on to determine its equity cost of capital:

Current Treasury-Bill Yield	Average S&P 500 Return 1926-2004	Average Treasury-Bill Yield 1926-2004
2.4%	12.3%	3.9%

What is the best estimate of your firm's equity cost of capital?

2. Your firm manufactures keyboards for Dell. It has 20 million shares trading at $50 per share, an equity beta of 1.8, $500 million of AA-rated bonds with a yield-to maturity of 7% and a coupon rate of 10%, and intends to maintain this degree of leverage. The firm is considering expanding its manufacturing operations in Phoenix by producing voting booths. The tax rate is 35%, T-bonds are yielding 5%, and the market risk premium is 8.6% above T-bonds. The only public voting machine manufacturer has 75% debt financing and an equity beta of 1.2. What cost of capital should be used to evaluate the project?

3. Investor #1 is considering adding one of the following stocks into a diversified portfolio. Investor #2 is considering investing all of his money in one of the following stocks.

Stock	Beta	Standard Deviation
El Paso Electric	0.65	56%
General Electric	1.20	34%

Which one of the stocks is least risky to each of these investors?

4. You call your personal retirement portfolio the S&P 3, a value-weighted portfolio with $1 million invested in the 3 stocks below. Every quarter you rebalance the portfolio to return it to its equally weighted state. Determine how many shares should be invested in each stock as of 12/31/2006.

Stock	12/31/2006 Price	Shares Outstanding
Starbucks	$30	1 billion
Goldman Sachs	$150	400 million
Nordstrom	$50	200 million

5. In mid-2009, Amco Corp. had outstanding 8-year bonds with a yield to maturity of 8% and a BB rating. If corresponding risk-free rates were 3%, and the market risk premium is 5%, estimate the expected return of Amco's debt.

Solutions to Questions and Problems

1. The CAPM is typically applied using the current Treasury yield as the risk-free rate, and the historical market risk premium as measured by the average return on the S&P 500 minus the average return on corresponding term Treasury securities.

$$E[R_i] = r_i = r_f + \beta_i^{Mkt}(E[R_{Mkt}] - r_f) = 2.4\% + 1.4(12.3\% - 3.9\%) = 14.2\%$$

2. First, determine your capital structure.

E = the market value of equity = $50(20 \text{ million}) = \$1 \text{ billion}$

D = the market or book value of long-term debt = $500 million

Next, find the cost of equity.

First, unlever the equity beta of the voting booth manufacturer. The unlevered beta, β_U, measures the market risk of the firm without leverage, which is equivalent to the beta of the firm's assets. Since the comparison firm has 75% debt, you can use $D = .75$ and $E = .25$.

$$\beta_{assets} = \beta_{unlevered} = \beta_{equity}\left(\frac{E}{E + D}\right) = 1.2\left(\frac{.25}{.25 + .75}\right) = 0.30$$

Now, lever the Beta with your capital structure:

$$\beta_{equity} = \beta_{assets}\left(1 + \frac{D}{E}\right) = 0.30\left(1 + \frac{.50}{1}\right) = 0.45.$$

You can now use the CAPM to estimate your cost of equity.

$$r_E = r_f + \beta(E[r_{mkt}] - r_f) = .05 + 0.45(.086) = .0887 = 8.87\%$$

For the debt cost of capital, you can use the current yield-to-maturity, 7%, which reflects the market's required return on your bonds and the AA-rated bonds have a very small probability of default.

Finally, determine the after-tax weighted-average cost of capital.

$$\text{WACC} = \frac{D}{D+E} r_D (1-t) + \frac{E}{D+E} r_E = \frac{.5}{.5+1}(.07)(1-0.35) + \frac{1}{.5+1}(.0887)$$
$$= .01517 + .0591 = .074, \text{ or } 7.4\%$$

3. Investor #1 should select El Paso Electric because it has a lower beta, and beta measures the amount of risk that a stock will add to a diversified portfolio.

   Since investor #2 does not have a diversified portfolio, beta is not the correct measure of risk. In this situation, General Electric is the least risky because it has lower total risk as measured by standard deviation. However, investor #2 should not expect to be compensated for bearing a higher level of risk.

4. The total value of all 3 stocks is:

$$= (\$30 \times 1,000,000) + (\$150 \times 400,000,000) + (\$50 \times 200,000,000) = \$100 \text{ billion}$$

Stock	Portfolio Weight	Number of Shares
Starbucks	$\dfrac{\$30 \times 1,000,000,000}{100,000,000,000} = 30\%$	$\dfrac{0.30 \times \$1,000,000}{\$30} = 10,000$
Goldman Sachs	$\dfrac{\$150 \times 400,000,000}{100,000,000,000} = 60\%$	$\dfrac{0.60 \times \$1,000,000}{\$150} = 4,000$
Nordstrom	$\dfrac{\$50 \times 200,000,000}{100,000,000,000} = 10\%$	$\dfrac{0.10 \times \$1,000,000}{\$50} = 2,000$

5. Given the low rating of debt, as well as the recessionary economic conditions at the time, we know the yield to maturity of KB Home's debt is likely to significantly overstate its expected return. Using the recession estimates in Table 12.3 and an expected loss rate of 60%, from Eq. 12.7, we have:

$$r_d = (1-p)y + p(y-L) = y - p \times L$$
$$= \text{Yield to Maturity} - \text{Prob(default)} \times \text{Expected Loss Rate}$$
$$= 8.5\% - 8\%(0.60) = 3.2\%$$

CHAPTER 13

Investor Behavior and Capital Market Efficiency

Chapter Synopsis

13.1 Competition and Capital Markets

When the market portfolio is efficient, all stocks are on the security market line and have an alpha of zero. When a stock's alpha is not zero, investors can improve upon the performance of the market portfolio. As we saw in Chapter 11, the Sharpe ratio of a portfolio will increase if we buy stocks whose expected return exceeds their required return—that is, if we buy stocks with positive alphas. Similarly, we can improve the performance of our portfolio by selling stocks with negative alphas.

Thus, as savvy investors attempt to trade to improve their portfolios, they raise the price and lower the expected return of the positive-alpha stocks, and they depress the price and raise the expected return of the negative-alpha stocks, until the stocks are once again on the security market line and the market portfolio is efficient.

Notice that the actions of investors have two important consequences. First, while the CAPM conclusion that the market is always efficient may not literally be true, competition among savvy investors who try to "beat the market" and earn a positive alpha should keep the market portfolio close to efficient much of the time. In that sense, we can view the CAPM as an approximate description of a competitive market. Second, trading strategies that take advantage of non-zero alpha stocks may exist, and by doing so actually can beat the market.

13.2 Information and Rational Expectations

If news that alters a stock's expected return is publically announced, there are likely to be a large number of investors who receive this news and act on it. Similarly, anybody who hears the news will not want to sell at the old prices. The only way to remove this imbalance is for the price to rise so that the alpha is zero. Note that in this case it is quite possible for the new prices to come about without trade. That is, the competition between investors is so intense that prices move before any investor can actually trade at the old prices, so no investor can profit from the news.

In order to profit by buying a positive-alpha stock, there must be someone willing to sell it. Under the CAPM assumption of homogenous expectations, which states that all investors have the same information, it would seem that all investors would be aware that the stock had a positive alpha and none would be willing to sell. In reality, investors have different information and spend varying amounts of effort researching stocks. Consequently, we might expect that sophisticated investors would learn that a stock has a positive alpha, and that they would be able to purchase shares from more naïve investors.

However, even differences in the quality of investors' information will not necessarily be enough to generate trade in this situation. An important conclusion of the CAPM is that investors should hold the market portfolio (combined with risk-free investments), and this investment advice does not depend on the quality of an investor's information or trading skill. Even naïve investors with no information can follow this investment advice, and as the following example shows, by doing so they can avoid being taken advantage of by more sophisticated investors.

Because the average portfolio of all investors is the market portfolio, the average alpha of all investors is zero. If no investor earns a negative alpha, then no investor can earn a positive alpha, and the market portfolio must be efficient. As a result, the CAPM does not depend on the assumption of homogeneous expectations. Rather it requires only that investors have **rational expectations**, which means that all investors correctly interpret and use their own information, as well as information that can be inferred from market prices or the trades of others.

For an investor to earn a positive alpha and beat the market, some investors must hold portfolios with negative alphas. Because these investors could have earned a zero alpha by holding the market portfolio, we reach the following important conclusion:

> The market portfolio can be inefficient (so it is possible to beat the market) only if a significant number of investors either:
>
> 1. Do not have rational expectations so that they misinterpret information and believe they are earning a positive alpha when they are actually earning a negative alpha, or
>
> 2. Care about aspects of their portfolios other than expected return and volatility, and so are willing to hold inefficient portfolios of securities.

13.3 The Behavior of Individual Investors

One of the most important implications of our discussion of risk and return is the benefit of diversification. By appropriately diversifying their portfolios, investors can reduce risk without reducing their expected return. In that sense, diversification is a "free lunch" that all investors should take advantage of.

Despite this benefit, evidence suggests that individual investors fail to diversify their portfolios adequately. Evidence from the U.S. Survey of Consumer Finances shows that, for households that held stocks, the median number of stocks held by investors in 2001 was four, and 90% of investors held fewer than ten different stocks.

There are a number of potential explanations for this behavior. One is that investors suffer from a familiarity bias, so that they favor investments in companies they are familiar with. Another is that investors have relative wealth concerns and care most about the performance of their portfolio relative to that of their peers. This desire to "keep up with the Joneses" can lead investors to choose undiversified portfolios that match those of their colleagues or neighbors. In any case, this underdiversification is one important piece of evidence that individual investors may choose suboptimal portfolios.

Another bias comes from the finding that uninformed individuals tend to overestimate the precision of their knowledge. An implication of this overconfidence hypothesis is that, assuming they have no true ability, investors who trade more will not earn higher returns. Instead, their performance will be worse once we take into account the costs of trading (due to both commissions and bid-ask spreads). An implication of this overconfidence hypothesis is that, assuming they have no true ability, investors who trade more will not earn higher returns. Instead, their performance will be worse once we take into account the costs of trading (due to both commissions and bid-ask spreads).

In order for the behavior of uninformed investors to have an impact on the market, there must be patterns to their behavior that lead them to depart from the CAPM in systematic ways, thus imparting systematic uncertainty into prices. For investors' trades to be correlated in this way, they must share a common motivation.

13.4 Systematic Trading Biases

Investors tend to hold on to stocks that have lost value and sells stocks that have risen in value since the time of purchase. We call this tendency to hang on to losers and sell winners the **disposition effect.**

Studies also show that individuals are more likely to buy stocks that have recently been in the news, engaged in advertising, experienced exceptionally high trading volume, or have had extreme (positive or negative) returns.

In addition, investors appear to put too much weight on their own experience rather than considering all the historical evidence. As a result, people who grow up and live during a time of high stock returns are more likely to invest in stocks than people who grow up and live during a time of low stock returns.

An alternative reason why investors make similar trading errors is that they are actively trying to follow each other's behavior. This phenomenon, in which individuals imitate each other's actions, is referred to as **herd behavior.** Traders might herd in their portfolio choices because they might believe others have superior information that they can take advantage of by copying their trades; they may choose to herd in order to avoid the risk of underperforming their peers; and professional fund managers may face reputational risk if they stray too far from the actions of their peers.

Regardless of why individual investors choose not to protect themselves by holding the market portfolio, the fact that they don't has potential implications for the CAPM. If individual investors are engaging in strategies that earn negative alphas, it may be possible for a few more sophisticated investors to take advantage of this behavior and earn positive alphas.

13.5 The Efficiency of the Market Portfolio

In order for sophisticated investors to profit from investor mistakes, two conditions must hold. First, the mistakes must be sufficiently pervasive and persistent to affect stock prices. Second, there must be limited competition to exploit these non-zero alpha opportunities. If competition is too intense, these opportunities will be quickly eliminated before any trader can take advantage of them in a significant way.

If enough other investors are not paying attention, perhaps one can profit from public news announcements. However, investors should not expect this to be the case. Evidence shows that investors trying to profit from such news announcements quickly incorporate the implications of the news into the market prices. Since the average investor earns an alpha of zero, before including trading costs, beating the market should require special skills, such as better analysis of information or lower trading costs.

Numerous studies report that the actual returns to investors of the average mutual fund have a negative alpha. This suggests that mutual fund managers do not have the special skills, such as better analysis of information, necessary to find stocks that consistently beat the market and suggests that the market is largely efficient. Further, mutual funds generate trading costs and charge management fees, which further erode investors' returns.

Some researchers further categorize such tests as *weak form*, *semi-strong form*, and *strong form efficiency*. Weak form efficiency states that it should not be possible to profit by trading on information in past prices. Semi-strong form efficiency states that it should not be possible to consistently profit by trading on any public information, such as news announcements or analysts' recommendations. Finally, strong form efficiency states that it should not be possible to consistently profit even by trading on private information.

13.6 Style-Based Anomalies and the Market Efficiency Debate

- Portfolios of small stocks (those with a low market capitalizations = stock price x shares outstanding) have higher average returns. This empirical result is called the size effect.

- Portfolios of stocks with high book-to-market ratios (the ratio of the book value of equity to the market value of equity) have higher average returns.

- Portfolios of stocks that performed well in the previous year have higher average returns in the following year. Trading to take advantage of this relation is called a momentum strategy.

Over the years since the discovery of the CAPM, it has become increasingly clear to researchers and practitioners alike that by forming portfolios based on market capitalization, book-to-market ratios, and past returns, investors can construct trading strategies that have a positive alpha. Given these results, we are left to draw one of two conclusions.

1. Investors are systematically ignoring positive-NPV investment opportunities. That is, the CAPM correctly computes required risk premiums, but investors are ignoring opportunities to earn extra returns without bearing any extra risk, either because they are unaware of them or because the costs to implement the strategies are larger than the NPV of undertaking them.
2. The positive-alpha trading strategies contain risk that investors are unwilling to bear but the CAPM does not capture. That is, a stock's beta with the market portfolio does not adequately measure a stock's systematic risk, and so the CAPM does not correctly compute the risk premium.

The only way a positive-NPV opportunity can persist in a market is if some barrier to entry restricts competition. The existence of these trading strategies has been widely known for more than fifteen years. Not only is the information required to form the portfolios readily available, but many mutual funds follow momentum-based and market capitalization/book-to-market–based strategies. Hence, the first conclusion does not seem likely.

That leaves the second possibility: The market portfolio is not efficient, and therefore a stock's beta with the market is not an adequate measure of its systematic risk. Stated another way, the profits (positive alphas) from the trading strategy are really returns for bearing risk that investors are averse to and the CAPM does not capture.

13.7 Multifactor Models of Risk

The expected return of any marketable security can be written as a function of the expected return of the efficient portfolio:

$$E[R_i] = r_i = r_f + \beta_i^{\text{efficient portfolio}}(E[R_{\text{efficient portfolio}}] - r_f)$$

However, identifying an efficient portfolio is difficult to measure because expected returns and the standard deviations of a portfolio cannot be measured with great accuracy. Fortunately, it is not actually necessary to identify the efficient portfolio itself; all that is required is to identify a collection of portfolios from which the efficient portfolio can be constructed. The risk premium of any marketable security can then be written as the sum of the risk premium of each portfolio multiplied by the sensitivity of the stock with that portfolio—the factor betas, β_S^1 and β_S^2:

$$E[R_S] = r_f + \beta_S^1(E[R_1] - r_f) + \beta_S^2(E[R_2] - r_f)$$

where beta is measured relative to portfolios 1 and 2 which capture different **risk factors.** Thus, when more than one portfolio is used to measure market risk, the model is known as a **multifactor model,** and the model can be extended to any number of portfolios. The portfolios themselves can be thought of as either the risk factors or a portfolio of stocks correlated with an unobservable risk factor. This particular form of the multifactor model was originally developed by Stephen Ross and is referred to as the **Arbitrage Pricing Theory** (APT).

The most common portfolio to use in a multifactor model is the market portfolio, which just needs to capture at least some components of systematic risk. Other popular portfolios are the **small-minus-big (SMB) portfolio,** the **high-minus-low (HML) portfolio,** and the **momentum portfolio,** which are generally constructed as follows.

- **SMB.** Firms below the median market value of NYSE firms each month form an equally weighted portfolio, S, and firms above the median market value form an equally weighted portfolio, B. A trading strategy that each year buys portfolio S and finances this position by short selling portfolio B has historically produced positive risk-adjusted returns.

- **HML.** Each year firms with book-to-market ratios less than the 30th percentile of NYSE firms are used to form an equally weighted portfolio called the low portfolio, L. Firms with book-to-market ratios greater than the 70th percentile of NYSE firms form an equally weighted-portfolio called the high portfolio, H. A trading strategy that each year takes a long position in portfolio H, which it finances with a short position in portfolio L, has produced positive risk-adjusted returns.

- **Momentum.** Each year stocks are ranked by their return over the last year, and a portfolio is constructed that goes long on the top 30% of stocks and short on the bottom 30%. This trading strategy requires holding this portfolio for a year, and this process is repeated annually. The resulting portfolio is known as the **prior one-year momentum portfolio (PR1YR).**

Berk (1995) provides the following explanation for the size effect. When the market portfolio is not efficient, some stocks will plot above the SML, and some will plot below this line. All else equal, a positive alpha implies that the stock also has a relatively higher expected return. A higher expected return implies a lower price—the only way to offer a higher expected return is for investors to buy the stock's dividend stream at a lower price. A lower price means a lower market capitalization. Thus, when the market portfolio is not efficient, you should expect to observe the size effect.

All portfolios except the market portfolio are referred to as **self-financing** portfolios because the long position is financed by taking a short position, and because they require no net investment.

The collection of these four portfolios is currently the most popular choice for the multifactor model and is sometimes referred to as the **Fama-French-Carhart (FFC) factor model**, where:

$$E[R_s] = r_f + \beta_s^{Mkt}(E[R_{Mkt}] - r_f) + \beta_s^{SMB}E[R_{SMB}] + \beta_s^{HML}E[R_{HML}] + \beta_s^{PR1YR}E[R_{PR1YR}]$$

The FFC factor specification was identified a little more than ten years ago. Although it is widely used in academic literature to measure risk, much debate persists about whether it really is a significant improvement over the CAPM.

13.8 Methods Used in Practice

All of the techniques are imprecise, and there is no model of expected returns that gives an exact estimate of the cost of capital. John Graham and Campbell Harvey surveyed 392 CFOs and found that 73.5% of the firms use the CAPM to calculate the cost of capital. They also found that larger firms were more likely to use the CAPM. About one third reported using a multifactor model to calculate the cost of capital.

Appendix: Building a Multifactor Model

If an efficient portfolio can be constructed out of a collection of well-diversified portfolios, the collection of portfolios will correctly price assets. To keep things simple, assume that we have identified two portfolios that we can combine to form an efficient portfolio called **factor portfolios** and denote their returns by R_{F1} and R_{F2}. The efficient portfolio consists of some (unknown) combination of these two factor portfolios, represented by portfolio weights x_1 and x_2:

$$R_{eff} = x_1 R_{F1} + x_2 R_{F2}$$

To see that we can use these factor portfolios to measure risk, consider regressing the excess returns of some stock s on the excess returns of *both* factors:

$$R_s - r_f = \alpha_s + \beta_s^{F1}(R_{F1} - r_f) + \beta_s^{F2}(R_{F2} - r_f) + \varepsilon_s$$

We write the excess return of stock s as the sum of a constant, α_s, plus the variation in the stock that is related to each factor, and an error term ε_s that has an expectation of zero and is uncorrelated with either factor. The error term represents the risk of the stock that is unrelated to either factor.

If we can use the two factor portfolios to construct the efficient portfolio, then the constant term α_s is zero. To see why, consider a portfolio in which we buy stock s, then sell a fraction β_s^{F1} of the first factor portfolio and β_s^{F2} of the second factor portfolio, and invest the proceeds from these sales in the risk-free investment. This portfolio, which we call P, has return

$$R_p = R_s - \beta_s^{F1}R_{F1} - \beta_s^{F2}R_{F2} + (\beta_s^{F1} + \beta_s^{F2})r_f$$
$$= R_s - \beta_s^{F1}(R_{F1} - r_f) - \beta_s^{F2}(R_{F2} - r_f)$$

The return of this portfolio is

$$R_p = r_f + \alpha_s + \varepsilon_s.$$

That is, portfolio P has a risk premium of α_s and risk given by ε_s. Now, because ε_s is uncorrelated with each factor, it must be uncorrelated with the efficient portfolio. But recall from Chapter 11 that *risk that is uncorrelated with the efficient portfolio is firm-specific risk that does not command a risk premium*. Therefore, the expected return of portfolio P is r_f, which means α_s must be zero.

Setting α_s equal to zero and taking expectations of both sides of the equation we get the following two-factor model of expected returns:

$$E[R_s] = r_f + \beta_s^{F1}\left(E[R_{F1}] - r_f\right) + \beta_s^{F2}\left(E[R_{F2}] - r_f\right).$$

Selected Concepts and Key Terms

Alpha

The difference between a security's expected return and its CAPM required return from the security market line. According to the CAPM, all stocks and securities should be on the security market line and have an alpha of zero. If some securities have a non-zero alpha, the market portfolio is not efficient, and its performance can be improved by buying securities with positive alphas and selling those with negative alphas.

Arbitrage Pricing Theory (APT), Multifactor Model

When more than one portfolio is used to measure systematic risk, the model is known as a multifactor model. The portfolios themselves can be thought of as either the risk factors or as portfolios of stocks correlated with unobservable risk factors. The Arbitrage Pricing Theory is a form of multifactor model originally developed by Stephen Ross.

Disposition Effect

The empirically documented tendency for investors to hold on to stocks that have lost value and sells stocks that have risen in value since the time of purchase.

Fama-French-Carhart (FFC) Factor Specification

Because using the portfolios, SMB, HML, and momentum, along with the market, were identified by Eugene Fama, Kenneth French, and Mark Carhart, this specification of the multi-factor model is sometimes referred to as the Fama-French-Carhart (FFC) factor model.

Herd Behavior

The tendency of individual investors to imitate each other's actions. Traders might herd in their portfolio choices because they might believe others have superior information that they can take advantage of by copying their trades; they may choose to herd in order to avoid the risk of underperforming their peers; and professional fund managers may face reputational risk if they stray too far from the actions of their peers.

High-Minus-Low (HML) Portfolio

A portfolio often used in factor models that equals to the return on high book-to-market firms minus the return on low book-to-market firms. Each year firms with book-to-market ratios less than the 30th percentile of NYSE firms are used to form an equally weighted portfolio called the low portfolio, L. Firms with book-to-market ratios greater than the 70th percentile of NYSE firms form an equally weighted portfolio called the high portfolio, H. A trading strategy that each year takes a long position in portfolio H, which it finances with a short position in portfolio L, has produced positive risk-adjusted returns.

Momentum Strategy

Buying stocks that performed well in the prior period, often six months or a year, and holding them for the next period.

Prior One-Year Momentum (PR1YR) Portfolio

A portfolio often used in factor models. To form this portfolio, each year stocks are ranked by their return over the last year and a portfolio is constructed that goes long on the top 30% of stocks and short on the bottom 30%. This trading strategy requires holding the portfolio for a year, and this process is repeated annually.

Rational Expectations

An economic theory that can be used to model how investors impound information in stock prices. In the context of the CAPM, it implies that although investors may have different information regarding expected returns, correlations, and volatilities, they correctly interpret the information contained in market prices and adjust their estimates of expected returns in a rational way.

Semi-Strong Form Efficiency

The theory that consistent profits should not be possible from trading on any public information, such as news announcements or analysts' recommendations.

Size Effect

The observation that small stocks have positive CAPM alphas, which was first discovered in 1981 by Rolf Banz in "The Relationship between Return and Market Values of Common Stock," *Journal of Financial Economics* 9 (March 1981): 3–18.

Small-Minus-Big (SMB) Portfolio

A portfolio often used in factor models equal to the return on small firms minus the return on big firms. Firms below the median market value of NYSE firms each month form an equally weighted portfolio, S, and firms above the median market value form an equally weighted portfolio, B. A trading strategy that buys portfolio S and finances this position by short selling portfolio B is the SMB portfolio has historically produced positive risk-adjusted returns.

Strong Form Efficiency

The theory that it should not be possible to consistently profit even by trading on private information.

Weak Form Efficiency

The theory that it should not be possible to profit by trading on information in past prices by, for example, selling winners and hanging on to losers.

Concept Check Questions and Answers

13.1.1. If investors attempt to buy a stock with a positive alpha, what is likely to happen to its price and expected return? How will this affect its alpha?

As savvy investors attempt to trade to improve their portfolios, they raise the price and lower the expected return of the positive-alpha stocks, and they depress the price and raise the expected return of the negative-alpha stocks, until the stocks are once again on the security market line, the market portfolio is efficient, and all stocks have zero alpha.

13.1.2. What is the consequence of investors exploiting non-zero alpha stocks for the efficiency of the market portfolio?

Competition among savvy investors who try to "beat the market" and earn a positive alpha should keep the market portfolio close to efficient much of the time.

13.2.1. How can an uninformed or unskilled investor guarantee themselves a non-negative alpha?

Naïve investors with no information can hold the market portfolio (combined with risk-free investments) to ensure a non-negative alpha.

13.2.2. Under what conditions will it be possible to earn a positive alpha and beat the market?

For an investor to earn a positive alpha and beat the market, some investors must hold portfolios with negative alphas.

13.3.1. Do investors hold well-diversified portfolios?

There is much evidence that individual investors fail to diversify their portfolios adequately. Evidence from the U.S. Survey of Consumer Finances shows that, for households that held stocks, the median number of stocks held by investors in 2001 was four, and 90% of investors held fewer than ten different stocks.

13.3.2. Why is the high trading volume observed in markets inconsistent with the CAPM equilibrium?

Because the market portfolio is a value-weighted portfolio, it is also a passive portfolio in the sense that an investor does not need to trade in response to daily price changes in order to maintain it. Thus, if all investors held the market, we would see relatively little trading volume in financial markets.

13.3.3. What must be true about the behavior of small, uninformed investors for them to have an impact on market prices?

In order for the behavior of uninformed investors to have an impact on the market, there must be patterns to their behavior that lead them to depart from the CAPM in systematic ways, thus imparting systematic uncertainty into prices. For investors' trades to be correlated in this way, they must share a common motivation.

13.4.1. What are several systematic behavioral biases that individual investors fall prey to?

Investors tend to hold on to stocks that have lost value and sells stocks that have risen in value since the time of purchase. We call this tendency to hang on to losers and sell winners the disposition effect. Studies also show that individuals are more likely to buy stocks that have recently been in the news, engaged in advertising, experienced exceptionally high trading volume, or have had extreme (positive or negative) returns. In addition, investors appear to put too much weight on their own experience rather than considering all the historical evidence. As a result, people who grow up and live during a time of high stock returns are more likely to invest in stocks than people who grow up and live during a time of low stock returns.

13.4.2. What implication might these behavioral biases have for the CAPM?

Regardless of why individual investors choose not to protect themselves by holding the market portfolio, the fact that they don't has potential implications for the CAPM. If individual investors are engaging in strategies that earn negative alphas, it may be possible for a few more sophisticated investors to take advantage of this behavior and earn positive alphas.

13.5.1. Should uninformed investors expect to make money by trading based on news announcements?

If enough other investors are not paying attention, perhaps one can profit from public news announcements. However, investors should not expect this to be the case. Evidence shows that investors trying to profit from such news announcements quickly incorporate the implications of the news into the market prices.

13.5.2. If fund managers are talented, why do the returns of their funds to investors not have positive alphas?

Numerous studies report that the actual returns to investors of the average mutual fund have a negative alpha. This suggests that mutual fund managers do not have the special skills, such as better analysis of information, necessary to find stocks that consistently beat the market and suggests that the market is largely efficient. Further, mutual funds generate trading costs and charge management fees, which further erode investors' returns.

13.6.1. What does the existence of a positive-alpha trading strategy imply?

There are two different implications. 1) The positive-alpha trading strategies contain risk that investors are unwilling to bear but the CAPM does not capture. That is, a stock's beta with the market portfolio does not adequately measure a stock's systematic risk, and so the CAPM does not correctly compute the risk premium. 2) Investors are systematically ignoring positive-NPV investment opportunities. That is, the CAPM correctly computes required risk premiums, but investors are ignoring opportunities to earn extra returns without bearing any extra risk, either because they are unaware of them or because the costs to implement the strategies are larger than the NPV of undertaking them.

13.6.2. If investors have a significant amount of non-tradeable (but risky) wealth, why might the market portfolio not be efficient?

If investors have a significant amount of non-tradeable wealth, this wealth will be an important part of their portfolios, but will not be part of the market portfolio of tradeable securities. In such a world, the market portfolio of tradeable securities will likely not be efficient.

13.7.1. What is the advantage of a multifactor model over a single factor model?

Multifactor models have a distinct advantage over single-factor models in that it is much easier to identify a collection of portfolios that captures systematic risk than just a single portfolio.

13.7.2. How can you use the Fama-French-Carhart factor specification to estimate the cost of capital?

The Fama-French-Carhart factor specification identifies the collection of four portfolios that are most commonly used in a multifactor model. These portfolios include the market portfolio, small-minus-big portfolio, high-minus-low portfolio, and prior one-year momentum portfolio.

13.8.1. Which is the most popular method used by corporations to calculate the cost of capital?

John Graham and Campbell Harvey surveyed 392 CFOs and found that 73.5% of the firms use the CAPM to calculate the cost of capital and that larger firms were more likely to use the CAPM.

13.8.2. What other techniques do corporations use to calculate the cost of capital?

John Graham and Campbell Harvey surveyed 392 CFOs and found that about one third reported using a multifactor model to calculate the cost of capital. Two other methods that some firms in the survey reported using are historical average returns (40%) and the dividend discount model (16%).

Examples with Step-by-Step Solutions

Solving Problems

Quantitative problems using the concepts in this chapter may require determining if stocks are over- or undervalued according to the CAPM and interpreting stock alphas. They may also involve finding the cost of capital using a factor model, such as the Fama-French-Carhart model. Below are examples of each.

Examples

1. Suppose that a firm with a stock price of $80 just announced that it expects to pay a $100 per share liquidating dividend in 1 year, although the exact amount of the dividend depends on the performance of the company this year. Assume that the CAPM is a good description of stock price returns and that the stock's beta is 1.5, the market's expected return is 12%, and the risk-free rate is 5%.
   [A]   Is the stock priced correctly now?
   [B]   What is the alpha of the stock?
   [C]   What would you expect to happen to the stock price in the market after the announcement?

   Step 1. Determine the stock's expected return.

   $$E[R] = r_f + \beta_i^{Mkt}(R_{Mkt} - r_f) = .05 + 1.5(.12 - .05) = 0.148 = 15.5\%$$

   Step 2. Determine the value of the stock.

   $$P_0 = \frac{\$100}{1.155} = \$86.58$$

   Thus, the stock is undervalued by $86.58 - $80 = $6.58.

Step 3. To determine the stock's alpha, find the stock's expected return.

$$P_0 = \$86.58 = \frac{\$100}{1+r} \Rightarrow 1+r = \frac{\$100}{\$80} = 1.25 \Rightarrow r = 25\%$$

Thus, the alpha is 25% – 15.5% = 9.5%.

Step 4. Predict what would happen in an efficient market.

Since the stock has a positive alpha, investors should now increase the market price to $86.58. Thus, when the stock begins trading after the announcement, you should not expect to be able to buy the stock for a price below $86.58.

2. **Assume that the CAPM is a good description of stock price returns. You observe the following information for three stocks:**

	Beta	Expected Return
Ford	1.4	18%
General Electric	1.0	12%
Yahoo!	2.8	22%

Based on the stocks' alphas, which should you buy if the market's expected return is 12% and the risk-free rate is 5%?

Step 1. Calculate the CAPM expected returns on each stock.

$$E[R_{Ford}] = r_f + \beta_i^{Mkt}(R_{Mkt} - r_f) = .05 + 1.4(.12 - .05) = 0.148 = 14.8\%$$

$$E[R_{GE}] = r_f + \beta_i^{Mkt}(R_{Mkt} - r_f) = .05 + 1.0(.12 - .05) = 0.120 = 12.0\%$$

$$E[R_{Yahoo!}] = r_f + \beta_i^{Mkt}(R_{Mkt} - r_f) = .05 + 2.8(.12 - .05) = 0.246 = 24.6\%$$

Step 2. Calculate the alpha of each stock.

$$\alpha_i = E[R_i] - r_i = E[R_i] - \left(r_f + \beta_i^{Mkt}(E[R_{Mkt}] - r_f)\right)$$

$$\alpha_{Ford} = 18\% - 14.8\% = 3.2\%$$

$$\alpha_{GE} = 12\% - 12\% = 0\%$$

$$\alpha_{Yahoo!} = 22\% - 24.6\% = -2.6\%$$

So you should buy Ford because it has a positive alpha.

3. **Based on the Fama-French-Carhart factor model, which of the following stocks has the most systematic risk? If the risk-free rate is 5%, what are the firms' equity costs of capital?**

Factor	Stock A	Stock B
MKT	1.26	0.45
SMB	-0.43	0.33
HML	-0.38	0.23
PR1YR	-0.33	-0.35

Mean Monthly Return 1926-2005

MKT – r_f	0.64%
SMB	0.17%
HML	0.53%
PR1YR	0.76%

Step 1. The stock with the most systematic risk has the highest risk premium, so the risk premiums for stocks A and B must be calculated.

First, the monthly risk premiums:

RP_A= 1.26(0.64) + –0.43(0.17) + –0.38(0.53) + –0.33(0.76)   = 0.281%

RP_B= 0.45(0.64) + 0.33(0.17) + 0.23(0.53) + –0.35(0.76)   = 0.200%

Then the annual risk premiums,

RP_A = (1 + 0.00281)^{12} – 1 = 3.4%

RP_B = (1 + 0.00200)^{12} – 1 = 2.4%

So, stock A has the highest risk premium and thus the most systematic risk.

Step 2. Calculate the equity cost of capital for each firm.

The expected return can be calculated based on the FFC factor model:

$$E[R_S] = r_f + \beta_S^{Mkt}(E[R_{Mkt}] - r_f) + \beta_S^{SMB}E[R_{SMB}] + \beta_S^{HML}E[R_{HML}] + \beta_S^{PR1YR}E[R_{PR1YR}]$$

$$E[R_A] = 0.05 + 0.034 = 8.4\%$$

$$E[R_B] = 0.05 + 0.024 = 7.4\%$$

Questions and Problems

1. What are the three types of portfolios discussed in this chapter that have had positive CAPM alphas.

2. Explain the Berk (1995) explanation for the size effect.

3. Describe the factors in the Fama-French-Carhart factor model.

4. How is the small-minus-big (SMB) factor in the Fama-French-Carhart factor model estimated?

5. How is the high-minus-low (HML) factor in the Fama-French-Carhart factor model estimated?

Solutions to Questions and Problems

1. The three types of portfolios that have positive CAPM alphas are small firms (firms with a low stock market capitalization), firms with high book value of equity-to-market value of equity ratios, and firms with positive momentum (i.e. high returns in the prior period).

2. When the market portfolio is not efficient, you should expect to observe the size effect. When the market portfolio is not efficient, some stocks will plot above the SML, and some will plot below this line. All else equal, a positive alpha implies that the stock also has a relatively higher expected return. A higher expected return implies a lower price—the only way to offer a higher expected return is for investors to buy the stock's dividend stream at a lower price. A lower price means a lower market capitalization. Thus, when a financial economist forms a

portfolio of stocks with low market capitalizations, that collection contains stocks that will likely have higher expected returns and, if the market portfolio is not efficient, positive alphas.

3. The factors in the Fama-French-Carhart factor model are as follows.

- **The market.** This is similar to the CAPM market portfolio.

- **SMB (the small-minus-big portfolio).** This factor equals the return on small capitalization firms minus the return on large capitalization firms.

- **HML (the high-minus-low portfolio).** This factor equals to the return on high book-to-market firms minus the return on low book-to-market firms.

- **Momentum.** This factor measures the return on a stock over a prior period, such as one year.

4. Firms below the median market value of NYSE firms each month form an equally weighted portfolio, S, and firms above the median market value form an equally weighted portfolio, B.

5. Each year firms with book-to-market ratios less than the 30th percentile of NYSE firms are used to form an equally weighted portfolio called the low portfolio, L. Firms with book-to-market ratios greater than the 70th percentile of NYSE firms form an equally weighted portfolio called the high portfolio, H.

CHAPTER 14

Capital Structure in a Perfect Market

Chapter Synopsis

14.1 Equity Versus Debt Financing

A firm's **capital structure** refers to the debt, equity, and other securities used to finance its fixed assets. Equity and debt are the securities most commonly used. When equity is used without debt, the firm is said to be **unlevered**. Otherwise, the firm is **levered** and the amount of debt determines the firm's degree of **leverage**. Equity in a firm that also has debt outstanding is called **levered equity**.

The optimal capital structure is the one that maximizes the value of the firm. In an influential 1958 paper, Franco Modigliani and Merton Miller argued that, with perfect capital markets, the total value of a firm does not depend on its capital structure.

14.2 Modigliani-Miller I: Leverage, Arbitrage, and Firm Value

Modigliani and Miller (MM) showed that their capital structure propositions below hold in a **perfect capital market**, which is a market with the following set of conditions:

1. Investors and firms can trade the same set of securities at competitive market prices equal to the present value of their future cash flows.

2. There are no taxes, transaction costs, or issuance costs associated with security trading.

3. A firm's financing decisions do not change the cash flows generated by its investments nor do they reveal new information about them.

Under these conditions, MM demonstrated the following result regarding capital structure in determining firm value referred to as:

MM Proposition I

In a perfect capital market, the total value of a firm is equal to the market value of the total cash flows generated by its assets and is not affected by its choice of capital structure.

MM proved their result by arguing that, in perfect capital markets, the total cash flow paid out to all of a firm's security holders is equal to the total cash flow generated by the firm's assets. Therefore, by the Law of One Price, the firm's securities and its assets must have the same total market value. Thus, as long as the firm's choice of securities does not change the cash flows generated by its assets, this decision will not change the total value of the firm or the amount of capital it can raise.

Even if investors prefer an alternative capital structure to the one chosen by the firm, MM demonstrated that the firm's capital structure is still irrelevant because investors can borrow or lend on their own and achieve the same result. For example, an investor who would like more leverage can add leverage to his or her own portfolio. When investors use leverage in their own portfolios to adjust the leverage choice made by the firm, we say that they are using **homemade leverage**. As long as investors can borrow or lend at the same interest rate as the firm, homemade leverage is a perfect substitute for the use of leverage by the firm.

A hypothetical **market value balance sheet** lists all assets and liabilities of the firm at their market values instead of their historical costs. The market value balance sheet captures the idea that value is created by a firm's choice of assets and investments. By choosing positive-NPV projects that are worth more than their initial investment, the firm can enhance its value. Holding the cash flows generated by the firm's assets fixed, the choice of capital structure does not change the value of the firm. Instead, it merely divides the value of the firm into different securities.

14.3 Modigliani-Miller II: Leverage, Risk, and the Cost of Capital

By holding a portfolio of the firm's equity and debt, you can replicate the cash flows from holding unlevered equity. Because the return of a portfolio is equal to the weighted average of the returns of the securities in it, this equality implies the following relation between the returns of levered equity (R_E), debt (R_D), and unlevered equity (R_U):

$$R_U = \frac{E}{E+D}R_E + \frac{D}{E+D}R_D \Rightarrow R_E = R_U + \frac{D}{E}(R_U - R_D).$$

This equation shows that the levered equity return equals the unlevered return, plus an additional effect due to leverage. This leads to higher returns on levered equity when the firm performs well, but causes a lower return when the firm does poorly. The amount of additional risk depends on the amount of leverage, measured by the firm's market value debt-equity ratio, D/E. Because this relation holds for realized returns, it holds for the expected returns as well (denoted by r in place of R). This observation leads to:

MM Proposition II

The cost of levered equity is equal to the cost of unlevered equity plus a premium that is proportional to the market value debt-equity ratio as provided in the equation above.

The cost of capital of the firm's assets should equal the return that is available on other investments with similar risk. The weighted average of the firm's equity and debt cost of capital is the firm's **weighted average cost of capital (WACC)**, which equals:

$$r_{wacc} \equiv \frac{E}{E+D} r_E + \frac{D}{E+D} r_D .$$

With perfect capital markets, a firm's WACC is independent of its capital structure and is equal to its unlevered equity cost of capital.

The effect of leverage on the risk of a firm's securities can also be expressed in terms of beta. Because unlevered equity is equivalent to a portfolio of debt and levered equity, and because the beta of a portfolio is the weighted average of the betas of the securities within it, the following relation exists:

$$\beta_U = \frac{E}{E+D} \beta_E + \frac{D}{E+D} \beta_D .$$

The **unlevered beta** (β_U) measures the market risk of the firm without leverage, which is equivalent to the beta of the firm's assets. The unlevered beta therefore measures the market risk of the firm's business activities, ignoring any additional risk due to leverage.

When a firm changes its capital structure without changing its investments, its unlevered beta will remain unaltered. However, its equity beta will change to reflect the effect of the capital structure change on its risk, and the **levered beta** (β_E) can be calculated as:

$$\beta_U = \frac{E}{E+D} \beta_E + \frac{D}{E+D} \beta_D \Rightarrow \beta_E = \beta_U + \frac{D}{E}(\beta_U - \beta_D)$$

It is often assumed that the debt beta is zero, so:

$$\beta_E = \beta_U + \frac{D}{E} \beta_U = \beta_U \left(1 + \frac{D}{E}\right)$$

Holding cash has the opposite effect of leverage. Thus, leverage of the firm should be measured in terms of its **net debt** = debt − cash and risk free securities.

14.4 Capital Structure Fallacies

There are at least two incorrect arguments that are sometimes cited in favor of leverage.

- One fallacy is that when leverage increases a firm's expected earnings per share (EPS), it will cause the firm's stock price to increase. However, with perfect capital markets, an increase in EPS is accompanied by an increases risk the shareholders are exposed to and MM proposition I holds.

- Another fallacy is that issuing equity will dilute existing shareholders' ownership, so debt financing should be used instead. In this context, earnings **dilution** refers to the idea that if the firm issues new shares, the cash flows generated by the firm must be divided among a larger number of shares, thereby reducing the value of each individual share. The problem with this line of reasoning is that it ignores the fact that the cash raised by issuing new shares will increase the firm's assets. As long as the capital raised is invested in zero-NPV investments, the value per share will not change.

14.5 MM: Beyond the Propositions

The MM propositions have greatly influenced finance research and practice. Perhaps more important than the specific propositions themselves is the approach that MM took to derive them. Proposition I was one of the first arguments to show that the Law of One Price could have strong implications for security prices and firm values in a competitive market; it marks the beginning of the modern theory of corporate finance.

Their results can be interpreted as the **conservation of value principle** for financial markets: With perfect capital markets, financial transactions neither add nor destroy value, but instead represent a repackaging of risk (and therefore return). It implies that any financial transaction that appears to be a good deal in terms of adding value either is likely too good to be true or is exploiting some type of market imperfection.

Selected Concepts and Key Terms

Capital Structure

The relative proportions of debt, equity, and other securities used to finance a firm's fixed assets.

Conservation of Value Principle

With perfect capital markets, financial transactions neither add nor destroy value, but instead represent a repackaging of risk (and therefore return). It implies that any financial transaction that appears to be a good deal in terms of adding value either is likely too good to be true or is exploiting some type of market imperfection.

Dilution

The idea that if the firm issues new shares, the cash flows generated by the firm must be divided among a larger number of shares, thereby reducing the value of each individual share.

Homemade Leverage

When investors use leverage in their own portfolios to adjust the leverage choice made by the firm.

Market Value Balance Sheet

A form of balance sheet that lists all assets and liabilities of the firm at their market values instead of their historical costs as on a standard balance sheet. Unlike a traditional balance sheet, all assets and liabilities of the firm are included—even intangible assets such as reputation, brand name, or human capital.

Leveraged Recapitalization

When a firm issues debt and uses the proceeds to repurchase a significant percentage of its outstanding shares.

Levered Equity

Equity in a firm that also has debt outstanding.

Net Debt

Since holding cash is essentially the opposite of having debt, the amount of debt a firm effectively has is equal to its debt minus its cash and risk-free securities, which can be referred to as its net debt.

Unlevered Beta

The market risk of a firm's business activities, ignoring any additional risk due to leverage, which is equivalent to the beta of the firm's assets.

Unlevered Equity

Equity in a firm that has no debt outstanding.

Weighted Average Cost of Capital

The weighted average of the firm's equity and debt cost of capital, which should equal the return that is available on other investments with similar risk.

Concept Check Questions and Answers

14.1.1. Why are the value and cash flows of levered equity less than if the firm had issued unlevered equity?

The cash flows and value of levered equity are smaller than those of unlevered equity because debt payments must be made before any payments are made to equity holders.

14.1.2. How does the risk and cost of capital of levered equity compare to that of unlevered equity? Which is the superior capital structure choice in a perfect capital market?

The risk and the cost of capital of levered equity are higher than those of unlevered equity even when there is no risk that the firm will default. In a perfect market, equity financing and debt financing are equal because the total value of the firm is not affected by its choice of capital structure.

14.2.1. Why are investors indifferent to the firm's capital structure choice?

As long as the firm's choice of securities does not change the cash flows generated by its assets, this decision will not change the total value of the firm or the amount of capital it can raise. Further, investor's can create whatever capital structure they want by using homemade leverage to adjust the firm's capital structure.

14.2.2. What is a market value balance sheet?

A market value balance sheet is similar to an accounting balance sheet, with two important distinctions. First, all assets and liabilities of the firm are included—even intangible assets such as reputation, brand name, or human capital that are missing from a standard accounting balance sheet. Second, all values are current market values rather than historical costs.

14.2.3. In a perfect capital market, how will a firm's market capitalization change if it borrows in order to repurchase shares? How will its share price change?

The total value of the equity will decrease by the amount of stock that is repurchased, but the value per share will remain the same.

14.3.1. How do we compute the weighted average cost of capital of a firm?

The weighted average cost of capital is computed by summing the weighted average of the firm's equity and debt cost of capital.

14.3.2. With perfect capital markets, as a firm increases its leverage, how does its debt cost of capital change? Its equity cost of capital? Its weighted average cost of capital?

With perfect capital markets, as a firm increases its leverage, its debt and equity costs of capital both increase, but its weighted average cost of capital remains constant because more weight is put on the lower cost debt.

14.4.1. If a change in leverage raises a firm's earnings per share, should this cause its share price to rise in a perfect market?

No. Even though the firm's earnings per share increase with leverage, due to the additional risk, shareholders will demand a higher return. These effects cancel out, so the price per share is unchanged.

14.4.2. True or false: When a firm issues equity, it increases the supply of its shares in the market, which should cause its share price to fall.

False. As long as the firm sells the new shares of equity at a fair price, there will be no gain or loss to shareholders associated with the equity issue itself. The money taken in by the firm as a result of the share issue exactly offsets the dilution of the shares.

14.5.1. Consider the questions facing Dan Harris, CFO of EBS, at the beginning of this chapter. What answers would you give based on the Modigliani-Miller Propositions? What considerations should the capital structure decision be based on?

Based on the Modigliani-Miller propositions in a perfect market, Dan Harris, CFO of EBS, should answer that the total value of EBS is not affected by its choice of capital structure. In other words, the value of EBS is the same whether $50 million is raised by selling shares of EBS stock or by borrowing. Capital structure only affects a firm's value because of its impact on some type of market imperfection.

14.5.2. State the conservation of value principle for financial markets.

The conservation of value principle for financial markets states that with perfect capital markets, financial transactions neither add nor destroy value, but instead represent a repackaging of risk and return.

Examples with Step-by-Step Solutions

Solving Problems

Problems using this chapter's ideas may involve using Modigliani and Miller's proposition I (in a perfect capital market, the total value of a firm is equal to the market value of the total cash flows generated by its assets and is not affected by its choice of capital structure) to show the effects of changing a firm's capital structure on the value of the firm and its securities. See example 1 below. Problems may also involve using Modigliani and Miller's proposition II (the cost of capital of levered equity is equal to the cost of capital of unlevered equity plus a premium that is proportional to the market value debt-equity ratio) to show how the equity cost of capital increases with leverage. See example 2 below. Finally, problems may require accounting for the effect of leverage on the risk of a firm's securities in terms of beta. See example 3 below.

Examples

1. You are trying to decide whether your firm should use debt financing under different assumptions regarding the amount of debt in its capital structure. The firm's assets will generate an expected EBIT of $800,000 per year (beginning one year from today) in perpetuity. The firm will make no new capital or working capital investments and all assets are fully depreciated. The assets have a beta of 1.5, the risk-free rate is 5%, and the market risk premium, $(E[R_{Mkt}] - r_f)$, is 10%. You can issue bonds at par paying an annual coupon at a 5% annual rate. The firm has 100,000 shares outstanding. There are no corporate taxes or other market imperfections.

    [A] What is the value of the firm with no debt? What is the stock value per share?

    [B] What is the value of the firm if it issues $3 million of debt and uses the proceeds to repurchase 75,000 shares for $40 (75,000 × $40 = $3 million)? What is the stock value per share? Should the firm issue the debt?

    Step 1. Determine the unlevered equity cost of capital.

    The equity cost of capital is $E[R_i] = r_f + \beta_i^{Mkt}(E[R_{Mkt}] - r_f) = 5\% + 1.5(10\%) = 20\%.$

    Step 2. Determine the free cash flows of the unlevered firm.

    Since the firm will make no new investments and has no depreciation, FCF = NI each year.

EBIT	$800,000
– Tax @ 0%	0
Net income	800,000

    Step 3. Determine the value of the unlevered firm.

    Since the cash flows are a perpetuity, $PV = \dfrac{FCF}{r} = \dfrac{\$800,000}{0.20} = \$4$ million

    Step 4. Determine the value per share.

    $\text{Value per share} = \dfrac{V^U}{\text{Shares Outstanding}} = \dfrac{\$4,000,000}{100,000} = \$40$

    Step 5. Determine the value of the levered firm.

    By MM proposition I:

    $V^L = V^U = \$4$ million

    Step 6. Determine the equity value per share.

    The total equity value is $V^L - D = \$4,000,000 - \$3,000,000$, so:

    $\text{Value per share} = \dfrac{4,000,000 - 3,000,000}{100,000 - 75,000} = \$40$

    Thus, the firm should be indifferent between issuing the debt based on these assumptions.

2. Your firm has no debt financing and a market value of equity of $60 billion. The stock's beta is 1.2, the risk-free rate is 5%, and the historical market risk premium, $(E[R_{Mkt}] - r_f)$, is 6%. There are no corporate taxes or other market imperfections.

    [A] What is the equity cost of capital based on the CAPM?

    [B] What is the firm's weighted average cost of capital (WACC)?

[C] The firm is considering three different recapitalizations by issuing $10 billion, $30 billion, or $50 billion in 6% bonds, and using the proceeds to repurchase equity. Calculate the WACC and equity cost of capital in each of these three new capital structures.

Step 1. The unlevered cost of equity can be found using the CAPM.

$$E[R_i] = R_E = r_f + \beta_i^{Mkt}(E[R_{Mkt}] - r_f) = 0.05 + 1.2(0.06) = 12.2\%$$

Step 2. Since $D = 0$, $r_{WACC} = r_E$.

$$r_{wacc} = \frac{E}{E+D}r_E + \frac{D}{E+D}r_D = \left(\frac{60}{60+0}\right)0.122 + \left(\frac{0}{60+0}\right)r_D = 12.2\%$$

Step 3. Calculate r_{WACC} and r_E for each of the proposed capital structures.

By Miller and Modigliani's proposition II, the WACC will remain at 12.2%, but the r_E will vary according to the equation:

$$r_{WACC} = \frac{E}{E+D}r_E + \frac{D}{E+D}r_D \Rightarrow r_E = r_U + \frac{D}{E}(r_U - r_D)$$

By Miller and Modigliani's proposition I, the value of the firm will remain the same, so the new capital structures will have D/E ratios of 10/50, 30/30, and 50/10. The costs of equity capital under the three capital structures are:

$$r_E^{\$10\ billion} = 0.122 + \frac{10}{50}(0.122 - 0.06) = 13.4\%$$

$$r_E^{\$30\ billion} = 0.122 + \frac{30}{30}(0.122 - 0.06) = 18.4\%$$

$$r_E^{\$50\ billion} = 0.122 + \frac{50}{10}(0.122 - 0.06) = 43.2\%$$

3. Your firm is considering building a casino, and you are trying to determine the cost of capital in the industry. You have collected the following information on firms in the casino industry.

Company	Beta	Stock Price	Number of Shares	Debt
MGM Mirage	1.10	$72.67	143 million	$5.6 billion
Mandalay Resort Group	0.95	$70.43	65 million	$3.0 billion
Caesars Entertainment	1.20	$19.88	304 million	$4.6 billion

The risk-free rate is 5%, and the historical market risk premium, $(E[R_{Mkt}] - r_f)$, is 6%. There are no corporate taxes or other market imperfections.

[A] What is the equity cost of capital for an unlevered firm in the industry?
[B] What is the equity cost of capital for a firm in the industry with a debt-to-equity ratio of 1?

Step 1. Measure the unlevered betas.

The unlevered beta, β_U, measures the market risk of the firm without leverage, which is equivalent to the beta of the firm's assets. The unlevered beta therefore measures the market risk of the firm's business activities, ignoring any additional risk due to leverage, and can be estimated using:

$$\beta_U = \frac{E}{E + D} \beta_E + \frac{D}{E + D} \beta_D$$

Assuming that the debt betas are close to zero, leads to:

$$\beta_U \approx \frac{E}{E + D} \beta_E$$

E, the market value of equity, can be calculated as stock price × number of shares:

Company	Stock Price	Number of Shares	E
MGM Mirage	$72.67	143 million	$10.4 billion
Mandalay Resort Group	$70.43	65 million	$4.6 billion
Caesars Entertainment	$19.88	304 million	$6.0 billion

Now, unlevered betas can be calculated:

$$\beta_U^{MGM} = \frac{10.4}{10.4 + 5.6} 1.10 = 0.72$$

$$\beta_U^{Mandalay} = \frac{4.6}{4.6 + 3.0} 0.95 = 0.58$$

$$\beta_U^{Caesars} = \frac{6.0}{6.0 + 4.6} 1.2 = 0.68$$

Step 3. Calculate the unlevered equity cost of capital based on the average unlevered betas of the comparable firms.

The average unlevered beta is $\dfrac{0.72 + 0.58 + 0.68}{3} = 0.66$.

The equity cost of capital can be determined from the CAPM:

$$E[R] = r_f + \beta_i^{Mkt}(E[R_{Mkt}] - r_f) = 0.05 + 0.66(0.06) = 9.0\%$$

Step 4. Calculate the levered beta when D/E = 1.0.

When a firm changes its capital structure without changing its investments, its unlevered beta will remain unaltered. However, its equity beta will change to reflect the effect of the capital structure change on its risk, and the levered beta can be calculated as:

$$\beta_U = \frac{E}{E + D} \beta_E + \frac{D}{E + D} \beta_D \Rightarrow \beta_E = \beta_U + \frac{D}{E}(\beta_U - \beta_D)$$

Assuming that the debt beta is zero:

$$\beta_E = \left(1 + \frac{D}{E}\right) \beta_U = \left(1 + \frac{1}{1}\right) 0.66 = 1.32.$$

Step 5. Calculate the levered equity cost of capital based on the average unlevered beta of the comparable firms levered to reflect a *D/E* ratio of 1.0.

The equity cost of capital can now be determined from the CAPM:

$$E[R] = r_f + \beta_i^{Mkt}(E[R_{Mkt}] - r_f) = 0.05 + 1.32(0.06) = 12.9\%$$

Questions and Problems

1. A firm expects unlevered free cash flow of $10 million each year. Its unlevered cost of capital is 10%. The firm also has outstanding debt of $35 million, and it expects to maintain this level of debt permanently. There are no corporate taxes or other market imperfections.
   [A]   What is the firm's value of without leverage?
   [B]   What is the firm's value with the $35 million of debt? How much is the equity worth in this case?

2. An unlevered firm has 50 million shares outstanding and a stock price of $20. The firm plans to unexpectedly announce that it will issue $500 million in 10% coupon rate debt financing and use the proceeds to repurchase shares. The debt level is expected to remain at this level. There are no corporate taxes or other market imperfections.
   [A]   What is the firm's market value before the announcement?
   [B]   What is the market value of the firm after the debt is issued, but before the shares are repurchased?
   [C]   What is the share price just before the share repurchase? How many shares will be repurchased at this price? What is the share price after the share repurchase?

3. An unlevered firm has a beta of 0.75. The risk-free rate is 5% and the historical market risk premium, $(E[R_{Mkt}] - r_f)$, is 6%. There are no corporate taxes or other market imperfections.
   [A]   What is the equity cost of capital for an unlevered firm?
   [B]   What is the equity cost of capital for a firm with a debt-to-equity ratio of 2.0?

4. A levered firm has a beta of 1.5. The firm has a stock price of $50, 10 million shares outstanding, and $500 million of 6% coupon rate debt that sells at par. The risk-free rate is 5% and the historical market risk premium, $(E[R_{Mkt}] - r_f)$, is 6%. There are no corporate taxes or other market imperfections.
   [A]   What is the weighted average cost of capital of the levered firm?
   [B]   If the firm issued enough stock to buy back all of the debt, how much would the weighted average cost of capital and equity cost of capital change?

5. You are considering entering a new industry. The only publicly traded company has a beta of 2.5 and a debt-to-equity ratio of 2.2. Your firm uses 100% equity financing. What is the equity cost of capital your firm should use to evaluate the project? The risk-free rate is 6% and the historical market risk premium, $(E[R_{Mkt}] - r_f)$, is 5%. There are no corporate taxes or other market imperfections.

Solutions to Questions and Problems

1. [A] $V^U = \dfrac{10}{0.10} = \$100\,\text{million}$

   [B] $V^L = V^U = \$100$ million, $D = \$35$ million and $E = \$65$ million.

2. [A] $V^U = \$20 \times 50$ million $= \$1$ billion
   [B] $V^L = V^U = \$1$ billion

   [C]   Share price $= \dfrac{\$1\,\text{billion}}{50\,\text{million}} = \$20$.

   They will repurchase $\dfrac{\$500\,\text{million}}{\$20} = 25$ million shares.

After the share repurchase, $E = V^L - D =$ \$1 billion $-$ \$500 million $=$ \$500 million, and the value per share equals:

$$\frac{\$500 \text{ million}}{25 \text{ million}} = \$20$$

3. [A] $\quad r_E = r_f + \beta_i\,(E[R_{Mkt}] - r_f) = 0.05 + 0.75(0.06) = 9.5\%$

   [B] $\quad$ Assuming the debt beta is zero:

   $$\beta_E = \left(1 + \frac{D}{E}\right)\beta_U = \left(1 + \frac{2}{1}\right)0.75 = 2.25.$$

   $$r_E = r_f + \beta_i^{Mkt}(E[R_{Mkt}] - r_f) = 0.05 + 2.25(0.06) = 18.5\%$$

4. [A] $\quad r_E = r_f + \beta_i^{Mkt}(E[R_{Mkt}] - r_f) = 0.05 + 1.5(0.06) = 14\%$

   $$r_{wacc} = \frac{E}{E+D}r_E + \frac{D}{E+D}r_D = \left(\frac{500}{500+500}\right)0.14 + \left(\frac{500}{500+500}\right)0.06 = 10\%$$

   [B] $\quad$ The WACC would not change.
   The new equity cost of capital would be 10%, so it would fall be 4%.

5. Assuming that the debt betas are close to zero, leads to:

   $$\beta_U \approx \frac{E}{E+D}\beta_E = \frac{1}{1+3.2}2.5 = 0.78$$

   $$E[R_i] = R_E = r_f + \beta_i^{Mkt}(E[R_{Mkt}] - r_f) = 0.06 + 0.78(0.05) = 9.9\%$$

CHAPTER 15

Debt and Taxes

Chapter Synopsis

15.1 The Interest Tax Deduction

A C-Corporation pays taxes on profits after interest payments are deducted, but it pays dividends from after-tax net income. Thus, the tax code provides an incentive for the use of debt financing.

An **interest tax shield** is the amount a firm would have paid in taxes if it did not have interest expense. The size of the interest tax shield equals interest expense × the tax rate.

15.2 Valuing the Interest Tax Shield

The differential taxing of interest and dividends represents a market imperfection not considered in the original MM propositions. Given the availability of an interest tax shield, MM Proposition I can be restated in the presence of corporate taxes such that: The total value of the levered firm exceeds the value of the firm without leverage due to the present value of the tax savings from debt:

$$V^L = V^U + \text{PV(Interest Tax Shield)}$$

If a firm has a permanent, constant amount of debt, D, a marginal tax rate of τ_c, and a risk-free debt cost of capital of $r_D = r_f$, then the interest tax shield equals:

$$\text{PV(Interest Tax Shield)} = \frac{\tau_c \times \text{Interest}}{r_f} = \frac{\tau_c \times (r_f \times D)}{r_f} = \frac{\tau_c \times (\cancel{r_f} \times D)}{\cancel{r_f}} = \tau_c \times D$$

The tax deductibility of interest lowers the effective cost of debt financing for the firm. If the interest on debt is tax deductible, then an interest rate r is equivalent to an effective after-tax rate of $r \times (1 - \tau_c)$. To account for the benefit of the interest tax shield, the WACC can be restated to account for the after-tax cost of debt:

$$r_{wacc} = \frac{E}{E+D}r_E + \frac{D}{E+D}r_D(1-\tau_c).$$

15.3 Recapitalizing to Capture the Tax Shield

Consider a firm that has 20 million shares outstanding, a stock price of $15, no debt, and a 35% tax rate. The firm has had consistently stable earnings and management believes that they can borrow as much as $100 million. They are considering a leveraged recapitalization in which they would use the borrowed funds to repurchase $100 million/$15 = 6.67 million shares. They expect that the tax savings from this transaction will boost the stock price and benefit shareholders.

Without leverage, the firm's market value is the value of its unlevered equity. Assuming the current stock price is the fair price for the shares without leverage:

$$V^U = (20 \text{ million shares}) \times (\$15) = \$300 \text{ million}.$$

With $100 million in permanent debt, the present value of the firm's future tax savings is $\tau_c \times D = 0.35(\$100 \text{ million}) = \$35$ million and the levered firm value is:

$$V^L = V^U + PV(\text{Interest Tax Shield}) = \$300 \text{ million} + \$35 \text{ million} = \$335 \text{ million}.$$

The equity value, net of the $100 million of debt, is:

$$E = V^L - D = \$335 \text{ million} - \$100 \text{ million} = \$235 \text{ million} \Rightarrow P = \frac{\$235 \text{ million}}{20 - 6.67} = \$17.625.$$

Since the shares were repurchased at $15, the 13.33 million remaining shareholders get all of the $35 million tax shield, which equals $35 million/13.33 million = $2.625 per share.

More realistically, once investors know the recap will occur, the share price will rise immediately to a level that reflects the $35 million value of the interest tax shield that the firm will receive, $235 million/20 million = $16.75 per share. The benefit of the interest tax shield now goes to all 20 million of the original shares outstanding for a total benefit of $1.75/share × 20 million shares = $35 million.

15.4 Personal Taxes

Personal taxes may offset the corporate tax benefits of leverage. Investors are generally taxed on interest income from debt and dividend income from a stock; they are also taxed on capital gains when they sell a stock but may delay incurring those taxes indefinitely.

Every $1 received after taxes by debt holders from interest payments costs equity holders $1 $\times (1 - \tau^*)$ on an after tax basis, in which τ^*, the **effective tax advantage of debt**, equals:

$$\tau^* = \frac{(1-\tau_i)-(1-\tau_c)(1-\tau_e)}{(1-\tau_i)} = 1 - \frac{(1-\tau_c)(1-\tau_e)}{(1-\tau_i)}$$

where τ_e is the personal tax rate on equity income and τ_i is the personal tax rate on interest income. Now, the tax shield in a year is $\tau^* \times$ interest expense, and the value of a levered firm with permanent debt is

$$V^L = V^U + \tau^* \times D.$$

When there are no personal taxes, or when $\tau_e = \tau_i$, then $\tau^* = \tau_c$. However, when $\tau_e < \tau_i$, as it is today, then $\tau^* < \tau_c$ and there is a tax benefits of leverage.

15.5 Optimal Capital Structure with Taxes

In recent years, U.S. firms have shown a clear preference for debt as a source of external financing. In fact, the overall net equity issues has been negative, meaning that the value of shares that firms have bought back is greater than the value of the shares they have issued. Even though firms have not issued new equity, the market value of equity has risen over time such that average firm's debt as a fraction of the firm's value has remained reasonably stable at 35% to 40%. In 2005, debt accounted for about 36% of U.S firms' capital structures; however, the use of debt varied significantly by industry. Firms in growth industries like high technology carry very little debt, whereas airlines, automakers, and utilities, have high leverage ratios.

There is no corporate tax benefit from incurring interest payments that exceed EBIT. In fact, because interest payments constitute a tax disadvantage at the investor level when $\tau_i > \tau_e$, investors will pay higher individual taxes with excess leverage, making them worse off. Thus, it is optimal to borrow until interest equals EBIT to take full advantage of the corporate tax deduction of interest, but avoid the tax disadvantage of excess leverage at the personal level.

Since there are other provisions in the tax laws for deductions and tax credits, such as depreciation, investment tax credits, and operating loss carryforwards, some firms rely less heavily on the interest tax shield. However, even after considering alternate tax shields, firms have far less leverage than theory would predict at this point in the analysis. In the next chapter, factors that may help explain such apparently suboptimal behavior, such as bankruptcy costs, are considered.

Selected Concepts and Key Terms

Interest Tax Shield

The amount that a firm would have paid in taxes if it did not have interest expense. The size of the interest tax shield each period equals interest expense × the tax rate.

Concept Check Questions and Answers

15.1.1. With corporate income taxes, explain why a firm's value can be higher with leverage even though its earnings are lower.

A firm can be better off even though its earnings are lower because the total amount available to all investors is higher with leverage. The value of a firm is the total amount it can raise from all investors, not just equity holders. So, if the firm can pay out more in total with leverage, it will initially be able to raise more total capital.

15.1.2. What is the interest tax shield?

The interest tax shield is the gain to investors from the tax deductibility of interest payments. It is the additional amount that a firm would have paid in taxes if it did not have leverage.

15.2.1. With corporate taxes as the only market imperfection, how does the value of the firm with leverage differ from its value without leverage?

The total value of the levered firm exceeds the value of the firm without leverage due to the present value of the tax savings from debt.

15.2.2. How does leverage affect a firm's weighted average cost of capital?

Corporate taxes lower the effective cost of debt financing, which translates into a reduction in the weighted average cost of capital. The magnitude of the reduction in the WACC is proportional to the amount of debt financing. The higher the firm's leverage, the more the firm exploits the tax advantage of debt, and so the lower its WACC.

15.3.1. How can shareholders benefit from a leveraged recap when it reduces the total value of equity?

Although a leveraged recap reduces the total value of equity, shareholders capture the benefits of the interest tax shield upfront. The stock price rises at the announcement of the recap.

15.3.2. How does the interest tax shield enter into the market value balance sheet?

The total market value of a firm's securities must equal the total market value of the firm's assets. In the presence of corporate taxes, we must include the interest tax shield as one of the firm's assets on the market value balance sheet.

15.4.1. Under current law (in 2009), why is there a personal tax disadvantage of debt?

Just like corporate taxes, personal taxes reduce the cash flows to investors and diminish firm value. Personal taxes thus have the potential to offset some of the corporate tax benefits of leverage. Currently, in the United States and many other countries, interest income is taxed more heavily than capital gains from equity.

15.4.2. How does the personal tax disadvantage of debt change the value of leverage for the firm?

Personal taxes offset some of the corporate tax benefits of leverage and thus reduce the value of leverage for the firm.

15.5.1. How does the growth rate of a firm affect the optimal fraction of debt in the capital structure?

The optimal fraction of debt, as a proportion of a firm's capital structure, declines with the growth rate of the firm.

15.5.2. Do firms choose capital structures that fully exploit the tax advantages of debt?

The empirical results of international leverage indicate that firms do not fully exploit the tax advantages of debt because the interest expense of the average firm is well below its taxable income

Examples with Step-by-Step Solutions

Solving Problems

Problems using this chapter's ideas often involve calculating the after-tax cost of debt, the after-tax weighted-average cost of capital, the interest tax shield, and finding the present value of the interest tax shield and the value of a levered firm. Applications include considering the consequences on shareholder value of a leveraged recapitalization, which involves issuing debt which is then used to repurchase shares. Problems may also involve considering the effects of personal taxes.

Examples

1. You are trying to decide whether your firm should use debt financing under different assumptions regarding the amount of debt in its capital structure. The firm's assets will generate an expected EBIT of $800,000 per year (beginning one year from today) in perpetuity. The firm will make no new capital or working capital investments and all assets are fully depreciated. The assets have a beta of 1.5, the risk-free rate is 5%, and the market risk premium is 10%. You can issue bonds at par paying an annual coupon at a 5% annual rate. The corporate tax rate is 50%, and the firm has 100,000 shares outstanding.
   [A]   What is the value of the firm with no debt? What is the stock value per share?
   [B]   What is the value of the firm if it issues $1.5 million of debt and uses the proceeds to repurchase 75,000 shares for $20 (75,000 × $20 = $1.5 million)? What is the stock value per share? Should the firm issue the debt?

Step 1. Determine the unlevered equity cost of capital.

The equity cost of capital is $E[R_i] = r_f + \beta_i^{Mkt}(E[R_{Mkt}] - r_f) = 5\% + 1.5(10\%) = 20\%$.

Step 2. Determine the free cash flows of the unlevered firm.

Since the firm will make no new investments and has no depreciation, FCF = NI each year.

EBIT	$800,000
− Tax @ 50%	400,000
Net income	400,000

Step 3. Determine the value of the unlevered firm.

Since the cash flows are a perpetuity, $PV = \dfrac{FCF}{r} = \dfrac{\$400,000}{0.20} = \$2$ million

Step 4. Determine the value per share.

$$\text{Value per share} = \frac{V^U}{\text{Shares Outstanding}} = \frac{\$2,000,000}{100,000} = \$20$$

Step 5. Determine the value of the levered firm.

$$V^L = V^U + PV(\text{Tax shield}) = \$2,000,000 + \frac{D(r_D)(\tau_c)}{r_D}$$

$$= \$2,000,000 + \frac{\$1,500,000(0.05)(0.50)}{0.05} = \$2,750,000$$

Step 6. Determine the equity value per share.

The total equity value is $V^L - D = \$2,750,000 - \$1,500,000$, and the number of shares repurchased is $1,500,000/$20=75,000, so:

$$\text{Value per share} = \frac{2,750,000 - 1,500,000}{100,000 - 75,000} = \$50.$$

Thus, the firm should issue the debt based on these assumptions because it leads to an increase in the share price of $\dfrac{\$50 - \$20}{\$20} = 150\%$.

2. **Wrigley Inc. had $1 billion in EBITDA in 2006. The firm is unlevered and has a market value of equity of $12 billion and a tax rate of 40%. Consider the effect on the value of the firm of the following debt issuances. Assume that all proceeds will be used to buy back stock.**
   [A]   **Issuing $6 billion of 8% coupon rate 5-year bonds which repay the principal in 5 years.**
   [B]   **Issuing $6 billion of 8% coupon rate permanent bonds.**
   [C]   **Issuing $6 billion of 8% coupon rate bonds, with amount of bonds increasing by 5% every year forever.**

Step 1. Determine the value of the levered firm for the 5-year bonds.

Since annual interest is 0.08($6 billion) = $480 million, the annual tax shield is $480 million × 0.40 = $192 million for five years.

$$V^L = V^U + \text{PV(Interest Tax Shield)} = \$12\text{ billion} + \$192\text{ million}\left(\frac{1}{.08}\right)\left[1 - \frac{1}{.08(1.08)^5}\right]$$

$$= \$12\text{ billion} + \$0.8\text{ billion} = \$12.8\text{ billion}$$

Step 2. Determine the value of the levered firm for the permanent bonds.

Now, the $192 million tax shield is a perpetuity.

$$V^L = V^U + \text{PV(Interest Tax Shield)} = \$12\text{ billion} + \left[\frac{\$192\text{ million}}{.08}\right]$$

$$= \$12\text{ billion} + 2.4\text{ billion} = \$14.4\text{ billion}$$

Step 3. Determine the value of the levered firm for the bonds that increase by 5% every year forever.

Now, the $14 million tax shield is the first cash flow in a growing perpetuity.

$$V^L = V^U + \text{PV(Interest Tax Shield)} = \$12\text{ billion} + \left[\frac{\$192\text{ million}}{.08 - .05}\right]$$

$$= \$12\text{ billion} + 6.4\text{ billion} = \$18.5\text{ billion}$$

3. **Best Buy is equally likely to have EBIT this coming year of $1 billion, $1.5 billion, or $2 billion. Its corporate tax rate is 35%, and investors pay a 15% tax rate on income from equity and a 30% tax rate on interest income.**
   [A]   **What is the effective interest tax shield (considering both personal taxes and corporate taxes) if interest expense is $500 million this year?**
   [B]   **At what level of interest expense does the effective tax advantage of debt disappear?**

Step 1. Determine the effective tax rate if all of the interest will be used to shield taxes.

$$\tau^* = 1 - \frac{(1 - \tau_c)(1 - \tau_e)}{1 - \tau_i} = 1 - \frac{(1 - 0.35)(1 - 0.15)}{1 - 0.30} = 21.1\%$$

Step 2. Determine the effective tax shield if interest expense is $500,000.

Tax shield $= \tau^* \times$ Interest expense $= 0.211 \times \$500,000 = \$105,357$

Step 3. Determine when the effective tax rate is negative by considering different levels of interest expense.

Interest expense	Probability of NI > 0	$E[\tau_C]$	τ^*
$500,000,000	1.0	0.350	0.21
$1,000,000,000	1.0	0.350	0.21
$1,500,000,000	$\frac{2}{3}$	0.233	0.07
$2,000,000,000	$\frac{1}{3}$	0.117	-0.07

So for an interest expense up to $1.5 billion, there is a tax advantage. For interest expense over $1.5 billion, there is an expected effective tax <u>dis</u>advantage for debt financing.

Questions and Problems

1. A firm expects free cash flow of $10 million each year. Its corporate tax rate is 35%, and its unlevered cost of capital is 10%. The firm also has outstanding debt of $35 million, and it expects to maintain this level of debt permanently.
    [A]   What is the firm's value without leverage?
    [B]   What is the firm's value with the $35 million of debt?

2. A firm is considering permanently adding $100 million of debt to its capital structure. The corporate tax rate is 35%.
    [A]   Absent personal taxes, what is the value of the interest tax shield from the new debt?
    [B]   If investors pay a tax rate of 40% on interest income, and a tax rate of 20% on income from dividends and capital gains, what is the value of the interest tax shield from the new debt?

3. An unlevered firm has 50 million shares outstanding and a stock price of $20. The firm plans to unexpectedly announce that it will issue $500 million in 10% coupon rate debt financing and use the proceeds to repurchase shares. The debt level is expected to remain at this level. The tax rate is 35%.
    [A]   What is the firm's market value before the announcement?
    [B]   What is the market value of the firm after the repurchase?
    [C]   What is the share value after the repurchase assuming that the shares can be repurchased at $20 per share?

4. Suppose the corporate tax rate is 35%, and investors pay a tax rate of 15% on income from dividends or capital gains and a tax rate of 28% on interest income. Your firm plans to issue $1 billion in perpetual 10% coupon bonds. The firm has historically paid all net income out as dividends; however, in order to pay this interest expense, the firm will cut its dividend.
    [A]   How much will bondholders receive after paying taxes on the interest they earn?
    [B]   By how much will the firm need to cut its dividend each year to pay this interest expense?
    [C]   By how much will this cut in the dividend reduce equity holders' annual after-tax income?
    [D]   How much less will the government receive in total tax revenues each year?
    [E]   What is the effective tax advantage of debt with this amount of leverage?

5. Your unlevered firm will have a certain EBIT every year of $80 million. Every year it will spend $10 million on capital expenditures, invest $10 million in net working capital, and have $28 million in depreciation. The corporate tax rate is 35%, and the firm's cost of capital is 11%.
    [A]   If the firm's free cash flow is expected to grow by 5% per year, what is the value of its equity today?

[B]   If the debt cost of capital is 10%, what amount of borrowing would maximize the value of the firm? What would the value of the firm be then?

Solutions to Questions and Problems

1. [A] $V^U = \dfrac{10}{0.10} = \$100 \text{ million}$

   [B] $V^L = V^U + \tau_c D = 100 + 0.35 \times 30 = \$110.5 \text{ million}$

2. [A]   PV(Interest Tax Shield) = $\tau_c D$ = 35% × 100 = \$35 million.

   [B] $\tau^* = 1 - \dfrac{(1-0.35)(1-0.20)}{1-0.40} = 13.33\%$

   PV(Interest Tax Shield) = $\tau_c D$ = 13.33% × 100 = \$13.33 million

3. [A] V^U = \$20 × 50 million = \$1 billion

   [B] V^L = V^U + PV(Tax Shield) = \$1 billion + $\dfrac{\$500 \text{ million}(0.10)(0.35)}{0.10}$ = \$175 million

   = \$1.175 billion.

   [C]   E = V^L – D = \$1.175 billion – \$500 million = \$675 million

   They will repurchase $\$\dfrac{500 \text{ million}}{\$20} = 25 \text{ million shares}$.

   The share price is thus $= \dfrac{\$1.175 \text{ billion} - 500 \text{ million}}{50 \text{ million} - 25 \text{ million}} = \$27$.

4. [A]   \$100 million × (1 – .28) = \$72 million each year
   [B]   An interest expense of \$100 million per year reduces net income by 100(1 – .35) = \$65 million after corporate taxes. So, dividends will be \$65 million less.
   [C]   \$65 million dividend cut ⇒ \$65 × (1 – .15) = \$55.25 million per year.
   [D]   Interest taxes = .28 × 100 million = \$28 million
   Less corporate taxes = .35 × 100 million = \$35 million
   Less dividend taxes = .15 × 65 million = \$9.75 million
   ⇒ Government tax revenues change by 28 – 35 – 9.75 = –\$16.75 million

   [E] $\tau^* = 1 - \dfrac{(1-0.35)(1-0.15)}{1-0.28} = 23.3\%$

5. [A] $FCF = EBIT \times (1-\tau) + Dep - Capex - \Delta NWC = 80 \times (1-0.35) + 28 - 10 - 10 = \$60$

   $V^U = E = \dfrac{60}{0.11 - 0.05} = \$1 \text{ billion}$

   [B]   The firm can pay \$80 million in interest, so it can borrow:

   $\dfrac{\$80 \text{ million}}{0.10} = \$800 \text{ million at } 10\%.$

   $V^L = \$1 \text{ billion} + \dfrac{\$800 \text{ million}(0.10)(0.35)}{0.10} = \$1.28 \text{ billion}$

CHAPTER 16

Financial Distress, Managerial Incentives, and Information

Chapter Synopsis

In the previous two chapters it was shown that, in an otherwise perfect capital market in which firms pay taxes, the optimal capital structure includes debt such that earnings before interest and taxes equals interest. This allows the firm to avoid paying taxes and maximizes firm value. This chapter discusses how including market imperfections other than taxes in the analysis leads to the conclusion that firms should often borrow less than this amount.

16.1 Default and Bankruptcy in a Perfect Market

A firm is in **default** when it fails to make the required interest or principal payments on its debt. When a firm fails to satisfy another of the contractual requirements in the debt contract, such as an accounting ratio falling below a defined threshold, it may trigger so-called technical default. The occurrence or likelihood of either type of default often leads to a firm filing for bankruptcy protection under the 1978 Bankruptcy Reform Act to prevent creditors from immediately seizing collateral.

With perfect capital markets, Modigliani and Miller's Proposition I still applies because bankruptcy alone does not lead to a reduction in the firm's total value to investors. With perfect capital markets, bankruptcy simply shifts the ownership of the firm from equity holders to debt holders without changing the total value available to all investors.

16.2 The Costs of Bankruptcy and Financial Distress

The U.S. bankruptcy code was created to organize the bankruptcy process so that creditors are treated fairly and the value of the assets is not needlessly destroyed. According to the provisions of the 1978 Bankruptcy Reform Act, U.S. firms can file for two forms of bankruptcy protection: Chapter 7 or Chapter 11.

■ In a **Chapter 7 liquidation**, a trustee is appointed to oversee the liquidation of the firm's assets through an auction. The proceeds from the liquidation are used to pay the firm's creditors, and the firm ceases to exist.

■ In a **Chapter 11 reorganization**, a firm files for bankruptcy protection and all pending collection attempts are automatically suspended in a procedure called an **automatic stay**. The firm's existing management continues to operate the business and is given 120 days to propose a reorganization plan, which specifies the treatment of each creditor of the firm. In addition to cash payment, creditors may receive new debt or equity securities under the plan. The value of the cash and securities will generally be less than the amount each creditor was owed, but is hopefully more than they would receive if the firm was shut down immediately and liquidated, and any going concern value was destroyed. The creditors must vote to accept the plan using a specific process, and it must be approved by the court.

Unlike in prefect capital markets, a firm in bankruptcy generally incurs direct and indirect costs.

■ **Direct costs of bankruptcy** include out-of-pocket costs associated with defaulting on the contractual obligations in a debt contract, and going through the court supervised bankruptcy processes as defined in chapter 11 (reorganization) or chapter 7 (liquidation) of the 1978 Bankruptcy Reform Act. The costs may include court, lawyer, accountant, and investment banker fees incurred in the process. While difficult to quantify, studies estimate these costs as 3-4% of asset value.

■ **Indirect costs of bankruptcy** may include: a loss of customers that value post-sale services, a loss of willing suppliers, difficulty retaining and recruiting employees, and forced sales of assets at reduced prices. The costs are particularly difficult to quantify, but one study estimates these costs to be as high as 20% of firm value.

16.3 Financial Distress Costs and Firm Value

Direct and indirect costs of financial distress represent an important departure from Modigliani and Miller's assumption of perfect capital markets. Levered firms risk incurring financial distress costs that reduce the cash flows available to investors. When securities are fairly priced, the original shareholders of a firm pay the present value of the costs associated with bankruptcy and financial distress.

16.4 Optimal Capital Structure: The Trade-off Theory

In the **trade-off theory of capital structure**, debt should be chosen to maximize the value of the levered firm, V^L, which equals the value of the unlevered firm, V^U, plus the present value of any interest tax shield, net of the present value of other imperfections:

$V^L = V^U$ + PV(Interest tax shield) – PV(Direct costs of bankruptcy) – PV(Indirect costs of bankruptcy) – PV(Agency costs of debt) + PV(Agency benefits of debt).

16.5 Exploiting Debt Holders: The Agency Costs of Leverage

Agency costs are losses in value associated with having an agent with different interests work on behalf of the principals, or owners. In the context of a firm with leverage, a conflict of interest may exist because investment decisions may have different consequences for debt holders and equity holders.

In some circumstances, managers may have an incentive to take actions, such as excessive risk taking, under-investment, or cashing out, that benefit equity holders but harm the firm's creditors and lower the total value of the firm. For example, managers acting on behalf of the shareholders may engage in excessive risk taking and accept negative NPV projects because the cost of failure is largely borne by the debt holders if the project fails to generate sufficient cash flow to pay the interest and principal, and control of the firm is effectively turned over to the debt holders.

16.6 Motivating Managers: The Agency Benefits of Leverage

Using debt financing as a source of capital can also enhance a firm's value beyond just the tax shields from interest. For example, managers (the agents of the shareholders) of unlevered firms with excessive free cash flow, beyond what is needed to fund all positive NPV projects, may be motivated to spend the cash on things that benefit themselves, such as corporate jets and value-decreasing acquisitions, for the sake of empire building. If such firms have high leverage, they will have less free cash flow and thus less of an opportunity to make such value-decreasing investments.

In addition, when managers are shareholders in their firm, shareholder concentration can be maintained by issuing new debt instead of new equity, or increased by replacing some equity with debt. Managers that own a higher percentage of a firm's equity will have a better chance of making decisions that maximize the value of the stockholders' investment.

16.7 Agency Costs and the Trade-off Theory

The trade-off theory implies that mature, low-growth firms with stable cash flows and tangible assets should use more debt because they can use the tax shields and would incur lower costs if distress occurs, while firms with unstable cash flows and lots of intangible assets should use little or no debt because the probability and cost of financial distress are high. It also implies that, if securities are fairly priced, the original shareholders of the firm pay the present value of the costs associated with bankruptcy and financial distress, so firms often try to take actions, such as including protective covenants in debt contracts, to minimize these costs.

16.8 Asymmetric Information and Capital Structure

Asymmetric information exists when managers' information about the firm and its future cash flows is superior to that of external investors. This situation can lead to **adverse selection** in which buyers tend to discount the price they are willing to pay for a firm's securities because investors cannot determine whether a firm is over- or undervalued.

In the presence of adverse selection, it has been theoretically shown that there is a tendency for only the most overvalued firms to issue securities, and investors will assume that all issuers are likely to be overvalued. This adverse selection can be attenuated if the firm can provide some kind of credible signal. One way to make a signal credible is to make it too costly for all but higher valued firms to use it. One such signal firms can use, is to adopt a high level of leverage to signal to investors that they are undervalued. This signal is too costly for lower valued firms to send, because it will lead to higher expected costs of financial distress, causing these firm's values to fall.

The existence of asymmetric information and adverse selection is supported by three pieces of empirical evidence:

[1]   An issuer's stock price falls by about 2% to 3% when a new equity issue is announced, suggesting that the market knows that issuing firms are likely to be overvalued;

[2]   Firms tend to issue new stock after a large price run-up and, based on their post-issue performance, they appear to have been overvalued when they issued; and

[3]   Firms tend to issue new equity when the degree of information asymmetry is smallest, such as following earnings announcements.

The **pecking order hypothesis** theorizes that, due to asymmetric information and the likelihood of perceived adverse selection, managers of firms raising capital prefer using retained earnings, and then turn to less risky debt before external equity in order to avoid the market perceiving them as being overvalued, and trying to issue overvalued securities.

While difficult to test directly, this pecking order hypothesis is consistent with the finding that the vast majority of investment is funded by retained earnings, with net external financing amounting to less than 30% of capital expenditures in most years. Also, firms on average repurchase more equity than they issue, whereas they are net issuers of debt. These observations are also consistent with the trade-off theory of capital structure, but there is substantial evidence that firms do not follow a strict pecking order, as firms often issue equity even when borrowing is possible.

16.9 Capital Structure: The Bottom Line

The optimality of a firm's capital structure depends on market imperfections, such as taxes, financial distress costs, agency costs, and asymmetric information.

■   Of all the different possible imperfections that drive capital structure, the most significant is likely to be taxes. The interest tax shield allows firms to repay investors and avoid the corporate tax.

■   Financial distress may lead to other consequences that reduce the value of the firm. Firms must, therefore, balance the tax benefits of debt against the costs of financial distress.

■   Agency costs and benefits of leverage are also important determinants of capital structure. Too much debt can motivate managers and equity holders to take excessive risks or underinvest in a firm. When free cash flows are high, too little leverage may encourage wasteful spending.

■   A firm must also consider the potential signaling and adverse selection consequences of its financing choice. Because bankruptcy is costly for managers, increasing leverage can signal managers' confidence in the firm's ability to meet its debt obligations.

Finally, it is important to recognize that because actively changing a firm's capital structure (for example, by selling or repurchasing shares or bonds) entails transactions costs, firms may be unlikely to change their capital structures unless they depart significantly from the optimal level. As a result, most changes to a firm's debt-equity ratio are likely to occur passively, as the market value of the firm's equity fluctuates with changes in the firm's stock price.

Selected Concepts and Key Terms

Default

When a firm fails to make the required interest or principal payments on its debt. When a firm fails to satisfy another of the contractual requirements in the debt contract, such as an accounting ratio falling below a defined threshold, it may trigger so-called technical default. The occurrence or likelihood of either type of default often leads to a firm filing for bankruptcy protection under the 1978 Bankruptcy Reform Act to prevent creditors from immediately seizing collateral.

Bankruptcy

A court supervised reorganization of the firm's financial claims governed by the 1978 Bankruptcy Reform Act. The bankruptcy code was created to organize this process so that creditors are treated fairly and the value of the assets is not needlessly destroyed by letting creditors seize assets in a piecemeal fashion. U.S. firms can file for bankruptcy protection using the Chapter 7 Liquidation or Chapter 11 Reorganization provisions.

Chapter 7 Liquidation

A liquidation of the firm's assets as specified in Chapter 7 of the 1978 Bankruptcy Reform Act. A trustee is appointed to oversee the liquidation of the firm's assets through an auction. The proceeds from the liquidation are used to pay the firm's creditors according to their order in the legal seniority, and the firm ceases to exist.

Chapter 11 Reorganization

A reorganization of the firm's financial claims as governed by Chapter 11 of the 1978 Bankruptcy Reform Act. After a firm files for bankruptcy protection, all pending collection attempts are automatically suspended, and the firm's existing management continues to operate the business and is given the opportunity to propose a reorganization plan, which specifies the treatment of each creditor of the firm. In addition to cash payment, creditors may receive new debt or equity securities of the firm under the plan. The value of the cash and securities will generally be less than the amount each creditor was owed, but is hopefully more than they would receive if the firm was shut down immediately and liquidated and any going concern value was destroyed. The creditors must vote to accept the plan using a specific process, and it must be approved by the court.

Trade-off Theory

A theory that attempts to explain how firms should choose the capital structure that maximizes the value of the firm. In this theory, the total value of the levered firm equals the value of the firm without leverage plus the present value of the tax savings from debt, less the present value of financial distress costs (direct costs of bankruptcy, indirect costs of bankruptcy, agency costs of debt) plus the present value of the agency benefits of debt.

Agency Costs

Losses in value associated with having an agent with different interests work on behalf of the principals, or owners. In the context of a firm with leverage, a conflict of interest may exist because investment decisions may have different consequences for debt holders and equity holders. In some circumstances, managers may have an incentive to take actions, such as excessive risk taking, under-investment, or cashing out, that benefit equity holders but harm the firm's creditors and lower the total value of the firm. For example, managers acting on behalf of the shareholders may engage in excessive risk-taking and accept negative NPV projects because the cost of failure is largely borne by the debt holders, if the project fails to generate sufficient cash flow to pay the interest and principal, and control of the firm is effectively turned over to the debt holders.

Asset Substitution Problem

When shareholders can gain by making negative-NPV investments or decisions that sufficiently increase the firm's risk.

Debt Overhang

When a firm may be unable to finance new, positive-NPV projects because it faces financial distress.

Free Cash Flow Hypothesis

The view that wasteful spending is more likely to occur when firms have high levels of free cash flow, or cash flow in excess of what is needed after making all positive NPV investments and payments to debt holders. When cash is tight, managers will be more highly motivated to run the firm as efficiently as possible. Under this hypothesis, leverage may increase firm value by reducing wasteful investment by managers because it commits the firm to making future interest payments reducing excess cash flow.

Management entrenchment

The view that managers care most about keeping their jobs, and they are more likely to engage in wasteful investment when their position within the firm is secure. Because managers are more likely to lose their job in the event of financial distress, increasing leverage and the risk of distress may help to control wasteful investment.

Asymmetric information.

Asymmetric information exists when managers' information about the firm's level of risk and its future cash flows is superior to that of outside investors. As a result, managers may have better information than investors about the true value of the firm's securities. One way an undervalued firm can credibly convey its higher value to investors is by making statements about the firm's future prospects that investors and analysts can ultimately verify. If the penalties for intentionally deceiving investors are large such that they cannot be mimicked by lower-valued firms, investors will generally believe such statements and the information asymmetry will be attenuated.

Adverse selection

The idea that buyers will tend to discount the price they are willing to pay for a good when there is asymmetric information—the seller has private information about the value of the good. In such markets, it is likely that the market will generally contain low-quality goods. In the context of capital structure, investors will discount the price they are willing to pay for a firm's securities when there is asymmetric information, because investors cannot determine whether a firm is over- or undervalued. In the presence of adverse selection, it can be shown that there is a tendency for only the most overvalued firms to issue securities.

Moral Hazard

The idea that individuals will change their behavior if they are not fully exposed to its consequences. For example, equity holders may take excessive risk or pay excessive dividends if the negative consequences will be borne by bondholders.

Signaling theory of debt

In the presence of asymmetric information, the idea that firms can use high leverage as a way to signal to investors that they are undervalued. This signal may be too costly for lower valued firms to send because it will lead to higher expected costs of financial distress, causing these firms' values to fall.

Pecking order hypothesis

The idea that in the presence of asymmetric information and the likelihood of perceived adverse selection, managers will choose to issue the safest security they can and only issue new equity as a last resort. In this theory, firms raising capital prefer using retained earnings, and then turn to debt before equity to avoid the market perceiving them as being overvalued—attempting to issue overvalued securities.

Concept Check Questions and Answers

16.1.1. With perfect capital markets, does the possibility of bankruptcy put debt financing at a disadvantage?

No. The total value to all investors does not depend on the firm's capital structure. Investors as a group are not worse off because a firm has leverage. While it is true that bankruptcy results from a firm having leverage, bankruptcy alone does not lead to a greater reduction in the total value to investors. Thus, there is no disadvantage to debt financing, and a firm will have the same total value and will be able to raise the same amount initially from investors with either choice of capital structure.

16.2.2. Does the risk of default reduce the value of the firm?

With perfect capital markets, the risk of default does not reduce the value of the firm. While it is true that bankruptcy results from a firm having leverage, bankruptcy alone does lead to a greater reduction in the total value to investors.

16.2.1. If a firm files for bankruptcy under Chapter 11 of the bankruptcy code, which party gets the first opportunity to propose a plan for the firm's reorganization?

If a firm files for bankruptcy under Chapter 11, the firm's existing management is given the first opportunity to propose a reorganization plan.

16.2.2. Why are the losses of debt holders, whose claims are not fully repaid, not a cost of financial distress, whereas the loss of customers who fear the firm will stop honoring warranties is?

The losses of debt holders whose claims are not fully repaid are not considered as the cost of financial distress, because the firms in financial distress will often attempt to avoid filing for bankruptcy, by first negotiating directly with creditors. In contrast, the loss of customers, who fear the firm will stop honoring warranties, is the indirect cost of financial distress. Because bankruptcy may enable firms to walk away from future commitments to their customers, customers may be unwilling to purchase products whose values depend on future support or service from the firms.

16.3.1. Armin incurred financial distress costs only in the event that the new product failed. Why might Armin incur financial distress costs even before the success or failure of the new product is known?

Armin may incur several financial distress costs, even before the success or failure of the new product is known, because the original shareholders of the firm pay the present value of costs associated with bankruptcy and financial distress. Although debt holders bear them in the end, shareholders pay the present value of the costs of financial distress upfront.

16.3.2. True or False: If bankruptcy cost are only incurred once the firm is in bankruptcy and its equity is worthless, then these costs will not affect the initial value of the firm.

False. The value of the firm is reduced by the present value of the expected bankruptcy costs. Thus, shareholders should be concerned about financial distress costs that will be borne by debt holders because debt holders recognize that, when the firm defaults, they will not be able to get the full value of assets. As a result, they will pay less for the debt initially.

16.4.1. What is the "trade-off" in the trade-off theory?

The trade-off theory states that the total value of a levered firm equals the value of the firm without leverage, plus the present value of the tax savings from debt, less the present value of financial distress costs. There is a trade-off between the benefits of debt and the costs of financial distress.

16.4.2. According to the trade-off theory, all else being equal, which type of firm has a higher optimal level of debt: a firm with very volatile cash flows or a firm with very safe, predictable cash flows?

According to the trade-off theory, a firm with very safe, predictable, cash flow is likely to have a higher optimal level of debt because it has a low probability of default.

16.5.1. Why do firms have an incentive to both take excessive risk and under-invest when they are in financial distress?

They may take excessive risk because they may effectively be gambling with the debt holders money. They may underinvest because they believe that the value of the projects they fund may convey to the debt holders in the event of bankruptcy.

16.5.2. Why would debt holders desire covenants that restrict the firm's ability to pay dividends, and why might shareholders also benefit from this restriction?

Debt holders put such restriction on the firm to protect themselves from being exploited by management. Shareholders might also benefit from this restriction because it prevents the firm from taking a negative-NPV project, an overinvestment problem.

16.6.1. In what ways might managers benefit by overspending on acquisitions?

Managers might benefit by overspending on acquisitions because they prefer to run large firms rather than small ones. Managers of large firms tend to earn higher salaries, and they may also have more prestige and garner greater publicity.

16.6.2. How might shareholders use the firm's capital structure to prevent this problem?

For managers to engage in wasteful investment, they must have the cash to invest. Only when cash is tight will managers be motivated to run the firm as efficiently as possible. Therefore, shareholders can increase leverage to reduce the likelihood that a firm will pursue wasteful investments. Leverage increases firm value because it commits the firm to making future interest payments, thereby reducing excess cash flows and wasteful investment by managers.

16.7.1. Describe how the management entrenchment can affect the value of the firm.

The management entrenchment theory of capital structure states that managers choose a capital structure to avoid the discipline of debt, and to maintain their own job security. Thus managers seek to minimize leverage to prevent the job loss that would accompany financial distress, and thereby reduce the value of the firm.

16.7.2. Coca-Cola Enterprises is almost 50% debt financed, while Intel, a technology firm, has no net debt. Why might these firms choose such different capital structures?

The optimal level of debt varies with the characteristics of a firm. Firms with high research and development costs and future growth opportunities, such as Intel, typically maintain low debt levels. On the other hand, mature, low-growth firms with stable cash flows and tangible assets, such as Coca-Cola Enterprises, often fall into the high-debt category. These firms tend to have high free cash flow with few good investment opportunities. Thus the tax shield and incentive benefits of leverage are likely to be high.

16.8.1. How does asymmetric information explain the negative stock price reaction to the announcement of an equity issue?

There is asymmetric information between managers and investors. Managers know more than shareholders about the firm's profitability and future cash flows. Managers only issue equity if they have negative information about the firm's future prospects. Investors are aware that managers have private information about the firm; therefore, investors will discount the stock price they are willing to pay due to adverse selection.

16.8.2. Why might firms prefer to fund investments using retained earnings or debt rather than issuing equity?

Managers who perceive that the firm's equity is underpriced will have a preference to fund investment using retained earnings, or debt, rather than equity. This result is called the pecking order hypothesis.

16.9.1. Consider the differences in leverage across industries shown in Figure 15.7. To what extent can you account for these differences?

Leverage varies a lot across industries due to market imperfections such as taxes, financial distress costs, agency costs, and asymmetric information.

16.9.2. What are some reasons firms might depart from their optimal capital structure, at least in the short run?

The reasons that explain why firms may depart from their optimal capital structure are markets' imperfections, such as taxes, financial distress costs, agency costs, asymmetric information, and transaction costs.

Examples with Step-by-Step Solutions

Solving Problems

Problems using the concepts in this chapter can generally be solved by determining the effect on shareholders' wealth by a particular decision, by applying the equation:

$V^L = V^U + $ PV(Interest tax shield) − PV(Direct costs of bankruptcy) − PV(Indirect costs of bankruptcy) − PV(Agency costs of debt) + PV(Agency benefits of debt)

To successfully apply this equation, it is important to interpret how the information in the problem is related to the equation's terms in each application. A problem will not generally have all of these imperfections, but the equation tells you what to look for. For example, in problem 1 below, the problem states that "if the firm issues the debt, the firm estimates that the expected present value of direct costs of bankruptcy would be $1 million" but it doesn't mention other imperfections. If a problem involves a change in the number of shares, you may need to quantify the value change on a per-share basis. Some problems have effects related to the Asymmetric Information and Capital Structure discussion; problem 3 below shows how to handle these effects in this framework.

Examples

1. Managers of an unlevered firm that is expected to produce $1 million in free cash flow each year are considering making a $5 million investment that is expected to produce $1 million in unlevered free cash flow every year forever, beginning in one year. The firm would issue $5 million in permanent debt with a 5% annual interest rate to finance the project. The tax rate is 35%, the firm has 1 million shares, and the unlevered cost of equity is 10%. If the firm issues the debt, the firm estimates that the expected present value of direct costs of bankruptcy would be $1 million.

   [A] Explain whether managers of the unlevered firm should take the project.

   [B] If the project had a $0 NPV, would it change your answer?

   Step 1. Determine the value of the unlevered firm's shares before it makes the investment, to compare to the value per share *with* the project. The value of the firm is the present value of the firm's free cash flows at the unlevered cost of equity, and can be calculated using the present value of a perpetuity equation with $C = \$1$ million and $r = 10\%$.

   $$V^U = \frac{C}{r} = \frac{FCF}{r_S^{Unlevered}} = \frac{\$1 \text{ million}}{0.10} = \$10 \text{ million}$$

   So, the per share value = $10 million/1 million = $10.

   Step 2. Determine the value per share after the firm issues the debt and makes the investment, by considering the trade-off theory equation.

   $V^L = V^U$ + PV(Interest tax shield) – PV(Direct costs of bankruptcy) – PV(Indirect costs of bankruptcy) – PV(Agency costs of debt) + PV(Agency benefits of debt)

   The relevant terms are the value of the unlevered firm, which now produces an expected $2 million in unlevered free cash flow, the present value of the interest tax shield, and the direct costs of bankruptcy:

   $V^L = V^U$ + PV(Interest tax shield) – PV(Direct costs of bankruptcy) – 0 – 0 + 0

   $$= \frac{FCF}{r_S^{Unlevered}} + \frac{Debt(r_d)(t_c)}{r_d} - PV(\text{Direct costs of bankruptcy})$$

   $$= \frac{\$2 \text{ million}}{.10} + \frac{\$5 \text{ million}(.05)(.35)}{.05} - \$1 \text{ million} = \$20 + \$1.75 - \$1 = \$20.75 \text{ million}$$

   The value of equity (net of the new debt) equals $20.75 – $5 = $15.75 million.

   Thus, the new stock price would be $15.75 million/1 million = $15.75.

The managers should take the project to maximize the shareholders' wealth. The direct costs of bankruptcy are more than offset by the increase in firm value and the tax shield.

Step 3. Determine the value per share after the firm issues the debt, if the NPV of the project was $0. In this case, the new project would be worth $5 million, since it must be worth exactly what it cost.

The value of the unlevered firm would be $10 million + $5 million = $15 million. The value of the firm would now be:

$$V^L = V^U + PV(\text{Interest tax shield}) - PV(\text{Direct costs of bankruptcy}) - 0 - 0 + 0$$

$$= \$15 \text{ million} + \frac{\text{Debt}(r_d)(t_c)}{r_d} - PV(\text{Direct costs of bankruptcy})$$

$$= \$15 \text{ million} + \frac{\$5 \text{ million}(.05)(.35)}{.05} - \$1 \text{ million} = \$15 + \$1.75 - \$1 = \$15.75 \text{ million}$$

The value of equity (net of the new debt) now equals: $15.75 – $5 = $10.75 million.

Thus, the new stock price would be $10.75 million/1 million = $10.75.

The managers should still take the project to maximize the shareholders' wealth The direct costs of bankruptcy are more than offset by the tax shield alone.

2. **Managers of an unlevered firm expected to generate free cash flow of $10 million each year, are considering issuing $25 million of permanent 10% interest debt and using the proceeds to repurchase equity. If the firm issues the debt, it expects to lose some of its best, low-cost suppliers due to the firm's lower credit quality, and thus estimates a loss of $1 million of free cash flow per year. The firm's tax rate is 35%, and the required return on the firm's unlevered free cash flow is 10%. Explain whether managers of the unlevered firm should issue the debt.**

Step 1. Determine the value of the unlevered firm's stock so you can determine the change in value due to the project.

Using the present value of a perpetuity equation: $V^U = \dfrac{\$10 \text{ million}}{.10} = \$100 \text{ million}$

So, the value per share is $100 million/$1million = $100.

Step 2. Determine the value of the firm after it issues the debt, by considering the trade-off theory equation:

$V^L = V^U + PV(\text{Interest tax shield}) - PV(\text{Direct costs of bankruptcy}) - PV(\text{Indirect costs of bankruptcy}) - PV(\text{Agency costs of debt}) + PV(\text{Agency benefits of debt})$

The relevant terms now include the present value of the interest tax shield on the permanent debt and the present value of the indirect costs of financial distress from the loss of suppliers, which amounts to $1 million per year:

$$V^L = V^U + PV(\text{Interest tax shield}) - 0 - PV(\text{Indirect costs of bankruptcy}) - 0 + 0$$

$$= \$100 + \frac{\text{Debt}(r_d)(t_c)}{r_d} - \frac{\text{Annual indirect cost}}{.10} = \$100 + \frac{\$25(.10)(.35)}{.10} - \frac{\$1}{.10} = \$98.75 \text{ million}$$

The value of equity (net of the new debt) now equals $98.75 – $25 = $73.75 million.

Assuming that the shares were repurchased at the $100 per share value found in step 1, they would have repurchased $25 million/$100 = 250,000 shares.

Thus, the new stock price would be $73.75 million / 0.75 million = $98.33, and the managers should not issue the debt because it will lower shareholders' wealth. The indirect costs of bankruptcy are greater than the tax shield.

3. **Your unlevered firm is considering buying a new warehouse for $10 million to facilitate an expansion in the same line of business. Your firm has 1 million shares valued at $20 in the stock market, and you estimate that the present value of cash flows from the expansion is $15 million.**

   [A]   **If there is symmetric information between both the firm's managers and stock market investors, what should the stock price be if the firm issues $10 million of new stock at $20 to immediately purchase the warehouse? Should the firm issue the stock and take the project?**

   [B]   **Suppose there is asymmetric information between the firm's managers and stock market investors regarding the value of both the firm and the new project. Assume that investors, who are aware that overvalued firms tend to issue stock, will lower their estimate of the firm value by 3%. Also assume that the skeptical investors also assume the capital raised will be invested to earn exactly the required return (i.e. there is a zero NPV). What would the stock price be if the firm issues $10 million of new stock after announcing the stock issuance to immediately purchase the warehouse? Should the firm issue the stock and take the project?**

   [C]   **Suppose the firm decides to issue $10 million of permanent 5% annual interest rate debt to finance the project, and there is symmetric information regarding the new project's value. What would the stock price be if the firm issues the debt to immediately purchase the warehouse? Should the firm issue the debt and take the project?**

Step 1. To answer part A, determine the new per-share value by finding the post-issue value of the firm and the number of shares that would be issued.

The new firm value would change by the present value of cash flows from the expansion: $15 million. So, the new firm value is $20(1 million) + $15 million = $35 million.

The firm would have to issue $10 million/$20 = 500,000 shares, so there would be 1.5 million shares outstanding.

Thus, the new stock price would be $35 million/1.5 million = $23.33, and the firm should issue the stock and take the project to maximize shareholders' value. With symmetric information, firms should always take positive NPV projects.

Step 2. To answer part B, determine the new per-share value by finding the post-issue value of the firm and the number of shares that would be issued.

Investors would lower the value of the shares in the market by 3% to $19.40, and the firm would have to issue $10 million/$19.40 = 515,464 shares.

The new firm market value would also reflect the market's perception that the NPV of the new project is $0. So, the new firm value is $20(1 million)(1 − .03) + $10 million + $0 = $29.4 million.

Thus, the new stock price would be $29.4 million/1.515464 million = $19.40, and the firm should not issue the stock and take the project because it would reduce shareholders' wealth.

Step 3. To answer part C, determine the new per-share value by finding the post-issue value of the levered firm without the project:

$$V^L = V^U + \text{PV(Interest tax shield)}$$

$$= \$20(1 \text{ million}) + \frac{\text{Debt}(r_d)(t_c)}{r_d} = \$20 \text{ million} + \frac{\$10 \text{ million}(.05)(.35)}{.05} = \$23.5 \text{ million}$$

The new market value of the firm would also increase by the present value of the cash flows from the expansion: $15 million. So, the new firm value is $23.5 million + $15 million = $38.5 million.

The value of equity (net of the new debt) equals: $38.5 − $10 = $28.5.

Thus, the new stock price would be $28.5 million/1 million = $28.50, and the firm should issue the debt and take the project because it would increase shareholders' value.

Questions and Problems

1. Coca-Cola Bottlers Inc. owns bottling plants across the country. This year, they expect to generate $2 billion in EBIT, and they expect that EBIT will grow at a 3% annual rate beginning in the year following this coming year. The firm uses no debt financing, has 500 million shares that trade on the New York Stock Exchange, and has an equity beta of 0.5. The risk-free rate is 5%, and the market risk premium is 10%.

   If it chooses, the firm can issue bonds paying an annual coupon at a 5% annual rate. If it issues bonds, it issues perpetual bonds which pay interest every year at a 5% rate but never repays principal. The tax rate is 30%.

   [A] What is the stock value per share of the (unlevered) firm?
   [B] The firm is considering the following pure capital structure change. It plans to issue $7 billion of debt and use the proceeds to repurchase shares at the value that you found above in part A. The firm has no probability of bankruptcy. Should the firm perform the restructuring?

2. In problem 1, if the firm's debt wasn't riskless, and the firm needed to declare bankruptcy because it could not pay its interest expense, what is the minimum present value of bankruptcy costs that would make issuing the bonds a bad idea?

3. An unlevered firm with 1 million shares trading at $20 in the stock market is considering issuing $5 million of debt and using the proceeds to repurchase stock. If the firm pays 40% of its taxable income in taxes every year, and it is able to purchase the shares at the current market value, what is the most that the present value of financial distress costs could be, such that this restructuring is not a good idea?

4. An unlevered firm with 1 million shares trading at $20 in the stock market, is considering issuing $5 million of debt and using the proceeds to repurchase stock. The firm pays 40% of

its taxable income in taxes every year and believes that the present value of the potential financial distress costs will be $1 million. After the announcement of the planned restructuring, mangers are concerned that the stock price may rise. What is the highest average price the firm could repurchase shares for, such that the restructuring is a good idea for the remaining shareholders?

5. The pecking order hypothesis is based on the existence of asymmetric information and the likelihood of perceived adverse selection for firms issuing equity. Discuss empirical evidence that is consistent with this theory.

Solutions to Questions and Problems

1. [A]   The value of the unlevered firm is the present value of a growing perpetuity with $g = 3\%$.
The free cash flow in the first year is $2 million$(1 - t) = \$1.4$ million.
The required return from the CAPM is: $5\% + .5(10\%) = 10\%$.
So, the $V^U = [1.4] / (.1 - .03) = \$20$ million,
And, the price per share = $20/.5 = \$40$

   [B] $V^L = V^U + PV(\text{Interest tax shield}) = \$20 + [7(.05).3] / .05] = \$20 + \$2.1 = \$22.1$ million

The value of the equity (net of the debt) is now $\$22.1 - \$7 = \$15.1$ million.

There were 7 million$/\$40 = 175,000$ shares repurchased.

So, the price per share is 15.1 million/number of shares $= \$15.1/(.5 - .175) = \$46.46$ and the firm should go forward with the restructuring.

2. $V^L = V^U + PV(\text{Interest tax shield}) - PV(\text{Direct costs of bankruptcy})$

so the maximum size of the cost of financial distress is equal to:

PV(Interest tax shield) $= [7(.05).3]/.05] = \$2.1$ million.

3. Since the shares are being purchased at the pre-announcement value, any gain or loss accrues to the remaining shareholders.

$V^L = V^U + PV(\text{Interest tax shield}) - PV(\text{Financial distress costs})$

so the firm value will fall when PV(Interest tax shield) < PV(Financial distress costs)

since PV(Interest tax shield) $= \dfrac{\text{Debt}(r_D)\tau_C}{r_D} = 5(0.4) = \$2$ million

If the firm believes that the present value of the financial distress costs is above $2 million, it should not go forward with restructuring.

4.   Price per share $= \dfrac{V^L - D}{1 \text{ million} - (\text{repurchased shares})}$

$$= \dfrac{[V^U + PV(\text{Interest tax shield}) - PV(\text{Financial distress costs})] - D}{1 \text{ million} - (\text{repurchased shares})}$$

> $20 to make it a good idea.

V^U = $20 million, D = $5 million, PV(Financial distress costs) = $1 million, and

$$PV(\text{Tax shield}) = \frac{\text{Debt}(r_d)(\tau_c)}{r_d} = \frac{\$5(r_d)(0.40)}{r_d} = \$2 \text{ million}$$

$$\text{The number of repurchased shares} = \left[\frac{\$5 \text{ million}}{\text{Average price}} \right]$$

$$\text{So, set price per share} = \frac{[\$20m + 2m \ -1m] - 5m}{1 \text{ million} \ - \left[\dfrac{\$5 \text{ million}}{\text{Average price}} \right]} = \$20 \text{ ; solve for average price.}$$

$$\Rightarrow 16m = 20 - \left[\frac{\$100 \text{ million}}{\text{Average price}} \right]$$

$(\text{Average price}) \$4 = \$100 \Rightarrow$ Average price $= \$25.$

If you can buy the shares for less than $25, then the repurchase would benefit shareholders.

5. The pecking order hypothesis is consistent with the finding that the vast majority of investment is funded by retained earnings, with net external financing amounting to less than 30% of capital expenditures in most years. Also, firms on average repurchase more equity than they issue, whereas they are net issuers of debt.

The existence of asymmetric information and adverse selection is supported by three pieces of empirical evidence:

[1] An issuer's stock price falls by about 2% to 3% when a new equity issue is announced, suggesting that the market knows that issuing firms are likely to be overvalued;

[2] Firms tend to issue new stock after a large price run-up and, based on their post-issue performance, they appear to have been overvalued when they issued; and

[3] Firms tend to issue new equity when the degree of information asymmetry is smallest, such as following earnings announcements.

Chapter 17

Payout Policy

Chapter Synopsis

17.1 Distributions to Shareholders

A corporation's **payout policy** determines if and when it will distribute cash to its shareholders by issuing a **dividend** or undertaking a **stock repurchase.**

To issue a dividend, the firm's board of directors must authorize the amount per share that will be paid on the **declaration date.** The firm pays the dividend to all shareholders of record on the **record date.** Because it takes three business days for shares to be registered, only shareholders who purchase the stock at least three days prior to the record date receive the dividend. As a result, the date two business days prior to the record date is known as the **ex-dividend date;** anyone who purchases the stock on or after the ex-dividend date will not receive the dividend. Finally, on the **payable** (or **distribution**) **date,** which is generally about a month after the record date, the firm pays the dividend.

Just before the ex-dividend date, the stock is said to trade **cum-dividend.** After the stock goes ex-dividend, new buyers will not receive the current dividend, and the share price will reflect only the dividends in subsequent years. In a perfect capital market, when a dividend is paid, the share price drops by the amount of the dividend when the stock begins to trade ex-dividend.

Most dividend-paying corporations pay them at quarterly intervals. Companies typically increase the amount of their dividends gradually, with little variation. Occasionally, a firm may pay a one-time, **special dividend** that is usually much larger than a **regular dividend.**

An alternative way to pay cash to investors is through a share repurchase, in which a firm uses cash to buy shares of its own outstanding stock. These shares are generally held in the corporate treasury and can be resold in the future.

- An **open market repurchase**, in which a firm buys its own shares in the open market, is the most common way that firms repurchase shares.

- A firm can also use a **tender offer repurchase** in which it offers to buy shares at a pre-specified price during a short time period at typically a 10% to 20% premium.

- In a **Dutch auction repurchase,** a firm lists different prices at which it is prepared to buy shares, and shareholders indicate how many shares they are willing to sell at each price. The firm then pays the lowest price at which it can buy back the desired number of shares.

- A firm may also negotiate a purchase of shares directly from a major shareholder in a **targeted repurchase.**

17.2 Comparison of Dividends and Share Repurchases

In perfect capital markets, a stock's price will fall by the amount of the dividend when a dividend is paid, and a share repurchase has no effect on the stock price. In addition, by selling shares or reinvesting dividends, an investor can effectively create any cash dividend desired and can sell stock in the open market without a share repurchase. As a result, investors are indifferent between the various payout methods the firm might employ.

The Modigliani and Miller dividend irrelevance proposition states that in perfect capital markets, holding the investment policy of a firm fixed, the firm's choice of dividend policy is irrelevant and does not affect share value.

17.3 The Tax Disadvantage of Dividends

Taxes are an important market imperfection that affects dividend policy.

- When the tax rate on dividend exceeds the tax rate on capital gains, the optimal dividend policy is for firms to pay no dividends and use share repurchases for all payouts.

- Recent changes to the tax code have equalized the tax rates on dividends and capital gains. However, long-term investors can defer the capital gains tax until they sell, so there is still a tax advantage for share repurchases over dividends for most investors.

The fact that firms continue to issue dividends despite their tax disadvantage is often referred to as the **dividend puzzle.**

17.4 Dividend Capture and Tax Clienteles

While many investors have a tax preference for share repurchases rather than dividends, the strength of that preference depends on the difference between the dividend tax rate and the capital gains tax rate that each investor faces. The effective dividend tax rate, τ_d^*, which measures the net tax cost to the investor per dollar of dividend income received, is equal to:

$$\tau_d^* = \left(\frac{\tau_d - \tau_g}{1 - \tau_g} \right)$$

where τ_d is the tax on dividend income and τ_g is the tax rate on capital gains. When $\tau_d^* > 0$, investors would be better off with a share repurchase instead of dividends.

The effective dividend tax rate varies across investors for several reasons such as income level, investment horizon, tax jurisdiction, and type of investment account. Different investor tax rates create **clientele effects.** For example, individuals in the highest tax brackets have a preference for stocks that pay low or no dividends, whereas corporations, which are only taxed on 30% of dividend income, generally have a preference for stocks with high dividends.

17.5 Payout Versus Retention of Cash

With perfect capital markets, Modigliani and Miller payout policy irrelevance holds that as long as a firm without positive NPV projects invests excess cash flows in financial securities, the firm's choice of payout versus retention is irrelevant and does not affect the value of the firm.

However, in the presence of corporate taxes, it is generally costly for a firm to retain excess cash because the interest is taxable income for the corporation. Stockholders are better off if the corporation pays the cash out so it can be invested by the investors before taxable interest is incurred. After accounting for investor taxes, there remains a substantial tax disadvantage for retaining excess cash.

Nevertheless, firms may want to hold cash balances in order to help minimize the transaction costs of raising new capital when they have future potential cash needs. However, there is no benefit to shareholders for firms to hold cash in excess of future investment needs.

In addition to the tax disadvantage of holding cash, agency costs may arise, as managers may be tempted to spend excess cash on inefficient investments and perks. Thus, dividends and share repurchases may help minimize the agency problem of wasteful spending when a firm has excess cash. Without pressure from shareholders, managers may also choose to horde cash in order to reduce the firm's leverage and increase their job security.

17.6 Signaling with Payout Policy

When managers have better information than investors do regarding the future prospects of a firm, their payout decisions may signal this information.

Firms typically undertake **dividend smoothing** by maintaining relatively constant dividends, and they increase dividends much more frequently than they cut them. If a firm uses dividend smoothing, its dividend choice may contain information regarding management's expectations of future earnings.

- When a firm increases its dividend, it sends a positive signal to investors that management expects to be able to afford the higher dividend for the foreseeable future.

- When a firm cuts its dividend, it may signal that there it is necessary to reduce the dividend to save cash.

The idea that dividend changes reflect managers' views about a firm's future earnings prospects is called the **dividend signaling hypothesis.**

Studies of the market's reaction to dividend changes are consistent with this hypothesis. For example, during the period 1967–1993, firms that raised their dividend by 10% or more saw their stock prices rise by 1.3% after the announcement, while those that cut their dividend by 10% or more experienced a price decline of 23.71%.

17.7 Stock Dividends, Splits, and Spin-offs

In a **stock split**, shareholders receive additional shares in the firm and the stock price generally falls proportionally with the size of the split. For example, in a 2-for-1 stock split, the firm's stock price will fall by half or 50%. The typical motivation for a stock split is to keep the share price in a range thought to be attractive to small investors. If the stock price is deemed too low, firms can use a **reverse stock split,** which decreases the number of shares outstanding and results in a higher share price.

Stock splits are generally accomplished using a **stock dividend.** When shareholders receive additional shares of stock in the firm itself, the stock dividend has the same effect as s stock split; when they receive shares of a subsidiary, it is called a **spin-off.**

Selected Concepts and Key Terms

Bird in the Hand Hypothesis

Paying higher current dividends will lead to a higher stock price because shareholders prefer current dividends to future ones with the same present value. However, with perfect capital markets, shareholders can generate an equivalent cash flow at any time by selling shares. Thus, the dividend choice of the firm should not matter, and this hypothesis is generally believed to be a fallacy.

Clientele Effect

Individuals in the highest tax brackets have a preference for stocks that pay low or no dividends, whereas tax-free investors and corporations have a stronger preference for stocks with high dividends. Thus, a firm's dividend policy may be optimized for the tax preference of its investor clientele.

Declaration Date

The date a corporation announces that it will pay dividends to all shareholders of record on the record date.

Dividend Puzzle

The fact that firms continue to issue dividends despite their general tax disadvantage.

Dividend Signaling Hypothesis

The idea that dividend changes reflect managers' views about a firm's future earnings prospects. When a firm increases its dividend, it sends a positive signal to investors that management expects to be able to afford the higher dividend for the foreseeable future. When a firm cuts its dividend, it may be signaling that it is necessary to reduce the dividend to save cash.

Dividend-Capture Theory

The theory that, absent transaction costs, investors can trade shares at the time of the dividend so that non-taxed investors receive the dividend. Thus, non-taxed investors need not hold the high-dividend-paying stocks all the time; it is only necessary that they hold them when the dividend is actually paid.

Dutch Auction Share Repurchase

A method of repurchasing shares in which a firm lists different prices at which it is prepared to buy shares, and shareholders indicate how many shares they are willing to sell at each price. The firm then pays the lowest price at which it can buy back its desired number of shares.

Ex-Dividend Date

The date two business days prior to the record date; anyone who purchases the stock on or after the ex-dividend date will not receive the dividend.

Greenmail

A targeted share repurchase from an investor threatening a takeover.

Payable Date, Distribution Date

The date the firm mails dividend checks to the registered shareholders. Generally about a month after the record date.

Payout Policy

The procedure a firm uses to distribute cash to its shareholders by either issuing a dividend or undertaking a stock repurchase.

Record Date

The date a stockholder must own a stock in order receive the dividend.

Special Dividend

A one-time dividend that is usually much larger than a regular dividend.

Spin-Off

The distribution of shares of stock in a subsidiary to existing shareholders on a pro rata basis as a stock dividend.

Stock Dividend

A payment to shareholders in which each shareholder that owns the stock before it goes ex-dividend receives additional shares of stock of the firm itself (a stock split) or of a subsidiary (a spin-off).

Stock Split

A transaction in which shareholders receive additional shares in the firm. The stock price generally falls proportionally with the size of the split. For example, in a 2-for-1 stock split, the firm's stock price will fall by 50%. The typical motivation for a stock split is to keep the share price in a range thought to be attractive to small investors. If the stock price is deemed too low, firms can use a reverse stock split, which decreases the number of shares outstanding resulting in a higher share price.

Concept Check Questions and Answers

17.1.1. How is a stock's ex-dividend date determined, and what is its significance?

Because it takes three business days for shares to be registered, only shareholders who purchase the stock at least three days prior to the record date receive the dividend. As a result, the date two business days prior to the record date is known as the ex-dividend date; anyone who purchases the stock on or after the ex-dividend date will not receive the dividend.

17.1.2. What is a Dutch auction share repurchase?

In the Dutch auction share repurchase, a firm lists different prices at which it is prepared to buy and shareholders indicate how many shares they are willing to sell at each price. The firm then pays the lowest price at which it can buy back its desired number of shares.

17.2.1. True or False: When a firm repurchases its own shares, the price rises due to the decrease in the supply of shares outstanding.

False. When a firm repurchases its own shares, the supply of shares is reduced, but the value of the firm's assets declines when it spends its cash to buy the shares. If the firm repurchases its shares at their market prices, these two effects offset each other, and the share price is unchanged.

17.2.2. In a perfect capital market, how important is the firm's decision to pay dividends versus repurchase shares?

As Modigliani and Miller make clear, the value of a firm ultimately derives from its underlying free cash flow. A firm's free cash flow determines the level of payouts that it can make to its investors. In a perfect capital market, whether these payouts are made through dividends or share repurchases does not matter.

17.3.1. What is the optimal dividend policy when the dividend tax rate exceeds the capital gain tax rate?

The optimal dividend policy when the dividend tax rate exceeds the capital gain tax rate is to pay no dividends at all.

17.3.2. What is the dividend puzzle?

The dividend puzzle refers to the fact that firms continue to pay dividends despite their tax disadvantage.

17.4.1. Under what conditions will investors have a tax preference for share repurchases rather than dividends?

While many investors have a tax preference for share repurchases rather than dividends, the strength of that preference depends on the difference between the dividend tax rate and the capital gains tax rate that they face. Tax rates vary across investors for several reasons, including income level, investment horizon, tax jurisdiction, and type of investment account.

17.4.2. What does the dividend-capture theory imply about the volume of trade in a stock around the ex-dividend day?

The dividend-capture theory states that absent transaction costs, investors can trade shares at the time of the dividend so that non-taxed investors receive the dividend. An implication of this theory is that we should see large volumes of trade in a stock around the ex-dividend day, as high-tax investors sell and low tax-investors buy the stock in anticipation of the dividend, and then reverse those trades just after the ex-dividend date.

17.5.1. Is there an advantage for a firm to retain its cash instead of paying it out to shareholders in perfect capital markets?

No. In perfect capital markets, if a firm invests excess cash flows in financial securities, the firm's choice of payout versus retention is irrelevant and does not affect the initial share price.

17.5.2. How do corporate taxes affect the decision of a firm to retain excess cash?

Corporate taxes make it costly for a firm to retain excess cash. When the firm receives interest from its investment in financial securities, it owes taxes on the interest. Thus, cash is equivalent to negative leverage, and the tax advantage of leverage implies a tax disadvantage to holding cash.

17.6.1. What possible signals does a firm give when it cuts its dividend?

According to the dividend signaling hypothesis, when a firm cuts the dividend, it gives a negative signal to investors that the firm does not expect that earnings will rebound in the near term and so it needs to reduce the dividend to save cash. Also, a firm might cut its dividend to exploit new positive-NPV investment opportunities. In this case, the dividend decrease might lead to a positive stock price reaction.

17.6.2. Would managers acting in the interests of long-term shareholders be more likely to repurchase shares if they believe the stock is undervalued or overvalued?

If managers believe the stock is currently undervalued, a share repurchase is a positive-NPV investment. Managers will clearly be more likely to repurchase shares if they believe the stock to be undervalued.

17.7.1. What is the difference between a stock dividend and a stock split?

Stock dividends of 50% or higher are generally referred to as stock splits. In both cases, a firm does not pay out any cash to shareholders.

17.7.2. What is the main purpose of a reverse split?

The main purpose of a reverse split is to increase the stock price by reducing the number of shares outstanding. If the price of the stock falls too low, a company can use a reverse split to bring the price in any range the company desires.

Examples with Step-by-Step Solutions

Solving Problems

Problems in this chapter may involve determining the effects of a dividend payment or a share repurchase on the value of a corporation's shares in perfect capital markets. They may also require determining the effects for different types of investors (or clientele) when personal taxes are considered. You should also understand why there is generally a tax disadvantage to holding excess cash and be able to account for the effects of a stock split on share values.

Examples

1. **Arizona Public Service Corporation (APS) expects to generate $50 million in free cash flow next year, and this amount is expected to grow by 3% indefinitely. APS has no debt and has accumulated $200 million of excess cash on its balance sheet. The firm's unlevered cost of equity is 8%, and it has 40 million shares outstanding. Would shareholders be better off if the cash was paid out as a dividend or if the cash was used to repurchase shares? There are no taxes or other market imperfections.**

   Step 1. The value per share before a dividend or repurchase must be determined.

Since there is no debt, the value per share equals:

$$P = \frac{\text{Enterprise value}}{\text{40 million shares}} = \frac{\overbrace{\left(\frac{\$50 \text{ million}}{(0.08\text{-}0.03)}\right)}^{\text{PV(Future FCFs)}} + \overbrace{\$200 \text{ million}}^{\text{Excess Cash}}}{\text{40 million}} = \$30$$

Step 2. Determine the value to an investor that holds a share until the ex-dividend date.

They could pay a $\dfrac{\$200 \text{ million}}{\text{40 million}} = \$5$ dividend.

The ex-dividend price equals $\dfrac{\text{Enterprise value}}{\text{40 million shares}} = \dfrac{\overbrace{\left(\frac{\$50 \text{ million}}{(0.08\text{-}0.03)}\right)}^{\text{PV(Future FCFs)}}}{\text{40 million}} = \$25.$

So the value to an investor that holds a share until the ex-dividend date is $5 + $25 =$30.

Step 2. Determine the value per share after the proposed repurchase.

Assuming the shares are repurchased at the current value of $30, the firm can repurchase:

$$\frac{\$200 \text{ million}}{\$30} = 6.66\overline{6} \text{ million shares.}$$

The post-repurchase price equals $\dfrac{\text{Enterprise value}}{\text{40 million shares}} = \dfrac{\overbrace{\left(\frac{\$50 \text{ million}}{(0.08-0.03)}\right)}^{\text{PV(Future FCFs)}}}{33.33\overline{3} \text{ million}} = \$30.$

Step 4. Determine what the firm should do.

Since capital markets are perfect, the stock price falls by the amount of the dividend when a dividend is paid and a share repurchase has no effect on the stock price. Thus, the firm's choice of dividend policy is irrelevant, and the value per share is $30 in any case.

2. **Arizona Public Service Corporation (APS) expects to generate $50 million in free cash flow next year, and this amount is expected to grow by 3% indefinitely. APS has no debt and has accumulated $200 million of excess cash on its balance sheet. The firm's unlevered cost of equity is 8%, and it has 40 million shares outstanding. Would shareholders be better off if the cash was paid out as a dividend or if the cash was used to repurchase shares? The only market imperfections are personal taxes on dividends (at 15%) and capital gains (also at 15%). The average investor bought the shares at the initial public offering price of $15.**

Step 1. The value per share before a dividend or repurchase must be determined.

Since there is no debt, the value per share equals:

$$P = \frac{\text{Enterprise value}}{\text{40 million shares}} = \frac{\overbrace{\left(\frac{\$50 \text{ million}}{(0.08\text{-}0.03)}\right)}^{\text{PV(Future FCFs)}} + \overbrace{\$200 \text{ million}}^{\text{Excess Cash}}}{\text{40 million}} = \$30$$

Step 2. Determine the value to an investor that holds a share until the ex-dividend date.

They could pay a $\dfrac{\$200 \text{ million}}{40 \text{ million}} = \$5$ dividend, with an after-tax value of $\$5(1 - 0.15) = \$4.25$.

The ex-dividend price equals $\dfrac{\text{Enterprise value}}{40 \text{ million shares}} = \dfrac{\overbrace{\left(\dfrac{\$50 \text{ million}}{(0.08 - 0.03)}\right)}^{\text{PV(Future FCFs)}}}{40 \text{ million}} = \$25.$

So, the value to an investor that holds a share until the ex-dividend date is:

$4.25 + $25 = $29.25 and total taxes paid is 40 million × $5 × 0.15 = $30 million.

Step 3. Determine the value per share after the repurchase.

Assuming the shares are repurchased at the current value of $30, the firm can repurchase:

$\dfrac{\$200 \text{ million}}{\$30} = 6.66\overline{6} \text{ million shares.}$

The post-repurchase price equals $\dfrac{\text{Enterprise value}}{40 \text{ million shares}} = \dfrac{\overbrace{\left(\dfrac{\$50 \text{ million}}{(0.08 - 0.03)}\right)}^{\text{PV(Future FCFs)}}}{33.33\overline{3} \text{ million}} = \$30.$

However the value to the value to the $6.66\overline{6}$ million investors that sold is:

$30 – ($30 – $15)0.15 = $27.75, and total taxes paid is $6.66\overline{6} \times (\$30 - \$15)0.15 = \$15$ million.

Step 4. Determine what the firm should do.

The optimal payout policy is to neither pay dividends nor repurchase shares. However, repurchasing shares is preferred to paying dividends because investors are only taxed on the capital gain and incur $15 million less in taxes.

3. **Microsoft has $30 billion in excess cash, which is invested in Treasury bills paying 5% interest. The board of directors is considering either paying a dividend immediately or paying a dividend in one year.**
   [A] **In a perfect capital market, which option will shareholders prefer?**
   [B] **If the corporate tax rate on interest is 35%, individual investors pay a tax rate on dividends of 15% and a tax rate of 30% on interest income, and institutional investors pay no taxes, which option will shareholders prefer?**

Step 1. Determine the value of each option to shareholders in perfect markets.

If Microsoft pays an immediate dividend, the shareholders receive $30 billion today.

If it pays the dividend in one year, it will be able to pay:

$30 billion × (1.05) = $31.5 billion.

This is the same value as if shareholders had received a $30 billion dividend and invested the $30 billion in Treasury bills themselves.

Thus, shareholders are indifferent about whether the firm pays the dividend immediately or retains the cash.

Step 2. Determine the value of each option with taxes if all investors are individual investors.

If Microsoft pays an immediate dividend, shareholders receive $30 billion today, but they only receive $30 billion × (1 – 0.15) = $25.50 billion after taxes.

If it invests the cash for one year, it will earn 0.05(1 – 0.35) = 3.25% and it will be able to pay:

$30 billion × (1.0325) = $30.975 billion and shareholders would receive:

$30.975 billion × (1 – 0.15) = $26.33 billion in a year 1 dividend after taxes.

Investors would have been able to earn 0.05(1 – 0.3) = 3.5% on their $25.5 after-tax dividend payment and thus have $25.5(1.035) = $26.39 billion.

Thus, individual investors would be slightly better off with the immediate dividend.

Step 3. Determine the value of each option with taxes if all investors are institutional investors.

If Microsoft pays an immediate dividend, shareholders receive $30 billion today.

If it invests the cash for one year, it will earn 0.05(1 – 0.35) = 3.25% and it will be able to pay:

$30 billion × (1.0325) = $30.975 billion in a year 1 dividend.

Investors would have been able to earn 5% on their $30 dividend payment and thus have $30(1.05) = $31.5 billion.

Thus, institutional investors would be better off by $525 million with the immediate dividend.

Questions and Problems

1. Below are the current tax rates for different investors: an individual investor who holds stocks for one year; a pension fund; and a corporation, which can exclude 70% of dividend income from taxes.

Investor	Dividend Tax Rate	Capital Gain Tax Rate
Individual investors	15%	15%
Pension funds	0%	0%
Corporations	0.35%(1 – 0.7)=10.5%	35%

    Calculate the effective dividend tax rates each type of investor, and explain what this means for each investor's preference for dividends.

2. Suppose that Apple computer, which is currently trading for $90 per share, has the following types of stock splits.
    [A]   A 3-for-1 stock split.
    [B]   A 1-for-4 reverse split.
    [C]   A 50% stock dividend.

    Calculate the value of 1,000 shares before and after the split.

3. An unlevered corporation has $100 million of excess cash and 50 million shares outstanding with a current market price of $20 per share. The board of directors has declared a special dividend of $100 million.

   [A] What is the ex-dividend price of a share in a perfect capital market?

   [B] If the board instead decided to use the cash to do a one-time share repurchase, what is the price of the shares once the repurchase is complete in a perfect capital market?

   [C] What do stockholders want the firm to do?

4. Southwest Natural Gas is expected to pay a constant dividend of $4 per share per year in perpetuity. All investors require an 8% return on the stock. Individual investors pay a 20% tax on dividends, but there is no capital gains tax. Institutional investors pay no taxes on dividends or capital gains.

   [A] What is the value of a share of a share of the stock?

   [B] What kinds of investors would be expected to hold the stock?

5. How can firms use dividends to signal information about the firm's value?

Solutions to Questions and Problems

1. Individual investor $\tau_d^* = \left(\dfrac{\tau_d - \tau_g}{1 - \tau_g} \right) = \dfrac{0.15 - 0.15}{1 - 0.15} = 0\%$

   Thus, they are indifferent between receiving dividends or capital gains. However, paying dividends forces all stockholders to pay taxes on the income—even if they do not want the income now. In addition, long-term investors can defer the capital gains tax until they sell, so there is still a tax advantage for share repurchases over dividends for most investors. Thus, stockholders would still generally prefer selling shares to recognize taxable income on their own.

   Pension fund $\tau_d^* = \left(\dfrac{\tau_d - \tau_g}{1 - \tau_g} \right) = \dfrac{0}{1 - 0} = 0\%$

   So pension funds are indifferent between receiving dividends or capital gains.

   Corporation $\tau_d^* = \left(\dfrac{\tau_d - \tau_g}{1 - \tau_g} \right) = \dfrac{0.105 - 0.35}{1 - 0.35} = -38\%$

   Thus, corporations prefer to receive dividends due to their advantageous taxation.

2. The value is $1,000 \times \$90 = \$90,000$ before the splits.

   [A] Since the number of shares increases threefold, the value per share must be one-third its pre-split value.

   $P = \left(\dfrac{1}{3} \right) \$90 = \$30$

   There are now 3,000 shares, so $V = 3,000 \times \$30 = \$90,000$.

   [B] Since the number of shares decreases by one-fourth, the value per share must be four times its pre-split value.

   $P = 4 \times \$90 = \$360$

   There are now 250 shares, so $V = 250 \times \$360 = \$90,000$.

[C]   Since the number of shares increases by 50%, the value per share must be $1/1.5 = 2/3$ its pre-split value.

$$P = \left(\frac{2}{3}\right)\$90 = \$60$$

There are now 1,500 shares, so $V = 1,500 \times \$60 = \$90,000$.

3. [A] They could pay a $\dfrac{\$100 \text{ million}}{50 \text{ million}} = \$2$ dividend

$$P = \frac{\text{PV(Future cash flows)} + \overbrace{\$100 \text{ million}}^{\text{Excess Cash}}}{50 \text{ million}} = \$20 \Rightarrow \text{PV(Future cash flows)} = \$900 \text{ million}$$

The ex-dividend price is:

$$P = \frac{\text{PV(Future cash flows)}}{50 \text{ million}} = \frac{\$900 \text{ million}}{50 \text{ million}} = \$18$$

Since $\$20 = \$18 + \$2$, the shareholders are no better off.

[B]   Assuming the shares are repurchased at the current value of $20, the firm can repurchase:

$$\frac{\$100 \text{ million}}{\$20} = 5 \text{ million shares.}$$

The post-repurchase price equals $\dfrac{\text{Enterprise value}}{45 \text{ million shares}} = \dfrac{\overbrace{\$900 \text{ million}}^{\text{PV(Future FCFs)}}}{45 \text{ million}} = \$20.$

So shareholders are no better off.

[C]   The firm's choice of dividend policy is irrelevant, and the value per share is $20 in any case.

4. [A] $P^{\text{Individual Investors}} = \dfrac{\$4(1 - 0.20)}{0.08} = \$40$

$P^{\text{Institutional Investors}} = \dfrac{\$4}{0.08} = \$50$

[B]   The clientele for the stock is likely to be institutional investors such as pension funds, insurance companies, and endowments.

5. The idea that dividend changes reflect managers' views about a firm's future earnings prospects is called the dividend signaling hypothesis.

■   When a firm increases its dividend, it sends a positive signal to investors that management expects to be able to afford the higher dividend for the foreseeable future.

■   When a firm cuts its dividend, it may signal that there it is necessary to reduce the dividend to save cash.

Studies of the market's reaction to dividend changes are consistent with this hypothesis. For example, during the period 1967–1993, firms that raised their dividend by 10% or more saw their stock prices rise by 1.34% after the announcement, while those that cut their dividend by 10% or more experienced a price decline of 23.71%.

CHAPTER 18

Capital Budgeting and Valuation with Leverage

Chapter Synopsis

18.1 Overview of Key Concepts

There are three discounted cash flow valuation methods: the weighted average cost of capital (WACC) method, the adjusted present value (APV) method, and the flow-to-equity (FTE) method. Despite differences in implementation, all methods can be used to determine the same correct project or firm value. In the next three sections, three assumptions will be made:

1. The project has average risk, so the project's cost of capital can be assessed based on the risk of the firm.

2. The firm's debt-equity ratio is constant, so its weighted average cost of capital will not fluctuate due to leverage changes.

3. Corporate taxes are the only market imperfection. Imperfections such as costs of financial distress, agency costs and benefits of debt, and issuance costs are not significant at the level of debt chosen.

These assumptions will be relaxed in the final sections of the chapter.

18.2 The Weighted Average Cost of Capital Method

The WACC method calculates the total value of the equity and debt by discounting unlevered free cash flows at the WACC, r_{wacc}. The key steps in the WACC valuation method are:

1. Determine the free cash flows of the firm or project.

2. Compute the after-tax WACC as

$$r_{wacc} = \frac{E}{E+D}r_E + \frac{D}{E+D}r_D(1-\tau_c)$$

where E is the market value of equity, r_E is equity cost of capital, D is the market value of debt (net of cash), r_D is the debt cost of capital, and τ_c is the marginal corporate tax rate.

3. Compute the value of the firm or project, including the tax benefit of leverage, by discounting the free cash flows such that

$$V_0^L = \sum_{t=0}^{T} \frac{FCF_t}{(1+r_{wacc})}$$

The intuition of the WACC method is that the firm's weighted average cost of capital represents the average return the firm must pay to its investors (both debt and equity holders) on an after-tax basis. Thus, an acceptable project should generate an expected return of at least the firm's weighted average cost of capital. The WACC method incorporates the tax savings associated with using debt in the r_{wacc} calculation, which uses the after-tax cost of debt.

18.3 The Adjusted Present Value Method

In the adjusted present value (APV) method, the total value of an investment is determined by first calculating its unlevered value and then adding the value of the interest tax shield and deducting any costs that arise from other market imperfections. The key steps in the APV valuation method are as follows:

1. Determine the free cash flows of the investment.

2. Determine the investment's value without leverage (V^U) by discounting its free cash flows at the unlevered cost of capital, r_U. With a constant debt-equity ratio,

$$r_U = \text{Pretax WACC} = \frac{E}{E+D}r_E + \frac{D}{E+D}r_D$$

3. Determine the present value of the interest tax shield. Given the expected debt on date t, D_t, the interest tax shield at time t is $\tau_c \times D_t$. If a constant debt-equity ratio is maintained, r_U is the appropriate discount rate to use top discount the tax shields.

4. Add the present value of the interest tax shield to the unlevered value and subtract the present value of any financial distress, agency, and issuance costs:

$$V^L = APV = V^U + PV(\text{interest tax shield}) - PV(\text{Financial distress, agency, and Issuance costs})$$

The APV method may be easier to apply than the WACC method when the firm does not maintain a constant debt-equity ratio and the level of debt in the future is known.

However, the APV method is generally more complicated to apply than the WACC method when a firm uses a constant leverage ratio because you need to know the debt level to compute the interest tax shield, but with a constant debt-equity ratio you need to know the project's value to compute the debt level. As a result, implementing the APV approach with a constant debt-equity ratio requires solving for the project's debt and value simultaneously.

18.4 The Flow-to-Equity Method

In the flow-to-equity (FTE) valuation method, the free cash flows available to equity holders, after taking into account all payments to and from debt holders, are discounted using the levered equity cost of capital. The key steps in the flow-to-equity method for valuing a levered investment are as follows:

1. Determine the **free cash flow to equity** (FCFE) of the investment as

$$\text{FCFE} = \text{FCF} - \overbrace{(1 - \tau_c) \times (\text{Interest payments})}^{\text{After-tax interest expense}} + (\text{Net borrowing})$$

2. Determine the equity cost of capital, r_E.

3. Compute the equity value, E, by discounting the free cash flow to equity using the equity cost of capital.

The FTE method has the same disadvantage associated with the APV approach: You need to know the debt level to compute the interest tax shield, but with a constant debt-equity ratio you need to know the project's value to compute the debt level.

18.5 Project-Based Costs of Capital

The methods discussed above assumed that both the risk and the leverage of the project under consideration matched those characteristics for the firm as a whole. However, specific projects often have different risk and leverage than the average investment made by the firm.

The cost of capital should reflect the risk of owning assets used in the project. The cost of capital for a specific industry can be estimated by studying single-division firms in that industry. If the unlevered cost of capital for the industry happens to be known, then r_E can be inferred as:

$$r_U = \frac{E}{E + D} r_E + \frac{D}{E + D} r_D \Rightarrow r_E = r_U + \frac{D}{E}(r_U - r_D)$$

Once the equity cost of capital is known, the division's WACC can be determined. The same r_{wacc} estimate can be calculated directly using

$$r_{wacc} = r_U - \left(\frac{D}{E + D}\right) \tau_c r_D$$

If r_U is not known, then the CAPM can be used to determine r_E. First, unlever the comparison firm's beta as:

$$\beta_U = [E/(E + D)]\beta_E + [D/(E + D)]\beta_D.$$

The unlevered beta can be used in the CAPM to estimate the unlevered cost of capital to use in the APV method. For the WACC and FTE methods, the unlevered beta can be relevered to reflect the firm's capital structure as:

$$\beta_E = \beta_U + [D/E](\beta_U - \beta_D).$$

The levered beta, β_E, can be used in the CAPM to determine the industry equity cost of capital, and then the division's WACC can be determined.

To determine the cost of capital for a project, the amount of debt associated with the project must be determined based on the incremental financing needed if the firm takes on the project.

- The incremental financing of a project need not correspond to the financing that is directly tied to the project. For example, a project financed with a mortgage for 90% of its value by a firm with a policy to maintain a 40% debt-to-value ratio will reduce debt elsewhere in the firm. In that case, the appropriate debt-to-value ratio to use when evaluating the project is 40%, not 90%.

- A firm's leverage should be evaluated based on its debt net of any excess cash.

- When a firm's dividend payouts and share repurchases are set in advance and will not be affected by a project's free cash flow, new projects are effectively 100% debt financed. Any cash requirement of the project will be funded using the firm's cash or borrowing, and any cash that the project produces will be used to repay debt or increase the firm's cash.

18.6 APV with Other Leverage Policies

When the firm has a **constant interest coverage ratio,** it keeps its interest payments to a target fraction of its FCF. Using the APV method, the value of a project for a firm in which k equals incremental interest payments as a target fraction of the project's free cash flow is given by constant interest coverage model:

$$V^L = APV = V^U + \text{PV(interest tax shield)} = V^U + \tau_c k \times V^U = (1 + \tau_c k)V^U$$

When the level of debt fluctuates with the value of the project, the project's unlevered cost of capital should be used to discount the tax shields. However, when a firm has a fixed debt schedule, the interest tax shields can be discounted using the debt cost of capital, r_D, since the amount of the debt will not fluctuate, and thus the tax shield is less risky than the project.

18.7 Other Effects of Financing

- If there are fees associated with securing a loan or issuing securities, they should be deducted when computing a project's value.

- If management believes that the equity will sell at a price that is less than its true value, this mispricing is a cost of the project for the existing shareholders and it should be deducted when determining a project's value.

- When the probability of financial distress is high, the estimated future free cash flows should be reduced by the expected costs associated with financial distress and agency problems.

- The probability of financial distress also raises the unlevered cost of capital. Since financial distress is more likely to occur when economic times are bad, the costs of distress cause the value of the firm to fall further in a market downturn. Financial distress costs, therefore, tend to increase the sensitivity of the firm's value to market risk, raising the unlevered cost of capital for highly levered firms.

18.8 Advanced Topics in Capital Budgeting

When the firm readjusts is debt annually, based on its expected future free cash flows, the discount rate used for the interest tax shield is r_D for the first period, because it is fixed, and then r_U from then on. The constant interest coverage model in this case becomes:

$$V^L = APV = V^U + \text{PV(interest tax shield)} = V^U + \tau_c k\left(\frac{1+r_U}{1+r_D}\right) \times V^U.$$

If investors are taxed on the income they receive from holding equity or debt, it will raise the return they require to hold those securities.

▨ The WACC method already accounts for personal taxes since the equity and debt cost of capital in the market already reflects the effects of investor taxes.

▨ The APV approach must be modified in the presence of personal taxes because it requires an estimate of the unlevered cost of capital. Thus, r_D and τ_c should be replaced by:

$$r_D^* \equiv r_D \frac{(1-\tau_i)}{(1-\tau_e)} \text{ and } \tau^* = 1 - \frac{(1-\tau_c)(1-\tau_e)}{(1-\tau_i)}.$$

Appendix: Foundations and Further Details

18A.1 Deriving the WACC Method

For a project financed by both debt and equity, a firm will have to pay investors a total of

$$E(1 + r_E) + D(1 + r_D).$$

Assume that the project generates free cash flows of FCF_1 at the end of the year, the interest tax shield of the debt provides a tax savings of $\tau_c \times$ (interest on debt) $\approx \tau_c\, r_D\, D$, and the investment will continue beyond next year with a continuation value of V_1^L. Thus, to satisfy investors, the project cash flows must be such that

$$E(1 + r_E) + D(1 + r_D) = FCF_1 + \tau_c r_D D + V_1^L$$

Because $V_0^L = E + D$, , we can write the WACC as:

$$r_{wacc} = \frac{E}{V_0^L} r_E + \frac{D}{V_0^L} r_E(1 - \tau_c).$$

The value of the project today can then be expressed as the present value of next period's free cash flows and continuation value:

$$V_0^L = \frac{FCF_1 + V_1^L}{1 + r_{wacc}}.$$

For a multi-year project, and assuming the WACC remains constant:

$$V_0^L = \frac{FCF_1}{1 + r_{wacc}} + \frac{FCF_2}{(1 + r_{wacc})^2} + \frac{FCF_3}{(1 + r_{wacc})^3} + \dots$$

That is, the value of a levered investment is the present value of its future free cash flows using the weighted average cost of capital.

18A.2 The Levered and Unlevered Cost of Capital

If an investor holds a portfolio of all of the equity and debt of the firm, then the investor will receive the free cash flows of the firm plus the tax savings from the interest tax shield. Since these are the same cash flows an investor would receive from a portfolio of the unlevered firm and a separate "tax shield" security that paid the investor the amount of the tax shield each period, these two portfolios generate the same cash flows, so by the Law of One Price they have the same market values:

$$V^L = E + D = V^U + T.$$

where T is the present value of the interest tax shield. Because these portfolios have equal cash flows, they must also have identical expected returns, which implies

$$Er_E + Dr_D = V^U r_U + Tr_T.$$

where r_T is the expected return associated with the interest tax shields. The relationship between r_E, r_D, and r_U will depend on the expected return r_T, which is determined by the risk of the interest tax shield.

18A.3 Solving for Leverage and Value Simultaneously

When we use the APV method, we need to know the debt level to compute the interest tax shield and determine the project's value. But if a firm maintains a constant debt-to-value ratio, we need to know the project's value to determine the debt level. When a firm maintains a constant leverage ratio, to use the APV method we must solve for the debt level and the project value simultaneously. While complicated to do by hand, it can be done in Excel using iteration.

The solution is to enter the debt capacity as an Excel formula that sets the debt capacity to be the desired percentage of the project's value. Now, the levered value depends on the debt capacity, and the debt capacity depends on the levered value, but Excel will keep calculating until the values for the debt capacity and levered value of the spreadsheet are consistent

Selected Concepts and Key Terms

Adjusted Present Value (APV)

A valuation method in which the total value of an investment is determined by first calculating its unlevered value and then adding the present value of the interest tax shields and deducting any costs that arise from other market imperfections.

Debt Capacity

The amount of debt at date t that is required to maintain the firm's target debt-to-value ratio.

Flow-to-Equity (FTE)

A valuation method in which the free cash flows available to equity holders, after taking into account all payments to and from debt holders, are discounted using the levered equity cost of capital.

Free Cash Flow to Equity (FCFE)

The free cash flow in a period that remains after subtracting the after-tax value of interest payments made in the period, adding the value of debt that was issued, and subtracting any debt repayments made.

Concept Check Questions and Answers

18.1.1. What are the three methods we can use to include the value of the tax shield in the capital budgeting decision?

The WACC valuation method, the adjusted present value (APV) valuation method, and the flow to equity valuation method.

18.1.2. In what situation is the risk of a project likely to match that of the overall firm?

This would generally be the case only if the firm is in one line of business. For a firm with multiple divisions, the risk of the projects in different divisions may be different.

18.2.1. Describe the key steps in the WACC valuation method.

The key steps in the WACC valuation method are: 1) determining the free cash flow of the investment; 2) compute the weighted average cost of capital; and 3) compute the value of the investments, including the tax benefit of leverage, by discounting the free cash flow of the investment using the WACC.

18.2.2. How does the WACC method take into account the tax shield?

It uses the after-tax debt cost of capital, thus accounting for the fact that interest expense is paid before taxes and results in an interest tax shield.

18.3.1. Describe the adjusted present value (APV) method.

The adjusted present value method is a valuation method in which we determine the levered value of an investment by first calculating its unlevered value, and then adding the value of the interest tax shield and deducting any costs that arise from other market imperfections.

18.3.2. At what rate should we discount the interest tax shield when a firm maintains a target leverage ratio?

When a firm maintains a target leverage ratio, future interest tax shields have similar risk to the project's cash flows, and so should be discounted at the project's unlevered cost of capital.

18.4.1. Describe the key steps in the flow to equity method for valuing a levered investment.

The key steps in the flow to equity method for valuing a levered investment are: 1) determine the free cash flow to equity of the investment; and 2) compute the equity value by discounting the free cash flow to equity using the equity cost of capital.

18.4.2. Why does the assumption that the firm maintains a constant debt-equity ratio simplify the flow-to-equity calculation?

Because we are using the same discount rate for the free cash flow and the tax shield, the cash flows of the project and the tax shield can be combined first and then discounted at the rate r_U.

18.5.1. How do we estimate a project's unlevered cost of capital when the project's risk is different from that of a firm?

When a project's risk is different from that of the firm as a whole, we must estimate its cost of capital separately from that of the firm. We estimate the project's unlevered cost of capital by looking at the unlevered cost of capital for other firms with similar market risk as the project.

18.5.2. What is the incremental debt associated with a project?

The incremental debt associated with a project is the change in a firm's total debt (net of cash) with the project versus without the project.

18.6.1. What condition must the firm meet to have a constant interest coverage policy?

A firm has a constant interest coverage policy if it sets debt to maintain its interest expenses as a fraction of free cash flow.

18.6.2. What is the appropriate discount rate for tax shields when the debt schedule is fixed in advance?

When debt levels are set according to a fixed schedule, the appropriate discount rate for the predetermined interest tax shields is the debt cost of capital.

18.7.1. How do we deal with issuance costs and security mispricing costs in our assessment of a project's value?

Issuance cost, as well as any costs or gains from mispricing of issued securities, should be included in the assessment of a project's value.

18.7.2. How would financial distress and agency costs affect a firm's use of leverage?

Financial distress costs are likely to lower the expected free cash flow of a project and raise its unlevered cost of capital. Taking these effects into account together with agency costs may limit a firm's use of leverage.

18.8.1. When a firm has pre-determined tax shields, how do we measure its net debt when calculating its unlevered cost of capital?

When debt is set according to a fixed schedule for some period of time, the interest tax shields for the scheduled debt are known, relatively safe cash flows. These safe cash flows will reduce the effect of leverage on the risk of the firm's equity. Thus, when a firm has pre-determined tax shields, we should deduct the value of these safe tax shields from the debt when measuring the firm's net debt.

18.8.2. If the firm's debt-equity ratio changes over time, can the WACC method still be applied?

When a firm does not maintain a constant debt-equity ratio for a project, the WACC method becomes more difficult to use, because when the proportion of debt financing changes, the project's equity cost of capital and WACC will not remain constant over time. With a bit of care, however, this method can still be used and, of course, will lead to same result as other methods.

Examples with Step-by-Step Solutions

Solving Problems

Problems may involve calculating the value of a firm or project using the weighted-average cost of capital (WACC) method, the adjusted present value (APV) method, or the flow-to-equity (FTE) method under the assumption that a firm uses a constant leverage ratio. Problem 1 below demonstrates how to use each of the methods and shows that each method leads to the same value.

Problems may also require determining the correct project or firm cost of capital. For projects in a different industry, or for non-public firms, the cost of capital for a specific industry can be estimated by studying single-division firms in that industry.

Other problems may apply the APV for a firm with a fixed debt schedule, a constant interest coverage ratio, or for a firm that adjusts its level of debt annually.

Examples

1. You are valuing a firm that you expect will have earnings before interest and taxes (EBIT) of $26 million every year beginning in one year. Each year, you expect that depreciation will equal capital spending and there will be no new required investments in working capital. The firm has 10 million shares outstanding, uses 50% debt financing, has a debt cost of capital of 6%, a beta of 0.8, and a tax rate of 50%. The risk-free rate is 6%, and the market risk premium is 5%.
   [A] What is the value per share using the weighted average cost of capital (WACC) method?
   [B] What is the value per share using the adjusted present value method (APV) method?
   [C] What is the value per share using the flow-to-equity (FTE) method?

Step 1. Determine the firm's unlevered free cash flows.

EBIT	$26,000,000
− Interest	0
EBT	26,000,000
− Taxes	13,000,000
Unlevered Net Income	13,000,000

Free Cash Flow

Plus: Depreciation	= Capital Spending
Less: Capital Spending	= Depreciation
Less: Increases in Working Capital	0
Free Cash Flow	$13,000,000

Step 2. Determine the after-tax weighted-average cost of capital (WACC).

The equity cost of capital can be determined from the CAPM.

$$r_E = r_f + \beta(E[R_{Mkt}] - r_f) = 0.06 + 0.80(0.05) = 10\%$$

The WACC can now be calculated as:

$$r_{wacc} = \frac{E}{E+D}r_E + \frac{D}{E+D}r_D(1-\tau_c) = 0.50(0.10) + 0.50(0.06)(1-0.50) = 6.5\%$$

Step 3. Determine the firm value, equity value, and value per share using the WACC method.

Since the firm's free cash flows are a perpetuity:

$$V_0^L = \sum_{t=1}^{T} \frac{FCF_t}{(1+r_{wacc})} = \frac{FCF}{r_{wacc}} = \frac{\$13,000,000}{0.065} = \$200\,million$$

The WACC method values the firm as a whole, so the equity value is:

$$E = V^L - D = \$200\,million - 0.50(\$200\,million) = \$100\,million$$

And the value per share is $\dfrac{\$100\,million}{10\,million} = \$10$.

Step 4. Determine the unlevered cost of capital to use for the APV method.

The unlevered equity beta, assuming that the debt beta is approximately zero, is:

$\beta_U = [E/(E+D)]\beta_E + [D/(E+D)]\beta_D \approx [E/(E+D)]\beta_E = 0.50(0.80) = 0.40$

So the unlevered cost of equity, which equals the unlevered cost of capital, is:

$r_E = r_f + \beta(E[R_{Mkt}] - r_f) = 0.06 + 0.40(0.05) = 8\%$

Step 5. Determine the firm value, equity value, and value per share using the APV method.

Assuming that the present value of financial distress, agency and issuance costs are zero:

$V^L = APV = V^U + PV(\text{Interest tax shield})$

$$= \frac{\$13\text{ million}}{0.08} + \frac{\$100(0.06)(0.50)}{0.08} = 162.50 + 37.50 = \$200\text{ million.}$$

The APV method values the firm as a whole, so the equity value is:

$E = V^L - D = \$200\text{ million} - 0.50(\$200\text{ million}) = \$100\text{ million.}$

And the value per share is $\dfrac{\$100\text{ million}}{10\text{ million}} = \$10.$

Step 6. Determine the annual free cash flow to equity (FCFE) for the FTE method.

EBIT	$26,000,000
– Interest (6% × $100 million)	6,000,000
EBT	20,000,000
– Taxes	10,000,000
Unlevered Net Income	10,000,000

Free Cash Flow

Plus: Depreciation	= Capital Spending
Less: Capital Spending	= Depreciation
Less: Increases in Working Capital	0
Plus: Net Borrowing	0
Free Cash Flow to Equity (FCFE)	$10,000,000

Step 7. Determine the equity value and value per share using the FTE method.

The equity value is the present value of the flows to equity, which are a perpetuity, discounted at the levered cost of equity:

$$E = \sum_{t=1}^{T} \frac{FCFE_t}{(1+r_E)} = \frac{FCFE}{r_E} = \frac{\$10,000,000}{0.10} = \$100\text{ million}$$

The FTE method values the firm as a whole, so the value per share is $\dfrac{\$100\text{ million}}{10\text{ million}} = \$10.$

2. **Suppose that the firm in problem 1 was expected to have a constant interest coverage ratio in which interest payments were going to be maintained at 50% of free cash flow. What would the value per share be now?**

Step 1. Determine which technique would be best to use.

The easiest method would be to use here is the constant interest coverage APV equation discussed in the chapter.

Step 2. The APV is now:

$$V^L = APV = V^U + \text{PV(interest tax shield)} = V^U + \tau_c k \times V^U = (1 + \tau_c k)V^U$$

$$= (1 + 0.50 \times 0.30)\left(\frac{\$13,000,000}{0.08}\right) = \$186.875$$

Step 3. Determine the value per share now.

The APV method values the firm as a whole, so the equity value is: $E = V^L - D$

The amount of debt, D, is now $\dfrac{\text{Interest expense}}{r_D} = \dfrac{0.30(13,000,000)}{0.06} = \$65$ million

Assuming that the firm currently has this much debt:

$E = V^L - D$ = \$186.875 million − \$65 million = \$121.875 million.

And the value per share is $\dfrac{\$121.875 \text{ million}}{10 \text{ million}} = \$12.1875$

3. **Suppose that firm in problem 1 adjusts its debt annually based on its expected future free cash flows such that its interest payments are maintained at 50% of free cash flow. What would the value per share be now?**

Step 1. Determine which technique would be best to use.

The easiest method would be to use now is the adjustment to the APV equation discussed in the chapter which values a firm assuming that it adjusts its debt annually based on its expected future free cash flows.

Step 2. The APV is now:

$$V^L = APV = V^U + \text{PV(interest tax shield)} = V^U + \tau_c k \left(\frac{1 + r_U}{1 + r_D}\right) \times V^U$$

$$= 162.50 + 0.50(0.30)\left(\frac{1.08}{1.06}\right) \times 162.50 = \$187.335$$

Step 3. Determine the value per share now.

The APV method values the firm as a whole, so the equity value is: $E = V^L - D$

The amount of debt, D, is now $\dfrac{\text{Interest expense}}{r_D} = \dfrac{0.30(13,000,000)}{0.06} = \$65$ million

Assuming that the firm currently has this much debt:

$E = V^L - D$ = \$187.335 million − \$65 million = \$122.335 million.

And the value per share is $\dfrac{\$122.335 \text{ million}}{10 \text{ million}} = \$12.23.$

The value is slightly higher than the value in problem 2 because the discount rate used for the interest tax shield is r_D for the first period because it is fixed, and then r_U from then on.

Questions and Problems

1. You are evaluating a project that costs $5 million. The project is expected to generate free cash flow of $1 million the first year, and this free cash flow is expected to be the same every year. The levered equity cost of capital of 17%, the firm has a debt cost of capital of 5%, and a tax rate of 40%. Your firm maintains a debt-equity ratio of 1.0.
   [A]   What is the NPV of the project including any tax shields from leverage?
   [B]   How much debt will the firm initially take on as a result of the project?
   [C]   How much of the project's value is attributable to the present value of interest tax shields?

2. As in problem 1, you are evaluating a project that costs $5 million. The project is expected to generate free cash flow of $1 million the first year, and this free cash flow is expected to be the same every year. The levered equity cost of capital of 17%, the firm has a debt cost of capital of 5%, and a tax rate of 40%. Your firm maintains a debt-equity ratio of 1.0.
   [A]   What is the free cash flow to equity for this project?
   [B]   What is its NPV computed using the FTE method? How does it compare with the NPV based on the WACC method?

3. In year 1, your firm is expected to report $10 million in earnings before interest and taxes (EBIT). The market expects that EBIT will grow at a rate of 3% per year forever. The firm will never make new capital investments and will not change net working capital. The firm currently has $50 million in risk-free debt, and it plans to keep a constant ratio of debt to equity every year, so that the debt will also grow by 3% per year. The corporate tax rate equals 40%, the risk-free rate is 5%, the expected return on the market is 10%, and the asset beta for this industry is 0.60. Using the APV method, what is your firm's total market value? What is the value of the equity?

4. Nordstrom is spinning off its casual clothing segment, and you are trying to determine the value of the spun-off entity. You estimate that the division's free cash flow in the coming year to be $100 million, and you expect the free cash flows will grow by 3% per year in subsequent years. Because the spin-off isn't publicly traded yet, you do not have an accurate assessment of the division's equity beta. However, you do have beta data for Gap, Inc., a firm it closely resembles. Gap has an equity beta of 1.1, a debt beta of 0.10, and a debt-equity ratio of 0.20. Nordstrom has a beta of 2.2 and a debt-equity ratio of 1.0, and the spun-off firm will maintain this leverage ratio and has been told by its investment bankers that the debt cost of capital will be 6%. The corporate tax rate is 40%, the risk-free rate is 5%, and the expected return on the market portfolio is 10%.
   [A]   Estimate the division's WACC.
   [B]   Estimate the spun off unit's share value based on the 100 million that will be outstanding after the spinoff.

5. As in problem 1, you are evaluating a project that costs $5 million. The project is expected to generate free cash flow of $1 million the first year, and this free cash flow is expected to be the same every year. The levered equity cost of capital of 17%, the firm has a debt cost of capital of 5%, and a tax rate of 40%. Your firm maintains a debt-equity ratio of 1.0.
   [A]   If the project was funded exclusively by obtaining a $5 million bank loan, what WACC should be used to evaluate the project?
   [B]   Suppose that the firm intends to maintain a debt-equity ratio of 1.0 and the debt associated with this project will be fixed at 50% of its value. What is the value of the tax shield now?

Solutions to Questions and Problems

1. [A] $r_{wacc} = \dfrac{E}{E + D}r_E + \dfrac{D}{E + D}r_D(1 - \tau_c) = 0.50(0.17) + 0.50(0.05)(1 - 0.40) = 10\%$

$NPV = \sum_{t=1}^{T} \dfrac{FCF_t}{(1 + r_{wacc})} = -\$5 \text{ million} + \dfrac{FCF}{r_{wacc}} = -5 \text{ million} + \dfrac{\$1 \text{ million}}{0.10} = \$5 \text{ million}$

   [B]   The firm is financed with 50% debt, so D = 0.50(10) = \$2.5 million.

   [C]   PV(Interest tax shield) = $\dfrac{\$2.5(0.05)(0.40)}{0.10} = \$0.50 \text{ million}$

2. [A] FCFE = FCF − $\overbrace{(1 - \tau_c) \times (\text{Interest payments})}^{\text{After-tax interest expense}}$ + (Net borrowing)

   $=\$1 \text{ million} - (1 - .40)[5 \times 0.05] = \$0.85 \text{ million}$

   [B] $E = \sum_{t=1}^{T} \dfrac{FCFE_t}{(1 + r_E)} = \dfrac{FCFE}{r_E} = \dfrac{\$0.85 \text{ million}}{0.17} = \$5 \text{ million}$

   So, the NPV is −\$5 million + 2(\$5 million) = \$5 million—the same as when using the WACC method.

3. $r_E = r_f + \beta(E[R_{Mkt}] - r_f) = 0.05 + 0.60(0.05) = 8\%$

   $V^L = APV = V^U + PV(\text{interest tax shield}) =$

   $= \dfrac{\$10 \text{ million}}{0.08 - 0.03} + \dfrac{\$50 \text{ million}(0.05)(0.40)}{0.08 - 0.03} = 200 + 20 = \$220 \text{ million}$

   E = 220 − 50 = \$170 million

4. [A]   Unlever the Gap beta:

   $\beta_U = [E / (E + D)]\beta_E + [D / (E + D)]\beta_D = [1 / (1 + .2)]1.1 + [.2 / (1 + .2)]0.10 = 0.933$

   Relever the beta to reflect the division's debt-equity ratio of 1.0.

   $\beta_E = \beta_U + [D / E](\beta_U - \beta_D) = 0.933 + 1(0.933 - 0.10) = 1.77$

   Calculate the levered cost of equity:

   $r_E = r_f + \beta(E[R_{Mkt}] - r_f) = 0.05 + 1.76(0.05) = 13.8\%$

   Calculate the WACC:

   $r_{wacc} = \dfrac{E}{E + D}r_E + \dfrac{D}{E + D}r_D(1 - \tau_c) = 0.50(0.138) + 0.50(0.06)(1 - 0.40) = 8.7\%$

   [B] $V_0^L = \sum_{t=1}^{T} \dfrac{FCF_t}{(1 + r_{wacc})} = \dfrac{FCF}{r_{wacc} - g} = \dfrac{\$100 \text{ million}}{0.087 - 0.03} = \$1.75 \text{ billion}$

   The WACC method values the firm as a whole, so the equity value is:

   $E = V^L - D = \$1.75 \text{ billion} - 0.50(\$1.75 \text{ billion}) = \$875 \text{ million}.$

   And the value per share is $\dfrac{\$875 \text{ million}}{100 \text{ million}} = \$8.75.$

5. [A] The loan will reduce debt elsewhere in the firm, so the appropriate debt-to-value ratio to use when evaluating the project is 50% of the project's value, not 100%.

So $r_{wacc} = \dfrac{E}{E + D} r_E + \dfrac{D}{E + D} r_D (1 - \tau_c) = 0.50(0.17) + 0.50(0.05)(1 - 0.40) = 10\%$

   [B] When a firm has a fixed debt schedule, the interest tax shields can be discounted using the debt cost of capital, r_D, since the amount of the debt will not fluctuate and thus the tax shield is less risky than the project.

$$\text{PV(Interest tax shield)} = \frac{\$5(0.05)(0.40)}{0.05} = \$2.0 \text{ million}$$

CHAPTER 19

Valuation and Financial Modeling: A Case Study

Chapter Synopsis

19.1 Valuation Using Comparables

A valuation using comparable publicly traded firm valuation multiples may be used as a preliminary way to estimate the value of a firm. However, this technique generally ignores important differences between firms, such as levels of operating efficiency and growth prospects.

19.2 The Business Plan

While comparable firm valuation multiples provide a useful starting point, the value of a firm or project depends on its future performance. Thus, it is necessary to study the firm or project's operations, investments, and capital structure, and to assess its potential for improvements and future growth.

19.3 Building the Financial Model

A financial model may be used to project the future cash flows from an investment. A **pro forma** income statement projects the firm's future income statements based on a set of assumptions.

The financial model should also consider future working capital needs and capital expenditures. Based on these estimates, future free cash flows as well as pro forma balance sheets and statements of cash flows can be forecast.

19.4 Estimating the Cost of Capital

To value an investment, the investment's risk needs to be assessed and an estimate of the appropriate cost of capital must be determined. One method for estimating the equity cost of capital is to use the CAPM. The unlevered beta can be used in the CAPM to estimate the unlevered cost of capital to use in the APV method. The firm or comparison firm's beta can be unlevered using:

$$\beta_U = [E / (E + D)]\beta_E + [D / (E + D)]\beta_D \approx [E / (E + D)]\beta_E.$$

For the WACC and FTE methods, the unlevered beta can be relevered to reflect the firm's capital structure as:

$$\beta_E = \beta_U + [D / E](\beta_U - \beta_D) \approx \beta_U[1 + (D / E)].$$

The levered beta can be used in the CAPM to determine the industry equity cost of capital, and then the firm's WACC can be determined.

19.5 Valuing the Investment

For a firm or project with an infinite life, free cash flows are generally forecast for several years until a constant rate of growth is expected to begin in year T. These FCFs are then discounted back to time zero individually as lump sums.

Next, the firm's continuation, or terminal, value at the end of the forecast horizon must be estimated. One common method of estimating the terminal value is to assume a constant expected growth rate, g, and a constant debt-equity ratio, to calculate the discounted cash flow value of the cash flows from time $T+1$ to infinity, valued at time T:

$$\text{Enterprise Value in Year } T = V_T^L = \frac{FCF_{T+1}}{r_{wacc} - g}$$

Another method of determining the terminal value is to use a valuation multiple based on comparable firms. It is informative to use both the discounted cash flow approach and the multiples approach when estimating a realistic terminal value estimate.

While the NPV method is the most reliable approach for evaluating an investment, practitioners often use cash multiples as an alternative valuation method. The cash multiple for an investment is the ratio of the total cash received to the total cash invested:

$$\text{Cash Multiple} = \frac{\text{Total Cash Received}}{\text{Total Cash Invested}}$$

The obvious weakness of the cash multiple approach is that it does not depend on the amount of time it takes to receive the cash, nor does it account for the risk of the investment. It is therefore useful only for comparing deals with similar time horizons and risk.

19.6 Sensitivity Analysis

Sensitivity analysis is useful for evaluating the uncertainty of estimates used in a valuation. By computing the value based on different variable estimates, the impact of this uncertainty on the value of the firm or project can be estimated.

Appendix: Compensating Management

Firms may use a management incentive plan to reward management for good performance. This may be in the form of an equity stake that would be vested over a period of years. Because the payment to the managers is an equity claim, to compute its present value we must use an equity cost of capital. To compute the equity cost of capital r_E, we use Eq. 18.20, which applies when the debt levels of the firm follow a known schedule:

$$r_E = r_U + \frac{D - T^s}{E}(r_U - r_D).$$

We then compute the cost of management's equity share by discounting at this rate:

$$\text{Cost of Management's Share}_t = \frac{\text{Cost of Management's Share}_{t-1}}{1 + r_E(t)}.$$

Once we have determined the cost of management's equity share, it can be deducted from the total value of the equity.

Selected Concepts and Key Terms

Pro Forma Forecasts

Projections of future income statements, balance sheets, or statements of cash flows for a firm or project based on a set of assumptions.

Cash Multiple, Multiple of Money, Absolute Return

The ratio of the total cash received to the total cash invested.

Unlevered P/E Ratio

A P/E ratio that is calculated by dividing continuing enterprise value by unlevered net income.

Concept Check Questions and Answers

19.1.1. What is the purpose of the valuation using comparables?

The purpose of the valuation using comparables is to estimate the value of a firm by comparing it to firms in a similar line of business.

19.1.2. If the valuation using comparables indicates the acquisition price is reasonable compared to other firms in the industry, does it establish that the acquisition is a good investment opportunity?

No, the valuation using comparables ignores important differences among firms such as operating efficiency and growth prospects. The valuation using comparables should be used as a preliminary way to estimate the value of a firm.

19.2.1. What are the different operational improvements KKP plans to make?

KKP plans to cut administrative costs immediately and redirect resources to new product development, sales, and marketing.

19.2.2. Why is it necessary to consider these improvements to assess whether the acquisition is attractive?

Whether the acquisition is attractive and is a successful investment for KKP depends on Ideko's post-acquisition performance. Thus, it is necessary to look in detail at Ideko's operation, investments, and capital structure, and to assess its potential for improvements and future growth.

19.3.1. What is a pro forma income statement?

A pro forma income statement is an income statement that is not based on actual data but, instead, depicts the firm's financials under a given set of hypothetical assumptions.

19.3.2. How do we calculate the firm's free cash flow, and the free cash flow to equity?

To compute free cash flow, we first adjust net income by adding back the after-tax interest payments associated with the net debt in its capital structure, adding back depreciation, and then deducting increases in net working capital and capital expenditures. To calculate the free cash flow to equity, we add net borrowing (increases to net debt) to the free cash flow of firm, and then deduct the after-tax interest expense.

19.4.1. What is a standard approach to estimate an equity beta?

The standard approach to estimating an equity beta is to determine the historical sensitivity of the stock's return to the market's returns by using linear regression to estimate the slope coefficient of the straight line.

19.4.2. How do we estimate a firm's unlevered cost of capital using data from comparable publicly traded firms?

To estimate a firm's unlevered cost of capital using data from comparable publicly traded firms, we first estimate the equity cost of capital for the comparable firms, and then estimate the unlevered cost of capital for each firm based on its capital structure. The unlevered costs of capital of the comparable firms are next used to estimate the unlevered cost of capital for the target firm.

19.5.1. What are the main methods of estimating the continuation value of the firm at the end of the forecast horizon?

The main methods of estimating the continuation value of the firm at the end of the forecast horizon are the multiples approach and the discounted cash flow valuation approach using the WACC method.

19.5.2. What are the potential pitfalls of analyzing a transaction like this one based on its IRR or cash multiple?

There are potential pitfalls with the IRR and cash multiple methods. First, there is no single cost of capital to compare to the IRR because the firm's leverage ratio changes over time, which will also change the risk of its equity. Besides, the cash multiple does not depend on the amount of time it takes to receive the cash, nor does it account for the risk of the investment. It is therefore useful only for comparing deals with similar time horizons and risks.

19.6.1. What is the purpose of the sensitivity analysis?

The purpose of using sensitivity analysis is to evaluate the uncertainty of estimates used for valuation, and the impact of this uncertainty on the value of the deal.

19.6.2. Table 19.20 shows the sensitivity analysis for KKP's investment in Ideko. Given this information, do you recommend the acquisition of Ideko?

Yes, we recommend the acquisition of Ideko. With an assumption of an exit EBITDA multiple of 9.1, KKP will have a good profit on its $53 million investment in Ideko, and the IRR of 33.3% is very high. Even with a very low exit multiple of 6.0, KKP will approximately break even on its investment in Ideko.

Examples with Step-by-Step Solutions

Solving Problems

All of the problems in this chapter relate to the Ideko case study discussed in the chapter, and generally involve applications that require the use of the Ideko spreadsheet.

Most problems involve varying the assumptions used in a discounted cash flow valuation using the APV and FTE methods, with five years of forecasted data and a growing perpetuity or EBITDA multiple terminal value. The problems generally require manipulating the original spreadsheet used in the chapter's case study by changing one or more of the variables to achieve some specific result. Problem 1 below provides an example of what this process is like. Problems may also involve using comparable valuation multiples to value a project or firm. Problem 2 below provides an example of calculating and using valuation multiples.

Examples

1. **In the valuation of Ideko, direct labor is estimated as $18 per unit in the base year and growing at 4% in 2006-2010. New information suggests that labor costs should be $22 per unit and grow at 5%. How does this affect the valuation using the WACC method?**

   Step 1. Determine what needs to be changed.

   The assumption affects the forecasted income statements, which affect the unlevered free cash flow calculations. Once these are updated with the new assumptions, the valuation can be revised.

   Step 2. Revise the pro forma income statements for 2006-2010.

   Changing the labor cost, changes the income statements as follows:

		2005	2006	2007	2008	2009	2010
INCOME STATEMENT ($000s)							
1	Sales	75,000	88,358	103,234	119,777	138,149	158,526
2	Cost of Goods Sold						
3	Raw Materials	(16,000)	(18,665)	(21,593)	(24,808)	(28,333)	(32,193)
4	Direct Labor Costs	(22,000)	(26,681)	(32,089)	(38,327)	(45,506)	(53,754)
5	**Gross Profit**	37,000	43,012	49,551	56,642	64,310	72,579
6	Sales & Marketing	(11,250)	(14,579)	(18,582)	(23,356)	(27,630)	(31,705)
7	Administration	(13,500)	(13,254)	(15,485)	(16,769)	(17,959)	(20,608)
8	**EBITDA**	12,250	15,180	15,484	16,517	18,721	20,266
9	Depreciation	(5,500)	(5,450)	(5,405)	(6,865)	(7,678)	(7,710)
10	**EBIT**	6,750	9,730	10,079	9,652	11,043	12,555
11	Interest Expense (net)	(75)	(6,800)	(6,800)	(6,800)	(7,820)	(8,160)
12	**Pretax Income**	6,675	2,930	3,279	2,852	3,223	4,395
13	Income Tax	(2,336)	(1,025)	(1,148)	(998)	(1,128)	(1,538)
14	**Net Income**	4,339	1,904	2,131	1,854	2,095	2,857

Step 3. Revise the forecasted free cash flow forecasts for 2006–2010.

Free cash flows are now:

	A	B	C	D	E	F	G	H	I
151				**2005**	**2006**	**2007**	**2008**	**2009**	**2010**
152	**Free Cash Flow ($000s)**								
153	1	**Net Income**		1,904	2,131	1,854	2,095	2,857
154	2	Plus: After-Tax Interest Expense		4,420	4,420	4,420	5,083	5,304
155	3	**Unlevered Net Income**		6,324	6,551	6,274	7,178	8,161
156	4	Plus: Depreciation		5,450	5,405	6,865	7,678	7,710
157	5	Less: Increases in NWC		3,325	(3,768)	(4,215)	(4,834)	(5,408)
158	6	Less: Capital Expenditures		(5,000)	(5,000)	(20,000)	(15,000)	(8,000)
159	7	**Free Cash Flow of Firm**		10,099	3,188	(11,076)	(4,978)	2,463

Step 4. Recalculate the terminal value in 2010.

Using a 9.1× EBITDA multiple, as was done in the base case in the text, results with:

	A	B	C	D	E	F	G
184	**Continuation Value: Multiples Approach ($000s)**						
185	1	EBITDA in 2010	20,266				
186	2	EBITDA multiple	9.1x				
187	3	**Terminal Enterprise Value**	**184,416**				
188	4	Debt	(120,000)				
189	5	**Terminal Equity Value**	**64,416**				

Step 5. Recalculate the enterprise value and equity value.

Discounting the free cash flows using the APV method results in:

	A	B	C	D	E	F	G	H	I
215				**2005**	**2006**	**2007**	**2008**	**2009**	**2010**
216	**APV Method ($ millions)**								
217	1	Free Cash Flow			10,099	3,188	(11,076)	(4,978)	2,463
218	2	**Unlevered Value V^u**		**116,131**	**117,645**	**126,222**	**149,920**	**169,890**	**184,416**
219	3	Interest Tax Shield			2,380	2,380	2,380	2,737	2,856
220	4	**Tax Shield Value T^s**		**10,428**	**8,757**	**6,972**	**5,067**	**2,674**	-
221	5	**APV: $V^L = V^u + T^s$**		**126,559**	**126,402**	**133,194**	**154,987**	**172,564**	**184,416**
222	6	Debt		(100,000)	(100,000)	(100,000)	(115,000)	(120,000)	(120,000)
223	7	**Equity Value**		**26,559**	**26,402**	**33,194**	**39,987**	**52,564**	**64,416**

Step 6. Summarize the result.

The change in labor cost has a large impact. The 2005 equity value falls from $113 million to $27 million. Now, given the $53 million cost to acquire Ideko's equity, the deal no longer looks attractive.

2. **Given the new forecasts in problem 1, recalculate the 2005 valuation multiples in order to determine the firm's value relative to the comparison firms.**

Step 1. Recalculate the 2005 valuation multiples.

Variable	2005 Value in Million
Sales	$75
EBITDA	$12.3
Net Income	$4.3
Enterprise Value	$126.6
Value of Equity	$26.6

Multiple	Variables	2005 Value
P/E	Value of Equity/Net Income	6.2
EV/Sales	Enterprise Value/Sales	1.7
EV/EBITDA	Enterprise Value/EBITDA	10.3

Step 2. Compare the multiples to the comparable firms.

Ideko Ratio	Luxottica (Proposed)	Sporting Goods Oakley, Inc.	Group	Nike, Inc.	Industry
P/E	6.2	24.83	28.03	18.23	20.33
EV/Sales	1.7	2.03	2.73	1.53	1.43
EV/EBITDA	10.3	11.63	14.43	9.33	11.43

Step 3. Make conclusions.

Now, Ideko's P/E ratio is much lower than the industry. The revised labor estimate drops the P/E down from 21.6 in the original valuation and makes Ideko's equity appear to be relatively undervalued.

The EV/Sales multiple falls from 2.0 to 1.7 and is now closer to Nike and the industry.

The EV/EBITDA multiple rises from 9.1 to 10.3. This is due to the fact that the level of profitability falls at a greater rate than enterprise value. The firm now has a lower relative valuation than the comparable firms, other than Nike and the industry at large.

CHAPTER 20

Financial Options

Chapter Synopsis

20.1 Option Basics

A **financial option** gives its owner the right, but not the obligation, to buy or sell a financial asset at a fixed price on or until a specified future date.

■ A **call option** gives the owner the right to buy an asset.

■ A **put option** gives the owner the right to sell the asset.

When a holder of an option enforces the agreement and buys or sells the asset at the agreed-upon price, the holder is said to be **exercising an option.** The option buyer, or holder, holds the right to exercise the option and has a long position in the contract. The option seller, or writer, sells (or writes) the option and has a short position in the contract. The **exercise,** or **strike,** price is the price the contract allows the owner to buy or sell the asset.

The most commonly traded options are written on stocks; however, options on other financial assets also exist, such as options on stock indices like the S&P 500. Using an option to reduce risk is called **hedging.** Options can also be used to **speculate,** or bet on the future price of an asset.

American options allow their holders to exercise the option on any date up to and including a final date called the expiration date. **European options** allow their holders to exercise the option only on the **expiration date.** Although most traded options are American, European options trade in a few circumstances. For example, European options written on the S&P 500 index exist.

A call options with a strike price below the current stock price is **in-the money,** as is a put option with a strike price above the current stock price. Call options with strike prices above the current stock price are **out-of-the money,** as are put options with strike prices below the current stock price.

20.2 Option Payoffs at Expiration

The value of a call (C) and a put (P) at expiration are:

$$C = \max(S - K, 0) \text{ and } P = \max(K - S, 0)$$

where S is the stock price at expiration, K is the exercise price, and max is the maximum of the two quantities in the parentheses.

The writer of a put or call has cash flows that are the opposite of the buyer's cash flows. Because an investor who is long an option will not exercise an option that is out-of-the-money, an option writer can only have a negative payoff once the option is written.

Investors may combine options in a portfolio to undertake various strategies. For example, a **straddle** involves buying a put and a call at the same exercise price, and can be used by investors who expect the stock to be very volatile and move up or down a large amount, but who do not necessarily have a view on which direction the stock will move. Conversely, investors who expect the stock to end up near the strike price may choose to sell a straddle.

Another strategy, called **portfolio insurance,** involves using options to ensure that a stock or portfolio does not fall below a certain level.

- If you want to ensure that the value of a stock does not fall below $50, you could buy a **protective put** with a $50 strike price. If the stock is above $50, you keep the stock, but if it is below $50, you can exercise your put and sell the stock for $50.

- Instead of holding a share of stock and a put, you could get the same payoff by purchasing a risk-free zero coupon bond with a face value of $50 and a European call option with a strike price of $50. In this case, if the stock is below $50, you receive the payoff from the bond; if the stock is above $50, you can exercise the call and use the payoff from the bond to buy the stock for the strike price of $50.

The idea that you can accomplish this same objective two ways is the basis for put-call parity, which is discussed next.

20.3 Put-Call Parity

Consider the two different ways to construct portfolio insurance:

1. Purchase the stock and a put.

2. Purchase a bond and a call.

Because both positions provide exactly the same payoff, the Law of One Price requires that they must have the same price. The relation of the price of a European call option in terms of the price of a European put, the underlying stock, and a zero-coupon bond is known as:

Put-Call Parity

$$C = P + S - PV(K) - PV(Div)$$

where $PV(Div)$ is the present value of the stock's future dividends. It says that the price of a European call equals the price of the stock plus an otherwise identical put minus the price of a bond that matures on the exercise date of the option. In other words, you can think of a call as a combination of a levered position in the stock, $S - PV(K)$, plus insurance against a drop in the stock price offered by the put.

20.4 Factors Affecting Options Prices

The **intrinsic value** of an option is the value it would have if it expired immediately. Options can have values above this value in relation to several boundaries:

- If an American option is worth less than its intrinsic value, arbitrage profits could be made by purchasing the option and immediately exercising it. Thus, an American option cannot be worth less than its intrinsic value, and it cannot be worth less than a European option since it can be exercised at any time.

- A put option cannot be worth more than its strike price because the maximum payoff for a put option occurs if the stock becomes worthless.

- A call option cannot be worth more than the stock itself.

The **time value** of an option is the difference between the current option price and its intrinsic value.

- For American options, the longer the time to the exercise date, the more valuable the option because of the greater likelihood of very high or very low returns for the stock.

- The value of an option also generally increases with the volatility of the stock because of the greater likelihood of very high or very low returns for the stock.

20.5 Exercising Options Early

The price of a call option on a non-dividend-paying stock always exceeds its intrinsic value. Thus, it is never optimal to exercise a call option on a non-dividend-paying stock early—you are always better off just selling the option. Since the right to exercise the call early is worthless, an American call on a non-dividend-paying stock has the same price as a European call.

The right to exercise an option on dividend-paying stocks early is generally valuable for both calls and puts. Since the price of the stock drops to reflect dividends paid, the value of a call option falls at this time. However, unlike the owner of the stock, the option holder does not get the dividend. Thus, by exercising early and holding the stock, the owner of the call option can capture the dividend. Because a call should only be exercised early to capture the dividend, it will only be optimal to do so just before the stock's ex-dividend date.

20.6 Options and Corporate Finance

If the firm's value is below the value of its debt outstanding, the firm must declare bankruptcy, and the equity holders receive nothing. If the firm's value exceeds the value of the debt, the equity holders get whatever is left once the debt has been repaid. Thus, a share of stock can be thought of as a call option on the assets of a firm with a strike price equal to the value of debt.

Similarly, debt can be thought of as owning the firm and having sold a call option with a strike price equal to the required debt payment. If the value of the firm exceeds the required debt payment, the call will be exercised and the debt holders will receive the required debt payment and give up the firm. If the value of the firm does not exceed the required debt payment, the call will be worthless, the firm will declare bankruptcy, and the debt holders will be entitled to the firm's assets.

Selected Concepts and Key Terms

American Options

Options that allow their holders to exercise the option on any date up to and including a final date called the expiration date.

At-the-Money Options

Call or put options with strike prices equal to the current stock price.

Call Option

A contract that gives the owner the right (but not the obligation) to buy an asset.

Credit Default Swap (CDS)

In a credit default swap, the buyer pays a premium to the seller (often in the form of periodic payments) and receives a payment from the seller to make up for the loss if the underlying bond defaults. Investment banks developed and began trading CDSs in the late 1990s as a means to allow bond investors to insure the credit risk of the bonds in their portfolios. Many hedge funds and other investors soon began using these contracts as a means to speculate on the prospects of the firm and its likelihood of default even if they did not hold its bonds.

European Options

Options that allow their holders to exercise the option only on the expiration date. Although most traded options are American, European options trade in a few circumstances.

Exercising an Option

When a holder of an option enforces the agreement and buys or sells the share of stock at the agreed-upon price.

Expiration Date

The final date an option can be exercised.

Financial Option

A contract that gives its owner the right, but not the obligation, to purchase or sell a financial asset at a fixed price at some future date.

Hedging with Options

Using an option to reduce risk.

In-the-Money Options

Call options with strike prices above the current stock price, and put options with strike prices below the current stock price.

Intrinsic Value of an Option

The value an option would have if it expired immediately.

Open Interest

The total number of contracts written on an option contract.

Open Premium

The market price of an option.

Option Writer

The investor who sells (or writes) the option and has a short position in the contract.

Out-of-the-Money Options

Call options with strike prices below the current stock price, and put options with strike prices above the current stock price.

Portfolio Insurance, Protective Put

Holding a stock (or stock index) and a put option on the same stock (or stock index). In addition to buying such a protective put, the same effect can be achieved by purchasing a bond and a call option.

Put Option

A contract that gives the owner the right, but not the obligation, to sell an asset.

Put-Call Parity

The relation of the price of a European call option in terms of the price of a European put, the underlying stock, and a zero-coupon bond: $C = P + S - PV(K) - PV(Div)$.

Straddle

A strategy that involves buying a put and a call at the same exercise price. It can be used by investors who expect the stock to be very volatile and move up or down a large amount, but who do not necessarily have a view on which direction the stock will move.

Strike (Exercise) Price

The price the contract allows the owner to buy or sell the asset thus exercising the option.

Time Value of an Option

The difference between the current option price and its intrinsic value.

Concept Check Questions and Answers

20.1.1. What is the difference between an American option and a European option?

An American option allows the holder to exercise on any date up to and including the expiration data, while a European option allows the holder to exercise only on the expiration date.

20.1.2. Does the holder of an option have to exercise it?

No, a holder of an option will exercise only when it is beneficial to the holder. If the option is out-of-the-money on the expiration date, the holder will not exercise the option.

20.1.3. Why does an investor who writes (shorts) an option have an obligation?

Because the writer of the option has the obligation to fulfill the contract and will have to buy or sell the stock to the buyer of the option in the event that it is exercised.

20.2.1. What is a straddle?

A straddle is a combination consisting of a call and a put with the same strike price and the same expiration date.

20.2.2. Explain how you can use put options to create portfolio insurance. How can you create portfolio insurance using call options?

You can create portfolio insurance by purchasing put options on a portfolio of stocks. Or you can achieve exactly the same effect by purchasing a bond and a call option.

20.3.1. Explain put-call parity.

Put-call parity relates the value of a call to the value of the stock, the bond, and the put with the same strike price and the same maturity date. It says that the price of a European call equals the price of the stock plus an otherwise identical put minus the price of a bond that matures on the exercise date of the option.

20.3.2. If a put option trades at a higher price from the value indicated by the put-call parity equation, what action should you take?

If a put trades at a higher price from the value indicated by the put-call parity, you can arbitrage by selling the overvalued put and stock and simultaneously buying the call option. You are guaranteed to make a profit while taking no risk.

20.4.1. What is the intrinsic value of an option?

The intrinsic value is the immediate exercise value. The intrinsic value of a call is the current stock price minus the strike price, while the intrinsic value of a put is the strike price minus the current stock price.

20.4.2. Can a European option with a later exercise date be worth less than an identical European option with an earlier exercise date?

Yes, a European option with a later exercise date can trade for less than an identical European option with an earlier exercise date. For example, suppose the stock price of XYZ goes to zero due to a bankruptcy. The one-month European put is worth more than the one-year European put because you can exercise and get your money sooner.

20.4.3. How does the volatility of a stock affect the value of puts and calls written on the stock?

The value of both put and call options increases with volatility of the underlying stock price.

20.5.1. Is it ever optimal to exercise an American call on a non-dividend paying stock early?

No, you should not exercise an American call on a non-dividend paying stock early. You are better off selling the call rather than exercising it.

20.5.2. When may it be optimal to exercise an American put option early?

It can be optimal to exercise a deep-in-the-money American put option.

20.5.3. When might it be optimal to exercise an American call early?

For the deep-in-the-money calls, when the present value of the dividends is larger than the interest earned.

20.6.1. Explain how equity can be viewed as a call option on the firm.

A share of stock can be thought of as a call option on the assets of the firm with strike price equal to the value of debt outstanding.

20.6.2. Explain how debt can be viewed as an option portfolio.

The debt holders can be viewed as owning the firm and having sold a call option with strike price equal to the required debt payment. If the value of the firm exceeds the required debt payment, the call will be exercised so the debt holders receive the strike price and give up the firm. If the cash flow of the firm does not exceed the required debt payment, the call is worthless, the firm declares bankruptcy, and the debt holders are entitled to the firm's assets.

Examples with Step-by-Step Solutions

Solving Problems

Problems in this chapter may involve constructing basic option intrinsic value payoff diagrams like in problem 1 below. Other problems require understanding put-call parity, like in example 2 below. You should also be familiar with factors affecting option values and basic option pricing boundaries. Finally, problems may involve understanding how corporate equity and debt securities can be viewed as a portfolio of securities including options as in example 3 below.

Examples

1. Microsoft is currently trading for $27. There are traded put and call options with a strike price of $25, and you are considering different trading strategies.
   - [A] If you buy a call option with a $25 exercise price, what is the intrinsic value payoff diagram? Is the option in the money? What is the intrinsic value of a contract for 100 options?
   - [B] If you buy a put option with a $25 exercise price, what is the intrinsic value payoff diagram? Is the option in the money? What is the intrinsic value of a contract for 100 options?
   - [C] If you buy a straddle by buying a call option and a put option with a $25 exercise price, what is the intrinsic value payoff diagram? Is the strategy in the money? What is the intrinsic value of a contract for 100 options?

Step 1. Determine the payoff diagram of the call option.

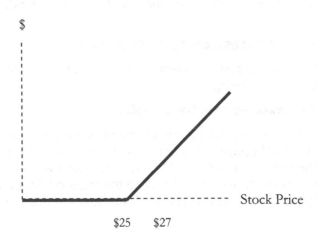

The call option is in the money since the strike price is below the stock price.

The contract has an intrinsic value of 100($27 – $25) = $200.

Step 2. Determine the payoff diagram of the put option.

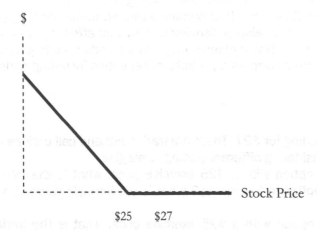

The put option is out of the money since the strike price is below the stock price.

The contract has an intrinsic value of 100($0) = $0.

Step 3. Determine the payoff diagram of the straddle.

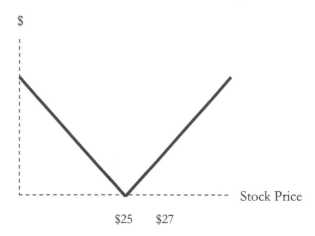

The straddle is always in the money, unless the stock price is $25.

The contract has an intrinsic value of 100($27 − $25) + 100($0)= $200.

2. **Your investment bank often deals with CEOs who want to hedge their stock options in the firm where they work. One of your clients, the CEO of a non-dividend-paying public company that has no publicly traded put options, wants to purchase a one-year European put option on his firm's stock with a strike price of $100. Another dealer is willing to write a one-year European call option on the stock with a strike price of $100 and sell you the call option for $12 per share. The stock is trading for $109 per share, and the one-year risk-free interest rate is 3.09%. What price should you offer to sell the put option?**

Step 1. Determine how to go about pricing the put option.

Since you can replicate the payoff of the put option, you can determine the cost to replicate the option using put-call parity.

Step 2. Use put-call parity and determine the strategy you must use to replicate the put option payoff.

Using put-call parity,

$$C = P + S - PV(K) - PV(Div),$$

you can replicate the payoff of the one-year put option with a strike price of $100 as:

$$C = P + S - PV(K) - 0 \implies P = C - S + PV(K).$$

So you must buy a call with a strike price of $100, short sell the stock, and buy a one-year zero-coupon bond with a face value of $100.

Step 3. Verify that the final payoff of the portfolio of the three securities matches the payoff of a call option.

With this combination, you have the following final payoff depending on the stock price in one year:

	Stock Price in One Year (P)	
	Above $100	Below $100
Long the Call Option	P – $100	0
Short the Stock	– P	– P
Long the Bond	$100	$100
Portfolio	$0	$100 – P
Sell Put Option	$0	–($100 – P)
Total Payoff	$0	$0

Therefore, you can sell the put option and have a future payoff of zero no matter what happens.

Step 4. Use put-call parity and solve for the price of the put such that you break even.

$$P = C - S + PV(K) = -\$12 + \$110 - \frac{\$100}{1.0309} = \$1.00$$

Thus, as long as you sell the put for more than $1.00, you will make a profit.

3. **Using diagrams, explain and demonstrate how corporate securities can be viewed as the following options:**
   [A]   Equity can be viewed as a call option on a firm.
   [B]   Debt can be viewed in terms of a call option on a firm.
   [C]   Debt can be viewed in terms of a put option on the firm.

Step 1. Diagram how equity can be viewed as a call option on a firm.

On the maturity date of the debt, if the value of the firm is larger than the value of the debt, D, investors will pay back the debt and keep the difference for themselves. If the value of the firm is lower than the value of the debt, investors will be forced to handover the assets to lenders, and end up with a zero payoff.

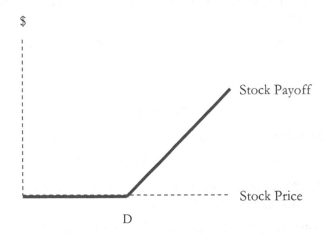

Step 2. Diagram how debt can be viewed in terms of a call option on a firm.

Debt holders can be viewed as being long on the assets of the firm and short on a call option with a strike price equal to the value of the debt, D.

If the value of the firm exceeds the required debt payment, the call will be exercised; the debt holders will therefore receive the strike price (the required debt payment) and give up the firm. If the value of the firm does not exceed the required debt payment, the call will be worthless, the firm will declare bankruptcy, and the debt holders will be entitled to the firm's assets.

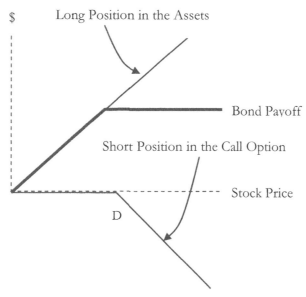

Step 3. Diagram how debt can be viewed in terms of a put option.

Debt can be viewed as a combination of being short a put option with a strike price equal to the value of debt, *D*, and long a risk-free bond with a face value equal to the value of the debt.

When the firm's assets are worth less than the required debt payment, the put is in-the-money; the owner of the put option will therefore exercise the option and receive the difference between the required debt payment and the firm's asset value. This leaves the portfolio holder (debt holder) with just the assets of the firm. If the firm's value is greater than the required debt payment, the put is worthless, leaving the portfolio holder with the required debt payment.

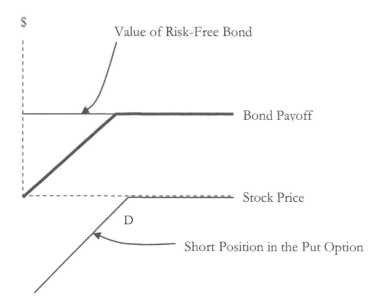

Questions and Problems

1. You own a 1,000 call options on Apple stock with a strike price of $70 that expire in exactly one month.
   [A]   If the stock is trading at $95 in one month, what is the payoff of the options?
   [B]   If the stock is trading at $50 in one month, what is the payoff of the options?
   [C]   Draw a payoff diagram showing the value of one call option at expiration as a function of the stock price at expiration.

2. You are undertaking a so-called strangle strategy and are long both a call and a put on the same stock with the same exercise date. The exercise price of the call is $15 and the exercise price of the put is $10.
   [A]   Plot the intrinsic value of this combination as a function of the stock price on the exercise date.
   [B]   What is the strategy's maximum loss?

3. Intel stock is currently trading for $20 per share. A one-year European put option on Intel with a strike price of $15 is currently trading for $0.50. If the one-year risk-free interest rate is 5%, what is the value of a one-year European call option on Intel with a strike price of $15? (Intel pays no dividends.)

4. General Electric (GE) stock is currently trading for $50 per share. A one-year European call option with a strike price of $55 is currently trading for $8.00. GE is expected to pay dividends of $2.00 this year. If the one-year risk-free interest rate is 5%, what is the value of a one-year European put option on GE with a strike price of $55?

5. Suppose you want to insure against the possibility that the price of Apple stock will drop below $75. Describe how you can accomplish this objective using:
   [A]   put options, and
   [B]   a bond and a call option.

Solutions to Questions and Problems

1. [A]   1,000(95 − 70) = $5,000
   [B]   1,000(0) = $0
   [C]

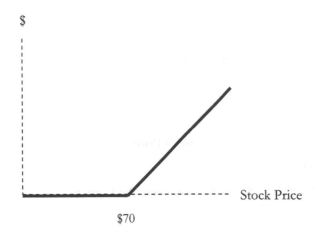

2. [A]

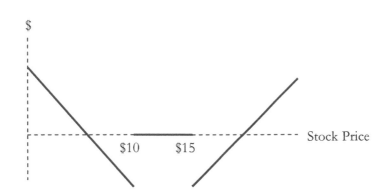

[B] The maximum loss is $0 based on the intrinsic values.

3. Using put-call parity:

$$C = P + S - PV(K) = \$0.50 + \$20 - \frac{\$15}{1.05} = \$6.21$$

4. Using put-call parity, and assuming that dividend is paid in one year and that the risk-free rate is the correct rate to use to find the present value of the dividend:

$$C = P + S - PV(K) - PV(Div) \Rightarrow P = C - S + PV(K) + PV(Div)$$

$$= \$8.00 - \$55 + \frac{\$55}{1.05} + \frac{\$2.00}{1.05} = \$7.29$$

5. [A]   You can purchase a European put option with a strike price of $75. If Apple is above $75, you keep the stock, but if it is below $75, you exercise your put and sell it for $75. Thus, you get the upside, but are insured against a drop in the price.

   [B]   Instead of holding a share of Apple stock and a put, you could get the same payoff by purchasing a risk-free zero coupon bond with a face value of $75 and a European call option with a strike price of $75. In this case, if Apple is below $75, you receive the payoff from the bond. If Apple is above $75, you can exercise the call and use the payoff from the bond to buy the stock for the strike price of $75.

CHAPTER 21

Option Valuation

Chapter Synopsis

21.1 The Binomial Option Pricing Model

The **Binomial Option Pricing Model** makes the simplifying assumption that at the end of each period, the stock price has only two possible values.

Using this assumption, the value of a single-period option can be determined by calculating the cost to construct a **replicating portfolio**, which is a portfolio of other securities that has exactly the same value in one period as the option. Since the option and the portfolio have the same payoffs, the Law of One Price implies that the current value of the call and the replicating portfolio must be equal.

For example, consider a European call option that expires in one period with an exercise price of $50 (today's price) in which the price will increase or decrease by $10. The option payoff can be summarized on a **binomial tree**—a timeline with two branches at every date representing the possible events that could happen at those times:

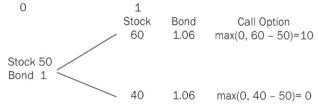

	0	1		
		Stock	Bond	Call Option
		60	1.06	max(0, 60 – 50)=10
Stock 50				
Bond 1				
		40	1.06	max(0, 40 – 50)= 0

To create a replicating portfolio using a stock and a bond, the value of the portfolio must match the value of the option in each state. Thus, the value of the portfolio must be $10 in the up state and $0 in the down state. Assuming the risk-free rate is 6%, the replicating portfolio must satisfy:

$$60\Delta + 1.06B = 10, \text{ and}$$

$$40\Delta + 1.06B = 0.$$

where Δ is the number of shares of stock purchased, and B is the initial investment in the bond. Solving these two simultaneous equations results in $\Delta = 0.50$ and $B = -18.87$. Thus, the value of the portfolio today is $6.13—the cost of 0.5 shares less the amount borrowed: $0.5 \times \$50 - 18.87 = \$25 - \$18.87$.

In general, the value of a call using the binomial model is:

$$C = S\Delta + B$$

where

$$\Delta = \frac{C_u - C_d}{S_u - S_d} \text{ and } B = \frac{C_d - S_d\Delta}{1 + r_f}.$$

in which S is the current stock price, S_u is the stock price in the up state, S_d is the stock price in the down state, C_u is the option value in the up state, and C_d is the option value in the down state. The term Δ can be interpreted as the sensitivity of the option's value to changes in the stock price.

Extending the binomial model to more than one period requires forecasting an S_u and an S_d at each binomial tree node. The example above can be extended to two periods as follows:

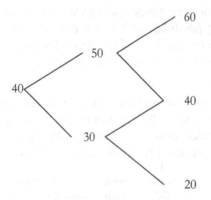

Starting at the end of the tree and working backwards, an option value can be calculated at each node by using the general option valuation model.

■ At time 2, the option expires, so its value is $10 if the stock price goes up to $60, and zero otherwise.

■ If the stock price has gone up to $50 at time 1, C = $6.13 as shown above.

■ If the stock price has gone down to $30, the option is worthless.

Thus, at time 0, $C_u = \$6.13$ and $C_d = \$0$, so the initial value of the call at time 0 is:

$$C = S\Delta + B = 40(0.3065) - 8.67 = \$3.59 \,.$$

because

$$\Delta = \frac{C_u - C_d}{S_u - S_d} = \frac{6.13 - 0}{50 - 30} = 0.3065, \text{ and } B = \frac{C_d - S_d \Delta}{1 + r_f} = \frac{0 - 30(0.3065)}{1.06} = -8.67$$

The replicating portfolio must be adjusted at the end of each period by making the necessary portfolio adjustments. Such a **dynamic trading strategy** requires no net investment, and it ensures that the value of the portfolio is $10 if the stock goes up to $60, and is zero otherwise, at time 2.

By decreasing the length of each period, and increasing the number of periods in the binomial tree, a realistic model for the stock price can be developed. However, for European call and put options, as the length of each period shrinks to zero, and the number of periods per year grows to infinity; the results of the binomial option pricing model can be calculated using a single, simple formula: The Black-Scholes formula, which is considered next.

21.2 The Black-Scholes Option Pricing Model

The Black-Scholes price of a call option on a non-dividend-paying stock is:

$$C = S\Delta + B = S \times N(d_1) - PV(K) \times N(d_2).$$

where $N(d)$ is the cumulative normal distribution evaluated at d (the probability that a normally distributed variable is less than d) and:

$$d_1 = \frac{\ln[S/PV(K)]}{\sigma\sqrt{T}} + \frac{\sigma\sqrt{T}}{2} \text{ and } d_2 = d_1 - \sigma\sqrt{T}.$$

$PV(K)$ is the present value of a risk-free zero-coupon bond that pays K on the expiration date of the option. Since an American call option on a non-dividend-paying stock always has the same price as a European option, the Black-Scholes formula can be used to price American or European call options on non-dividend-paying stocks.

To use the model, only five parameters are needed: the stock price, the strike price, the exercise date, the risk-free interest rate, and the standard deviation (volatility) of the stock. Everything except the stock's volatility can be observed. Importantly, the stock's expected return is not needed; because a stock's volatility is much easier to measure (and forecast) than its expected return, the Black-Scholes formula is generally very precise.

Using put-call parity, the Black-Scholes price of a put option on a non-dividend-paying stock is:

$$P = C = P + S - PV(K) \Rightarrow P = \overbrace{S \times N(d_1) - PV(K) \times N(d_2)}^{C} - S + PV(K)$$

$$= PV(K)[1 - N(d_2)] - S[1 - N(d_1)].$$

The holder of a European call option does not receive any dividends, but the stock price tends to drop by the amount of the dividend when the stock goes ex-dividend. Thus, the final stock price must be lowered by the present value of any dividends paid prior to the expiration date. The Black-Scholes formula can be modified for European options on dividend-paying stocks by replacing S with S* = S – PV(Div). Often the stock is assumed to pay a dividend that is proportional to its stock price, with q equal to the stock's (compounded) dividend yield until the expiration date, such that S* = S/(1 + q).

The volatility of the stock can be estimated using: (1) the stock's historical standard deviation, or (2) the **implied volatility** of the stock. The implied volatility can be found by observing the market price of an option and, after using the other four required variables, solving for volatility in the Black-Scholes formula.

The call **option delta** (Δ) is $N(d_1)$; it is the change in the price of an option given a $1 change in the price of the stock. Because Δ is always between 0 and 1, the change in the call price is always less than the change in the stock price. The put option delta is $-[1 - N(d_1)]$. Since Δ always between 0 and 1, B is always between 0 and K. Thus, put options on a positive beta stock will have a negative beta.

21.3 Risk-Neutral Probabilities

Risk-neutral probabilities are the probabilities that equate the expected value of the payoffs of an asset discounted by the risk-free rate to the asset's price today. These probabilities can be used to price any other asset for which the payoffs in each state are known.

In a binomial tree, the risk-neutral probability that the stock price will increase is given by:

$$\rho = \frac{(1+r_f)S - S_d}{S_u - S_d}$$

In the equation, ρ is not the actual probability of the stock price increasing. Instead, it represents how the actual probability would have to be adjusted to keep the stock price the same in a risk-neutral world. For this reason, ρ and $(1-\rho)$ are referred as risk-neutral probabilities. They are also known as **state-contingent prices**, **state prices**, or **martingale prices**.

A **derivative security** is a security whose payoff depends solely on the prices of other marketed assets. Values of derivative securities can be obtained by discounting the expected cash flows computed using the risk-neutral probabilities at the risk-free rate.

The risk-neutral pricing method is the basis for a common technique for pricing derivative assets called **Monte Carlo simulation**. In this method, the expected payoff of the derivative security is estimated by calculating its average payoff after simulating many random paths for the underlying stock price. In the randomization, the risk-neutral probabilities are used, and so the average payoff can be discounted at the risk-free rate, to estimate the derivative security's value.

21.4 Risk and Return of an Option

To measure the risk of an option, its beta can be computed. The beta of an option can also be calculated as the beta of an option-replicating portfolio.

Since the beta of a portfolio is the weighted average beta of the securities that make up the portfolio:

$$\beta_{option} = \frac{S\Delta}{S\Delta + B}\beta_S + \frac{B}{S\Delta + B}\beta_B = \frac{S\Delta}{S\Delta + B}\beta_S$$

since the replicating portfolio consists of $S \times \Delta$ dollars invested in the stock, B dollars invested in the bond, and the risk-free bond's beta is zero.

For a call option, Δ is greater than zero and B is less than zero. Thus, for stocks with positive betas, calls will have larger betas than the underlying stock, while puts will have negative betas.

21.5 Corporate Applications

To derive an expression for the beta of equity when the beta of debt is not zero, the idea that equity can be viewed as a call option on the firm's assets can be used. If you let A be the value of the firm's assets, E be the value of equity, and D be the value of debt, then because equity is a call option on the assets of the firm, $E = S\Delta + B$ where $A = E + D = S$. Substituting these expressions into the beta of the option equation above yields an expression for the beta of equity that does not assume the beta of debt is zero:

$$\beta_E = \Delta \frac{A}{E} \beta_U = \Delta \left(1 + \frac{D}{E} \right) \beta_U .$$

When the debt is riskless, the firm's equity is always in-the-money and $\Delta = 1$.

When the beta of debt is nonzero, the Black-Scholes formula can be used to unlever the equity beta of the firm and find the beta of debt. Debt, D, is equal to a portfolio consisting of a long position in the assets of the firm and a short position in its equity. The beta of debt is the beta of this portfolio is:

$$\beta_D = \frac{A}{D} \beta_U - \frac{E}{D} \beta_E = (1 - \Delta) \frac{A}{D} \beta_U = (1 - \Delta) \left(1 + \frac{E}{D} \right) \beta_U .$$

Selected Concepts and Key Terms

Binomial Option Pricing Model

A technique for pricing options that was derived by John Cox, Stephen Ross, and Mark Rubinstein in: "Option Pricing, A Simplified Approach," *Journal of Financial Economics* 7(3) (1979): 229–263. The model makes the simplifying assumption that at the end of the next period, the stock price has only two possible values. The value of a single-period option can be determining the cost to construct a replicating portfolio—a portfolio of other securities that has exactly the same value in one period as the option. Since they have the same payoffs, the Law of One Price implies that the current value of the call and the replicating portfolio must be equal.

Binomial Tree

A timeline with two branches at every date representing the possible events that could happen at those times.

Black-Scholes Option Pricing Model

A technique for pricing options that was derived by Fischer Black and Myron Scholes in: "The Pricing of Options and Corporate Liabilities," *Journal of Political Economy,* 81, 1973. To use the model, only five parameters are needed: the stock price, the strike price, the exercise date, the risk-free interest rate, and the standard deviation (volatility) of the stock. Everything except the stock's volatility can be observed. Importantly, the stock's expected return is not needed; because a stock's volatility is much easier to measure (and forecast) than its expected return, the Black-Scholes formula can be very precise.

Cumulative Normal Distribution

The probability of how likely the value of a normally distributed random variable will occur.

Derivative Security

A security whose payoff depends solely on the prices of other assets.

Dynamic Trading Strategy

A strategy that forms a replicating portfolio every period to ensure that the value of the portfolio is the same as the option at the expiration date.

Implied Volatility

The standard deviation found by observing the market price of an option and, after using the other required variables, solving for volatility in the Black-Scholes formula.

Leverage Ratio

The ratio of the amount invested in the stock position in the replicating portfolio to the value of the replicating portfolio, $S\Delta / (S\Delta + B)$.

Replicating Portfolio

A portfolio of other securities that has exactly the same value in one period as the option. Risk-Neutral Probabilities, Martingale Prices, State Prices, State-Contingent Prices Probabilities that equate the expected value of the payoffs of an asset discounted by the risk-free rate to the asset's price today. These probabilities can be used to price any other asset for which the payoffs in each state are known.

Concept Check Questions and Answers

21.1.1. What is the key assumption of the binomial option pricing model?

That at the end of the each period the stock price has only two possible values.

21.1.2. Why don't we need to know the probabilities of the states in the binominal tree in order to solve for the price of the option?

Because the probability of future states depends on investors' beliefs and is difficult to estimate, we do not need to know the probabilities of the states in the binominal tree to solve for the price of the option.

21.1.3. What is a replicating portfolio?

A replicating portfolio is a portfolio of other securities that has exactly the same value in one period as the option. By the Law of One price, the value of the option today must equal the value of the replicating portfolio.

21.2.1. What are the inputs of the Black-Scholes option pricing formula?

The inputs of the Black-Scholes option pricing formula are the stock price, the strike price, the exercise date, the risk-free rate, and the volatility of the stock.

21.2.2. What is the implied volatility of a stock?

It is the standard deviation that makes the Black-Scholes option pricing formula value equal to the market value of an option based on a given stock price, strike price, exercise date, and risk-free rate.

21.2.3. How does the delta of a call option change as the stock price increases?

It increases.

21.3.1. What are risk-neutral probabilities? How can they be used to value options?

Risk-neutral probabilities are the probabilities that equate the expected value of the payoffs of an asset discounted by the risk-free rate, to the asset's price today. These probabilities can then be used to price any other asset for which the payoffs in each state are known.

21.3.2. Does the binominal model or Black-Scholes model assume that investors are risk neutral?

No, the binominal model and Black-Scholes model do not assume that investors are risk neutral. These models work for any set of investor preferences, including risk-neutral investors.

21.4.1. Is the beta of a call greater or smaller than the beta of the underlying stock?

The beta of a call always exceeds the beta of the underlying stock if the stock has positive beta.

21.4.2. What is the leverage ratio of a call?

The leverage ratio is the ratio of the amount of money in the stock position in the replicating portfolio over the value of the replicating portfolio. The leverage ratio of a call is always greater than one, but out-of-the-money calls have higher leverage ratios than in-the-money calls.

21.5.1. How can we estimate the beta of debt?

Since debt is equal to a portfolio consisting of a long position in the assets of the firm and the short position in its equity, we can estimate beta of debt as the weighted average beta of the assets and the equity in this portfolio.

21.5.2. The fact that equity is a call option on the firm's assets leads to what agency costs?

It may lead to an asset substitution problem because the value of the equity call option increases with the firm's volatility. Thus, equity holders may have an incentive to take excessive risk. Also, since equity holders gain less than $1 for each $1 increase in the value of the firm's assets, they may have reduced incentive to invest, causing an underinvestment problem.

Examples with Step-by-Step Solutions

Solving Problems

Problems using the ideas in this chapter most importantly involve valuing options using either the binomial model or the Black-Scholes model. The first 2 problems below provide examples. Problems may require using risk-neutral probabilities to value options using the binomial model as demonstrated in problem 3 below.

You may also be required to calculate the beta and leverage ratio of a put or call option. Finally, a problem may require the calculation of the beta of risky debt. The Questions and Problems section below provides examples of these applications of option pricing methodology.

Examples

1. **Microsoft is trading for $30 today. In each of the next two years, you believe that the price can either go up by $3 or down by $2. Assume that the risk-free rate is 5% and that Microsoft pays no dividends.**
   [A]   What is the value of a two-year European call option with a $30 strike price?
   [B]   What is the value of a two-year European put option with a $30 strike price?

   Step 1. Determine which model to use.

   Since the up and down movements can be determined each period, the binomial model can be used.

   Step 2. Draw the call's payoff diagram.

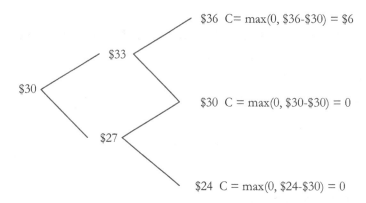

$36 C= max(0, $36-$30) = $6

$33

$30 C = max(0, $30-$30) = 0

$30

$27

$24 C = max(0, $24-$30) = 0

   Step 3. Determine the value of the call after the first period in the up state using the binomial model.

   $C = S\Delta + B$, where:

   $$\Delta = \frac{C_u - C_d}{S_u - S_d} = \frac{6-0}{36-30} = 1 \text{ and } B = \frac{C_d - S_d\Delta}{1+r_f} = \frac{0-30(1)}{1.05} = -28.57$$

   So, $C_u = S\Delta + B = \$33(1) - 28.57 = \$4.42$.

   Step 4. Determine the value of the call after the first period in the down state using the binomial model.

   $$\Delta = \frac{C_u - C_d}{S_u - S_d} = \frac{0-0}{30-24} = 0 \text{ and } B = \frac{C_d - S_d\Delta}{1+r_f} = \frac{0-24(0)}{1.05} = 0$$

   So, $C_d = S\Delta + B = \$27(0) + 0 = \$0$.

   Step 5. Determine the value of the call at time zero using the up- and down-state call values.

   $$\Delta = \frac{C_u - C_d}{S_u - S_d} = \frac{4.42-0}{33-27} = 0.74 \text{ and } B = \frac{C_d - S_d\Delta}{1+r_f} = \frac{0-27(0.72)}{1.05} = -\$18.51$$

   So, $C_0 = S\Delta + B = \$30(0.74) - \$18.51 = \$3.69$.

   Step 6. Determine the value of the put using put-call parity.

   $$C = P + S - PV(K) \Rightarrow P = C - S + PV(K) = 3.69 - 30 + \frac{30}{1.05} = \$2.26.$$

2. **Microsoft is trading for $30 today. The stock's historical volatility (standard deviation) is 35% per year. Assume that the risk-free rate is 5% and Microsoft pays no dividends.**
   [A]   What is the value of a two-year European call option with a $30 strike price?
   [B]   What is the value of a two-year European put option with a $30 strike price?

   Step 1. Determine which model to use.

   The Black-Scholes formula can be used since an estimate of volatility is known.

   The value of the call option is:

   $$C = S \times N(d_1) - PV(K) \times N(d_2)$$

   Step 2. Calculate d_1.

   $S = \$30$, $K = \$30$, $T = 2$, $\sigma = 0.35$, and $PV(K) = PV(30) = 30e^{-rt} = 30e^{-0.05 \times 2} = 27.15$

   So, $d_1 = \dfrac{\ln[S/PV(K)]}{\sigma\sqrt{T}} + \dfrac{\sigma\sqrt{T}}{2} = \dfrac{\ln[30/30e^{-0.05\times2}]}{0.35\sqrt{2}} + \dfrac{0.35\sqrt{2}}{2} = \dfrac{0.10}{0.50} + \dfrac{0.50}{2} = 0.45$

   Step 3. Calculate d_2.

   $$d_2 = d_1 - \sigma\sqrt{T} = 0.45 - 0.35(1.41) = -0.05$$

   Step 4. Calculate $N(d_1)$ and $N(d_2)$.

   Using the NORMSDIST function in Excel:

   $N(d_1)$: =NORMSDIST(0.45) = 0.67

   $N(d_2)$: =NORMSDIST(-0.05) = 0.48

   Step 5. Calculate the call value.

   $$C = S \times N(d_1) - PV(K) \times N(d_2) = 30 \times 0.67 - 27.15 \times 0.48 = \$7.07.$$

   Step 6. Determine the put value using put-call parity.

   $$C = P + S - PV(K) \Rightarrow P = \overbrace{S \times N(d_1) - PV(K) \times N(d_2)}^{C} - S + PV(K), \text{ so}$$

   $$P = PV(K)[1 - N(d_2)] - S[1 - N(d_1)] = 27.15[1 - 0.48] - 30[1 - 0.67] = \$4.21.$$

3. **Microsoft is trading for $30 today. Next year, you believe that the price can either go up by $3 or down by $2. Assume that the risk-free rate is 5% and Microsoft pays no dividends. Calculate the risk-neutral probabilities and use them to price a call option with a strike price of $30.**

   Step 1. Determine the option payoff.

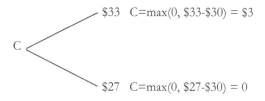

Step 2. Calculate the risk-neutral probabilities.

$$\rho = \frac{(1+r_f)S - S_d}{S_u - S_d} = \frac{(1.05)30 - 27}{33 - 27} = 0.75$$

$$(1-\rho) = 1 - 0.75 = 0.25$$

Step 3. Calculate the option value.

$$C = \frac{\rho C_u + (1-\rho)C_d}{1+r} = \frac{0.75(3) + (0.25)0}{1.05} = \$2.14$$

Step 4. Verify that this is the same value when using the binomial model.

$$C = S\Delta + B$$

where,

$$\Delta = \frac{C_u - C_d}{S_u - S_d} = \frac{3-0}{33-27} = 0.50 \text{ and } B = \frac{C_d - S_d\Delta}{1+r_f} = \frac{0 - 27(0.50)}{1.05} = -12.86$$

So, $C_u = S\Delta + B = \$30(0.50) - 12.86 = \$2.14$.

Questions and Problems

1. The current price of a stock is $100. In each of the next two years, this stock price will either go up by $20 or go down by $20. The stock pays no dividends. The one-year risk-free interest rate is 6% and will remain constant. Using the binomial model, calculate the price of a one-year call option on the stock with a strike price of $80.

2. Yahoo stock is trading for $40. The stock's historical volatility (standard deviation) is 70% per year. Assume that the risk-free rate is 5% and that the firm pays no dividends. What is the value of a six-month European call option with a $45 strike price?

3. Calculate the beta of the six-month Yahoo call option with a $45 strike price in problem 2 above. Assume that the volatility (standard deviation) is 70% per year, the risk-free rate is 5%, that the firm pays no dividends, and that Yahoo has a stock beta of 2.21. What is the option's leverage ratio?

4. Intel is contemplating issuing $40 billion in zero-coupon debt due in five years and using the proceeds to repurchase stock. Intel has a stock price of $20, 7 billion shares, an equity beta of 2.31 and the firm currently uses no leverage. The two-year risk-free rate is 5%. The implied volatility on at the money call options is 40%. Using the Black-Scholes model, estimate the debt and equity betas after the restructuring.

5. What are the value of the values of the put options in problems 1 and 2?

Solutions to Questions and Problems

1. Determine the value of the call after the first period in the up state using the binomial model.

$$\Delta = \frac{C_u - C_d}{S_u - S_d} = \frac{40-20}{140-100} = 0.50 \text{ and } B = \frac{C_d - S_d\Delta}{1+r_f} = \frac{20 - 100(0.50)}{1.06} = -28.30$$

So, $C_u = S\Delta + B = \$120(0.50) - 28.30 = \$31.70$.

Determine the value of the call after the first period in the down state using the binomial model.

So, $C_d = S\Delta + B$ = $80(0.50) – 28.30 = $11.70.

Determine the value of the call at time zero using the up- and down-state call values.

$$\Delta = \frac{C_u - C_d}{S_u - S_d} = \frac{31.70 - 11.70}{120 - 80} = 0.50 \text{ and } B = \frac{C_d - S_d\Delta}{1 + r_f} = \frac{21.70 - 80(0.50)}{1.06} = -\$17.26$$

So, $C_0 = S\Delta + B$ = $100(0.50) – $17.26 = 32.74.

2. S = $40, K = $45, T = 0.50, σ = 0.70, and PV(K) = PV(45) = $45e^{-rt}$ = $45e^{-0.05 \times 0.5}$ = $43.89

So, $d_1 = \dfrac{\ln[S/PV(K)]}{\sigma\sqrt{T}} + \dfrac{\sigma\sqrt{T}}{2} = \dfrac{\ln[40/43.89]}{0.70\sqrt{0.50}} + \dfrac{0.70\sqrt{0.50}}{2} = -0.19 + 0.25 = 0.06$

$d_2 = d_1 - \sigma\sqrt{T} = 0.06 - 0.70(0.71) = -0.44$

Using the NORMSDIST function in Excel:

$N(d_1)$: = NORMSDIST(0.06) = 0.52

$N(d_2)$: = NORMSDIST(–0.44) = 0.33

$C = S \times N(d_1) - PV(K) \times N(d_2) = 40 \times 0.52 - 43.89 \times 0.33$ = $6.32.

3. $\beta_{option} = \dfrac{S\Delta}{S\Delta + B}\beta_S$

S = $40, K = $45, T = 0.50, σ = 0.70, and PV(K) = PV(45) = $45e^{-rt}$ = $45e^{-0.05 \times 0.5}$ = $43.89

$\Delta = N(d_1); \ d_1 = \dfrac{\ln[S/PV(K)]}{\sigma\sqrt{T}} + \dfrac{\sigma\sqrt{T}}{2} = \dfrac{\ln[40/43.89]}{0.70\sqrt{0.50}} + \dfrac{0.70\sqrt{0.50}}{2} = -0.19 + 0.25 = 0.06$

$B = -PV(K) \times N(d_2); \ d_2 = d_1 - \sigma\sqrt{T} = 0.06 - 0.70(0.71) = -0.44$

Using the NORMSDIST function in Excel:

= NORMSDIST(d_1) = = NORMSDIST(0.06) = 0.52

= NORMSDIST(d_2) = = NORMSDIST(-0.44) = 0.33

$\Delta = N(d_1) = 0.52$

$B = -PV(K) \times N(d_2) = -43.89(0.33) = -14.48$

$\beta_{option} = \dfrac{S\Delta}{S\Delta + B}\beta_S = \dfrac{40(0.52)}{40(0.52) - 14.48}2.21 = 7.28$

4. $\beta_D = (1 - \Delta)\left(1 + \dfrac{E}{D}\right)\beta_U$

$\beta_E = \Delta\left(1 + \dfrac{D}{E}\right)\beta_U$

After the restructuring, D = $40 billion and E = $100 billion.

$S = 140$, $K = 40$, $T = 5$, $\sigma = 0.40$, and $PV(K) = PV(40) = 45e^{-rt} = 40e^{-0.05\times5} = 31.15$

$$d_1 = \frac{\ln[S/PV(K)]}{\sigma\sqrt{T}} + \frac{\sigma\sqrt{T}}{2} = \frac{\ln[140/31.15]}{0.40\sqrt{5}} + \frac{0.40\sqrt{5}}{2} = 1.68 + 0.45 = 2.13$$

$$d_2 = d_1 - \sigma\sqrt{T} = 2.13 - 0.40(2.24) = 1.23$$

Using the NORMSDIST function in Excel:

= NORMSDIST(d_1) = = NORMSDIST(2.13) = 0.98

= NORMSDIST(d_2) = = NORMSDIST(1.23) = 0.89

$\Delta = N(d_1) = 0.98$

$B = -PV(K) \times N(d_2) = -31.15(0.89) = 27.72$

$$\beta_D = (1-\Delta)\left(1+\frac{E}{D}\right)\beta_U = (1-0.98)\left(1+\frac{100}{40}\right)2.31 = 0.16$$

$$\beta_E = \Delta\left(1+\frac{D}{E}\right)\beta_U = 0.98\left(1+\frac{40}{100}\right)2.31 = 3.17$$

5. Determine the value of the put in problem 1 using put-call parity.

$$C = P + S - PV(K) \Rightarrow P = C - S + PV(K) = 32.74 - 100 + \frac{80}{1.06} = \$8.21$$

Determine the value of the put in problem 2 using put-call parity.

$$C = P + S - PV(K) \Rightarrow P = \overbrace{S \times N(d_1) - PV(K) \times N(d_2)}^{C} - S + PV(K), \text{ so}$$

$$P = PV(K)[1 - N(d_2)] - S[1 - N(d_1)] = 43.89[1 - 0.33] - 40[1 - 0.52] = \$10.21.$$

Chapter 22

Real Options

Chapter Synopsis

22.1 Real Versus Financial Options

A **real option** is the right, but not the obligation, to make a decision regarding an investment in real assets, such as to expand production capacity or abandon a project. While the underlying assets on which real options derive their value are generally not traded in competitive markets, like financial options, the principles of option valuation can often be used to determine their values.

The presence of real options can significantly increase the value of an investment opportunity, especially when there is a lot of uncertainty. Thus, to correctly evaluate an investment, the value of these options should be included in the analysis.

22.2 Decision Tree Analysis

A **decision tree** is a graphical representation of future decisions that contains: **decision nodes**, in which the decision maker has the option of what path to take, and **information nodes**, in which uncertainty is involved that is out of the decision maker's control.

Unlike a binomial tree used to price options with the binomial option pricing model, the decision maker must make a decision at each decision node so some of the uncertainty is under the control of the decision maker.

There are three kinds of real options that are most frequently encountered in practice: (1) the option to delay a project, (2) a growth option, and (3) the option to abandon a project.

22.3 The Option to Delay an Investment Opportunity

When there is not an option to wait, it is optimal to invest in any positive-NPV project immediately. When there exists the option of delaying the acceptance of a project, it is usually optimal to invest only when the NPV is substantially greater than zero.

■ By delaying an investment, you can base your decision on additional information. The option to wait is most valuable when there is a great deal of uncertainty regarding what the value of the investment will be in the future.

■ However, similar to the idea that it may be optimal to exercise a call option early on a dividend-paying stock, there may be value from the investment that is forgone by waiting.

22.4 Growth and Abandonment Options

A **growth option** is a real option to increase the size of a firm by investing in the future. Because these options have non-negative values, they often contribute significantly to the value of any firm that has future possible investment opportunities.

For example, by undertaking a project in a specific industry, a firm may acquire the opportunity to invest in new projects that firms outside the industry do not have easy access. This is called the **option to expand**. Many firms use this idea when they undertake large-scale projects. Rather than commit to the entire project initially, a firm experiments by undertaking the project in stages. It implements the project on a smaller scale first; if the small-scale project proves successful, the firm then exercises the growth option and expands the project.

Future growth opportunities are like a collection of real call options on potential projects. Since out-of-the-money calls are riskier than in-the-money calls, and because most growth options are likely to be out-of-the-money, the growth component of firm value is likely to be riskier than the ongoing assets of the firm. This observation might explain why small, young firms have higher returns than older, established firms. It also explains why R&D-intensive firms often have high costs of capital even when most of the R&D risk is idiosyncratic.

The Black-Scholes option pricing model might not price growth options correctly because the Black-Scholes formula values European options, while most growth options can be exercised at any time. An alternative approach, in which the flexibility afforded by future managerial decisions can be taken into account, is to value growth options using the binomial option pricing model.

An **option to abandon** can also add value to a project. For example, a project that may be profitable or unprofitable; depending on the realized market demand can be abandoned if demand proves to be too low. Thus, the firm can avoid the present value of the future negative cash flows while maintaining the option of continuing to operate the project if demand is sufficiently high.

A common option to abandon faced by homeowners is the option to prepay their mortgage and refinance their loan.

■ If, after the bank issues the mortgage, rates go down, the mortgage holder can prepay the mortgage and replace it with a new mortgage at a lower rate.

■ If rates go up after the mortgage is issued, the bank is stuck with a loan that is below the current market rate.

Since the bank has effectively written an option, they demand a higher rate on the loan than the rate they would demand if the mortgage did not have the abandonment option. In fact, an important reason that mortgage interest rates are higher than Treasury rates is because mortgages have an abandonment option that Treasuries do not have.

Similarly, corporate bonds are often callable, containing the option to pay of the face value before the maturity date. Thus, yields on equivalent non-callable bonds may offer a lower yield because the bond does not contain a written option.

22.5 Applications to Multiple Projects

Consider a firm that must choose between two mutually exclusive projects. In both cases, the projects are expected to save $3 million per year and the cost of capital is 10%.

■ The shorter project will cost $10 million to implement and last five years.

$$\underset{\text{5-year Project}}{\text{NPV}} = \frac{3}{0.10}\left(1 - \frac{1}{1.1^5}\right) - 10 = \$1.37 \text{ million}$$

■ The longer project will cost $17 million and last 10 years.

$$\underset{\text{10-year Project}}{\text{NPV}} = \frac{3}{0.10}\left(1 - \frac{1}{1.1^{10}}\right) - 17 = \$1.43 \text{ million}$$

With such mutually exclusive projects with different lives, the NPVs can be misleading because the calculations ignore the difference in these projects' life spans—the longer project is worth more partly because its benefits last longer. Whether these additional benefits are worth their additional NPV depends on what happens in the next five years.

Traditionally, managers have used the **equivalent annual benefit** method to choose between projects of different lives. This approach accounts for the difference in project lengths by calculating the constant payment over the life of the project that is equivalent to receiving the NPV today, and then selecting the project with the higher equivalent annual benefit. However, this method ignores the value of any real options because it assumes that the projects will always be replicated at their original terms.

Since the future cost of a machine is uncertain, there is an abandonment option to consider. Because of technological advances, machines may become more or less expensive and the firm only needs to replace the shorter project if it is advantageous to do so.

22.6 Rules of Thumb

In practice, carrying out a thorough real options analysis requires an extensive amount of time. Consequently, many firms resort to less time-consuming rules of thumb.

■ The **profitability index rule**. When an investment opportunity can be delayed, it is optimal to invest only when the NPV of the investment project is sufficiently high. Since it is often difficult to calculate precisely how high the NPV must be to optimally launch a project, some firms use the following rule of thumb: Invest whenever the profitability index = (NPV/initial investment) is at least 1.0 or higher. When the investment cannot be delayed, the optimal rule is to invest whenever the profitability index is greater than zero.

■ The **hurdle rate rule** states that a firm should invest whenever the NPV of the project is positive using the hurdle rate as the discount rate, where:

$$\text{Hurdle Rate} = \text{Cost of Capital} \times \frac{\text{Mortgage Rate}}{\text{Risk-Free Rate}}.$$

in which the **mortgage rate** is the rate on a risk-free annuity that is callable at any time. The mortgage rate exceeds the risk-free rate because mortgages carry an option to abandon by prepaying the loan. If the project has a positive NPV when using the mortgage interest rate as the discount rate, you can immediately get the benefits of the project and still take advantage of a lower rate if rates fall. Thus, it makes sense to invest immediately.

22.7 Key Insights from Real Options

Although a simple rule on how to account for all real options does not exist, there are a few simple principles that we have covered in this chapter. In closing, it is worth restating these principles:

- Out-of-the-Money Real Options Have Value.
- In-the-Money Real Options Need Not be Exercised Immediately.
- Waiting Is Valuable.
- Delay Investment Expenses as Much as Possible.
- Create Value by Exploiting Real Options.

Combining these insights, we find that by staging investments, and using clear, valuation-based methods to determine at each stage if the firm should abandon, defer, continue, or grow an investment opportunity, managers can substantially increase firm value.

Selected Concepts and Key Terms

Abandonment Option, Option to Abandon

The real option to discontinue a project.

Callable Annuity Rate

The rate on a risk-free annuity that can be repaid (or called) at any time.

Decision Tree, Decision Node, Information Node

A graphical representation of future decisions. A decision tree contains two kinds of nodes: **decision nodes**, in which the decision maker has the option of what path to take, and **information nodes,** in which uncertainty is involved that is out of the control of the decision maker. Unlike a binomial tree used to price options with the binomial option pricing model, the decision maker must make a decision at each decision node so some of the uncertainty is under the control of the decision maker.

Equivalent Annual Benefit

The constant payment over the life of the project that is equivalent to receiving the NPV today. The equivalent annual benefit rule involves selecting the mutually exclusive project with the higher equivalent annual benefit.

Growth Option

A real option to increase the size of a firm by investing in the future. Because these options have non-negative value, they often contribute significantly to the value of any firm that has future possible investment opportunities.

Hurdle Rate Rule, Hurdle Rate

The hurdle rate rule states that a firm should invest whenever the NPV of the project is positive using the hurdle rate as the discount rate, where:

$$\text{Hurdle Rate} = \text{Cost of Capital} \times \frac{\text{Callable Annuity Rate}}{\text{Risk-Free Rate}}.$$

If the project has a positive NPV when using the mortgage interest rate as the discount rate, you can immediately get the benefits of the project and still take advantage of a lower rate if rates fall. Thus, it makes sense to invest immediately.

Mutually Dependent Investments

A group of projects in which the value of one project depends upon the outcome of the others.

Profitability Index Rule

In the presence of the real option to delay, invest whenever the profitability index = (NPV/initial investment) is at least 1.0 or some higher threshold.

Real Option

The right, but not the obligation, to make a particular decision regarding an investment in real assets, such as to expand production capacity or abandon a project.

Sunk-Cost Fallacy

The idea that, once a manager makes a large investment, he should not abandon a project.

Concept Check Questions and Answers

22.1.1. What is the difference between a real option and a financial option?

A key distinction between a real option and a financial option is that real options, and the underlying assets on which they are based, are often not traded in a competitive market.

22.1.2. Why does a real option add value to an investment decision?

Because real options allow a decision maker to choose the most attractive alternative after new information has been learned.

22.2.1. What is the difference between an information node and a decision node on a decision tree?

Decision nodes are points in which the decision maker has the option of what path to take, and information nodes are points in which uncertainty is involved that is out of the decision maker's control.

22.2.2. What makes real options valuable?

The flexibility of making investment decisions at a later point of time makes real options valuable.

22.3.1. What is the economic trade-off between investing immediately or waiting?

By choosing to wait for more information, you give up any profits the project might generate in the interim. In addition, a competitor could use the delay to develop a competing product. The decision to wait, therefore, involves a trade-off between these costs and the benefit of remaining flexible.

22.3.2. How does the option to wait affect the capital budgeting decision?

When you do not have the option to wait, it is optimal to invest in any positive-NPV project. When you have the option of deciding when to invest, it is usually optimal to invest only when the NPV is substantially greater than zero.

22.4.1. Why can a firm with no ongoing projects, and investment opportunities that currently have negative NPVs, still be worth a positive amount?

A firm with no ongoing projects, and investment opportunities that currently have negative NPVs, can still be worth a positive amount if the firm has future possible investment opportunities, and thus future possible growing potential.

22.4.2. Why is it sometimes optimal to invest in stages?

It is sometimes optimal for firms to invest in stages when they undertake big projects. Rather than commit to the entire project initially, a firm experiments by undertaking the project in stages. It implements the project on a smaller scale first; if the small-scale project proves successful, the firm then exercises the option to grow the project.

22.4.3. How can an abandonment option add value to a project?

An abandonment option can add value to a project because a firm can drop a project if it turns out to be unsuccessful.

22.5.1. Why is it inappropriate to simply pick the higher NPV project when comparing mutually exclusive investment opportunities of different lengths?

It is inappropriate to simply pick the higher NPV project when comparing mutually exclusive investment opportunities of different lengths, because the future costs to replace the short-lived project and the future benefits the long-lived project can provide are uncertain.

22.5.2. What is a major shortcoming of the equivalent annual benefit method?

A major shortcoming of the equivalent annual benefit method is that it ignores the value of any real options, by assuming that the projects will be replaced at their original terms.

22.5.3. How can you decide the order of investment in a staged investment decision?

You can find the optimal order to stage mutually dependent projects by ranking each, from highest to lowest, according to the ratio of (1-PV(success))/PV(investments), where PV(success) is the value at the start of the project of receiving $1 if the project succeeds (i.e., the present value of the risk-neutral probability of success), and PV(investment) is the project's required investment, again expressed as a present value at the project's start.

22.6.1. Explain the profitability index rule of thumb.

The profitability index rule of thumb directs you to invest whenever the profitability index exceeds some predetermined number. When the investment cannot be delayed, the optimal rule is to invest whenever the profitability index is greater than zero. When there is an option to delay, invest only when the index is at least one.

22.6.2. What is the hurdle rate rule and what uncertainty does it reflect?

The hurdle rate rule computes the NPV using the hurdle rate, a discount rate higher than the cost of capital, and specifies that the investment should only be undertaken when the NPV computed in this way is positive. It reflects interest rate uncertainty.

Examples with Step-by-Step Solutions

Solving Problems

Problems may involve the consideration of the three most common kinds of real options: (1) the option to delay a project, (2) a growth option, and (3) the option to abandon a project. See problems 1 and 3 below for examples involving these options. Such problems may require the general ability to draw a decision tree by incorporating the information in a problem into decision and information nodes.

Problems also may entail deciding between mutually-exclusive projects with different lives when there is uncertainty about the cost of replicating the shorter-lived project in the future, as in problem 2 below. Finally, problems may require applying the profitability index and hurdle rate rules of thumb, as in examples in the Questions and Problems section below.

Examples

1. Nike has developed a prototype for a Nike-branded baseball that the firm plans to market to Major League baseball, college baseball, and high school baseball. They hope that the baseball is accepted as the new standard for most leagues, but the ball's rate of market adoption is uncertain. In order to have the ball ready in 1 year, Nike would have to invest $50 million to set up contractual relationships with third-party contract manufacturers in China. The ball's average total cost would be $0.50 and the selling price would be $1.50. Based on market surveys, Nike believes that there is a 25% chance of a high rate of adoption, in which 100 million balls will be sold annually forever, and a 75% chance of a low rate of adoption, in which 10 million balls will be sold annually forever. The adoption rate will be determined in one year when the first orders for the balls come in. The annual fixed costs associated with the project would be $30 million per year. Ignore tax effects and assume that Nike's cost of capital is at 10% and the risk-free rate is 5%.
   [A] What is the NPV of the project based on the project's expected future cash flows? Based on this measure, should Nike accept the project?
   [B] What is the embedded option in this project? Is the project worthwhile when considering the option?

Step 1. Calculate the NPV of the project.

Since the profit per ball is $1.50 – $0.50 = $1, the project's expected annual cash flow is:

0.25[$1(100 million)] + 0.75[$1(10 million)] – $30 million = $2.5 million.

So, NPV = –$50 million + $\frac{\$2.5 \text{ million}}{0.10}$ = –$50 million + $25 million = –$25 million.

Since the NPV is significantly below 0, the project should not be accepted.

Step 2. Identify the option in the project.

Since the project can be stopped if the demand is observed to be low in one year, the project has an option to abandon.

Step 3. Determine the value of the project in each state and the option payoff.

The NPV with high demand is: $-\$50 + \frac{\$70}{0.10} = -\$50 + \$700 = \$650 \text{ million.}$

The NPV with low demand is: $-\$50 + \frac{-\$22.5}{0.10} = -\$50 + -\$125 \text{ million} = -175 \text{ million.}$

The project value at time 0 and in the up and down states is:

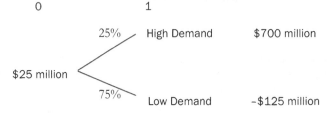

The option payoff is:

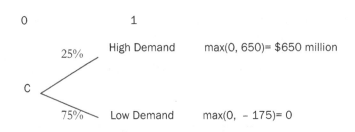

Step 4. Determine the risk-neutral probabilities.

$$\rho = \frac{(1 + r_f)S - S_d}{S_u - S_d} = \frac{(1.05)25 - -125}{700 - -125} = 0.18$$

$$(1 - \rho) = 1 - 0.18 = 0.82$$

Step 5. Calculate the option value using the binomial model.

$$C = \frac{\rho C_u + (1 - \rho)C_d}{1 + r} = \frac{0.18(650) + (0.82)0}{1.05} = \$111 \text{ million}$$

Step 6. Make a conclusion.

The option to abandon makes the project worthwhile. The standard discounted cash flow NPV calculation, based on expected future cash flows, ignores the option's value.

2. Your firm recently purchased a hotel which is in poor condition, and you must decide between:
   [1]   A less-expensive refurbishing, in which carpets would be replaced and low-cost fixtures would be installed, and
   [2]   A more-expensive refurbishing, in which marble floors would be installed along with high-quality fixtures.

   Option 1 would cost $6 million today and produce $2 million per year in free cash flow for 5 years, at which time a new refurbishing would be required. Option 2 would cost $10 million today and produce $2 million per year in free cash flow for 10 years, at which time a new refurbishing would be required. Assume that the cost of capital is fixed at 10%.

   [A]   What is the NPV of each option? Why does NPV not allow you to make the correct decision in this case?
   [B]   Based on the Equivalent Annual Benefit of both options, which should be chosen?
   [C]   Assume that in five years, a less-expensive refurbishing is equally likely to cost either $6 million or $8 million, and last five more years generating $2 million per year. Now which option should be chosen?

Step 1. Determine the NPV of each option.

The NPV of the option 1 is:

$$NPV = -\$6\ million + \$2\ million\left[\frac{1}{.10} - \frac{1}{.10(1.10)^5}\right] = \$1.58\ million.$$

The NPV of the option 2 is:

$$NPV = -\$10\ million + \$2\ million\left[\frac{1}{.10} - \frac{1}{.10(1.10)^{10}}\right] = \$2.29\ million.$$

Since the projects are mutually exclusive and have different lives, comparing the NPVs will not determine which is more valuable. For example, the shorter project could be replicated again in 5 years and, if all assumptions were unchanged, the NPV at that time would be another $1.58 million.

Step 2. Determine the Equivalent Annual Benefit of each option.

The Equivalent Annual Benefit accounts for the difference in project lengths by calculating the constant payment over the life of the project that is equivalent to receiving the NPV today.

The Equivalent Annual Benefit (EAB) of the option 1 is:

$$EAB\left[\frac{1}{.10} - \frac{1}{.10(1.10)^5}\right] = \$1.58\ million \Rightarrow EAB = \$0.42\ million$$

The Equivalent Annual Benefit of the option 2 is:

$$EAB\left[\frac{1}{.10} - \frac{1}{.10(1.10)^{10}}\right] = \$2.29\ million \Rightarrow EAB = \$0.37\ million.$$

Based on this rule, option 1 should now be chosen because it has a higher EAB. This is true if, as the method implicitly assumes, you are able to refurbish the hotel for $5 million in 5 years.

Step 3. Draw a decision tree for the projects' refurbishing costs.

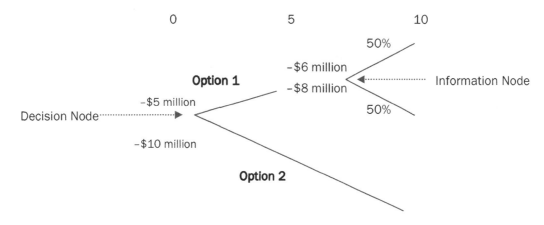

Step 4. Calculate the potential NPVs of repeating option 1 at time 5.

If the cost is $6 million, the NPV is $1.58 million again.

If the cost is $8 million:

$$NPV = -\$8\text{ million} + \$2\text{ million}\left[\frac{1}{.10} - \frac{1}{.10(1.10)^5}\right] = -\$0.42\text{ million}$$

Sine the NPV is negative, you would not refurbish the hotel if the cost was $8 million.

Step 5. Determine the NPV of option 1 today.

Based on the expected NPVs of replicating the project:

$$NPV = \$1.58\text{ million} + \frac{0.50 \times \$1.58\text{ million} + 0.50 \times \$0}{1.1^5} = \$2.07\text{ million.}$$

Step 6. Make a conclusion.

After considering the uncertainty regarding the cost of replicating the project, option 2 is actually more valuable, based on these assumptions.

3. **Fox Searchlight Pictures recently purchased a script for a new movie about a poker player. The movie would cost $30 million to produce. Given the growing popularity of the game, the producer believes it may be better to delay the start of production. The studio estimates that there is a 25% chance that the popularity of poker will increase in one year, and the movie would be expected to generate $40 million in the first year. Otherwise, the popularity of poker will be the same in one year and the movie would be expected to generate $20 million in the first year. In either case, the movie is expected to generate $5 million in the second year and decline by 5% per year forever. The cost of capital is fixed at 15% and the risk-free rate is 5%.**
   [A] **What is the NPV of the project based on the project's expected future cash flows?**
   [B] **What is the embedded option in this project? Is the project worthwhile when considering the option?**
   [C] **What should they do?**

Step 1. Calculate the NPV of the project.

The expected free cash flow in one year is 0.25[$40 million)] + 0.75[$20 million)] = $25 million, so:

$$NPV = -\$30\text{ million} + \frac{\$25\text{ million}}{1.15} + \frac{\left(\dfrac{\$5\text{ million}}{0.15+0.05}\right)}{1.15} = \$13.5\text{ million}$$

Step 2. Identify the option in the project.

The project has an option to delay.

The NPV of the project if there is an increase in popularity is:

$$PV = -\$30\text{ million} + \frac{\$40\text{ million}}{1.15} + \frac{\left(\dfrac{\$5\text{ million}}{0.15+0.05}\right)}{1.15} = \$26.5\text{ million}$$

The value of the project if there is no increase in popularity is:

$$PV = -30 + \frac{\$20 \text{ million}}{1.15} + \frac{\left(\dfrac{\$5 \text{ million}}{0.15+0.05}\right)}{1.15} = \$9.1 \text{ million}$$

Step 3. Determine the value of the project and option payoffs.

The project value, net of the initial investment is:

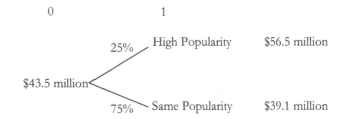

The option payoff is:

	0		1	
		25%	High Popularity	\$26.5 million
	C			
		75%	Same Popularity	\$9.1 million

Step 4. Calculate the risk-neutral probabilities.

$$\rho = \frac{(1+r_f)S - S_d}{S_u - S_d} = \frac{(1.05)43.5 - 39.1}{56.5 - 39.1} = 0.38$$

$$(1-\rho) = 1 - 0.38 = 0.62$$

Step 5. Calculate the option value.

$$C = \frac{\rho C_u + (1-\rho)C_d}{1+r} = \frac{0.38(26.5) + 0.62(9.1)}{1.05} = \$15 \text{ million}$$

Step 6. Conclusion.

The value today from waiting to invest in the movie next year is \$15 million. This value exceeds the NPV of \$13.5 million from investing today. Thus, they are better off waiting to invest.

Questions and Problems

1. 12 years ago, Merck developed a new drug for which it was awarded a 17-year patent, which now has 5 years remaining. The drug cures a disease that has been very rare, but there are signs that it is becoming more prevalent. If a \$3 million investment is made, the drug can be sold through a selected group of doctors this year generating a cash flow of \$500,000. Over the next 5 years, the risk-neutral probability that free cash flow will grow by 50% per year is 25%, and the risk-neutral probability that free cash flow will grow by 1% is 75%. After the

patent expires in 5 years, free cash flows will be zero. The risk-free rate is fixed at 10% and the cash flows are considered risk free because the project is not influenced by systematic risk factors. What is the NPV of the project if it is accepted today? What is the NPV of waiting to invest in one year when the rate of growth will be apparent? What should they do?

2. Fox Searchlight Pictures recently purchased a script for a new movie about a poker player. The movie would cost $30 million to produce. Given the growing popularity of the game, the producer believes it may be better to delay the start of production. The studio estimates that there is a 25% chance that the popularity of poker will increase in one year, and the movie would be expected to generate $40 million in the first year. Otherwise, the popularity of poker will be the same in one year and the movie would be expected to generate $20 million in the first year. In either case, the movie is expected to generate $5 million in the second year and decline by 5% per year forever. The cost of capital is fixed at 15%. Based on the profitability index rule of thumb, which states that only projects with profitability indices above 1 should be undertaken today, should the movie be made today?

3. A firm has an opportunity to bid for the drilling rights for 2 years on a tract of land. The cost of extracting oil is $62 per barrel and the price of oil is $60 per barrel. The standard deviation of the price of oil is 30% and the risk-free rate is 5%.
   [A]   Is the project acceptable according to the NPV rule?
   [B]   What is the option value per barrel? Use the Black-Scholes pricing model.
   [C]   What are the unrealistic assumptions that the Black-Scholes pricing model makes in this application?

4. Your firm is considering entering into a contract to become the official supplier of paper to the U.S. government for 20 years. For the right to become the official paper supplier, you would have to pay $100 million up front, and the government would agree to purchase paper resulting in a free cash flow of $11 million per year for 20 years. You consider the cash flows to be risk free since the agreement is with the U.S. government. No other firm is considering the offer, and you believe it would be available in the future if you don't take it today. The one-year risk-free interest rate is 7%, and today's rate on a risk-free perpetual bond is 8%. As in the appendix to the chapter, assume that interest rates will either be 10% or 6% in one year with risk-neutral probabilities of 64.375% and 35.625%, respectively. Compare the NPV of making the investment today, with the value of the call option on the project, to determine if you should invest today or wait.

5. As in problem 4, your firm is considering entering into a contract to become the official supplier of paper to the U.S. government for 20 years. For the right to become the official paper supplier, you would have to pay $100 million up front, and the government would agree to purchase paper resulting in a free cash flow of $11 million per year for 20 years. You consider the cashflows to be risk free since the agreement is with the U.S. government. No other firm is considering the offer, and you believe it would be available in the future if you don't take it today. The one-year risk-free interest rate is 7%, and today's rate on a risk-free perpetual bond is 8%. As in the appendix to the chapter, assume that interest rates will either be 10% or 6% in one year with risk-neutral probabilities of 64.375% and 35.625%, respectively, such that the mortgage rate (the rate of an equivalent perpetual bond that is repayable at any time) is 9.6%. Based on the hurdle rate rule of thumb, should they start today, or wait and see if rates drop, and then invest?

Solutions to Questions and Problems

1. Determine the discounted cash flow NPV if the investment is made today.

If the high growth rate state occurs, then the present value of the free cash flows is:

$$PV = C \times \left(\frac{1}{r-g}\right)\left(1-\left(\frac{1+g}{1+r}\right)^N\right) - 10 = 500{,}000 \times \left(\frac{1}{0.10-0.50}\right)\left(1-\left(\frac{1.50}{1.10}\right)^5\right)$$

$$= \$4{,}643{,}902$$

If the low growth rate state occurs, then the present value of the free cash flows is:

$$PV = C \times \left(\frac{1}{r-g}\right)\left(1-\left(\frac{1+g}{1+r}\right)^N\right) - 10 = 500{,}000 \times \left(\frac{1}{0.10-0.01}\right)\left(1-\left(\frac{1.01}{1.10}\right)^5\right)$$

$$= \$1{,}930{,}030$$

So the NPV based on the expected future cash flows is:

$$NPV = 0.25(4.64 \text{ million}) + 0.75(1.93 \text{ million}) - \$3 \text{ million} = -\$0.39 \text{ million} < 0.$$

Thus, the project is unacceptable according the NPV rule.

Determine the NPV of investing in one year.

Since only 4 years will be left on the patent, if the high growth rate state occurs, then the NPV at time 1 is:

$$PV = C \times \left(\frac{1}{r-g}\right)\left(1-\left(\frac{1+g}{1+r}\right)^N\right) - 10 = 500{,}000 \times \left(\frac{1}{0.10-0.50}\right)\left(1-\left(\frac{1.50}{1.10}\right)^4\right) - \$3 \text{ million}$$

$$= \$72{,}195$$

If the low growth rate state occurs, then the NPV at time 1 is:

$$PV = C \times \left(\frac{1}{r-g}\right)\left(1-\left(\frac{1+g}{1+r}\right)^N\right) - 10 = 500{,}000 \times \left(\frac{1}{0.10-0.01}\right)\left(1-\left(\frac{1.01}{1.10}\right)^4\right) - \$3 \text{ million}$$

$$= -\$1{,}393{,}036$$

Since the investment will only be made in the high growth state. The value today of this is:

$$NPV_0 = (0.25)\left(\frac{72{,}195}{1.1}\right) + .75(0) = \$16{,}385$$

Make a conclusion. The NPV of waiting one year is slightly positive, whereas the NPV of undertaking the investment today is negative, so they should wait a year.

2. The NPV is:

$$NPV = -\$30 \text{ million} + \frac{\$25 \text{ million}}{1.15} + \frac{\left(\dfrac{\$5 \text{ million}}{0.15+0.05}\right)}{1.15} = \$13.5 \text{ million}$$

The profitability index is:

$$PI = \frac{NPV}{\text{Initial Investment}} = \frac{\$13.5 \text{ million}}{\$30 \text{ million}} = 0.45.$$

Since the *PI* < 1, the investment should be delayed.

Note that this is the same conclusion made in example 3 above.

3. [A] Since the profit per barrel is negative, the NPV of *n* barrels is also negative, and it should be rejected.

   [B] Using Black-Scholes

$S = \$60$, $K = \$62$, $T = 2$, $\sigma = 0.30$, and PV(K) = PV(62) = $62e^{-rt}$ = $62e^{-0.05 \times 2}$ = 56.1

So, $d_1 = \dfrac{\ln[S/PV(K)]}{\sigma\sqrt{T}} + \dfrac{\sigma\sqrt{T}}{2} = \dfrac{\ln[60/56.1]}{0.30\sqrt{2}} + \dfrac{0.30\sqrt{2}}{2} = 0.158 + 0.212 = 0.37$

Calculate d_2.

$d_2 = d_1 - \sigma\sqrt{T} = 0.37 - 0.30(1.41) = -0.05$

Calculate $N(d_1)$ and $N(d_2)$.

Using the NORMSDIST function in Excel:

$N(d_1)$: = NORMSDIST(0.37) = 0.64

$N(d_2)$: = NORMSDIST(-0.05) = 0.48

Calculate the call value.

$C = S \times N(d_1) - PV(K) \times N(d_2) = 60 \times 0.64 - 56.1 \times 0.48 = \$11.07.$

   [C] Black-Scholes assumes that the option can only be exercised in two years. The firm can actually start or stop pumping at any time during the two years as the the price of oil changes. Modeling flexibility requires a complex binomial tree that shows the different paths that the price of oil might take.

4. The NPV of entering into the contract today at an 8% cost of capital is:

$$\text{NPV} = -\$100 \text{ million} + \$11 \text{ million} \left[\frac{1}{.08} - \frac{1}{.08(1.08)^{20}} \right] = -\$8 \text{ million}$$

The NPV of entering into the contract in one year if the cost of capital is 10% is:

$$\text{NPV} = -\$100 \text{ million} + \$11 \text{ million} \left[\frac{1}{.10} - \frac{1}{.10(1.10)^{20}} \right] = -\$6.4 \text{ million}$$

The NPV of entering into the contract in one year if the cost of capital is 6% is:

$$\text{NPV} = -\$100 \text{ million} + \$11 \text{ million} \left[\frac{1}{.06} - \frac{1}{.06(1.06)^{20}} \right] = \$26.2 \text{ million}$$

The payoff diagram is:

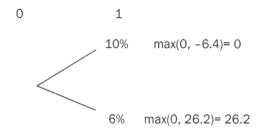

The option value is:

$$C = \frac{\rho C_u + (1 - \rho)C_d}{1 + r} = \frac{(0.64375)0 + (0.35625)26.2}{1.08} = \$8.6$$

So the value of the call option on the project is higher and you should delay the investment and invest in one year if interest rates fall.

5. The NPV at the hurdle rate is:

$$NPV = -\$100 \text{ million } + \$11 \text{ million} \left[\frac{1}{.096} - \frac{1}{.096(1.096)^{20}} \right] = -\$4.7 \text{ million } < 0$$

The rule of thumb suggests that you should delay the investment.

CHAPTER 23

Raising Equity Capital

Chapter Synopsis

23.1 Equity Financing for Private Companies

A private company can raise equity capital from several potential outside sources:

- **Angel investors** are individual investors—frequently friends or acquaintances of the entrepreneur—who buy equity in small private firms. Because their capital investment is often relatively large, they typically receive a sizeable equity share in the business and have substantial influence in the business decisions of the firm.

- **Venture capital firms** are limited partnerships formed to invest in the private equity of young firms. Institutional investors, such as pension funds, are typically the limited partners. Most general partners charge an annual management fee of 2% of the fund's committed capital plus 20% of any positive return they generate.

- **Institutional investors** may invest directly in private firms or they may invest indirectly by becoming limited partners in venture capital firms.

- **Corporate investors** are corporations that invest in private companies; they are often referred to as **corporate partners**, **strategic partners**, and **strategic investors**.

When a company sells equity to outside investors for the first time, it typically issues **convertible preferred stock.** This give investors all of the future benefits of common stock if things go well, and if the company runs into financial difficulties, the preferred stockholders have a senior claim on the assets of the firm.

Firms generally raise capital in different rounds. The **pre-money valuation** is the value of the shares outstanding prior to a new funding round at the price in the funding round. The **post-money value** is the value of the whole firm (old plus new shares) at the funding round price.

The method used by equity investors to realize a return from their initial equity investment is called an **exit strategy.** There are two general types of exit strategies: an acquisition by another firm or a public equity offering.

23.2 The Initial Public Offering

The process of selling stock to the public for the first time is called an initial public offering (IPO). Going public has advantages and disadvantages.

- The main advantages of going public are improved liquidity for the equity investors and better access to capital, both from the IPO proceeds and in subsequent equity offerings.

- A disadvantage of going public is that the equity holders of the corporation become more widely dispersed. This undermines investors' ability to monitor the company's management and thus represents a loss of control.

- Furthermore, once a company goes public, it must satisfy all of the increasingly stringent requirements of public companies. Organizations such as the Securities and Exchange Commission (SEC), the securities exchanges (including the New York Stock Exchange and the Nasdaq), and Congress (through the Sarbanes-Oxley Act of 2002) have adopted new standards that require more thorough financial disclosure, greater accountability, and more stringent requirements for the board of directors. Compliance with the new standards is costly and time-consuming for public companies.

After deciding to go public, managers of the company work with an **underwriter**, which is an investment banking firm that manages the offering and designs its structure. The shares that are sold in the IPO may either be new shares that raise capital, known as a **primary offering,** or existing shares that are sold by current shareholders, known as a **secondary offering.**

Typically, an issuer uses a **firm commitment** IPO in which the underwriter guarantees that it will sell all of the stock at the offer price. The underwriter purchases the entire issue at a slightly lower price than the offer price and then resells it at the offer price. The difference between the underwriter's purchase price and the offer price is the **spread**—the primary means of compensation for the underwriter.

The **lead underwriter** is the primary investment banking firm responsible for managing the IPO along with a group of other underwriters, collectively called the **syndicate**, to help market and sell the issue. Underwriters are responsible for marketing and pricing the IPO, as well as helping the firm with all of the necessary filings.

Issuers must file a **registration statement** that provides financial and other information about the company to investors prior to an IPO. Part of the registration statement, called the **preliminary prospectus** or **red herring,** is distributed before the stock is offered. Once the company has satisfied the SEC's disclosure requirements, the SEC approves the stock for sale to the general public. The company prepares the final registration statement and **final prospectus** containing all the details of the IPO, including the number of shares offered and the offer price.

To determine the offer price, underwriters work with the issuer to value the company using discounted cash flow and comparable multiple valuation techniques. Underwriters also gain valuation advice from potential investors during the **road show,** in which senior management and the lead underwriters travel around the country explaining the deal to their largest customers—mainly institutional investors such as mutual funds and pension funds.

At the end of the road show, customers provide non-binding indications of their demand. The underwriters then study the total demand and adjust the price until it is virtually certain that the issue will succeed. This process is called **book building**.

In most cases, the pre-existing shareholders are subject to a **lockup provision,** and they cannot sell their shares for 180 days after the IPO.

23.3 IPO Puzzles

There are four puzzling IPO characteristics:

1. On average, IPOs appear to be underpriced.

   On average, between 1960 and 2003, the price in the U.S. aftermarket was 18.3% higher at the end of the first day of trading as underwriters appear to use the information they acquire during the book-building stage to intentionally **underprice** the IPO.

   The most prominent explanation of underpricing is the manifestation of a form of adverse selection referred to as the **winner's curse.** An investor who requests shares in an IPO will "win" (get all the shares requested) when demand for the shares by others is low, and the IPO is more likely to perform poorly. However, the investor will get low allocations in the best IPOs because they are oversubscribed. This effect implies that it may be necessary for the underwriter to underprice its issues on average in order for less-informed investors to be willing to participate in IPOs.

2. The number of issues is highly cyclical.

   It appears that the number of IPOs is not solely driven by the demand for capital: When times are good, the market is flooded with new issues; when times are bad, the number of issues dries up. In some periods, firms and investors seem to favor IPOs; at other times, firms appear to rely on alternative sources of capital and financial economists are not sure why.

3. It is unclear why firms willingly incur such high costs.

   Almost all IPOs ranging in size from $20 million to $80 million pay an underwriting spread of 7%. It is difficult to understand how a $20 million issue can be profitably done for $1.4 million, while an $80 million issue requires paying fees of $5.6 million.

4. The long-run performance of a newly public company is poor.

   On average, a three- to five-year buy and hold strategy has been a bad investment.

23.4 The Seasoned Equity Offering

A **seasoned equity offering** (SEO) is the process in which a public firm issues new shares. An SEO involves many of the same procedures as an IPO. The main difference is that the price-setting process is not necessary because a market price for the stock already exists.

Two kinds of seasoned equity offerings exist: a cash offer and a rights offer.

- In a **general cash offer,** the firm offers the new shares to investors at large.

- In a **rights offer,** the firm offers the new shares only to existing shareholders. In the United States, almost all offers are cash offers, but the same is not true internationally. For example, in the United Kingdom, most seasoned offerings of new shares are rights offers.

On average, a firm's stock price falls by 2% to 3% when it announces an SEO. This price decline is consistent with the idea that a firm, concerned about the interests of its existing shareholders, will not issue stock if the firm is undervalued and tend only to issue stock that is overvalued. Thus, investors infer from the decision to have an SEO that the company is likely to be overvalued.

Stocks of firms having SEOs underperform following the offering. This is consistent with the explanation provided for why there is a negative reaction at the SEO issuance and suggests that the stock price decrease at the announcement is not large enough.

Selected Concepts and Key Terms

Angel Investors

Individual investors—frequently friends or acquaintances of the entrepreneur—who buy equity in small private firms. Because their capital investment is often relatively large, they typically receive a sizeable equity share in the business and have substantial influence in the business decisions of the firm.

Auction IPO

A very rarely used IPO method in which investors place bids in an auction process, which sets the highest price such that the number of bids at or above that price equals the number of offered shares. All winning bidders pay this price, even if their bid was higher.

Best-Efforts Offer

A rarely used IPO method in which the underwriter does not guarantee that the stock will be sold, but instead tries to sell the stock for the best possible price. Such deals may have an all-or-none clause in which the deal is called off if all of the shares are not sold.

Book Building

A process in which customers provide non-binding indications of their demand early in the IPO process. The underwriters then add up the total demand and adjust the price until it is virtually certain that the issue will succeed.

Carried Interest

The fee that general partners in a private equity firm make from taking a share of any positive return generated by the fund.

General Cash Offer

A method of issuing securities where a firm offers new shares to investors in exchange for cash.

Exit Strategy

The method used by equity investors to realize a return form their initial equity investment. There are two general types of exit strategies: an acquisition by another firm or a public equity offering.

Initial Public Offering (IPO)

The process of selling stock to the public for the first time.

Leveraged Buyout (LBO)

In a **leveraged buyout** (LBO), a group of private investors purchases all the equity of a public corporation.

Lockup

An agreement that forbids pre-IPO shareholders from selling their shares for a period—generally 180 days—after an IPO.

Over-Allotment Provision, Greenshoe Provision

An option which allows an underwriter to issue more 15% more shares in an IPO.

Post-Money Valuation

The value of the whole firm (old plus new shares) at the funding round price.

Pre-Money Valuation

The value of the shares outstanding prior to a new funding round at the price in the funding round.

Primary Offering

Shares that are sold in a security offering in which the proceeds go to the issuing firm.

Private Equity Firm

A firm that specializes in raising money and undertaking leveraged buyouts (LBOs) on behalf of investors in a private equity fund using the money raised for funding the equity portion of LBOs.

Rights Offer

A method of raising seasoned equity in which the firm offers new shares only to existing shareholders.

Road Show

A process in which senior management and the lead underwriters travel around the country explaining the deal to their largest customers—mainly institutional investors such as mutual funds and pension funds—before an IPO.

Seasoned Equity Offering (SEO)

The process in which a public firm issues new shares.

Secondary Offering

Shares that are sold in a security offering by stockholders in which the proceeds go to a stockholder instead of the issuing firm.

Spread

The difference between the underwriter's purchase price and the offer price in a security offering.

Syndicate

A group of underwriters responsible for managing the IPO process and marketing and selling the issue.

Tombstone

An advertisement in newspapers in which intermediaries advertise the sale of stock (both IPOs and SEOs). They were more important several years ago; today, investors become informed about the impending sale of stock by the news media, via a road show, or through the book-building process, so these tombstones are merely a ritual.

Underwriter

An investment banking firm that manages the security offering and designs its structure.

Venture Capital Limited Partnership

A limited partnership formed to invest in the private equity of young firms. Institutional investors, such as pension funds, are typically the limited partners. Most firms charge an annual management fee of 2% of the fund's committed capital plus 20% of any positive return they generate.

Winner's Curse

An explanation for the underpricing of IPOs. An investor who requests shares in an IPO will "win" (get all the shares you requested) when demand for the shares by others is low, and the IPO is more likely to perform poorly. However, the investor will get low allocations in the best IPOs because they are oversubscribed. This effect implies that it may be necessary for the underwriter to underprice its issues on average in order for less-informed investors to be willing to participate in IPOs.

Concept Check Questions and Answers

23.1.1. What are the main sources of funding for private companies to raise outside equity capital?

Private companies can raise outside equity capital from angel investors, venture capital firms, institutional investors, and corporate investors.

23.1.2. What is a venture capital firm?

A venture capital firm is a limited partnership that specializes in raising money to invest in the private equity of young firms.

23.2.1. What are some advantages and disadvantages of going public?

The main advantages of going public are improved liquidity for the equity investors and better access to capital, both from the IPO proceeds and in subsequent equity offerings. A disadvantage of going public is that the equity holders of the corporation become more widely dispersed, reducing investors' ability to monitor the company's management and thus represents a loss of control. Also, public firms must satisfy all of the increasingly stringent reporting requirements, which is costly and time-consuming.

23.2.2. Explain the mechanics of an auction IPO.

In an auction IPO, the company that goes public lets the market determine the price by auctioning off the company. Investors place bids over a set period of time. An auction IPO sorts the bids from high to low, and sells the stock at the highest price that will sell all of the offered shares. All winning bidders pay this price, even if they initially bid something higher.

23.3.1. List and discuss four characteristics about IPOs that financial economists find puzzling.

There are four IPO puzzles. First, on average IPOs appear to be underpriced: the price at the end of trading on the first day is often substantially higher than the IPO price. Second, the number of issues is highly cyclical. Third, the costs of the IPO are very high. Fourth, the long-run performance of a newly public company is poor.

23.3.2. What is a possible explanation for IPO underpricing?

The most prominent explanation of underpricing is the manifestation of a form of adverse selection referred to as the **winner's curse.** An investor who requests shares in an IPO will "win" (get all the shares requested) when demand for the shares by others is low, and the IPO is more likely to perform poorly. However, the investor will get low allocations in the best IPOs because they are oversubscribed. This effect implies that it may be necessary for the underwriter to underprice its issues on average in order for less-informed investors to participate in IPOs.

23.4.1. What is the difference between a cash offer and a rights offer for a seasoned equity offering?

In a cash offer, a firm offers the new shares to investors at large. In a right offer, a firm offers the new shares only to existing shareholders.

23.4.2. What is the average stock price reaction to an SEO?

Researchers have found that the stock price reaction to an SEO is negative on average. Often the value destroyed by the price decline can be a significant fraction of the new money raised.

Examples with Step-by-Step Solutions

Solving Problems

Problems may involve determining the pre-money valuation, the post-money valuation, and the fractional ownership interests surrounding a round of financing as in example 1 below. Other problems may involve understanding the mechanics of an auction IPO as in example 2. You should also be able to determine an initial IPO valuation based on comparable firm valuation multiples as in example 3. You should also understand the basic mechanics of a rights offering and be able to calculate the underwriter's spread in an IPO or SEO and the initial return (or underpricing) in an IPO. The Questions and Problems section provides examples of all of these applications.

Examples

1. You initially funded your start-up company by contributing $250,000 for 250,000 shares of stock. Since then, you have sold an additional 500,000 shares to angel investors. You are now considering raising even more capital from a venture capital limited partnership (VC). This VC would invest $4.5 million and would receive 750,000 newly issued shares.
   [A]   What is the pre-money valuation?
   [B]   What is the post-money valuation?
   [C]   What percentage will you own? What is the value of your shares?
   [D]   What percentage of the firm will the VC end up owning?

Step 1. Determine the pre-money valuation.

The pre-money valuation is the value of the shares outstanding prior to a new funding round at the price in the funding round.

The number of shares before the new round of financing from the VC is:

Stockholder	Number of Shares
You	250,000
Angels	500,000
Total	750,000

The VC is paying $4,500,000/750,000 = $6 per share, so the pre-money valuation is:

$6 × 750,000 = $4,500,000.

Step 2. Determine the post-money valuation.

The post-money value is the value of the whole firm (old plus new shares) at the funding round price.

The number of shares after the new round of financing from the VC is:

Stockholder	Number of Shares
You	250,000
Angels	500,000
Venture capital firm	750,000
Total	1,500,000

The VC is paying $4,500,000 / 750,000 = $6 per share, so the post-money valuation is:

$6 × 1,500,000 = $9,000,000.

Step 3. Determine your ownership stake and value after the new round of financing.

You own $\dfrac{250,000}{1,500,000} = 16.6\bar{6}\%$.

Your stake is worth 250,000 × $6 = $1,500,000.

Step 4. Determine the VC's ownership stake after the new round of financing.

The VC owns $\dfrac{750,000}{1,500,000} = 50\%$.

2. **Your firm is ready to issue stock in an initial public offering. You hope to raise $40 million by issuing 4 million shares at $10, but you are using an auction IPO so the auction will ultimately determine how much equity will be raised if 4 million shares are issued. After the deadline for submitting bids, the following bids were received:**

Price	Number of Shares
$12.00	200,000
11.50	300,000
11.00	500,000
10.50	1,500,000
10.00	2,000,000
9.50	3,000,000
9.00	4,500,000

Will you be able to raise $40 million?

Step 1. Determine the cumulative demand schedule.

Price	Number of Shares
$12.00	200,000
11.50	500,000
11.00	1,000,000
10.50	3,000,000
10.00	5,000,000
9.50	8,000,000
9.00	12,500,000

Step 2. Determine the winning price.

The offer price is the highest price such that the number of bids at or above that price equals the number of offered shares. All winning bidders pay this price, even if their bid was higher.

The winning price is thus $10.

All auction participants who bid prices higher than $10 will receive the number of shares they bid. However, since there are 2 million bids at $10, but only 1 million shares available to these bidders, the shares will have to be rationed. Shares will be awarded on a pro rata basis to bidders who bid $10.

3. **You are an investment banker preparing your PowerPoint presentation for the upcoming road show for a client in the satellite radio industry, iRadio. Last year, iRadio had sales of $300 million and EBITDA of $50 million. You have identified the following information for the two closest competitors, XM Satellite Radio and Sirius, which have recently gone public:**

Company	$\dfrac{\text{Enterprise Value}}{\text{EBITDA}}$	$\dfrac{\text{Enterprise Value}}{\text{Sales}}$
XM Satellite Radio	22.3	5.3
Sirius	24.8	7.6

XM, Sirius, and iRadio all have no debt. After the IPO, iRadio will have 50 million shares outstanding. Determine the comparable multiple valuations that should be included in the presentation.

Step 1. Determine the valuation based on the EBITDA multiples of the comparable firms.

The average comparable firm ratio is 23.6, thus the total equity value is:

50,000,000 × 23.6 = $1,180,000,000

and the value per share is:

$$\frac{\$1,180,000,000}{50,000,000} = \$23.60.$$

Step 2. Determine the revenue multiple relative valuation.

The average comparable firm ratio is 6.5, thus the total equity value is:

300,000,000 × 6.5 = $1,950,000,000

and the value per share is:

$$\frac{\$1,950,000,000}{50,000,000} = \$39.00.$$

Step 3. Make a conclusion.

Although a discounted cash flow analysis should also be conducted, based on the comparable firm multiples, the price range for iRadio stock is between $24 and $39 per share.

Questions and Problems

1. Starbucks has 800 million shares outstanding trading at $40 per share. They want to raise $2 billion and are considering using a rights offering.
   [A] If the offering requires 10 rights to purchase one share at $25 per share, how much will they raise? What is the value per share after the rights issue?
   [B] If the offering requires 8 rights to purchase one share at $20 per share, how much will they raise? What is the value per share after the rights issue?

2. eHealth plans to offer 5 million shares at $10 each with Morgan Stanley and Merrill Lynch serving as co-lead underwriters.
   [A] If the underwriters' spread is the standard 7%, how much will the firm raise?
   [B] If the first day's closing price is $12.44, how much is the issue underpriced by?

3. You initially funded your company by contributing nothing more than some software code you had written in graduate school. You then formed a corporation and raised $1 million in venture capital (VC) financing in exchange for 25% of the firm's equity. You are now considering raising more capital from the same VC firm. This VC would invest another $10 million in order to maintain the same fractional ownership.
   [A] What is the post-money valuation?
   [B] What is the value of your shares?

4. Your firm is conducting an auction IPO of 1 million shares. After the deadline for submitting bids, the following bids were received:

Price	Number of Shares
$6.00	0
5.75	10,000
5.50	40,000
5.25	350,000
5.00	600,000
4.75	1,000,000
4.50	1,500,000

   How much will the offering raise?

5. You are a mutual fund manager considering an IPO for a firm that produces hydroelectric energy that is expected to be priced at $12 per share. Last year, the firm had sales of $100 million and EBITDA of $5 million. You have identified the following information for the two closest competitors, Gulf Electric and Columbia Power:

Company	Price / Earnings	Price / Sales
Gulf Electric	26.2	2.2
Columbia Power	32.5	2.8

   After the IPO, the issuing firm will have 10 million shares outstanding. Based on the comparable firm multiples, is the IPO an attractive investment?

Solutions to Questions and Problems

1. [A] If investors exercise their rights, 800 million/10 = 80 million shares will be purchased at $25 raising $2 billion.
The value of the firm after the issue is 800 million × $40 + $2 billion = $34 billion.
The value per share is thus $34 billion/880 million = $38.64.

   [B] If investors exercise their rights, 800 million/8 = 100 million shares will be purchased at $20 raising $2 billion.
The value of the firm after the issue is 800 million × $40 + $2 billion = $34 billion.
The value per share is thus $34 billion/900 million = $37.78.

2. [A] The spread is the difference between the underwriter's purchase price and the offer price. In this case, it equals 0.07 × $10 per share = $0.70 per share. Thus the firm would raise $9.30 × 5 million = $46.5 million.

   [B] The underpricing, or initial return, equals:

$$\frac{\$12.44 - \$10}{\$10} = 24.4\%$$

3. [A] The post-money value is the value of the whole firm (old plus new shares) at the funding round price. Since the VC is contributing $10 million for 25% of the corporation's equity, the post-money valuation is 4 × $10 million = $40 million.

   [B] Determine your ownership stake and value after the new round of financing.
You own 75% of the equity, which is worth $30 million.

4. The cumulative demand schedule is:

Price	Number of Shares
$6.00	0
5.75	10,000
5.50	50,000
5.25	400,000
5.00	1,000,000
4.75	2,000,000
4.50	3,500,000

The offer price is the highest price such that the number of bids at or above that price equals the number of offered shares. All winning bidders pay this price, even if their bid was higher.

The winning price is thus $5 and you will raise $5 million before any fees.

5. Determine the P/E multiple relative valuation.

The average comparable firm ratio is 29.4, thus the total equity value is:

5,000,000 × 29.4 = $147,000,000

and the value per share is:

$$\frac{\$147,000,000}{10,000,000} = \$14.70.$$

Determine the revenue multiple relative valuation.

The average comparable firm P/S ratio is 2.5, thus the total equity value is:

$100,000,000 \times 2.5 = \$250,000,000$

and the value per share is:

$$\frac{\$250,000,000}{10,000,000} = \$25.00.$$

Based on the comparable firm multiples, the price of $10 looks attractive.

CHAPTER 24

Debt Financing

Chapter Synopsis

24.1 Corporate Debt

In order to issue public bonds, a prospectus must be produced that describes the details of the offering and includes an **indenture,** a formal contract between the bond issuer and a trust company. The trust company represents the bondholders and makes sure that the terms of the indenture are enforced.

While corporate bonds generally make semiannual coupon payments, corporations sometimes issue zero-coupon bonds as well. Most corporate bonds have maturities of 30 years or less, although in the past there have been original maturities of up to 999 years.

A bond's face value, typically $1,000, does not always correspond to the actual cash raised because of underwriting fees and the possibility that the bond may be issued at a discount to face value. If a coupon bond is issued at a discount, it is called an **original issue discount** (OID) bond.

Historically, most bonds were **bearer bonds,** and whoever physically held the bond certificate owned the bond. However, nearly all bonds that are issued today are **registered bonds.** The issuer maintains a list of all holders of its bonds and, on each coupon payment date, the bond issuer consults its list of registered owners and sends the owner the coupon payment.

Four types of corporate debt are typically issued: **notes**, **debentures, mortgage bonds,** and **asset-backed bonds.** Debentures and notes are unsecured debt and, in the event of bankruptcy, the holders have a claim to only the assets of the firm that are not already pledged as collateral on other debt. Notes typically have shorter maturities (less than ten years) than debentures. Asset-backed bonds and mortgage bonds are secured debt: Specific assets are pledged as collateral that bondholders have a direct claim to in the event of bankruptcy. Mortgage bonds are secured by real property, whereas asset-backed bonds can be secured by any kind of asset. Although the word "bond" is commonly used to mean any kind of debt security, technically a corporate bond must be secured.

A bondholder's priority in claiming assets in the event of default is known as the bond's **seniority.** Most debenture issues contain clauses restricting the company from issuing new debt with equal or higher priority than existing debt. When a firm conducts a subsequent debenture issue that has lower priority than its outstanding debt, the new debt is known as a **subordinated debenture.**

International bonds are classified into four broadly defined categories.

- **Domestic bonds** are bonds issued by a local entity and traded in a local market, but purchased by foreigners. They are denominated in the local currency.

- **Foreign bonds** are bonds issued by a foreign company in a local market and are intended for local investors. They are also denominated in the local currency. Foreign bonds in the United States are known as **Yankee bonds.** In other countries, foreign bonds also have special names. For example, in Japan they are called **Samurai bonds;** in the United Kingdom, they are known as **Bulldogs.**

- **Eurobonds** are international bonds that are not denominated in the local currency of the country in which they are issued.

- **Global bonds** combine the features of domestic, foreign, and Eurobonds and are offered for sale in several different markets simultaneously.

The **private debt** market is larger than the public debt market. Private debt has the advantage that it avoids the cost of registration but the disadvantage of being illiquid. There are two segments of the private debt market:

- A bank **term loan** may be issued by a single bank, or it may be a **syndicated loan** issued by a group of banks.

- A **private placement** is a bond issue that does not trade on a public market but rather is sold to a small group of investors. Because a private placement does not need to be registered, it is less costly to issue. Instead of an indenture, often a simple promissory note is sufficient. In 1990, the U.S. Securities and Exchange Commission (SEC) issued Rule 144A, which significantly increased the liquidity of certain privately placed debt. Private debt issued under this rule can be traded by large financial institutions among themselves.

24.2 Other Types of Debt

Sovereign debt is debt issued by national governments, such as U.S. Treasury securities, which represent the single largest sector of the U.S. bond market.

The U.S. Treasury issues five kinds of securities.

- **Treasury bills** are pure discount bonds that have original maturities of less than one year. Currently the Treasury issues bills with original maturities of 4, 13, and 26 weeks.

- **Treasury notes** are semi-annual coupon bonds with original maturities of between 1 and 10 years. The Treasury issues notes with maturities of 2, 3, 5, and 10 years at the present time.

- **Treasury bonds** are semiannual-paying coupon bonds with maturities longer than 10 years. Recently, the Treasury resumed sales of 30-year Treasury bonds with a bond that was issued on February 15, 2006; in the future, it plans to sell 30-year bonds four times a year, in February, May, August, and November.

- **TIPS** (Treasury Inflation-Protected Securities) are inflation-indexed bonds with maturities of 5, 10, and 20 years. These coupon bonds have an outstanding principal that is adjusted for inflation. Thus, although the coupon rate is fixed, the dollar coupon varies because the semiannual coupon payments are a fixed rate of the inflation-adjusted principal. The final repayment of principal at maturity is inflation-adjusted and also protected against deflation.

Treasury securities are initially sold to the public in an auction. All competitive bidders submit sealed bids in terms of the yield and the amount of bonds they are willing to purchase. The Treasury then accepts the lowest-yield competitive bids up to the amount required to fund the issue. The highest yield accepted is termed the **stop-out yield.** Noncompetitive bidders (usually individuals) just submit the amount of bonds they wish to purchase and are guaranteed to have their orders filled at the auction. All successful bidders (including the noncompetitive bidders) are awarded the same yield.

STRIPS (Separate Trading of Registered Interest and Principal Securities) are repackaged securities in which investment banks purchase Treasury notes and bonds and then resell each coupon and principal payment separately as a zero-coupon bond.

Agency securities are issued by a U.S. government agency, such as the Government National Mortgage Association (GNMA, or "Ginnie Mae"), or by a U.S. government-sponsored enterprise, such as the Student Loan Marketing Association ("Sallie Mae"). Although they are not generally backed by the full faith and credit of the U.S. government (Ginnie Mae is an exception because its issues do contain this explicit guarantee), many investors doubt that the government would allow any of its agencies to default; thus, they believe that these issues contain an implicit guarantee.

Most agency bonds are mortgage-backed securities that are **pass-through securities** in which each security is backed by an underlying **pool** of mortgages. When homeowners in the pool make their mortgage payments, this cash is passed through (minus servicing fees) to the bond holders.

Municipal bonds, which are issued by state and local governments, pay interest that is not taxable at the federal level and may be exempt from state and local taxes as well. They are often structured as **serial bonds** in which they are scheduled to mature serially over a number of years.

- **General obligation bonds** are backed by the full faith and credit of a local government.

- **Revenue bonds** are funded by specific revenues generated by projects that were initially financed by the bond issue, but they are not backed by the full faith and credit of a local government.

An **asset-backed security** (ABS) is a security that is made up of other financial securities. The security's cash flows come from the cash flows of the underlying financial securities that "back" it. We refer to the process of creating an asset-backed security by packaging a portfolio of financial securities and issuing an asset-backed security backed by this portfolio as **asset securitization.**

By far the largest sector of the asset-backed security market is the mortgage-backed security market. A **mortgage-backed security** (MBS) is an asset-backed security backed by home mortgages. U.S. government agencies, such as the Government National Mortgage Association (GNMA, or "Ginnie Mae"), are the largest issuers in this sector.

24.3 Bond Covenants

Covenants are restrictive clauses in a bond contract that limit the issuer from taking actions that may weaken its ability to repay the bonds. For example, covenants may restrict the ability of management to pay dividends, or they may limit the level of further indebtedness or specify that the issuer must maintain a minimum amount of working capital. If the issuer fails to live up to any covenant, the bond goes into default.

By including more covenants, issuers can reduce their cost of borrowing. The stronger the covenants in the bond contract, the less likely the issuer will default on the bond, and so the lower the interest rate investors will require to buy the bond.

24.4 Repayment Provisions

While an issuer can always retire one of its bonds early by repurchasing the bond in the open market, **callable bonds** give the issuer of the bond the right to retire all outstanding bonds on (or after) a specific **call date** for the **call price**, generally set at or above the bond's face value. If the call provision offers a cheaper way to retire the bonds, the issuer can forgo the option of purchasing the bonds in the open market and call the bonds instead.

Before the call date, investors anticipate the optimal strategy that the issuer will follow, and the bond price reflects this strategy.

- When market yields are high relative to the bond coupon, investors anticipate that the likelihood of exercising the call is low and the bond price is similar to an otherwise identical non-callable bond.

- When market yields are low relative to the bond coupon, investors anticipate that the bond will likely be called, so its price is close to the price of a non-callable bond that matures on the call date.

The **yield to call** (YTC) is the annual yield of a callable bond assuming that the bond is called at the earliest opportunity.

Some bonds are repaid through a **sinking fund** in which the issuer makes regular payments into a fund that is used to repurchase bonds. Bonds selling at a discount are repurchased in the open market; if a bond is trading at a premium, the bonds are repurchased at par in a lottery.

Convertible bonds give bondholders the right to convert the bond into stock at any time up to the maturity date of the bond. Thus a convertible bond can be thought of as a regular bond plus a warrant (a call option written by the company on new stock it will have to issue if the warrant is exercised), so a convertible bond is worth more than an otherwise identical straight bond.

At maturity, the strike price, or **conversion price,** of the embedded warrant in a convertible bond is equal to the face value of the bond divided by the **conversion ratio,** which equals the number of shares of common stock into which each bond can be converted. If the stock does not pay a dividend, then the holder of a convertible bond should wait until maturity before deciding whether to convert.

When convertible bonds are also callable, then if the issuer calls them, the holder can choose to convert rather than let the bonds be called. When the bonds are called, the holder faces exactly the same decision as he would on the maturity date of the bonds: He will choose to convert if the stock price exceeds the conversion price and let the bonds be called otherwise.

Selected Concepts and Key Terms

Agency Securities

Bonds issued by agencies of a U.S. government agency, such as the Government National Mortgage Association (GNMA, or "Ginnie Mae"), or by a U.S. government-sponsored enterprise, such as the Student Loan Marketing Association ("Sallie Mae"). Although they are not generally backed by the full faith and credit of the U.S. government (Ginnie Mae is an exception because its issues do contain this explicit guarantee), many investors doubt that the government would allow any of its agencies to default; thus, they believe that these issues contain an implicit guarantee.

Asset-Backed Bonds

Bonds secured by specific assets. In the event of default, the bondholders have a right to seize the assets that serve as collateral.

Asset-Backed Security (ABS)

An asset-backed security (ABS) is a security that is made up of other financial securities. The security's cash flows come from the cash flows of the underlying financial securities that "back" it.

Asset Securitization

The process of creating an asset-backed security by packaging a portfolio of financial securities and issuing an asset-backed security backed by this portfolio.

Balloon Payment

A large payment on a bond's maturity date used to retire the issue.

Bearer Bonds

Bonds in which the physical holder of the bond certificate is the owner of the bond.

Bulldogs

Bonds issued by a foreign company in the United Kingdom that are intended for local investors and denominated in pounds.

Callable bonds, Call date, Call price,

Bonds that give the issuer of the bond the right (but not the obligation) to retire all outstanding bonds on (or after) a specific **call date** for the **call price,** generally set at or above the bond's face value.

Convertible bonds, Conversion price, Conversion ratio

Bonds that give bondholders the right to convert the bond into stock at any time up to the maturity date for the bond. At maturity, the strike price, or **conversion price,** of the embedded warrant in a convertible bond is equal to the face value of the bond divided by the **conversion ratio,** which specifies the number of shares of common stock into which each bond can be converted.

Covenants

Restrictive clauses in a bond contract that limit the issuer from taking actions that may weaken its ability to repay the bonds.

Debentures

Unsecured bonds with maturities longer than ten years.

Eurobonds

International bonds that are not denominated in the local currency of the country in which they are issued.

Foreign Bonds

Bonds issued by a foreign company in a local market and intended for local investors and denominated in the local currency.

General Obligation Bonds

Municipal bonds that are backed by the full faith and credit of a local government.

Indenture

The formal contract between the bond issuer and a trust company. The trust company represents the bondholders and makes sure that the terms of the indenture are enforced.

Leveraged Buyout (LBO)

A group of private investors who purchase all the equity of a public corporation.

Mortgage Bonds

Bonds that are secured by real property.

Municipal Bonds

Bonds issued by state and local governments that pay interest that is not taxable at the federal level and may be exempt from state and local taxes as well.

Treasury Notes

Semi-annual coupon bonds with original maturities of between 1 and 10 years. The Treasury issues notes with maturities of 2, 3, 5, and 10 years at the present time.

Original Issue Discount (OID) Bonds

A bond that is issued at a discount to its face value.

Revenue Bonds

Municipal bonds funded by specific revenues generated by projects that were initially financed by the bond issue, but not backed by the full faith and credit of a local government.

Seniority

A bondholder's priority in claiming assets in the event of default

Sinking Fund

A feature of a bond issue in which the issuer makes regular payments into a fund administered by the trustee over the life of the bond that is used to repurchase bonds.

Sovereign Debt

Debt issued by national governments, such as U.S. Treasury securities

Stop-Out Yield

The highest yield accepted yield in a Treasury security auction. All successful bidders are awarded this yield.

STRIPS (Separate Trading of Registered Interest and Principal Securities)

The repackaging of Treasury notes and bonds in which each coupon and principal payment is sold separately as a zero-coupon bond.

Subordinated Debenture

A debenture issue that has lower priority than other outstanding debentures.

Syndicated Bank Loan

A bank loan issued by a group of banks in which one lead bank typically takes a small percentage of the loan and syndicates the rest to other banks.

TIPS (Treasury Inflation-Protected Securities)

Inflation-indexed bonds with maturities of 5, 10, and 20 years that have an outstanding principal that is adjusted for inflation. Thus, although the coupon rate is fixed, the dollar coupon varies because the semiannual coupon payments are a fixed rate of the inflation-adjusted principal. The final repayment of principal at maturity is also protected against deflation.

Yankee Bonds

Foreign bonds issued in the United States, intended for U.S. investors, and denominated in dollars.

Yield to Call (YTC)

The annual yield of a callable bond assuming that the bond is called at the earliest opportunity.

Concept Check Questions and Answers

24.1.1. List four types of corporate debt that are typically issued.

Four types of corporate debt that are typically issued are notes, debentures, mortgage bonds, and asset-backed bonds.

24.1.2. What are the four categories of international bonds?

International bonds consist of four categories: domestic bonds are bonds that are issued by a local entity and traded in a local market, but purchased by foreigners; foreign bonds are bonds issued by a foreign company in a local market and are intended for local investors; Eurobonds are international bonds that are not denominated in the local currency of the country which they are issued; and global bonds combine the features of domestic, foreign, and Eurobonds and are offered for sale in several different markets simultaneously.

24.2.1. List four different kinds of securities issued by the U.S. Treasury.

The U.S. Treasury issues four different kinds of securities: bills, notes, bonds, and Treasury Inflation-Protected Securities (TIPS).

24.2.2. What is the distinguishing characteristic of municipal bonds?

The distinguishing characteristic of municipal bonds is that the income on municipal bonds is not taxable at the federal level.

24.2.3. What is an asset-backed security?

A security that is made up of other financial securities. The security's cash flows come from the cash flows of the underlying financial securities that "back" it.

24.3.1. What happens if an issuer fails to live up to a bond covenant?

If the issuer fails to live up to any covenant, the bond goes into default. That event may lead the firm into bankruptcy.

24.3.2. Why can bond covenants reduce a firm's borrowing cost?

The stronger the covenants in the bond contract, the less likely the issuer will default on the bond, and so the lower the interest rate investors will require to buy the bond. That is, by including more covenants, issuers can reduce their costs of borrowing.

24.4.1. What is a sinking fund?

A sinking fund provision requires a company to make regular payments into a sinking fund administered by a trustee over the life of the bond. These payments are then used to repurchase bonds.

24.4.2. Do callable bonds have a higher or lower yield than otherwise identical bonds without a call feature? Why?

The issuer will exercise the call option only when the market rates are lower than the bond's coupon rate. Therefore, the holder of a callable bond faces reinvestment risk precisely when it hurts. This makes the callable bonds relatively less attractive to the bondholder than the identical non-callable bonds. Consequently, callable bonds will trade at a lower price and therefore have a higher yield than otherwise identical bonds without a call feature.

24.4.3. Why does a convertible bond have a lower yield than an otherwise identical bond without the option to convert?

A convertible bond has a lower yield than an otherwise identical bond without the option to convert because it has an embedded warrant. If the price of a firm were to rise subsequently so that the bondholders choose to convert, the current shareholders would have to sell an equity stake in their firm for below-market value. The lower interest rate is compensation for the possibility that this event will occur.

Examples with Step-by-Step Solutions

Solving Problems

Problems may involve determining the cash flows of Treasury Inflation-Protected Securities (TIPS) like in example 1 below. Problems may also require determining the yield to call (YTC) for a callable bond, as in example 2 below. Finally, problems may require the determination of the conversion price, conversion value, and optimal conversion strategy for a convertible bond as in example 3.

Examples

1. On July 15th, 2001 the Treasury issued 10-year Treasury Inflation-Protected Securities (TIPS) with a semi-annual coupon rate of 5% and a face value of $1,000. On that date, the Consumer Price Index (CPI), on which the inflation is protection based, was 176.5.
   [A]   If the CPI is at 247 on the maturity date, what coupon and principal will be paid?
   [B]   If the CPI is at 150 on the maturity date, what coupon and principal will be paid?

   Step 1. Determine the principal and interest if the CPI is at 247 at maturity.

   The CPI index appreciated by:

   $$\frac{247 - 176.5}{176.5} = 40\%$$

   Thus, the principal amount of the bond increased by 40% from $1,000 to $1,400.

   The semi-annual coupon payment is:

   $$\left(\frac{0.05}{2}\right) \times \$1,400 = \$35.00$$

   and the final payment of the principal is $1,400.

   Step 2. Determine the principal and interest if the CPI is at 150.

   The CPI index depreciated by:

   $$\frac{150 - 176.5}{176.5} = 15\%$$

   Thus, the principal amount of the bond decreased by 15% from $1,000 to $850.

   The semi-annual coupon payment is

   $$\left(\frac{0.05}{2}\right) \times \$850 = \$21.25.$$

   However, the final payment of the principal is protected against deflation. Thus, the original face value of $1,000 will be repaid.

2. Berkshire Hathaway has just issued 20-year, $1,000 face value, 6% semi-annual coupon bonds that are callable at 105% of par. The bond can be called in one year or anytime thereafter on a coupon payment date. The bonds are trading at 95% of par. What is the bond's yield to maturity (YTM) and yield to call (YTC)?

Step 1. Draw a time line showing the bond's payments.

Step 2. Calculate the yield to maturity based on holding the bond to maturity.

$$\$950 = \frac{30}{YTM}\left(1 - \frac{1}{(1+YTM)^{40}}\right) + \frac{1,000}{(1+YTM)^{40}} \Rightarrow YTM=3.2\%$$

So, the annual yield to maturity is 6.4%.

Step 3. Draw a time line showing the bond's payments if it is called at its first call date.

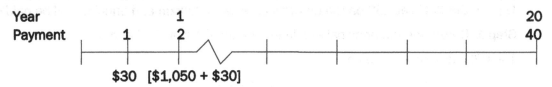

Step 4. Calculate the yield to call if it is called at its first call date

$$\$950 = \frac{30}{YTM}\left(1 - \frac{1}{(1+YTM)^{2}}\right) + \frac{1,050}{(1+YTM)^{2}} \Rightarrow YTM=8.2\%$$

So the annual yield to call is 16.4%.

3. **You own a convertible bond with a face value of $1,000 that is convertible into 20 shares of a stock that does not pay a dividend.**
   [A]   **What is the conversion ratio?**
   [B]   **What is the conversion price?**
   [C]   **If the stock is trading at $60 five years before the maturity date, should you convert the bond into stock?**
   [D]   **If the stock is trading at $60 at the maturity date, should you convert the bond into stock?**

Step 1. Determine the conversion ratio.

The conversion ratio is the number of shares of stock that the bond can be converted into. So the conversion ratio is 20.

Step 2. Determine the conversion price.

The conversion price of the embedded warrant in a convertible bond is equal to the face value of the bond divided by the conversion ratio, so:

The conversion price is $1,000/20 = $50.

Step 3. Determine the conversion value of the bond if the stock price is $60.

The value of 20 shares of stock is $60 × 20 = $1,200.

Step 4. Decide if you should convert the bond into stock if the stock is trading at $60 five years before the maturity date

If the stock does not pay a dividend, then it is never optimal to exercise a call early. Thus, the holder of a convertible bond should wait until the maturity date of the bond before deciding whether to convert.

Step 5. Decide if you should convert the bond into stock if it is at the maturity date.

Since the conversion value of the bond is worth more than $1,000, you should convert the bond into stock.

Questions and Problems

1. On Wednesday, January 29, 1997, the United States Treasury made its first issue of an inflation-linked bond which matured in January of 2007. The bonds had a semi-annual coupon rate of 3.375% and a face value of $1,000. On that date, the Consumer Price Index (CPI), on which the inflation protection based, was 160. On January 26, 2007, the CPI was 205. What coupon and principal was paid on that date?

2. Motorola has $1,000 face value, 9% semi-annual coupon bonds that mature in 7 years and are callable at 102% of par. The bond can be called in exactly 2 years or anytime thereafter on a coupon payment date. The bonds are trading for $1,075. What is the bond's yield to maturity and yield to call?

3. Your firm has the following capital structure:

Security	Face or Par Value
Debentures	$20 million
Stock	$1 million
Subordinated Debentures	$10 million
Mortgage Bonds	$40 million
Preferred Stock	$5 million

You have just filed for bankruptcy under Chapter 7 of the 1978 Bankruptcy Reform Act. A trustee has been appointed to oversee the liquidation of the firm's assets through an auction.

[A]   If the asset auction raises $45 million, including all real estate, how will the proceeds be allocated to the security holders?

[B]   If the asset auction raises $75 million, including all real estate, how will the proceeds be allocated to the security holders?

4. You own a convertible bond with a face value of $1,000 and a conversion ratio of 25. If the stock is trading at $37 at the maturity date, should you convert the bond into stock?

5. Draw a payoff diagram for a convertible bond with a face value of $1,000 and a conversion ratio of 25.
[A]   At the maturity date.
[B]   Two years before the maturity date. (An approximate diagram is sufficient here.)

Solutions to Questions and Problems

1. The CPI index appreciated by:

$$\frac{205-160}{160} = 28\%$$

Thus, the principal amount of the bond increased by 28% from $1,000 to $1,280.

The semi-annual coupon payment is:

$$\left(\frac{0.03375}{2}\right) \times \$1,280 = \$21.60.$$

and the final payment of the principal is $1,280.

2. The time line showing the bond's payments is.

The yield to maturity based on holding the bond to maturity is:

$$\$1,075 = \frac{45}{YTM}\left(1 - \frac{1}{(1+YTM)^{14}}\right) + \frac{1,000}{(1+YTM)^{14}} \Rightarrow YTM = 3.8\%$$

So, the annual yield to maturity is 7.6%.

The bond's payments if it is called at its first call date are.

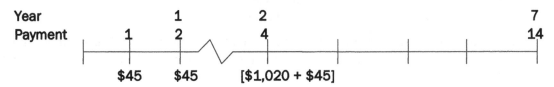

The yield to call if it is called at its first call date is:

$$\$1,075 = \frac{45}{YTM}\left(1 - \frac{1}{(1+YTM)^{4}}\right) + \frac{1,020}{(1+YTM)^{4}} \Rightarrow YTM = 2.96\%$$

So the annual yield to call is 5.9%.

3. [A] The proceeds from the liquidation are used to pay the firm's creditors according to their order in the legal seniority.

Security	Face or Par Value	Amount Received
Mortgage Bonds	$40 million	$40 million
Debentures	$10 million	$5 million
Subordinated Debentures	$10 million	$0
Preferred Stock	$5 million	$0
Stock	$1 million	$0

[B]   The proceeds from the liquidation are used to pay the firm's creditors according to their order in the legal seniority.

Security	Face or Par Value	Amount Received
Mortgage Bonds	$40 million	$40 million
Debentures	$10 million	$10 million
Subordinated Debentures	$10 million	$10 million
Preferred Stock	$5 million	$5 million
Stock	$1 million	$10 million

4. The conversion ratio is 25, so bond can be converted into 25 shares of stock.

The value of 25 shares of stock is $38 × 25 = $950. Since the conversion value of the bond is less more than $1,000, you should not convert the bond into stock.

5. [A]

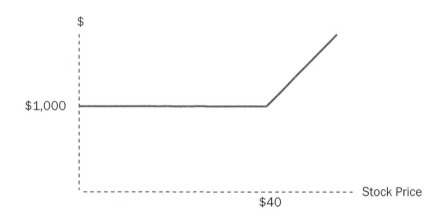

[B]

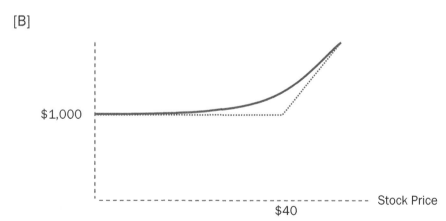

CHAPTER 25

Leasing

Chapter Synopsis

25.1 The Basics of Leasing

A lease is a contract between two parties.

- The **lessee** is liable for periodic payments in exchange for the right to use the asset.

- The **lessor** is the owner of the asset and is entitled to the lease payments in exchange for letting the lessee use the asset.

At the end of the contract term, the lease specifies who will retain ownership of the asset and at what terms. The lease also specifies any cancellation provisions, any options for renewal and purchase, and the obligations for maintenance and related servicing costs.

Many types of lease transactions are possible based on the relationship between the lessee and the lessor.

- In a **sales-type lease**, the lessor is the manufacturer of (or a primary dealer for) the asset.

- In a **direct lease**, the lessor is an independent company that specializes in purchasing assets and leasing them to customers.

- In a **sale and leaseback**, the lessee receives cash from the sale of the asset and then makes lease payments to retain the use of the asset.

- In a **leveraged lease**, the lessor borrows the initial capital for the purchase and uses the lease payments to pay interest and principal on the loan.

In some circumstances, the lessor is not an independent company but rather a separate business partnership, called a **special-purpose entity** (SPE), which is created by the lessee for the sole purpose of obtaining the lease. SPEs are commonly used in **synthetic leases**, which are designed to obtain specific accounting and tax treatment.

In a perfect market, the cost of leasing is equivalent to the cost of buying and reselling the asset:

$$PV(\text{Lease Payments}) = \text{Purchase Price} - PV(\text{Residual Value})$$

where the **residual value** is the market value of the asset at the end of the lease. Thus the amount of the lease payment will depend on the purchase price, the residual value, and the appropriate discount rate for the cash flows.

In a perfect market, the cost of leasing and then purchasing the asset is equivalent to the cost of borrowing to purchase the asset and making loan payments:

$$PV(\text{Lease Payments}) + PV(\text{Residual Value}) = PV(\text{Loan Payments}).$$

At the end of the lease, the lease may allow the lessee to obtain ownership of the asset for some price.

- A **fair market value** (FMV) lease gives the lessee the option to purchase the asset at its fair market value at the termination of the lease.

- In a **fair market value cap lease,** the lessee can purchase the asset at the minimum of its fair market value and a fixed price (the "cap").

- In a **$1.00 out lease,** ownership of the asset transfers to the lessee at the end of the lease for a nominal cost of $1.00.

- In a **fixed price lease,** the lessee has the option to purchase the asset at the end of the lease for a fixed price that is set in the lease contract.

25.2 Accounting, Tax, and Legal Consequences of Leasing

Absent market imperfections, leases represent another form of zero-NPV financing available to a firm, and the Modigliani-Miller propositions apply: Leases neither increase nor decrease firm value, but serve only to divide the firm's cash flows and risks in different ways. Thus, the decision to lease is often driven by real-world market imperfections related to the accounting, tax, and legal treatment of leasing.

The Financial Accounting Standards Board (FASB) distinguishes two types of leases based on the lease terms.

- In an **operating lease,** the lessee reports the lease payment as an operating expense and the lessee does not deduct a depreciation expense for the asset. The lessee does not report the asset on its balance sheet, but it must be disclosed in the footnotes of the financial statements.

- In a **capital** or **finance lease**, the asset acquired is listed on the lessee's balance sheet, and the lessee incurs depreciation expenses for the asset. In addition, the present value of the future lease payments is listed as a liability, and the interest portion of the lease payment is deducted as an interest expense.

The lease is treated as a capital lease if it satisfies any of the following conditions.

1. Title to the property transfers to the lessee at the end of the lease term.

2. The lease contains an option to purchase the asset at a bargain price that is substantially less than its fair market value.

3. The lease term is 75% or more of the estimated economic life of the asset.

4. The present value of the minimum lease payments at the start of the lease is 90% or more of the asset's fair market value.

Firms that prefer to keep a lease off of the balance sheet will often structure lease contracts to avoid these conditions.

The Internal Revenue Service (IRS) separates leases into two broad categories.

- In a **true tax lease,** the lessor receives the depreciation deductions associated with the ownership of the asset. The lessee can deduct the full amount of the lease payments as an operating expense, and these lease payments are treated as revenue for the lessor.

- In a **non-tax lease,** the lessee receives the depreciation deductions and can deduct the interest portion of the lease payments as an interest expense. The interest portion of the lease payment is interest income for the lessor.

IRS Revenue Ruling 55-540 provides the conditions that determine the tax classification of a lease. If the lease satisfies any of these conditions, it is treated as a non-tax lease.

1. The lessee obtains equity in the leased asset.

2. The lessee receives ownership of the asset on completion of all lease payments.

3. The total amount that the lessee is required to pay for a relatively short period of use constitutes an inordinately large proportion of the total value of the asset.

4. The lease payments greatly exceed the current fair rental value of the asset.

5. The property may be acquired at a bargain price in relation to the fair market value of the asset at the time when the option may be exercised.

6. Some portion of the lease payments is specifically designated as interest or its equivalent.

These rules attempt to identify cases in which a lease is likely to provide the lessee with use of the asset for a large fraction of its useful life and are designed to prevent the use of leases solely for tax avoidance.

The treatment of leased property in bankruptcy depends on its classification.

- If the lease is considered a **security interest,** the firm effectively owns the asset and the asset is protected against seizure. The lessor is then treated as any other secured creditor and must await the firm's reorganization or ultimate liquidation.

- If the lease is classified as a **true lease,** then the lessor retains ownership rights over the asset. Within 120 days of filing Chapter 11, the bankrupt firm must choose whether to assume or reject the lease. If it assumes the lease, it must settle all pending claims and continue to make all promised lease payments. If it rejects the lease, the asset must be returned to the lessor (with any pending claims of the lessor becoming unsecured claims against the bankrupt firm). Thus, if a lease contract is characterized as a true lease in bankruptcy, the lessor is in a somewhat superior position than a lender if the firm defaults.

The distinction is very similar to the accounting and tax distinctions. Operating and true tax leases are generally viewed as true leases by the courts, whereas capital and non-tax leases are more likely to be viewed as a security interest.

25.3 The Leasing Decision

For a non-tax lease, the lessee still receives the depreciation deductions, the same as when the asset is purchased. However, only the interest portion of the lease payment is deductible, so a non-tax lease is directly comparable to a traditional loan. It is therefore attractive to lease if it offers a better interest rate than would be available with a loan. To determine if it offers a better rate, you can discount the lease payments at the firm's pretax borrowing rate and compare it to the purchase price of the asset.

When evaluating a true-tax lease, you can compare leasing the asset to purchasing the asset using the following steps.

1. Compute the incremental cash flows for leasing versus buying, including the depreciation tax shield if buying and the tax deductibility of the lease payments if leasing.

2. Compute the NPV of leasing versus buying using equivalent leverage by discounting the incremental cash flows at the after-tax borrowing rate.

If the NPV is positive, then leasing does provide an advantage over debt financing.

Any differences in the maintenance and service arrangements or any cancellation or other lease options should also be included when comparing leasing versus a debt-financed purchase.

25.4 Reasons for Leasing

For a lease to be attractive to both the lessee and the lessor, the gains must come from some underlying economic benefits that the leasing arrangement provides, such as the following situations.

- **Tax Differences.** With a true tax lease, the lessee replaces depreciation and interest tax deductions with a deduction for the lease payments. Depending on the timing of the payments, one set of deductions may have a larger present value. A tax gain occurs if the lease shifts the more valuable deductions to the party with the higher tax rate. If the asset's tax depreciation deductions are more rapid than its lease payments, a true tax lease may be advantageous if the lessor is in a higher tax bracket than the lessee. If the asset's tax depreciation deductions are slower than its lease payments, there are potential tax gains from a true tax lease if the lessor is in a lower tax bracket than the lessee.

- **Reduced Resale Costs.** Lessors are often specialists at finding a new user for a leased asset and thus face lower costs.

- **Efficiency Gains from Specialization.** Lessors often have efficiency advantages over lessees in maintaining or operating certain types of assets.

- **Reduced Distress Costs and Increased Debt Capacity.** Assets leased using a true lease are not afforded bankruptcy protection and can be seized in the event of default, so a lessor may be able to offer more attractive financing through the lease than an ordinary lender could.

- **Transferring Risk.** Leasing allows the party best able to bear the uncertainty regarding the residual value of the leased asset to hold it.

- **Improved Incentives.** When the lessor is the manufacturer, a lease in which the lessor bears the risk of the residual value can improve incentives and lower agency costs. Such a lease provides the manufacturer with an incentive to produce a high-quality, durable product that will retain its value over time.

Some reasons that lessees and lessors cite for preferring leasing to purchasing are difficult to justify economically.

- **Reducing Leverage Through Off-Balance-Sheet Financing.** By avoiding the four criteria that define a capital lease for accounting purposes, a firm can avoid listing the long-term lease as a liability. However, whether they appear on the balance sheet or not, lease commitments are a liability for the firm and have the same effect on the risk and return characteristics of the firm as other forms of leverage. Most financial analysts and sophisticated investors understand this fact and consider operating leases (which must be listed in the footnotes of the financial statements) to be additional sources of leverage.

- **Avoiding Capital Expenditure Controls.** One reason some managers will choose to lease equipment rather than purchase it is to avoid the scrutiny that often accompanies large capital expenditures.

- **Preserving Capital.** A commonly cited advantage of leasing is that there is no down payment required, so the lessee can save cash for other needs. However, for most large corporations, the amount of leverage the firm can obtain through a lease is unlikely to exceed the amount of leverage the firm can obtain through a loan. Thus this benefit is likely to exist only for small or highly capital-constrained firms.

Selected Concepts and Key Terms

$1.00 Out Lease

A lease in which ownership of the asset transfers to the lessee at the end of the lease for a nominal cost of $1.00.

Capital (Finance) Lease

A lease in which the asset acquired is listed on the lessee's balance sheet, and the lessee incurs depreciation expenses for the asset. In addition, the present value of the future lease payments is listed as a liability, and the interest portion of the lease payment is deducted as an interest expense.

Direct Lease

A lease in which the lessor is an independent company that specializes in purchasing assets and leasing them to customers.

Fair Market Value (FMV) Lease, Fair Market Value Cap Lease

A lease that gives the lessee the option to purchase the asset at its fair market value at the termination of the lease. In a fair market value cap lease, the lessee can purchase the asset at the minimum of its fair market value and a fixed price (the "cap").

Fixed Price Lease

A lease in which the lessee has the option to purchase the asset at the end of the lease for a fixed price that is set upfront in the lease contract.

Lease-Equivalent Loan

A loan that is required to purchase an asset that leaves the purchaser with the same obligations as the lessee would have.

Lessee

The party in lease contract that is liable for periodic payments in exchange for the right to use the asset.

Lessor

The owner of a leased asset who is entitled to the lease payments in exchange for lending the asset.

Leveraged Lease

A lease in which the lessor borrows the initial capital for the purchase and uses the lease payments to pay interest and principal on the loan.

Non-Tax Lease

A lease in which the lessee receives the depreciation deductions and can deduct the interest portion of the lease payments as an interest expense. The interest portion of the lease payment is interest income for the lessor.

Operating Lease

A lease in which the lessee reports the lease payment as an operating expense and the lessee does not deduct a depreciation expense for the asset. The lessee does not report the asset on its balance sheet, but it must be disclosed in the footnotes of the financial statements.

Residual Value

The market value of the asset at the end of the lease.

Sale and Leaseback

A lease in which the lessee receives cash from the sale of the asset and then makes lease payments to retain the use of the asset.

Sales-Type Lease

A lease in which the lessor is the manufacturer (or a primary dealer) of the asset.

Special-Purpose Entity (SPE), Synthetic Lease

A separate business partnership created by the lessee for the sole purpose of obtaining the lease. SPEs are commonly used in synthetic leases, which are designed to obtain specific accounting and tax treatment.

True Lease

A lease in which the asset is not protected in the event that the lessee declares bankruptcy, and the lessor can seize the asset if lease payments are not made. If the lease is deemed a security interest by the bankruptcy court, then the asset is protected and the lessor becomes a secured creditor.

True Tax Lease

A lease in which the lessor receives the depreciation deductions associated with the ownership of the asset. The lessee can deduct the full amount of the lease payments as an operating expense, and these lease payments are treated as revenue for the lessor.

Concept Check Questions and Answers

25.1.1. In a perfect capital market, how is the amount of a lease payment determined?

In a perfect capital market, the cost of leasing is equivalent to the cost of purchasing and reselling the asset.

25.1.2. What types of lease options would raise the amount of the lease payment?

The following lease options would raise the amount of the lease payment: a $1.00 out lease, a fixed price lease, and a fair market value cap lease.

25.2.1. How is a $1.00 out lease characterized for accounting and tax purposes?

A $1.00 out lease is characterized as a capital lease for accounting and tax purposes because this lease contains an option to purchase the asset at a bargain price below its fair market value.

25.2.2. Is it possible for a lease to be treated as an operating lease for accounting purposes and as a non-tax lease for tax purposes?

Yes, it is possible for a lease to be treated as an operating lease for accounting purposes and a non-tax lease for tax purposes. This lease is called a synthetic lease and allows the lessee to deduct depreciation and interest expense for tax purposes, but the lessee does not need to report the asset on its balance sheet.

25.3.1. Why is it inappropriate to compare leasing to buying?

It is inappropriate to compare leasing to buying because leasing is a form of financing, and in order to evaluate a lease correctly, we should compare it to buying the asset using an equivalent amount of leverage.

25.3.2. What discount rate should be used for the incremental lease cash flows to compare a true tax lease to borrowing?

We can compare a true-tax lease to borrowing by discounting the incremental cash flow of leasing by the after-tax borrowing rate.

25.3.3. How can we compare a non-tax lease to borrowing?

A non-tax lease is attractive if it offers a better interest rate than would be available with a loan. To determine if the lease offers a better rate, we discount the lease payments at the firm's pre-tax borrowing rate and compare it to the purchase price of the asset.

25.4.1. What are some of the potential gains from leasing if the lessee plans to hold the asset for only a small fraction of its useful life?

If the lessee plans to hold the asset for only a small fraction of its useful life, the lessee is better off leasing the asset rather than buying when the asset is costly and time consuming to resell.

25.4.2. If a lease is not listed as a liability on the firm's balance sheet, does it mean that a firm that leases rather than borrows is less risky?

Even if a lease is not listed as a liability on the firm's balance sheet, a firm that leases is not less risky than a firm that borrows. A lease commitment is a liability for the firm. Therefore, a lease has the same effect on the risk-and-return characteristics of the firm as other forms of leverage.

Examples with Step-by-Step Solutions

Solving Problems

Problems may require the comparison of leasing versus buying as in example 1 below. Problems may also include market imperfections that may make leasing pay off for the lessor and the lessee. Example 2 below provides an example of this situation when the lessor and the lessee have differing tax rates. Problems may involve determining lease payments in perfect markets based on end-of-year lease options as in example 3 below. Some applications may require an understanding of different aspects of the accounting, tax, and legal consequences of leasing discussed above; the Questions and Problems section provides examples of these issues.

Examples

1. **Your firm will either purchase or lease a new $500,000 packaging machine from the manufacturer. If purchased, the machine will be depreciated straight-line over five years. You can lease the machine using a true tax lease for $125,000 per year for five years with the first payment today. Assume the machine has no residual value, the secured borrowing rate is 9%, and the tax rate is 35%. Should you buy or lease?**

   Step 1. Determine the cash flow consequences of buying the machine.

	0	1	2	3	4	5
Capital Expenditures	−500,000	—	—	—	—	—
Depreciation Tax Shield		35,000	35,000	35,000	35,000	35,000
Free Cash Flow	−500,000	35,000	35,000	35,000	35,000	35,000

   Step 2. Determine the cash flow consequences of leasing the machine.

	0.	1	2	3	4	5
Lease Payments	−125,000	−125,000	−125,000	−125,000	−125,000	—
Income Tax Savings	43,750	43,750	43,750	43,750	43,750	—
Free Cash Flow	−81,250	−81,250	−81,250	−81,250	−81,250	—

   Step 3. Determine the incremental cash flows of leasing versus buying.

	0.	1	2	3	4	5
Free Cash Flow Lease	−81,250	−81,250	−81,250	−81,250	−81,250	—
Less: Free Cash Flow Buy	−500,000	35,000	35,000	35,000	35,000	35,000
Lease − Buy	418,750	−116,250	−116,250	−116,250	−116,250	−35,000

   Step 4. Determine the NPV of leasing versus buying using the incremental cash flows

   The after-tax borrowing rate is 9%(1 − 0.35) = 5.85%.

   $$NPV = 418,750 + \frac{-116,250}{1.0585} + \frac{-116,250}{1.0585^2} + \frac{-116,250}{1.0585^3} + \frac{-116,250}{1.0585^4} + \frac{-35,000}{1.0585^5} = -\$11,796$$

Step 5. Make a conclusion.

You are better off buying, since the NPV of leasing is less than zero.

2. You need to buy a $100,000 machine for your business. You are aware that if the asset's tax depreciation deductions are slower than its lease payments, then there are potential tax gains from a true tax lease if the lessor is in a lower tax bracket than the lessee. Your brother's business only pays taxes at a 15% rate and can borrow at 8%. You have offered to use a true tax lease and pay him $23,600 in annual payments beginning today if he will buy the machine and then lease it to you. The machine has a 5-year straight line depreciation schedule, and after 5 years it would be worthless. You have an 8% borrowing rate and a 35% tax rate. Does it make sense for you and your brother if he buys the machine and leases it to you?

Step 1. Determine how to solve the problem.

You need to find the NPV of leasing instead of borrowing for your firm as well as the NPV for your brother's firm of buying the machine and leasing it to you. If both firms benefit, then it makes sense.

Step 2. Determine the incremental cash flows of leasing versus buying for you.

The cash flow consequences of buying the machine for you are as follows.

	0	1	2	3	4	5
Capital Expenditures	-100,000	—	—	—	—	—
Depreciation Tax Shield		7,000	7,000	7,000	7,000	7,000
Free Cash Flow	-100,000	7,000	7,000	7,000	7,000	7,000

The cash flow consequences of leasing the machine for you are as follows.

	0	1	2	3	4	5
Lease Payments	-23,600	-23,600	-23,600	-23,600	-23,600	—
Income Tax Savings	8,260	8,260	8,260	8,260	8,260	—
Free Cash Flow	-15,340	-15,340	-15,340	-15,340	-15,340	—

The incremental cash flows of leasing versus buying are:

	0	1	2	3	4	5
Free Cash Flow Lease	-15,340	-15,340	-15,340	-15,340	-15,340	—
Less: Free Cash Flow Buy	-100,000	7,000	7,000	7,000	7,000	7,000
Lease – Buy	84,660	-22,340	-22,340	-22,340	-22,340	-7,000

Step 3. Determine the NPV of leasing versus buying for you.

The after-tax borrowing rate is 8%(1 – 0.35) = 5.20%.

$$NPV = 84,660 + \frac{-22,340}{1.052} + \frac{-22,340}{1.052^2} + \frac{-22,340}{1.052^3} + \frac{-22,340}{1.052^4} + \frac{-7,000}{1.052^5} = \$377$$

Step 4. Determine the incremental cash flows of leasing versus buying for the lessor.

The lessor will buy the machine and lease it to you resulting in the following cash flows:

	0	1	2	3	4	5
Capital Expenditures	-100,000	—	—	—	—	—
Depreciation Tax Shield		3,000	3,000	3,000	3,000	3,000
Free Cash Flow	-100,000	3,000	3,000	3,000	3,000	3,000

	0	1	2	3	4	5
Lease Payments	23,600	23,600	23,600	23,600	23,600	–
Less: Income Tax	3,540	3,540	3,540	3,540	3,540	–
Free Cash Flow	20,060	20,060	20,060	20,060	20,060	–

The incremental cash flows of buying and then leasing the machine are as follows.

	0	1	2	3	4	5
Free Cash Flow of Buying	–100,000	3,000	3,000	3,000	3,000	3,000
Free Cash Flow of Leasing	20,060	20,060	20,060	20,060	20,060	–
Buy + Lease	–79,940	23,060	23,060	23,060	23,060	3,000

Step 5. Determine the NPV for the lessor.

The after-tax borrowing rate is 8%(1 – 0.15) = 6.8%.

$$NPV = -79,940 + \frac{23,060}{1.068} + \frac{23,060}{1.068^2} + \frac{23,060}{1.068^3} + \frac{23,060}{1.068^4} + \frac{3,000}{1.068^5} = \$682.$$

Step 6. Make a conclusion.

The NPV is slightly positive for both the lessee and the lessor, so it makes sense to arrange the lease. However, the NPVs are relatively small.

3. **You are considering leasing a $500,000 machine for 5 years. The machine's estimated residual value is $100,000. If the borrowing rate is 6% APR with monthly compounding, compute the monthly lease payment in a perfect market for the following leases:**
   [A]   A fair market value lease.
   [B]   A fair market value lease with a $50,000 cap.
   [C]   A $1.00 out lease.
   [D]   A fixed price lease with a $50,000 final price.

Step 1. Determine the lease payment for the fair market value lease.

$$PV(\text{Lease Payments}) = \text{Purchase Price} - PV(\text{Residual Value}) = \$500,000 - \frac{\$100,000}{(1.005)^{60}} = \$425,863$$

$$\$425,863 = L + L\left(\frac{1}{0.005} - \frac{1}{0.005(1.005)^{59}}\right) \Rightarrow L = \$8,192$$

Step 2. Determine the lease payment for the fair market value lease with a $50,000 cap.

$$PV(\text{Lease Payments}) = \text{Purchase Price} - PV(\text{Residual Value}) = \$500,000 - \frac{\$50,000}{(1.005)^{60}} = \$462,931.$$

$$\$462,931 = L + L\left(\frac{1}{0.005} - \frac{1}{0.005(1.005)^{59}}\right) \Rightarrow L = \$8,905$$

Step 3. Determine the lease payment for the $1.00 out lease.

$$PV(\text{Lease Payments}) = \text{Purchase Price} - PV(\text{Residual Value})$$

$$= \$500,000 - \frac{\$1}{(1.005)^{60}} \approx \$500,000$$

$$\$500,000 = L + L\left(\frac{1}{0.005} - \frac{1}{0.005(1.005)^{59}}\right) \Rightarrow L = \$9,618$$

Step 4. Determine the lease payment for the fixed price lease with a $50,000 final price.

PV(Lease Payments) = Purchase Price − PV(Residual Value)

$$= \$500,000 - \frac{\$50,000}{(1.005)^{60}} = \$462,931.$$

$$\$462,931 = L + L\left(\frac{1}{0.005} - \frac{1}{0.005(1.005)^{59}}\right) \Rightarrow L = \$8,905$$

Questions and Problems

1. Your firm will either purchase or lease a new $500,000 packaging machine from the manufacturer. If purchased, the machine will be depreciated straight line over five years. You can lease the machine **using a non-tax** lease for $125,000 per year for five years with the first payment today. Assume the machine has no residual value, the secured borrowing rate is 9%, and the tax rate is 35%. Should you buy or lease?

2. Your firm has the following balance sheet:

Assets		Liabilities & Equity	
Cash	1,000,000	Debt	10,000,000
Property, Plant & Equipment	19,000,000	Equity	10,000,000
Total Assets	20,000,000	Total Liabilities & Equity	20,000,000

You are about to buy a $5 million machine. What will the balance sheet look like if you use:

[A]   Equity.
[B]   An operating lease.
[C]   A capital lease.
[D]   A bank loan.

3. Your firm is considering purchasing a $10 million machine with a residual value of $500,000. The risk-free rate is 6% APR, and you operate in perfect capital markets.
[A]   What is the monthly lease rate on a 5-year lease with the first payment today?
[B]   What would the 5-year monthly loan payment be if you borrowed the purchase price?
[C]   Which option is better, buying or leasing?

4. Your firm will either purchase or lease a new $48,000 delivery truck. If purchased, the truck will be depreciated straight line over 4 years. You can lease the truck using a true tax lease for $13,000 per year for four years with the first payment today. Assume the machine has no residual value, the secured borrowing rate is 9%, and the tax rate is 40%. Should you buy or lease?

5. Your firm is considering leasing a $20,000 copy machine. The machine has an estimated economic life of five years and your secured borrowing rate is 9% APR with monthly compounding. Classify each lease below as a capital lease or operating lease for financial accounting reporting.
[A]   A five-year fair market value lease with payments of $400 per month.
[B]   A three-year fair market value lease with payments of $500 per month.

Solutions to Questions and Problems

1. With the lease payments you could borrow:

$$NPV = 125{,}000 + \frac{125{,}000}{1.09} + \frac{125{,}000}{1.09^2} + \frac{125{,}000}{1.09^3} + \frac{125{,}000}{1.09^4} = \$529{,}965.$$

Thus, you should borrow since you could raise more than $500,000 with those payments.

2. [A]

Assets		Liabilities & Equity	
Cash	1,000,000	Debt	10,000,000
Property, Plant & Equipment	24,000,000	Equity	15,000,000
Total Assets	25,000,000	Total Liabilities & Equity	25,000,000

[B]

Assets		Liabilities & Equity	
Cash	1,000,000	Debt	10,000,000
Property, Plant & Equipment	19,000,000	Equity	10,000,000
Total Assets	20,000,000	Total Liabilities & Equity	20,000,000

[C]

Assets		Liabilities & Equity	
Cash	1,000,000	Debt & Leases	15,000,000
Property, Plant & Equipment	24,000,000	Equity	10,000,000
Total Assets	25,000,000	Total Liabilities & Equity	25,000,000

[D]

Assets		Liabilities & Equity	
Cash	1,000,000	Debt	15,000,000
Property, Plant & Equipment	24,000,000	Equity	10,000,000
Total Assets	25,000,000	Total Liabilities & Equity	25,000,000

3. [A] PV(Lease Payments) = Purchase Price − PV(Residual Value)

$$= \$10 \text{ million} - \frac{\$500{,}000}{(1.005)^{60}} = \$9{,}629{,}314$$

$$\$9{,}629{,}314 = L + L\left(\frac{1}{0.005} - \frac{1}{0.005(1.005)^{59}}\right) \Rightarrow L$$

$$= \frac{\$9{,}629{,}314}{1 + \left(\frac{1}{0.005} - \frac{1}{0.005(1.005)^{59}}\right)} = \$185{,}235$$

[B] $\$10,000,000 = C\left(\dfrac{1}{0.005} - \dfrac{1}{0.005(1.005)^{60}}\right) \Rightarrow C$

$$= \dfrac{\$10,000,000}{\left(\dfrac{1}{0.005} - \dfrac{1}{0.005(1.005)^{60}}\right)} = \$193,328.02$$

[C] Both options are equivalent. The payment for the loan is larger, but you own the asset past 5 years.

4. Determine the cash flow consequences of buying the truck.

	0	1	2	3	4
Capital Expenditures	-50,000	—	—	—	—
Depreciation Tax Shield		4,800	4,800	4,800	4,800
Free Cash Flow	-50,000	4,800	4,800	4,800	4,800

Determine the cash flow consequences of leasing the machine.

	0	1	2	3	4
Lease Payments	-13,000	-13,000	-13,000	-13,000	—
Income Tax Savings	5,200	5,200	5,200	5,200	
Free Cash Flow	-7,800	-7,800	-7,800	-7,800	

Determine the incremental cash flows of leasing versus buying.

	0	1	2	3	4
Free Cash Flow Lease	-7,800	-7,800	-7,800	-7,800	—
Less: Free Cash Flow Buy	-50,000	4,800	4,800	4,800	4,800
Lease – Buy	42,200	-12,600	-12,600	-12,600	-4,800

Determine the NPV of leasing versus buying using the incremental cash flows

The after-tax borrowing rate is 9%(1 – 0.35) = 5.85%.

$$\text{NPV} = 42,200 + \dfrac{-12,600}{1.0585} + \dfrac{-12,600}{1.0585^2} + \dfrac{-12,600}{1.0585^3} + \dfrac{-4,800}{1.0585^4} = \$4,603$$

You are better off leasing, since the NPV of leasing is greater than zero.

5. The lease is treated as a capital lease if it satisfies any of the following conditions:

   1. Title to the property transfers to the lessee at the end of the lease term.

   2. The lease contains an option to purchase the asset at a bargain price that is substantially less than its fair market value.

   3. The lease term is 75% or more of the estimated economic life of the asset.

   The present value of the minimum lease payments at the start of the lease is 90% or more of the asset's fair market value.

   [A] The present value of the lease payments is:

   $$\text{PV(Lease Payments)} = \$400 + \$400\left(\dfrac{1}{0.0075} - \dfrac{1}{0.0075(1.0075)^{59}}\right) = \$19,4133.87$$

   This represents 19.4 / 20 = 97% of the value of the machine, so it is a capital lease.

[B] The present value of the lease payments is:

$$PV(\text{Lease Payments}) = \$500 + \$500\left(\frac{1}{0.0075} - \frac{1}{0.0075(1.0075)^{35}}\right) = \$15,841$$

This represents 15.8/20 = 79.2% of the value of the machine and no other condition is met, so it is an operating lease

CHAPTER 26

Working Capital Management

Chapter Synopsis

26.1 Overview of Working Capital

Any reduction in working capital requirements generates a positive free cash flow that the firm can distribute immediately to shareholders. Thus, a reduction in a firm's required investment in working capital can increase the value of the firm.

A firm's **cash cycle** is the length of time between when the firm pays cash to purchase its initial inventory and when it receives cash from the sale of the output produced from that inventory. The longer a firm's cash cycle, the more working capital it has, and the more cash it needs to carry to conduct its daily operations. The cash cycle can be measured by calculating the cash conversion cycle (CCC):

CCC = Inventory Days + Accounts Receivable Days − Accounts Receivable Days

where:

$$\text{Inventory Days} = \frac{\text{Inventory}}{\text{Average Daily Cost of Goods Sold}}$$

$$\text{Accounts Receivable Days} = \frac{\text{Accounts Receivable}}{\text{Average Daily Sales}}$$

$$\text{Accounts Payable Days} = \frac{\text{Accounts Payable}}{\text{Average Daily Cost of Goods Sold}}.$$

The firm's **operating cycle** is the average length of time between when a firm originally purchases its inventory and when it receives the cash back from selling its product. If the firm pays cash for its inventory, this period is identical to the firm's cash cycle. However, most firms buy their inventory on credit, which reduces the amount of time between the cash investment and the receipt of cash from that investment.

26.2 Trade Credit

When a firm allows a customer to pay for goods at some date later than the date of purchase, it creates an account receivable for the firm and an account payable for the customer. The credit that the firm is extending to its customer is known as **trade credit.**

If a supplier offers its customers trade credit terms of "net 30," payment is not due until 30 days from the date of the invoice, and the supplier is effectively letting the customer use its money for an extra 30 days.

The selling firm may also offer the buying firm a discount if payment is made early. The terms "2/10, net 30" mean that the buying firm will receive a 2% discount if it pays for the goods within 10 days; otherwise, the full amount is due in 30 days. Firms offer discounts to encourage customers to pay early so that the selling firm gets cash from the sale sooner. However, the amount of the discount also represents a cost to the selling firm because it does not receive the full selling price for the product.

Trade credit can be an attractive source of funds due to its simplicity and convenience. However, trade credit is like a loan from the selling firm to its customer. If a firm sells a product for $100 but offers its customer terms of 2/10, net 30, the customer can take advantage of the discount and pays $98 within the 10-day discount period. The customer also has the option to use the $98 for an additional 20 days (30 − 10 = 20). The interest rate for the 20-day term of the loan is $2/$98 = 2.04%. With a 365-day year, this rate over 20 days corresponds to an effective annual rate of

$$\text{Effective Annual rate (EAR)} = (1.024)^{365/20} - 1 = 44.6\%.$$

As long as the firm can obtain a bank loan at a lower interest rate, it would be better off borrowing at the lower rate and using the cash proceeds of the loan to take advantage of the discount offered by the supplier.

Collection float is the amount of time it takes for a firm to be able to use funds after a customer has paid for its goods. Firms can reduce their working capital needs by reducing their collection float. Collection float is determined by three factors.

- **Mail float:** How long it takes the firm to receive the check after the customer has mailed it.

- **Processing float:** How long it takes the firm to process the check and deposit it in the bank.

- **Availability float:** How long it takes before the bank gives the firm credit for the funds.

Firms can reduce collection float by streamlining in-house check-processing procedures and using automatic transfers from the customer's bank account to the firm's bank account.

Disbursement float is the amount of time it takes before payments to suppliers result in a cash outflow for the firm. Like collection float, it is a function of mail time, processing time, and check-clearing time. Although a firm may try to extend its disbursement float in order to lengthen its payables and reduce its working capital needs, it risks making late payments to suppliers.

The **Check Clearing for the 21st Century Act,** which became effective on October 28, 2004, is aimed at eliminating disbursement float due to the check-clearing process. Under the Act, banks can process check information electronically, and the funds are deducted from a firm's checking account on the same day that the firm's supplier deposits the check in its bank in most cases. Unfortunately, even though the funds are taken out of the check writer's account almost immediately under Check 21, the check recipient's account is not credited as quickly.

26.3 Receivables Management

Establishing a credit policy involves three steps.

1. Establishing credit standards

   Large firms perform this analysis in-house with their own credit departments. Small firms purchase credit reports from credit rating agencies such as Dun & Bradstreet. The decision of how much credit risk to assume plays a large role in determining how much money a firm ties up in its receivables. While a restrictive policy can result in a lower sales volume, the firm will have a smaller investment in receivables.

2. Establishing credit terms

   The firm decides on the length of the period before payment must be made (the "net" period) and chooses whether to offer a discount to encourage early payments. If it offers a discount, it must also determine the discount percentage and the discount period. If the firm is relatively small, it will probably follow the lead of other firms in the industry in establishing these terms.

3. Establishing a collection policy

   The content of this policy can range from doing nothing if a customer is paying late, to sending a polite letter of inquiry, to charging interest on payments extending beyond a specified period, to threatening legal action at the first late payment.

   The accounts receivable days is the average number of days that it takes a firm to collect on its sales. An **aging schedule** categorizes accounts by the number of days they have been on the firm's books. It can be prepared using either the number of accounts or the dollar amount of the accounts receivable outstanding. The aging schedule is also sometimes augmented by analysis of the payments pattern, which provides information on the percentage of monthly sales that the firm collects in each month after the sale.

26.4 Payables Management

A firm should choose to borrow using accounts payable only if trade credit is the cheapest source of funding. When a company has a choice between trade credit from two different suppliers, it should take the least-expensive alternative. In addition, a firm should always pay on the latest day allowed. Some firms ignore the payment due period and pay later, in a practice referred to as **stretching the accounts payable.**

26.5 Inventory Management

A firm needs its inventory to minimize the risk that the firm will not be able to obtain an input it needs for production because of factors such as seasonality in demand. The direct costs associated with inventory fall into three categories.

■ Acquisition costs are the costs of the inventory itself over the period being analyzed (usually one year).

■ Order costs are the total costs of placing an order over the period being analyzed.

■ Carrying costs include storage costs, insurance, taxes, spoilage, obsolescence, and the opportunity cost of the funds tied up in the inventory.

Some firms seek to reduce their carrying costs as much as possible. With "just-in-time" (JIT) inventory management, a firm acquires inventory precisely when needed so that its inventory balance is always zero, or very close to it.

26.6 Cash Management

Firm holds cash to meet day-to-day needs, to compensate for the uncertainty associated with its cash flows, and to satisfy bank requirements.

The amount of cash a firm needs to be able to pay its bills is sometimes referred to as a **transactions balance.** The amount of cash a firm holds to counter the uncertainty surrounding its future cash needs is known as a **precautionary balance.** A firm's bank may require it to hold a **compensating balance** in an account at the bank as compensation for services that the bank performs. Compensating balances are typically deposited in accounts that either earn no interest or pay a very low interest rate.

Selected Concepts and Key Terms

Aging Schedule

A schedule that categorizes accounts receivable by the number of days they have been on the firm's books. It can be prepared using either the number of accounts or the dollar amount of the accounts receivable outstanding.

Availability Float

How long it takes before the bank gives the firm credit for the funds.

Cash Conversion Cycle

Inventory Days + Accounts Receivable Days − Accounts Payable Days.

Cash Cycle

The length of time between when the firm pays cash to purchase its initial inventory and when it receives cash from the sale of the output produced from that inventory. The longer a firm's cash cycle, the more working capital it has, and the more cash it needs to carry to conduct its daily operations.

Check Clearing for the 21st Century Act (Check 21)

Effective on October 28, 2004, the Act's goal was to eliminate disbursement float due to the check-clearing process. Under the Act, banks can process check information electronically, and the funds are deducted from a firm's checking account on the same day that the firm's supplier deposits the check in its bank in most cases. Unfortunately, even though the funds are taken out of the check writer's account almost immediately under Check 21, the check recipient's account is not credited as quickly. As a result, the act does not eliminate collection float.

Collection Float

The amount of time it takes for a firm to be able to use funds after a customer has paid for its goods. Firms can reduce their working capital needs by reducing their collection float.

Compensating Balance

A minimum balance required by a bank as compensation for services that the bank performs. Compensating balances are typically deposited in accounts that either earn no interest or pay a very low interest rate.

Disbursement Float

The amount of time it takes before payments to suppliers result in a cash outflow for the firm. It is a function of mail time, processing time, and check-clearing time. Although a firm may try to extend its disbursement float in order to lengthen its payables and reduce its working capital needs, it risks making late payments to suppliers.

Mail Float

How long it takes the firm to receive the check after the customer has mailed it.

Operating Cycle

The average length of time between when a firm originally purchases its inventory and when it receives the cash back from selling its product. If the firm pays cash for its inventory, this period is identical to the firm's cash cycle. However, most firms buy their inventory on credit, which reduces the amount of time between the cash investment and the receipt of cash from that investment.

Precautionary Balance

The amount of cash a firm holds to counter the uncertainty surrounding its future cash needs.

Processing Float

How long it takes the firm to process the check and deposit it in the bank.

Trade Credit

The credit that a firm extends to its customers when a firm allows a customer to pay for goods at some date later than the date of purchase. When this happens, it creates an account receivable for the firm and an account payable for the customer.

Transactions Balance

The amount of cash a firm needs to be able to pay its bills.

Concept Check Questions and Answers

26.1.1. What is the difference between a firm's cash cycle and operating cycle?

A firm's cash cycle is the length of time between when the firm pays cash to purchase its initial inventory and when it receives cash from the sale of the output produced from that inventory. The operating cycle is the average length of time between when a firm originally purchases its inventory and when it receives the cash back from selling its products.

26.1.2. How does working capital impact a firm's value?

Working capital impacts a firm's value by affecting its free cash flow.

26.2.1. What does the term "2 / 10, Net 30" mean?

The term "2/10, Net 30" means that the buying firm will receive a 2% discount if it pays for the goods within 10 days; otherwise, the full amount is due in 30 days.

26.2.2. Why do companies provide trade credit?

Because a "cash-only" policy may cause them to lose customers to competing firms.

26.3.1. Describe three steps in establishing a credit policy.

Establishing a credit policy involves three steps: establishing credit standards (who the firm will extend credit to), establishing credit terms (the length of the period before payment must be made), and establishing a collection policy to deal with late payments.

26.3.2. What is the difference between accounts receivable days and an aging schedule?

Accounts receivable days are the average number of days that it takes a firm to collect on its sales. An aging schedule categorizes accounts by the number of days they have been on the firm's books.

26.4.1. What is accounts payable days outstanding?

It is the accounts payable balance expressed in terms of the number of days of cost of goods sold.

26.4.2. What are the costs of stretching accounts payable?

Suppliers may react to a firm whose payments are always late by imposing terms of cash on delivery (COD) or cash before delivery (CBD). The delinquent firm then bears the additional costs associated with these terms and may have to negotiate a bank loan to have the cash available to pay. The supplier may also discontinue business with the delinquent customer, leaving the customer to find another source, which may be more expensive or of lower quality. A poor credit rating might also result, making it difficult for the firm to obtain good terms with any other supplier.

26.5.1. What are the benefits and costs of holding inventory?

The benefit is that it helps minimize the risk that the firm will not be able to obtain an input it needs for production, especially when factors such as seasonality in demand mean that customer purchases do not perfectly match the most efficient production cycle. The direct costs of holding inventory are acquisition costs, order costs, and carrying costs.

26.5.2. Describe "just-in-time" inventory management.

With "just-in-time" inventory management, the firm acquires inventory precisely when needed so that its inventory balance is always zero, or very close to it.

26.6.1. List three reasons why a firm holds cash.

A firm holds cash to meet its day-to-day needs to compensate for the uncertainty associated with its cash flows and to satisfy bank requirements.

26.6.2. What trade-off does a firm face when choosing how to invest its cash?

When choosing how to invest its cash, a firm faces a return-risk trade-off. In fact, the firm may choose from a variety of short-term securities that differ somewhat with regard to their default risk and liquidity risk: The greater the risk, the higher the expected return on the investment. The financial manager must decide how much risk she is willing to accept in return for a higher yield.

Examples with Step-by-Step Solutions

Solving Problems

Problems may require understanding the components of a firm's working capital and determining the number of days in a firm's cash conversion cycle. You should also understand trade credit terms and be able to determine the cost of forgoing a trade credit discount. Finally, you should be able to construct an accounts receivable aging schedule.

Examples

1. Last year, Dell had sales of $57 billion, cost of goods sold of $46 billion, and the following end of year balance sheet (in billions):

Assets		Liabilities & Equity	
Cash	$9.0	Accounts Payable	$6.0
Accounts Receivable	7.5	Notes Payable	2.5
Inventory	0.5	Accrued Items	7.5
Total Current Assets	17.0	Total Current Liabilities	16.0
Net Plant, Property & Equipment	6.0	Long-term Debt	3.0
		Common Equity	4.0
Total Assets	$23.0	Total Liabilities & Equity	$23.0

[A] How much does Dell have invested in working capital?
[B] How long is Dell's cash cycle?
[C] If Dell had the industry average inventory days of 30, what would the cash cycle be?

Step 1. Determine net working capital.

Net working capital is current assets minus current liabilities, so Dell's investment in working capital is $17.0 – $16.0 = $1 billion.

Step 2. Determine the cash conversion cycle.

The cash conversion cycle (CCC) is equal to the inventory days plus the accounts receivable days minus the accounts payable days. Dell's cash conversion cycle is:

$$CCC = \frac{inventory}{average\ daily\ COGS} + \frac{accounts\ receivable}{average\ daily\ sales} - \frac{accounts\ payable}{average\ daily\ COGS}$$

$$CCC = \frac{\$0.5}{\left(\frac{\$46}{365}\right)} + \frac{\$7.5}{\left(\frac{\$57}{365}\right)} - \frac{\$6}{\left(\frac{\$46}{365}\right)}$$

= 4 days + 48 days - 48days = 4 days.

Step 3. Determine the cash conversion cycle if Dell had the industry average inventory days.

If Dell's inventory days had been 30 days, its cash conversion cycle would have been:

CCC = 30 days + 48 days – 48 days = 30 days.

2. **You have just purchased $30,000 worth of components from a supplier that offers credit terms of 3/10 net 30. If you pay today, how much you would pay? Should you pay today? What is the effective cost of the trade credit if you pay on day 30?**

Step 1. Determine the size of discounted payment.

The terms offer a 3% discount if you pay within 10 days. Thus, you would pay:

$$(1-0.03) \times \$30,000 = \$29,100.$$

However, since you would pay the same amount in 10 days, you should wait 10 days if you chose to take advantage of the discount.

Step 2. Determine the cost of using the trade credit by paying in 30 days.

If you wait until day 30, you will owe $30,000. Thus, you are paying $900 in interest for a 20-day loan (from day 10 to day 30). The interest rate over this period is:

$$\frac{\$900}{\$29,100} = 0.031 = 3.1\%.$$

The number of 20-day periods in a year is 365/20 = 18, so the effective annual cost of the trade credit is:

$$EAR = (1.031)^{18} - 1 = 73.2\%.$$

3. **Your company has the following accounts receivable:**

Customer	Accounts Receivable	Age in days
1	$50,000	25
2	70,000	55
3	90,000	30
4	110,000	2
5	40,000	22
6	20,000	22
7	80,000	44
8	30,000	76

The firm extends credit on terms of 1/15, net 45. Develop an aging schedule using 15-day increments through 60 days.

Step 1. Sort the accounts receivable customers by the age of their receivables.

Customer	Accounts Receivable	Age in days
4	110,000	2
5	40,000	22
6	20,000	22
1	$50,000	25
3	90,000	30
7	80,000	44
2	70,000	55
8	30,000	76

Step 2. Determine the Aging Schedule.

Percent of Days Outstanding	Accounts Receivable	Accounts Receivable
0-15	110,000	22.4
16-30	200,000	40.8
31-45	80,000	16.3
46-60	70,000	14.3
over 60	30,000	6.1
	490,000	100.0%

Questions and Problems

1. Last year, Ford had sales of $170 billion, cost of goods sold of $140 billion, and the following end of year balance sheet (in billions):

Assets		Liabilities & Equity	
Cash	$21.0	Accounts Payable	$25.0
Accounts Receivable	20.0	Notes Payable	15.5
Inventory	10.0	Accrued Items	7.5
Total Current Assets	51.0	Total Current Liabilities	48.0
Net Plant, Property		Long-term Debt	210.0
& Equipment	219.0	Common Equity	12.0
Total Assets	$270.0	Total Liabilities & Equity	$270.0

[A] How much does Ford have invested in working capital?
[B] How long is Ford's cash cycle?

2. You have just purchased inventory from a supplier that offers credit terms of 1/10 net 45. What is the effective cost of the trade credit if you pay on day 45?

3. What is the effective annual cost of credit terms of 1/15, net 45, if the firm stretches the accounts payable to 60 days?

4. Your company has the following accounts receivable:

Customer	Accounts Receivable	Age in days
1	$100,000	22
2	170,000	33
3	170,000	29
4	10,000	56
5	80,000	8
6	220,000	6
7	40,000	14
8	20,000	21
9	70,000	88

Develop an aging schedule using 15-day increments through 60 days.

5. Apple Computer had $16 billion in sales in 2005. Its cost of goods sold was $10 billion, and its average inventory balance was $500 million.
[A] What is Apple's inventory days ratio? What does it mean?
[B] Dell's turns over its inventory every four days. By how much would Apple reduce its investment in inventory if it could improve its inventory turnover ratio to match Dell?

Solutions to Questions and Problems

1. [A] Net working capital is current assets minus current liabilities, so Ford's investment in working capital is $51 − $48 = $3 billion.

   [B] The cash conversion cycle (CCC) is equal to the inventory days plus the accounts receivable days minus the accounts payable days. Ford's cash conversion cycle is:

$$\text{CCC} = \frac{\text{inventory}}{\text{average daily COGS}} + \frac{\text{accounts receivable}}{\text{average daily sales}} - \frac{\text{accounts payable}}{\text{average daily COGS}}$$

$$\text{CCC} = \frac{\$20}{\left(\frac{\$140}{365}\right)} + \frac{\$10}{\left(\frac{\$170}{365}\right)} - \frac{\$25}{\left(\frac{\$140}{365}\right)}$$

$$= 52 \text{ days} + 22 \text{ days} - 65 \text{days} = 9 \text{ days.}$$

2. The terms offer a 1% discount if you pay within 10 days. Thus, you would pay:

$$(1 - 0.01) \times \$X$$

If you wait until day 30, you will owe $X. Thus, you are paying $(0.01) \times \$X$ in interest for a 35-day loan (from day 10 to day 45). The interest rate over this period is:

$$\frac{(0.01) \times \$X}{(0.99) \times \$X} = 0.0101 = 1.01\%.$$

The number of 35-day periods in a year is 365/35 = 10.429, so the effective annual cost of the trade credit is:

$$\text{EAR} = (1.0101)^{10.429} - 1 = 11.0\%.$$

3. If they wait until day 60, they will owe $X. Thus, they are paying $(0.01) \times \$X$ in interest for a 50-day loan (from day 10 to day 60). The interest rate over this period is:

$$\frac{(0.01) \times \$X}{(0.99) \times \$X} = 0.0101 = 1.01\%.$$

The number of 50-day periods in a year is 365/35 = 7.30, so the effective annual cost of the trade credit is:

$$\text{EAR} = (1.0101)^{7.3} - 1 = 7.6\%.$$

4. Aging Schedule.

Days Outstanding	Accounts Receivable	Percent of Accounts Receivable
0-15	340,000	22.4
16-30	290,000	40.8
31-45	170,000	16.3
46-60	10,000	14.3
over 60	70,000	6.1
	880,000	100.0%

5. [A] The inventory days ratio is equal to the inventory divided by average daily cost of goods sold.

$$\text{Inventory Days} = \frac{\text{Inventory}}{\text{Average Daily COGS}} = \frac{\$500 \text{ million}}{\left(\dfrac{\$10 \text{ billion}}{365}\right)} = 18.25 \text{ days}$$

This implies that Apple's average inventory is around for about 18 days; i.e. it turns over inventory every 365/18.25 = 20 days.

[B] Apple could decrease its inventory days to 4 days by reducing its inventory to:

$$\text{Inventory Days} = \frac{\text{inventory}}{\text{average daily COGS}} = 4 = \frac{\$X \text{ million}}{\left(\dfrac{\$10 \text{ billion}}{365}\right)} \Rightarrow X = \$110 \text{ million}$$

Thus, Apple would reduce its inventory by $500 million − $110 million = $390 million.

CHAPTER 27

Short-Term Financial Planning

Chapter Synopsis

27.1 Forecasting Short-Term Financing Needs

The first step in short-term financial planning is to forecast the company's future cash flows. This exercise has two distinct objectives. First, a company forecasts its cash flows to determine whether it will have surplus cash or a cash deficit for each period. Second, management needs to decide whether that surplus or deficit is temporary or permanent.

When sales are concentrated during a few months, sources and uses of cash are likely to be seasonal. Firms in this position may find themselves with a sufficient surplus of cash during some months to compensate for a shortfall during other months. Occasionally, a company will encounter a negative or a positive cash flow shock in which cash flows are temporarily positive or negative for an unexpected reason.

27.2 The Matching Principle

In a perfect capital market, the choice of financing is irrelevant; thus, how the firm chooses to finance its short-term cash needs cannot affect value. In reality, important market frictions exist, such as the opportunity cost of holding cash in accounts that pay little or no interest and transactions costs from obtaining a loan to cover a cash shortfall. A firm can increase its value by adopting a policy that minimizes these kinds of costs.

The **matching principle** states that short-term needs should be financed with short-term debt and long-term needs should be financed with long-term sources of funds.

▪ **Permanent working capital** is the amount that a firm must keep invested in its short-term assets to support its continuing operations. Because this investment in working capital is required as long as the firm remains in business, it constitutes a long-term investment. The matching principle indicates that the firm should finance this permanent investment in working capital with long-term sources of funds.

- **Temporary working capital** is the difference between the actual level of investment in short-term assets and the permanent working capital investment. Because temporary working capital represents a short-term need, the firm should finance this portion of its investment with short-term financing.

In the long run, following the matching principle should help minimize a firm's transaction costs.

- Financing part or all of the permanent working capital with short-term debt is known as an **aggressive financing policy**. By relying on short-term debt the firm exposes itself to funding risk, which is the risk of incurring financial distress costs should the firm not be able to refinance its debt in a timely manner or at a reasonable rate.

- Financing short-term needs with long-term debt is known as a **conservative financing policy.**

27.3 Short-Term Financing with Bank Loans

Bank loans are typically initiated with a **promissory note,** which is a written statement that indicates the amount of the loan, the length of the loan, the payment convention, and the interest rate. In a single, end-of-period-payment loan, the firm pays interest on the loan and pays back the principal in one lump sum at the end of the loan.

The interest rate may be fixed or variable. The **prime rate** is the rate banks charge their most creditworthy customers. However, large corporations can often negotiate bank loans at an interest rate that is below the prime rate. Another common benchmark rate is the **London Inter-Bank Offered Rate,** or **LIBOR,** which is the rate of interest at which banks borrow funds from each other in the London inter-bank market. It is quoted for maturities of one day to one year for 10 major currencies. As it is a rate paid by banks with the highest credit quality, most firms will borrow at a rate that exceeds LIBOR.

Another common type of bank loan arrangement is a **line of credit,** in which a bank agrees to lend a firm any amount up to a stated maximum.

- An **uncommitted line of credit** is an informal agreement that does not legally bind the bank to provide the funds.

- A **committed line of credit** consists of a written, legally binding agreement that obligates the bank to provide the funds regardless of the financial condition of the firm (unless the firm is bankrupt) as long as the firm satisfies any restrictions in the agreement.

- A **revolving line of credit** is a committed line of credit that involves a solid commitment from the bank for a longer period of time, typically two to three years.

- A revolving line of credit with no fixed maturity is called **evergreen credit.**

These arrangements are typically accompanied by a **compensating balance** requirement (that is, a requirement that the firm maintain a minimum level of deposits with the bank) and restrictions regarding the level of the firm's working capital. The firm pays a commitment fee of 1/4% to 1/2% of the unused portion of the line of credit in addition to interest on the amount that the firm borrowed.

A **bridge loan** is another type of short-term bank loan that is often used to bridge the gap until a firm can arrange for long-term financing. For example, a real estate developer may use a bridge loan to finance the construction of a shopping mall.

With a **discount loan**, the borrower is required to pay the interest at the beginning of the loan period. The lender deducts interest from the loan proceeds when the loan is made.

Various loan fees charged by banks affect the effective interest rate that the borrower pays. A **loan origination fee**, where a firm pays a fee when the loan is initiated, reduces the amount of usable proceeds that the firm receives. A **compensating balance** requirement in the loan agreement reduces the usable loan proceeds.

27.4 Short-Term Financing with Commercial Paper

Commercial paper is short-term, unsecured debt used by large corporations; it is usually a cheaper source of funds than a short-term bank loan.

- With **direct paper,** the firm sells the security directly to investors.

- With **dealer paper,** dealers sell the commercial paper to investors in exchange for a spread (or fee) for their services.

Although the minimum face value is $25,000, most commercial paper has a face value of at least $100,000. The interest on commercial paper is typically paid by selling it at an initial discount.

The average maturity of commercial paper is 30 days and the maximum maturity is 270 days. Extending the maturity beyond 270 days triggers a registration requirement with the Securities and Exchange Commission (SEC), which increases issue costs and creates a time delay in the sale of the issue.

27.5 Short-Term Financing with Secured Financing

Businesses can also obtain short-term financing by using **secured loans** collateralized with short-term assets such as accounts receivables or inventory. Commercial banks, finance companies, and factors, which are firms that purchase the receivables of other companies, are the most common sources for secured short-term loans.

In a **pledging of accounts receivable agreement,** the lender reviews the invoices that represent the credit sales of the borrowing firm and decides which credit accounts it will accept as collateral for the loan, based on its own credit standards. The lender then lends the borrower some percentage of the value of the accepted invoices.

In a **factoring of accounts receivable** arrangement, the firm sells receivables to the lender (i.e., the factor), and the lender agrees to pay the firm the amount due from its customers at the end of the firm's payment period.

A factoring arrangement may be **with recourse,** meaning that the lender can seek payment from the borrower should the borrower's customers default on their bills. Alternatively, the financing arrangement may be **without recourse,** in which case the lender bears the default risk.

In a **floating lien, general lien,** or **blanket lien** arrangement, the loan is secured using all of the firm's inventory. With a **trust receipts loan,** distinguishable inventory items are held in a trust as security for the loan. In a **warehouse arrangement,** the inventory that serves as collateral for the loan is stored in a warehouse. The arrangement may call for a **public warehouse,** which is a business that exists for the sole purpose of storing inventory, or a **field warehouse,** which is operated by a third party but is set up on the borrower's premises.

Selected Concepts and Key Terms

Blanket Lien, Floating Lien, General Lien

When all of a firm's inventory is used to secure a loan.

Bridge Loan

A short-term bank loan that is often used to bridge the gap until a firm can arrange for long-term financing.

Commercial Paper, Direct Paper, Dealer Paper

Short-term, unsecured debt used by large corporations because it is usually a cheaper source of funds than a short-term bank loan. With direct paper, the firm sells the security directly to investors. With dealer paper, dealers sell the commercial paper to investors in exchange for a spread (or fee) for their services.

Evergreen Credit

A revolving line of credit with no fixed maturity.

Factoring of Accounts Receivable, Factors

A form of short-term financing in which a firm sells receivables to the lender (i.e., the factor), and the lender agrees to pay the firm the amount due from its customers at the end of the firm's payment period.

London Inter-Bank Offered Rate (LIBOR)

The rate of interest at which banks borrow funds from each other in the London inter-bank market that is quoted for maturities of one day to one year for 10 major currencies. It is a common benchmark rate used for floating-rate loans.

Matching Principle

The principle that short-term needs should be financed with short-term debt and long-term needs should be financed with long-term sources of funds.

Permanent Working Capital

The amount that a firm must keep invested in its short-term assets to support its continuing operations.

Pledging of Accounts Receivable

A method of securing a loan in which the lender reviews the invoices that represent the credit sales of the borrowing firm and decides which credit accounts it will accept as collateral for the loan, based on its own credit standards. The lender then typically lends the borrower some percentage of the value of the accepted invoices.

Prime Rate

The rate banks charge their most creditworthy customers. However, large corporations can often negotiate bank loans at an interest rate that is below the prime rate.

Temporary Working Capital

The difference between the actual level of investment in short-term assets and the permanent working capital investment.

Warehouse Arrangement

A method of securing a loan in which the inventory that serves as collateral for the loan is stored in a warehouse. The arrangement may call for a public warehouse, which is a business that exists for the sole purpose of storing inventory, or a field warehouse, which is operated by a third party but is set up on the borrower's premises.

Concept Check Questions and Answers

27.1.1. How do we forecast the firm's future cash requirements?

The first step in short-term financial planning is to forecast the company's future cash flows. When we analyze the firm's short-term financing needs, we typically examine its cash flows at quarterly intervals.

27.1.2. What is the effect of seasonalities on short-term cash flows?

Seasonal sales create large short-term cash flow deficits and surpluses. Therefore, firms need short-term financing to fund seasonal working capital requirements.

27.2.1. What is the matching principle?

The matching principle specifies that short-term needs for funds should be financed with short-term sources of funds, and long-term needs with long-term sources of funds.

27.2.2. What is the difference between temporary and permanent working capital?

A permanent working capital is the amount that a firm must keep invested in its short-term assets to support its continuous operations. A temporary working capital is the difference between the actual level of investment in short-term assets and the permanent working capital investment.

27.3.1. What is the difference between an uncommitted line of credit and a committed line of credit?

An uncommitted line of credit is an informal agreement that does not legally bind the bank to provide the funds. A committed line of credit consists of a written, legally binding agreement that obligates the bank to provide the funds regardless of the financial condition of the firm (unless the firm is bankrupt) as long as the firm satisfies any restrictions in the agreement.

27.3.2. Describe common loan stipulations and fees.

Common loan stipulations and fees include loan commitments fees, loan origination fees, and compensating balance requirements. A loan commitment fee is an interest charge on the unused portion of a committed line of credit. A loan origination fee is a fee that a bank charges to cover credit checks and legal fees. A compensating balance requirement means that the firm must hold a certain percent of the principal of the loan in an account at the bank.

27.4.1. What is commercial paper?

Commercial paper is a short-term, unsecured debt used by large corporations that is usually a cheaper source of funds than a short-term bank loan.

27.4.2. How is interest paid on commercial paper?

The interest on commercial paper is typically paid by selling it at an initial discount.

27.5.1. What is factoring of accounts receivable?

Factoring of accounts receivable means the firm sells receivables to the lender (i.e., the factor) and the lender agrees to pay the firm the amount due from its customers at the end of the firm's payment period.

27.5.2. What is the difference between a floating lien and a trust receipt?

In a floating lien arrangement, the entire inventory is used to secure the loan. This arrangement is risky to the lender because the value of the collateral securing the loan is reduced as inventory is sold. With a trust receipt loan, distinguishable inventory items are held in a trust as security for the loan. As these items are sold, the firm remits the proceeds from the sale to the lender in repayment of the loan.

Examples with Step-by-Step Solutions

Solving Problems

Problems using the concepts in this chapter may involve forecasting short-term working capital needs as in example 1 below. You should also be able to select between alternative sources of short-term financing that includes provisions such as compensating balances and loan origination fees as in example 2.

Examples

1. **Lehan Toys experiences a spike in demand leading into the holiday season. The following table contains financial forecasts in millions from August through February.**

	Aug	Sep	Oct	Nov	Dec	Jan	Feb
Net Income		$5	$5	$25	$55	$5	$5
Depreciation		2	3	3	4	5	4
Capital Expenditures		10	10	1	0	0	0
Levels of Working Capital							
Accounts Receivable	2	3	4	5	15	10	6
Inventory	2	2	4	10	8	4	2
Accounts Payable	5	6	4	3	2	2	2

During which months are the firm's seasonal working capital needs the greatest? When does it have surplus cash?

Step 1. Determine Lehan's working capital needs.

To determine the firm's seasonal working capital needs, calculate the changes in net working capital for the firm:

Changes in working capital	Month					
	Sep	Oct	Nov	Dec	Jan	Feb
Accounts receivable	$1	$1	$1	$10	-$5	-$4
Inventory	0	2	6	-2	-4	-2
Accounts payable	1	-2	-1	-1	0	0
Change in net working capital	$0	$1	$6	$7	-$9	-$6

From the table it can be seen that Lehan's working capital needs are highest in November and December due to an increase in its investment in accounts receivable and inventory in those months.

Step 2. Determine Lehan's cash position each month.

	Month					
	Sep	Oct	Nov	Dec	Jan	Feb
Net income	$5	$5	$25	$55	$5	$5
Plus: Depreciation	2	3	3	4	5	4
Minus: Changes in net working capital	0	1	6	7	-9	-6
Cash flow from operations	7	9	2	52	18	$15
Minus: Capital expenditures	10	10	0	1	0	0
Change in cash	-$3	-$1	$2	$51	$18	$15

Lehan has a need for cash in September and October and a surplus of cash in the last 4 months.

2. **Lehan Toys needs a $150,000 loan for the next 40 days. It is trying to decide which of three alternatives to use.**

Alternative A: Forgo the discount on its trade credit agreement that offers terms of 1/10, net 40.

Alternative B: Borrow the money from it current bank, which has offered to lend the firm $150,000 for 40 days at an APR of 9%. The bank will require a (no-interest) compensating balance of 5% of the face value of the loan and will charge a $3,000 loan origination fee.

Alternative C: Borrow the money from a new bank, which has offered to lend the firm $150,000 for 40 days at an APR of 8% with just a 3% loan origination fee.

Which alternative is the cheapest source of financing?

Step 1. Evaluate the cost of alternative A.

The terms offer a 1% discount if the firm pays within 10 days. Thus, you would pay:

(1 − 0.01) × $150,000 = $148,500.

If you wait until day 40, you will owe $150,000. Thus, you are paying $1,500 in interest for a 30-day loan (from day 40 to day 10). The interest rate over this period is:

$$\frac{\$1,500}{\$148,500} = 0.01 = 1.0\%.$$

The number of 30-day periods in a year is 365/30 = 12.2, so the effective annual cost of the trade credit is:

$$EAR = (1.01)^{12.2} - 1 = 12.9\%.$$

Step 2. Evaluate the cost of alternative B.

Lehan will actually need to borrow $153,000 in order to cover its $3,000 loan origination fee. Beyond that, it needs to have enough to meet the 5% compensating balance requirement. So the total amount that the firm must borrow is:

$$\text{Amount needed} = \frac{\$153,000}{1 - 0.05} = \$161,053.$$

At a 9% APR, the interest expense for the 40-day loan will be:

$$\frac{0.09}{365/40}(\$161,053) = \$1,588.$$

Since the loan origination fee is simply additional interest, the total interest on the 40-day loan is $1,588 + $3,000 = $4,588. The firm's usable proceeds from the loan are $150,000. So the interest rate for 40 days is:

$$\frac{\$4,588}{\$150,000} = 0.031 = 3.1\%.$$

The effective annual rate is thus $(1.031)^{365/40} - 1 = 32\%$.

Step 3. Evaluate the cost of alternative C.

Lehan will need to borrow $150,000(1.03) = $154,500 in order to cover the loan origination fee. An APR of 8% translates to an interest rate of $\frac{8\%}{365/40}$ = 0.9% for 40 days.

The interest expense for 40 days is 0.009 × $154,500 = $1,391 + $4,500 (from the origination fee).

The interest rate over 40 days is: $\frac{\$5,891}{\$150,000} = 3.9\%$

The effective annual rate is $(1.039)^{365/40} - 1 = 42\%$.

Step 4. Make a conclusion.

The option that provides the lowest effective annual rate is alternative A. Thus, Lehan should use the trade credit.

Questions and Problems

1. Your firm wants to borrow $1 million for one month. Using its inventory as collateral, it can obtain a 9% APR loan. The lender requires that a warehouse arrangement be used. The warehouse fee is $3,000, payable at the end of the month. What is the effective annual rate of this loan?

2. A firm issues three-month commercial paper with a $100,000 face value and receives $98,200. What is the effective annual rate of this loan?

3. You are considering borrowing $1 million for one month at an APR of 12%. The bank will require a (no-interest) compensating balance of 5% of the face value of the loan and will charge a $3,000 loan origination fee. What is your effective annual borrowing rate?

4. Your candy company experiences surges in demand during the holidays and around Valentine's Day. The following table contains financial forecasts in millions from August through February.

	Oct	Nov	Dec	Jan	Feb	Mar	Apr
Net Income		$2	$21	$2	$80	$2	$2
Depreciation		2	2	2	2	2	2
Capital Expenditures		2	2	2	2	2	2
Levels of Working Capital							
Cash	1	1	1	1	1	1	1
Accounts Receivable	2	2	20	10	70	10	2
Inventory	2	12	15	40	50	2	2
Accounts Payable	2	20	20	10	40	10	2

During which months are the firm's seasonal working capital needs the greatest? When does it have surplus cash?

5. What are the permanent working capital needs of the company in problem 4? What are the temporary needs?

Solutions to Questions and Problems

1. The monthly rate is 9%/12 = 0.75%. At the end of the month, you will owe:

$$\$1 \text{ million} \times 0.0075 = \$7,500.$$

Thus, with the warehouse fee of $3,000, you will pay $10,500 and the one month rate is:

$$\frac{\$10,500}{\$1 \text{ million}} - 1 = 1.05\%.$$

The effective annual rate is: $1.0105^{12} - 1 = 13.4\%$.

2. The amount of interest paid is $1,800.

The three month rate is:

$$\frac{\$1,800}{\$98,200} - 1 = 1.84\%.$$

The effective annual rate is: $1.0184^4 - 1 = 7.6\%$

3. You will need to borrow $1,003,000 to cover the loan origination fee.

You also need to have enough to meet the compensating balance requirement. So the total amount that you must borrow is:

$$\text{Amount needed} = \frac{\$1,003,000}{1-0.05} = \$1,055,789.$$

At a 12% APR, the interest expense for the one month loan will be:

$$\frac{0.12}{12} \times \$1,055,789 = \$10,558.$$

Since the loan origination fee is simply additional interest, the total interest on the one month loan is $10,558 + $3,000 = $13,558. The firm's usable proceeds from the loan is $1,000,000. So the interest rate for one month is:

$$\frac{\$13,558}{\$1,000,000} = 0.0136.$$

The effective annual rate is thus $(1.0136)^{12} - 1 = 17.5\%$.

4. To determine the firm's seasonal working capital needs, calculate the changes in net working capital for the firm:

Changes in working capital	Month					
	Nov	Dec	Jan	Feb	Mar	Apr
Cash	0	0	0	0	0	0
Accounts receivable	0	18	-10	60	-60	-8
Inventory	10	3	25	10	-48	0
Accounts payable	18	0	-10	30	-30	-8
Change in net working capital	$2	$21	$25	$40	-$78	$0

Next, determine the cash position each month.

	Month					
	Sep	Oct	Nov	Dec	Jan	Feb
Net income	$2	$21	$2	$80	$2	$2
Plus: Depreciation	2	2	2	2	2	2
Minus: Changes in net working capital	2	21	25	40	-78	0
Cash flow from operations	2	2	-21	42	82	$4
Minus: Capital expenditures	2	2	2	2	2	2
Change in cash	$0	$0	-$23	$40	$80	$2

The company has a large need for cash in October and a surplus of cash in December, January, and February.

5.

Working capital	Month					
	Nov	Dec	Jan	Feb	Mar	Apr
Cash	1	1	1	1	1	1
Accounts receivable	2	20	10	70	10	2
Inventory	12	15	40	50	2	2
Accounts payable	20	20	10	40	10	2
Net working capital	-$5	$16	$41	$81	$3	$3

The permanent level of working capital is likely about $3 million, the level in March and April. The firm's temporary working capital needs are very large, especially in January and February.

CHAPTER 28

Mergers and Acquisitions

Chapter Synopsis

28.1 Background and Historical Trends

The takeover market experiences **merger waves** that are generally characterized by a typical type of deal.

- The increase in activity in the 1960s is known as the conglomerate wave because firms typically acquired firms in unrelated businesses.

- The 1980s were known for hostile takeovers in which acquirers often purchased poorly performing conglomerates and sold off the individual business units.

- The 1990s wave is characterized by strategic, global deals involving companies in related businesses often designed to create strong firms on a scale that would allow them to compete globally.

Merger activity is greater during economic expansions and during bull markets. Many of the same technological and economic conditions that lead to a growing economy also apparently motivate managers to restructure assets through mergers and acquisitions.

28.2 Market Reaction to a Takeover

Most acquirers pay a substantial acquisition premium over the pre-takeover announcement price of the target firm.

- In mergers between 1973 and 1998, target shareholders experienced an average gain of 16% while acquirer shareholders have an average return of close to 0%.

- In tender offers between 1968 and 2001, target shareholders experience an average gain of 30% while acquirer shareholders have an average return of close to 0%.

28.3 Reasons to Acquire

Synergies are by far the most common justification that bidders give for the premium they pay for a target. Such synergies usually fall into two categories: cost reductions and revenue enhancements. Cost-reduction synergies are more common and easier to achieve because they generally translate into layoffs of overlapping employees and elimination of redundant resources. Revenue-enhancement synergies, however, are much harder to predict and achieve.

Specific sources of value may include the following.

- **Economies of scale and scope.** Economies of scale occur when the average total cost of production decreases as output increases. Economies of scope are savings that come from combining the production, marketing, and distribution of different types of related products.

- **Vertical integration** refers to the combination of two companies in the same industry that make products required at different stages of the production cycle.

- **Expertise.** Firms may use acquisitions to acquire expertise in particular areas to compete more efficiently.

- **Monopoly gains.** Merging with or acquiring a major rival may enable a firm to substantially reduce competition within the industry and thereby increase profits. Society as a whole bears the cost of monopoly strategies, so most countries have antitrust laws that limit such activity.

- **Efficiency gains** may be achieved through the elimination of duplication of the costs of running the firm. Acquirers also often argue that they can run the target firm more efficiently than existing management could.

- **Operating losses.** When a firm makes a profit, it must pay taxes on the profit. However, when it makes a loss, the government does not rebate taxes. Thus, a conglomerate may have a tax advantage over a single-product firm simply because losses in one division can offset profits in another division.

- **Diversification.** Since it is cheaper for investors to diversify their own portfolios than to have the corporation do it through acquisition, the only class of stockholders who can benefit from the diversification a merger generates are managers and other employees who bear the idiosyncratic risk of firm failure and may not hold well-diversified portfolios because they own a large amount of company stock.

- **Lower cost of debt or increased debt capacity.** All else being equal, larger firms, because they are more diversified, have a lower probability of bankruptcy. Consequently, they may have a higher debt capacity and a potentially lower borrowing cost.

28.4 The Takeover Process

An acquisition is only a positive-NPV project if the premium paid does not exceed the expected synergies. Valuing a target using comparable firm valuation multiples does not directly incorporate the operational improvements and other synergistic efficiencies that the acquirer intends to implement. Thus, a discounted cash flow valuation based on a projection of the expected cash flows that will result from the deal should be completed.

A **tender offer** is a public offer to purchase specified number of shares at a set price for a specified time period. A public target firm's board may not recommend that existing shareholders tender their shares, even when the acquirer offers a significant premium over the pre-offer share price. There is also the possibility that regulators might not approve the takeover. Because of this uncertainty about whether a takeover will succeed and the lapse of time when it will be accomplished, the market price does not rise by the amount of the premium when the takeover is announced.

In a cash transaction, the bidder simply pays for the target, including any premium, in cash. In a stock-swap transaction, the bidder pays for the target by issuing new stock and exchanges it for target stock. The price offered is determined by the exchange ratio—the number of bidder shares received in exchange for each target share. A stock-swap merger is positive NPV if:

$$\text{Exchange Ratio} < \frac{P_T}{P_A}\left(1 + \frac{S}{T}\right)$$

where P_T is the price of the target, P_A is the price of the acquirer, S is the synergies in the deal, and T is the value of the target.

Once a tender offer is announced, the uncertainty about whether the takeover will succeed adds volatility to the stock price. Traders known as **risk-arbitrageurs** speculate on the outcome of the deal. This potential profit arises from the difference between the target's stock price and the implied offer price, which is referred to as the **merger-arbitrage spread.** However, it is not a true arbitrage opportunity because there is a risk that the deal will not go through.

How the acquirer pays for the target affects the taxes of both the target shareholders and the combined firm. Any cash received in full or partial exchange for shares triggers an immediate tax liability for target shareholders. Target shareholders must pay a capital gains tax on the difference between the price paid for their shares in the takeover and the price they paid when they first bought the shares. If the acquirer pays for the takeover entirely by exchanging bidder stock for target stock, then the tax liability is generally deferred until the target shareholders actually sell their new shares of bidder stock.

If the acquirer purchases the target assets directly (rather than the target stock), then it may be able to step up the book value of the target's assets to the purchase price. This higher depreciable basis reduces future taxes through larger depreciation charges. Further, any goodwill created may be amortized for tax purposes over 15 years. The same treatment applies to a forward cash-out merger, where the target is merged into the acquirer and target shareholders receive cash in exchange for their shares.

Stock-swap mergers allow the target shareholders to defer their tax liability on the part of the payment made in acquirer stock, but they do not allow the acquirer to step up the book value of the target assets or amortize goodwill for tax purposes.

While the method of payment (cash or stock) affects how the value of the target's assets is recorded for tax purposes, it does not affect the combined firm's financial statements for financial reporting. The combined firm must mark up the value assigned to the target's assets on the financial statements by allocating the purchase price to target assets according to their fair market value. If the purchase price exceeds the fair market value of the target's identifiable assets, then the remainder is recorded as goodwill and is examined annually by the firm's accountants to determine whether its value has decreased.

For a merger to proceed, both the target and the acquiring board of directors must approve the deal and put the question to a vote of the shareholders of the target and generally shareholders of the acquiring firm as well.

28.5 Takeover Defenses

A **poison pill** is a rights offering that gives existing target shareholders the right to buy shares in either the target or the acquirer at a deeply discounted price once certain conditions are met. Because target shareholders can purchase shares at less than the market price, existing shareholders of the acquirer effectively subsidize their purchases. This subsidization makes the takeover so expensive for the acquiring shareholders that they choose not to pursue the deal unless the poison pill is removed, as often happens.

About two-thirds of public companies have a **staggered** (or **classified**) board in which only a fraction, say one-third, of the directors are up for election each year. Thus, even if the bidder's candidates win board seats, it will control only a minority of the target board. The length of time required to get control of the board can deter a bidder from making a takeover attempt when the target board is staggered. Most experts consider a poison pill combined with a staggered board to be the most effective defense available to a target company.

When a hostile takeover appears to be inevitable, a target company will sometimes look for a **white knight,** or an alternate company to acquire it. One variant on the white knight defense is the **white squire defense,** in which a large investor or firm agrees to purchase a substantial block of shares in the target with special voting rights.

Another defense against a takeover is a recapitalization, in which a company changes its capital structure to make itself less attractive as a target.

All mergers must be approved by regulators. In the United States, antitrust enforcement is governed by three main statutes.

- The Sherman Act of 1890 was passed in response to the formation of monopolies such as Standard Oil and prohibits mergers that would create a monopoly or undue market control.

- The Clayton Act was enacted in 1914 and strengthened the government's hand by prohibiting companies from acquiring the stock (or, as later amended, the assets) of another company if it would adversely affect competition.

- The Hart-Scott-Rodino (HSR) Act of 1976 requires that all mergers or acquisitions above a certain size must be approved by the government before the proposed takeovers occur.

28.6 Who Gets the Value Added from a Takeover?

Based on the average stock price reaction, it does not appear that the acquiring corporation generally captures the increase in value. Instead, the premium the acquirer pays is approximately equal to the value it adds, which means the target shareholders ultimately capture the value added by the acquirer. This is referred to as a **free rider problem,** and it discourages potential acquirers from even attempting to make a value-increasing acquisition bid.

One way to get around the free-rider problem is to buy the shares secretly in the market. However, SEC rules require that stockholders disclose their ownership when they acquire a 5% **toehold.**

Investors can also try and get around the free-rider problem by undertaking a leveraged buyout by borrowing the money to acquire a firm's shares and pledges the shares as collateral for the loan. In practice, premiums in LBO transactions are often quite substantial.

Another alternative is the **freezeout merger.** The laws on tender offers allow the acquiring company to freeze existing shareholders out of the gains from merging by forcing non-tendering shareholders to sell their shares for the tender offer price. An acquiring company makes a tender offer at an amount slightly higher than the current target stock price. If the tender offer succeeds, the acquirer gains control of the target and merges its assets into a new corporation, which is fully owned by the acquirer.

Selected Concepts and Key Terms

Conglomerate Merger

A merger in which the target and acquirer operate in unrelated industries.

Economies of Scale

A decrease in the average total cost of production as output increases.

Economies of Scope

A decrease in the average total cost of production from combining the production, marketing, and distribution of different types of related products.

Freezeout Merger

A merger in which the acquirer gains control of the target and merges its assets into a new corporation, which is fully owned by the acquirer. By offering a premium over the pre-tender offer price, the acquiring company forces non-tendering shareholders to sell their shares for the tender offer price. The bidder, in essence, gets complete ownership of the target for the tender offer price.

Golden Parachute

A lucrative severance package that is guaranteed to a firm's senior managers in the event that the firm is taken over and the managers are let go.

Horizontal Merger

A merger in which the target and acquirer operate in the same industries.

Poison Pill

A rights offering that gives existing target shareholders the right to buy shares in either the target or the acquirer at a deeply discounted price once certain conditions are met. Because target shareholders can purchase shares at less than the market price, existing shareholders of the acquirer effectively subsidize their purchases. This subsidization makes the takeover so expensive for the acquiring shareholders that they choose to pass on the deal unless the poison pill is removed, as often happens.

Proxy Fight

The process of attempting to convince target shareholders to unseat the target board by using their proxy votes to support the acquirers' candidates for election to the target board of directors.

Merger-Arbitrage Spread, Risk Arbitrage

The merger arbitrage spread is the difference between the current target stock price and the value of the pending merger consideration. Risk arbitrage is the process of attempting to profit from this spread that typically involves buying the target's stock and short-selling shares in the target's stock that will be paid in a stock-exchange merger upon consummation.

Staggered (Classified) Board

A board of directors structure in which a fraction of the directors are up for election each year.

Vertical Integration

The combination of two companies in the same industry that make products required at different stages of the production cycle.

Vertical Merger

A merger in which the target's industry buys or sells to the acquirer's industry.

White Knight

A large investor or firm that agrees to acquire a firm in order to fend off a takeover attempt from a bidder.

Concept Check Questions and Answers

28.1.1. What are merger waves?

Merger waves are peaks of heavy merger activity followed by quiet troughs of few transactions in the global takeover market.

28.1.2. What is the difference between a horizontal and vertical merger?

In a horizontal merger, the target and acquirer operate in the same industries. In a vertical merger, the target's industry buys or sells to the acquirer's industry.

28.2.1. On average, what happens to the target share price on the announcement of a takeover?

When a takeover is announced, the target shareholders enjoy a gain of 16% on average in their stock price.

28.2.2. On average, what happens to the acquirer share price on the announcement of a takeover?

When a takeover is announced, the acquirer shareholders see a loss of 1% on average in their stock price.

28.3.1. What are the reasons most often cited for a takeover?

The most often cited reasons for a takeover are economies of scale and scope, the control provided by vertical integration, the expertise gained from the acquired company, gaining monopolistic power, an improvement in operating efficiency, and benefits related to diversification such as increased borrowing capacity and tax savings.

28.3.2. Explain why diversification benefits and earnings growth are not good justifications for a takeover intended to increase shareholder wealth.

Diversification benefits and earnings growth are not good reasons for a takeover intended to increase shareholder wealth. Because most stockholders will already be holding a well-diversified portfolio, they get no further benefit from the firm diversifying through acquisition. Besides, it is possible to combine two companies to raise earnings per share, even when the merger itself creates no economic value. All that has happened is that the high-growth company, whose value lies in its potential to generate earnings in the future, has purchased a company for which most of the value lies in its current ability to generate earnings.

28.4.1. What are the steps in the takeover process?

The first step in the takeover process is that the bidder values the target company. Once the acquirer has completed the valuation process, it is in a position to make a tender offer, a public announcement of its intention to purchase a large block of shares for a specified price. Finally, for a merger to proceed, both the target and the acquiring board of directors must approve the deal and put the question to a vote of the shareholders of the target (and, in some cases, the shareholders of the acquiring firm as well).

28.4.2. What do risk arbitrageurs do?

Once a tender offer is announced, the uncertainty about whether the takeover will succeed adds volatility to the stock price. This uncertainty creates an opportunity for investors to speculate on the outcome of the deal. Traders known as risk-arbitrageurs, who believe that they can predict the outcome of a deal, take positions based on their beliefs.

28.5.1. What defensive strategies are available to help target companies resist an unwanted takeover?

Target companies can defend themselves in several ways to resist an unwanted takeover. The most effective defense strategy is the poison pill, which gives target shareholders the right to buy shares in either the target or the acquirer at a deeply discounted price. Another defense strategy is having a staggered board, which prevents a bidder from acquiring control over the board in a short period of time. Other defenses include looking for a friendly bidder (a white knight), making it expensive to replace management (a golden parachute), and changing the capital structure of the firm.

28.5.2. How can a hostile acquirer get around a poison pill?

Because the original poison pill goes into effect only in the event of a complete takeover (that is, a purchase of 100% of the outstanding shares), one way a hostile acquirer can get around it is not to do a complete takeover.

28.6.1. What mechanisms allow corporate raiders to get around the free rider problem in takeovers?

To get around the free rider problem in takeovers, corporate raiders can acquire a toehold in the target, attempt a leveraged buyout, or in the case when the acquirer is a corporation, offer a freezout merger.

28.6.2. Based on the empirical evidence, who gets the value added from a takeover? What is the most likely explanation of this fact?

The empirical evidence suggests that most of the value added appears to accrue to the target shareholders. The most likely explanation is the competition that exists in the takeover market. Once an acquirer starts bidding on a target company and it becomes clear that a significant gain exists, other potential acquirers may submit their own bids. The result is effectively an auction in which the target is sold to the highest bidder. Even when a bidding war does not result, an acquirer offers a large enough initial premium to forestall the process.

Examples with Step-by-Step Solutions

Solving Problems

Problems may require determining the dilution or accretion effect on earning per share as well as the effects on the P/E ratio of the acquirer in a merger as in example 1 below. You should also be able to determine how the exchange ratio in a stock-swap merger affects the NPV of an acquisition as in example 2. Finally, problems may involve the mechanics of a leveraged buyout (LBO) and the value consequences for LBO sponsors as in example 3.

Examples

1. Suppose that Google and General Electric (GE) both have earnings of $5 per share. General Electric is a mature company with few growth opportunities. GE has 1 million shares outstanding that are currently priced at $60 per share. Google is a young company with much more profitable growth opportunities; it has 1 million shares outstanding trading at $100 per share. Assume that Google acquires General Electric using its own stock, and the takeover adds no value.
   [A] In a perfect market, what is the value of Google after the acquisition?
   [B] At current market prices, how many shares must Google offer to GE's shareholders in exchange for their shares?
   [C] What is Google's earnings per share after the acquisition? Are Google's shareholders better or worse off?
   [D] Calculate Google's price-earnings ratio before and after the takeover. Are Google's shareholders better or worse off?

Step 1. Determine the value of Google after the acquisition.

Because the takeover adds no value, the post-takeover value of Google is just the sum of the values of the two separate companies:

100×1 million $+ 60 \times 1$ million $= \$160$ million.

Step 2. Calculate the required exchange ratio.

To acquire GE, Google must pay $60 million.

At its pre-takeover stock price of $100 per share, the deal requires issuing 600,000 shares. As a group, GE's shareholders will then exchange 1 million shares in GE for 600,000 shares in Google, so each shareholder will get 0.6 of a share in Google for each 1 share in GE.

Step 3. Determine EPS of the merged company.

The price per share of Google is still $100 after the takeover since the new value of the firm is $160 million and there are 1.6 million shares outstanding.

Prior to the takeover, both companies earned $5 share $\times$ 1 million shares = $5 million, so the combined corporation earns $10 million. There are 1.6 million shares outstanding after the takeover, so Google's post-takeover earnings per share equals:

$$\frac{\$10 \text{ million}}{1.6 \text{ million}} = \$6.25.$$

Thus, by acquiring GE, Google has raised its earnings per share by $1.25. However, the shareholders are no better off—their shares are still worth $100.

Step 4. Calculate the P/E ratio of Google before and after the deal.

Before: $\dfrac{P}{E} = \dfrac{\$100}{\$5} = 20$

After: $\dfrac{P}{E} = \dfrac{\$100}{\$6.25} = 16$

The price-earnings ratio has dropped to reflect the fact that after taking over GE, more of the value of Google comes from earnings from current projects than from its future growth potential. However, the shareholders are no worse off—their shares are still worth $100.

2. **At the time that Oracle announced plans to acquire Peoplesoft, Oracle stock was trading for $20 per share and Peoplesoft, which had 500 million shares outstanding, had a stock price of $15 per share. If the projected merger synergies were $5 billion, can Oracle offer a 1.5 Oracle shares for each Peoplesoft share in a stock swap and still generate a positive NPV?**

Step 1. Determine the maximum exchange ratio Oracle can offer based on the general formula in the chapter.

The exchange ratio must be less than $\dfrac{P_T}{P_A}\left(1+\dfrac{S}{T}\right)$

where P_T is the price of the target, P_A is the price of the acquirer, S is the synergies in the deal, and T is the value of the target.

Step 2. Determine the value of Peoplesoft stock before the merger as announced.

The equity value was: $15 × 500 million = $7.5 billion.

Step 3. Calculate the maximum exchange offer in this deal.

The exchange ratio must be less than $\dfrac{P_T}{P_A}\left(1+\dfrac{S}{T}\right) = \dfrac{\$15}{\$20}\left(1+\dfrac{\$5 \text{ billion}}{\$7.5 \text{ billion}}\right) = 1.25$

Step 4. Make a conclusion.

Thus, a 1.5× exchange offer would result in a negative-NPV investment for Oracle shareholders.

3. **A stock in a poorly managed firm in the grocery store industry is currently trading at $40 per share. The firm has 20 million shares outstanding and no debt. Your LBO firm believes that the value of the company could be increased by 50% if unprofitable stores were closed down. You decide to initiate a leveraged buyout and issue a tender offer for at least 50% of the outstanding shares.**
   [A] **If you use $400 million in debt, how much value can you extract?**
   [B] **If you use more debt, can you extract more value? What is the maximum value you can extract and still complete the deal?**

Step 1. Determine the current value of the target.

Currently, the value of the target is $40 × 20 million = $800 million.

Step 2. Determine the value in a deal financed with $400 million of debt.

The total value of the company will increase by 50% to $1.2 billion.

If you borrow $400 million and the tender offer succeeds, you will take control of the company and install new management that will close unprofitable stores.

The value of equity once the deal is done is the total value minus the debt outstanding:

Equity Value = 1.2 billion – 400 million = $800 million.

The value of the equity is the same as the pre-merger value. You own half the shares, which are worth $400 million, and paid nothing for them, so you have effectively captured all the value you anticipated adding to the target.

Step 3. Determine the maximum value you can extract and still complete the deal?

What if you borrowed more than $400 million? Assume you were able to borrow $450 million.

The value of equity after the merger would be

Equity Value = 1.2 billion – 450 = $750 million

This is lower than the pre-merger value.

Recall, however, that in the United States, existing shareholders must be offered at least the pre-merger price for their shares. Because existing shareholders anticipate that the share price will be lower once the deal is complete, all shareholders will tender their shares. This implies that you will have to pay $800 million for these shares. To complete the deal you will have to pay 800 – 450 = $350 million out of your own pocket. In the end, you will own all the equity, which is worth $750 million. You paid $350 million for it, so your profit is again $400 million. You cannot extract more value than the value you add to the company by taking it over.

Questions and Problems

1. Your company has earnings per share of $5 and 3 million shares outstanding that are trading for $25. You are thinking of buying a firm with earnings per share of $1 with 1 million shares outstanding and a price per share of $50. You will pay for the target by issuing new shares, but there are no expected synergies from the deal.
    [A]   What will your earnings per share be after the merger if you pay no premium?
    [B]   What will your earnings per share be after the merger if you pay a 30% premium?
    [C]   What explains the change in earnings per share in part [A]? Are your shareholders any better off?

2. [A]   What will the price-earnings ratio be for your firm in problem 1 after the merger if they pay no premium?
    [B]   How does this compare to the P/E ratio before the merger? How does this compare to the target's pre-merger P/E ratio?
    [C]   What explains the change in P/E ratios? Are your shareholders any better off?

3. If companies in the same industry as the target in problem 1 are trading at P/E multiples of 60 times earnings, what would be one estimate of an appropriate premium?

4. A corporation has announced plans to acquire a target in the same industry. The bidder is trading for $3 per share and target is trading for $2 per share and has a market

capitalization of $1 billion. If the projected synergies are $1 billion, what is the maximum exchange ratio NFF could offer in a stock swap and still generate a positive NPV?

5. You are evaluating a potential leveraged buyout of a company in a declining industry. The target's stock price is $2, and it has 100 million shares outstanding. You believe that if you buy the company and replace its management, its value will increase by 100%. You are considering acquiring the target in a leveraged buyout by offering $3 per share (financed with debt) for controlling ownership (50% of the shares) of the company.

[A] What will happen to the price of non-tendered shares after the offer?

[B] Given the answer in part [A], will shareholders tender their shares, not tender their shares, or be indifferent?

[C] What will your gain from the transaction be?

Solutions to Questions and Problems

1. [A] The target's shares are worth $50 and your shares are worth $25. You will have to issue 50/25 = 2 of your shares per share of the target to buy it.

That means that you have to issue 2 million new shares. After the merger, you will have a total of 5 million shares outstanding (the original 3 million plus the 2 million new shares).

Your total earnings will be $16 million after the merger. Thus, your new EPS will be $16 million / 5 million shares = $3.20.

[B] A 30% premium means that you will have to pay $65 per share. Thus, you will have to issue $65/$25 = 2.6 of your shares per share of the target which equals 2.6 million new shares.

With total earnings of $16 million and total shares outstanding after the merger of 5.6 million, you will have EPS of $16 million/5.6 million shares = $2.86.

[C] In part [A], the change in the EPS came from combining the two companies, one of which was earning $5 per share and the other was earning $1 per share. However, even though the target firm has one-fifth of your firm's EPS, it is trading for two-thirds of your firm's value.

This is possible if the target firm's earnings are less risky or if they are expected to grow more in the future. Thus, although your shareholders end up with lower EPS after the transaction, they have paid a fair price. The post merger share value is still ($75 million + $50 million)/5 million = $25. Thus, focusing on EPS alone cannot tell you whether shareholders are better or worse off.

2. [A] If you simply combine the two companies with no synergies, the total value of the company will be $75 million + $50 million = $125 million. You will have earnings totaling $16 million, so that your P/E ratio is $125 / $16 = 7.8.

[B] Your P/E ratio before the merger was $25 / $5 = 5.0

The target's P/E ratio was $50 / $1 = 50.0.

[C] By buying the target for its market price and creating no synergies, your shareholders are no better or worse off—the stock still has a value of ($75 million + $50 million)/5 million = $25. The transaction simply ends up with a company whose P/E ratio is between the P/E ratios of the two companies going into the transaction.

Focusing on metrics like the P/E ratio does not tell you whether you are better or worse off; even though your P/E went up from 5.0 to 7.8, your shareholders are no better or worse off.

3. The target has $1 in earnings per share, so if other companies in its industry are trading at 60 times earnings, then a starting point for a valuation of the target in this transaction would be $60 per share, implying a premium of:

$$\text{Premium} = \frac{\$60 - \$50}{\$50} = 20\%.$$

4. This problem can be answered by using the general equation in the text:

The exchange ratio must be less than $\frac{P_T}{P_A}\left(1 + \frac{S}{T}\right) = \frac{\$2}{\$3}\left(1 + \frac{\$1 \text{ billion}}{\$1 \text{ billion}}\right) = 1.3\overline{3}.$

This problem can also be solved by first calculating the number of shares of the target:

$$\text{Number of shares} = \frac{\$1,000,000,000}{\$2} = 500,000,000.$$

Including synergies, the target will be worth $1 billion + $1 billion = $2 billion, or $4 per share (= $2 billion/500 million).

Hence the maximum exchange ratio that can be offered is:

$$\text{Exchange ratio} = \frac{\$4}{\$3} = 1.3\overline{3}$$

Thus, a maximum exchange ratio of 1.33 of its share in exchange of each share of the target can be offered.

5. [A] The value should reflect the expected improvement that you will make by replacing the management, which you anticipate will double the firm's value, so the value of the company will be 2 × [$2 × 100 million] = $400 million.

If you buy 50% of the shares for $3 apiece, you will buy 50 million shares, paying $150 million. Since you will borrow this money, this means that the new value of the equity will be $400 million – $150 million in debt = $250 million. With 100 million shares outstanding, the price per share will be $2.50.

[B] Since the price of the shares after the tender offer, $2.50, is less than the $3 you are offering, everyone will want to tender their shares for $3.

[C] Assuming that everyone tenders their shares and you buy them all at $3 apiece, you will pay $150 million to acquire the company and it will be worth $400 million. You will own 100% of the equity, which will be worth $400 million – $150 million in debt = $250 million. Thus, your gain is $100 million since you paid $150 million.

CHAPTER 29

Corporate Governance

Chapter Synopsis

29.1 Corporate Governance and Agency Costs

Corporate governance is the system of controls, regulations, and incentives designed to maximize firm value and prevent fraud within a corporation. The role of the corporate governance system is to mitigate the conflict of interest that results from the separation of ownership and control in a corporation without unduly burdening managers with the risk of the firm.

An effective corporate governance system should provide incentives for taking the right action and punishments for taking the wrong action. The incentives come from owning stock in the company and from compensation that is sensitive to performance. Punishment comes when a board fires a manager for poor performance or fraud, or when, upon failure of the board to act, shareholders or raiders launch control contests to replace the board and management.

29.2 Monitoring by the Board of Directors

When the ownership of a corporation is widely held, no one shareholder has an incentive to bear the costs of monitoring management because they would bear the full cost of monitoring while the benefit is divided among all shareholders. Instead the shareholders as a group elect a board of directors to monitor managers. The directors themselves, however, may have the same conflict of interest—monitoring is costly and directors generally do not get significantly greater benefits than other shareholders from monitoring the managers closely. Consequently, shareholders understand that there are limits on how much monitoring they can expect from the board of directors.

There are three types of directors.

- **Inside directors** are employees, former employees, or family members of employees.

- **Gray directors** are individuals who are not as directly connected to the firm as insiders are, but who have existing or potential business relationships with the firm. Examples include bankers, lawyers, and consultants who are or may be retained by the firm.

- **Outside** (or **independent**) **directors** are neither managers nor are they likely to have current or potential business relationships with the firm. They are the most likely to make decisions solely in the interests of the shareholders.

A board is said to be **captured** when its monitoring duties have been compromised by connections or perceived loyalties to management. The longer a CEO has served, especially when that person is also chairman of the board, the more likely the board is to become captured.

29.3 Compensation Policies

In the absence of perfect monitoring, the conflict of interest between managers and stockholders can be mitigated by closely aligning their interests through the managers' compensation schemes. Managers' pay can be linked to the performance of a firm through bonuses based on accounting performance or grants of stock or stock options.

An influential study by Jensen and Murphy (1990) found that for every $1,000 increase in firm value, CEO pay changed an average of $3.25–$2.00 which came from changes in the value of the CEO's stock ownership. While many believe that this relation is too small, increasing the pay-for-performance sensitivity comes at the cost of burdening managers with risk. Thus, the optimal level of sensitivity depends on the managers' level of risk aversion, which is hard to measure.

The median value of options granted rose from less than $200,000 in 1993 to more than $1 million in 2001. The substantial use of stock and option grants in the 1990s greatly increased managers' pay-for-performance sensitivity; recent estimates put this sensitivity at $25 per $1,000 change in wealth.

Providing managers with such pay-for-performance sensitivity may provide an incentive to manipulate the release of financial forecasts so that bad news comes out before options are granted (to drive the exercise price down) and good news comes out after options are granted. Studies have found evidence of that practice.

Furthermore, many executives have engaged in a more direct form of manipulating their stock option compensation by **backdating** their option grants. Executives chose the grant date of a stock option retroactively, so that the date of the grant would coincide with a date when the stock price was at its low for the quarter or for the year. In mid-2006, SEC and U.S. Justice Department investigations into alleged backdating were ongoing for more than 70 firms. New SEC rules require firms to report option grants within two days of the grant date, which may help prevent further abuses.

29.4 Managing Agency Conflict

If all else fails, the shareholders' last line of defense against expropriation by self-interested managers is direct action. Perhaps the most extreme form of direct action that disgruntled shareholders can take is to hold a proxy contest and introduce a rival slate of directors for election to the board. This action gives shareholders an actual choice between the nominees put forth by management and the current board and a completely different slate of nominees put forth by dissident shareholders.

Any shareholder can also submit a resolution that is put to a vote at the annual meeting. A resolution could direct the board to take a specific action, such as to discontinue investing in a particular line of business or country, or remove a poison pill. Such resolutions rarely receive majority support, but if enough shareholders back the resolutions, they can be embarrassing for the board. Some large public pension funds, such as CalPERS (the California Public Employees Retirement System), take an activist role in corporate governance using such methods.

When internal governance systems such as ownership, compensation, board oversight, and shareholder activism fail, the one remaining way to remove poorly performing managers is by mounting a hostile takeover. Thus, the effectiveness of the corporate governance structure of a firm depends on how well protected its managers are from removal in a hostile takeover.

29.5 Regulation

The U.S. government has periodically passed laws that force minimum standards of governance in an attempt to improve the accuracy of information given both to boards and to shareholders.

The most recent major government regulation is the Sarbanes-Oxley Act of 2002 (SOX). Many of the problems at Enron, WorldCom, and elsewhere were kept hidden from boards and shareholders until it was too late. In the wake of these scandals, many people felt that the accounting statements of these companies, while often remaining true to the letter of GAAP, did not present an accurate picture of the financial health of a company. SOX is aimed at improving corporate governance by: 1) overhauling incentives and independence in the auditing process, 2) stiffening penalties for providing false information, and 3) forcing companies to validate their internal financial control processes.

SOX places strict limits on the amount of non-audit fees (consulting or otherwise) that an accounting firm can earn from the same firm that it audits. It also requires that audit partners rotate every five years and increases the criminal penalties for providing false information to shareholders.

Insider trading occurs when a person makes a trade based material, non-public information. If managers were allowed to trade on their information, their profits would come at the expense of outside investors, and as a result, outside investors would be less willing to invest in corporations. Insider trading regulations were passed to address this problem. The penalties for violating insider trading laws include jail time, fines, and civil penalties.

Only the U.S. Justice Department—on its own or at the request of the SEC—can bring charges that carry the possibility of a prison sentence. However, the SEC can bring civil actions if it chooses. In 1984, Congress stiffened the civil penalties for insider trading by passing the Insider Trading Sanctions Act, which allowed for civil penalties of up to three times the gain from insider trading.

29.6 Corporate Governance Around the World

Investor protection in the United States is generally seen as being among the best in the world. La Porta and Lopez-de-Silanes (1998) conclude that the degree of investor protection in other countries is largely determined by the legal origin of the country—specifically, whether its legal system was based on British common law (more protection) or French, German, or Scandinavian civil law (less protection).

In many other countries, the central conflict is between what are called "controlling shareholders" and "minority shareholders." In Europe, many corporations are run by families who own controlling blocks of shares. One way for families to gain control over firms even when they do not own more than half the shares is to issue **dual class shares** in which companies have more than one class of shares, and one class has superior voting rights over the other class.

While the U.S system focuses solely on maximizing shareholder welfare, most countries follow what is called the **stakeholder model,** giving explicit consideration to other stakeholders, such as employees. For example, countries such as Germany give employees board representation. Other countries have mandated works councils, local versions of labor unions that are to be informed and consulted on major corporate decisions. Some countries mandate employee participation in decision making in corporate constitutions.

29.7 The Trade-off of Corporate Governance

Corporate governance is a system of checks and balances with trade-offs between costs and benefits. As this chapter makes clear, this trade-off is very complicated. No one structure works for all firms. The costs and benefits of a corporate governance system also depend on cultural norms. An acceptable business practice in one culture can be unacceptable in another culture, and thus it is not surprising that there is such wide variation in governance structures across countries.

It is important to keep in mind that good governance is value enhancing and so, in principle, is something investors in the firm should strive for. Because there are many ways to implement good governance, one should expect firms to display—and firms do display—wide variation in their governance structures.

Selected Concepts and Key Terms

Backdating

The practice of choosing the grant date of a stock option retroactively so that the date of the grant would coincide with a date when the stock price was at its low for the quarter or for the year.

Captured Board

A board is said to be captured when its monitoring duties have been compromised by connections or perceived loyalties to management.

Corporate Governance

The system of controls, regulations, and incentives designed to maximize firm value and prevent fraud. The role of the corporate governance system is to mitigate the conflict of interest that results from the separation of ownership and control in a corporation without unduly burdening managers with the risk of the firm.

Gray Directors

Directors who are not as directly connected to the firm as insiders are, but who have existing or potential business relationships with the firm. For example, bankers, lawyers, and consultants who are already retained by the firm, or who would be interested in being retained may sit on a board. Their judgment could be compromised by their desire to keep the CEO happy.

Inside Directors

Directors who are employees, former employees, or family members of employees.

Insider Trading

Stock trading that is based material, non-public information. If managers were allowed to trade on their information, their profits would come at the expense of outside investors, and as a result, outside investors would be less willing to invest in corporations.

Outside (Independent) Directors

Directors who are not managers or likely to have current or potential business relationships with the firm. They are the most likely to make decisions solely in the interests of the shareholders.

Stakeholder Model

A system that gives governance power to stakeholders other than stockholders, such as employees. For example, countries such as Germany give employees board representation while other countries have mandated works councils, which are local versions of labor unions that are to be informed and consulted on major corporate decisions.

Concept Check Questions and Answers

29.1.1. What is corporate governance?

Corporate governance refers to the system of controls, regulations, and incentives designed to prevent fraud from happening.

29.1.2. What agency conflict do corporate governance structures address?

Agency conflict occurs when different stakeholders in a firm all have their own interests and these interests diverge.

29.2.1. What is the difference between gray directors and outside directors?

Grey directors are those who are not directly connected to the firm but have existing or potential business relationships with the firm. Outside directors or independent directors are neither directly connected to the firm nor have any business relationships with the firm.

29.2.2. What does it mean for a board to be captured?

A board is said to be captured when its monitoring duties have been compromised by connections or perceived loyalties to management.

29.3.1. What is the main reason for tying managers' compensation to firm performance?

By tying manager's compensation to firm performance, boards can better align managers' interests with those of shareholders.

29.3.2. What is the negative effect of increasing the sensitivity of managerial pay to firm performance?

Increasing the sensitivity of managerial pay to firm performance may give managers incentives to manipulate the stock price for a big compensation payout.

29.4.1. Describe and explain a proxy contest.

A proxy contest gives shareholders a choice between the nominees put forth by management and the current board, and a completely different slate of nominees put forth by dissident shareholders.

29.4.2. What is the role of takeovers in corporate governance?

When internal governance systems such as ownership, compensation, board oversight, and shareholder activism fail, the one remaining way to remove poorly performing managers is by mounting a hostile takeover. Thus, the effectiveness of the corporate governance structure of a firm depends on how well protected its managers are from removal in a hostile takeover.

29.5.1. Describe the main requirements of the Sarbanes-Oxley Act of 2002.

The Sarbanes-Oxley Act is intended to improve shareholder monitoring of managers by increasing the accuracy of their information. The Act does this by: 1) overhauling incentives and independence in the auditing process, 2) stiffening penalties for providing false information, and 3) forcing companies to validate their internal financial control processes.

29.5.2. What is insider trading, and how can it harm investors?

Insider trading occurs when a person makes a trade based on privileged information. By using this information, managers can exploit profitable trading opportunities that are not available to outside investors. If they were allowed to trade on their information, their profits would come at the expense of outside investors and, as a result, outside investors would be less willing to invest in corporations.

29.6.1. How does shareholder protection vary across countries?

Countries with British common law origin generally provide better shareholder protection than countries with civil law origin.

29.6.2. How can a minority owner in a business gain a controlling interest?

One way for a minority owner in a business to gain a controlling interest is to issue dual class shares with different voting rights. Another way is to create a pyramid structure.

CHAPTER 30

Risk Management

Chapter Synopsis

30.1 Insurance

Insurance is the most common method firms use to reduce risk. Many firms purchase **property insurance** to insure their assets against hazards such as fire, storm damage, vandalism, earthquakes, and other natural and environmental risks. Other common types of insurance include the following.

- **Business liability insurance,** which covers the costs that result if some aspect of the business causes harm to a third party or someone else's property;

- **Business interruption insurance,** which protects the firm against the loss of earnings if business operations are interrupted due to fire, accident, or some other insured peril; and

- **Key personnel insurance**, which compensates the firm for the loss or unavoidable absence of crucial employees in the firm.

When a firm buys insurance, it transfers the risk of the loss to an insurance company, which charges a premium to take on that risk.

In a perfect market, insurance companies should compete until they are just earning a fair return and the NPV from selling insurance is zero. If r_L is the appropriate cost of capital given the risk of the loss, the **actuarially fair premium** is:

$$\text{Insurance Premium} = \frac{\Pr(\text{Loss}) \times E[\text{Payment in the event of a loss}]}{1 + r_L}.$$

The cost of capital r_L depends on the risk being insured. If the risk is fully diversifiable, such as fire insurance, the beta is zero and $r_L = r_f$. For risks that cannot be fully diversified, the cost of capital r_L will include a risk premium. Insurance for non-diversifiable hazards is generally a negative beta asset because it pays off in bad times. Thus, r_L is less than the risk-free rate, leading to a higher insurance premium.

In a perfect market, insurance is a zero-NPV investment. Although insurance allows the firm to divide its risk in a new way, the firm's total risk—and, therefore, its value—remains unchanged. Thus, just like a firm's capital structure, the value of insurance must come from reducing the cost of market imperfections, such as reduced costs of financial distress, tax savings, increased debt capacity, and improved managerial incentives and risk assessment.

Market imperfections, such as insurance company operating expenses, also raise the cost of insurance above the actuarially fair price. The Insurance Information Institute estimates that operating expenses for the property and casualty insurance industry amounted to approximately 25% of premiums charged. A second factor that raises the cost of insurance is adverse selection because firm's seeking insurance will tend be riskier. Third, an agency cost known as **moral hazard** in which insured firms will tend to decide to take more risk raises the cost. The Insurance Research Council estimates that moral hazard costs account for about 11% of premiums.

Insurance companies try to mitigate adverse selection and moral hazard costs by screening applicants to assess their risk and investigating losses to look for evidence of fraud or deliberate intent. Insurance companies also structure their policies to reduce these costs. For example, most policies include both a deductible, which is the initial amount of the loss that is not covered by insurance, and policy limits, which limit the amount of the loss that is covered regardless of the extent of the damage.

30.2 Commodity Price Risk

Risk can also be reduced by hedging with contracts or transactions that provide the firm with cash flows that have lower volatility. For example:

- Long-term supply contracts can be used to lock in future prices;
- **Vertical integration** can be used by buying a key supplier; and
- **Futures contracts** can be used lock in future prices.

A futures contract is an agreement to trade an asset on some future date at a set price. They are traded anonymously on an exchange at a publicly observed market price and are generally very liquid. Both the buyer and the seller can get out of the contract at any time by selling it to a third party at the current market price.

In a perfect market, commodity supply contracts and futures contracts are zero-NPV investments that do not change the value of the firm. However, hedging commodity price risk can benefit the firm by reducing the costs of other frictions. Just as with insurance, the potential benefits include reduced costs of financial distress, tax savings, increased debt capacity, and improved managerial incentives and risk assessment.

30.3 Exchange Rate Risk

Multinational firms face the risk of currency exchange rate fluctuations.

Most exchange rates are **floating rates** and change constantly depending on the quantity supplied and demanded for each currency in the market. The supply and demand for each currency is driven by the activity of firms trading goods, trading by currency market investors, and actions of central banks in each country.

Fluctuating exchanges rates cause a problem known as the **importer–exporter dilemma** for firms doing business in international markets. If neither party in an international transaction will accept the exchange rate risk, the transaction may be difficult or impossible to negotiate.

A **currency forward contract** is a contract that sets the exchange rate in advance. It is usually written between a firm and a bank; however, the bank will generally enter into a second forward contract with offsetting exposure to eliminate its risk.

A currency forward contract specifies: 1) an exchange rate, 2) an amount of currency to exchange, and 3) a delivery date on which the exchange will take place. The exchange rate set in the contract is referred to as the **forward exchange rate.** By entering into a currency forward contract, a firm can lock in an exchange rate in advance and reduce or eliminate its exposure to fluctuations in a currency's value.

An alternative method to accomplish the same objective is to use a **cash-and-carry strategy** which, for a dollars-to-Euros contract, consists of the following three simultaneous trades.

1. Borrow euros today using a one-year loan with the interest rate, r_ϵ.

2. Exchange the euros for dollars today at the spot exchange rate.

3. Invest the dollars today for one year at the interest rate, $r_\$$.

In one year, you will owe euros (from the loan in transaction 1) and receive dollars (from the investment in transaction 3). Thus, you have converted euros in one year to dollars in one year, just as with the forward contract.

Because the forward contract and the cash-and-carry strategy accomplish the same conversion, by the Law of One Price they must do so at the same rate. Combining the rates used in the cash-and-carry strategy leads to the following no-arbitrage formula for the forward exchange rate called **covered interest parity**:

$$\underbrace{F_T}_{\substack{\$ \text{ in } T \text{ years} \\ \epsilon \text{ in } T \text{ years}}} = \underbrace{S}_{\substack{\$ \text{ today} \\ \epsilon \text{ today}}} \times \underbrace{\frac{(1 + r_\$)^T}{(1 + r_\epsilon)^T}}_{\substack{\$ \text{ in } T \text{ years}/\$ \text{ today} \\ \epsilon \text{ in } T \text{ years}/\epsilon \text{ today}}}$$

Currency options are another method that firms commonly use to manage exchange rate risk. The same pricing methodologies discussed in Chapter 21, including the Black-Scholes and binomial models, can be applied to currency options. In this case, the underlying asset is the currency, so the spot exchange rate is used in place of the stock price and the foreign interest rate you earn while holding the currency is analogous to the dividend yield for a stock so:

$$C = \frac{S}{(1 + r_\epsilon)^T} \times N(d_1) - \frac{K}{(1 + r_\$)^T} \times N(d_2)$$

where d_1 and d_2 are calculated using the fact that $S^*/PV(K) = F_T/K$:

$$d_1 = \frac{\ln[F_T/K]}{\sigma\sqrt{T}} + \frac{\sigma\sqrt{T}}{2} \text{ and } d_2 = d_1 - \sigma\sqrt{T}.$$

30.4 Interest Rate Risk

Firms that borrow must pay interest on their debt, so an increase in interest rates raises firms' borrowing costs and can reduce their profitability. In addition, many firms have fixed long-term future liabilities, such as capital leases or pension fund liabilities. A decrease in interest rates raises the present value of these liabilities and can lower the value of the firm. Thus, when interest rates are volatile, interest rate risk is a concern for many firms.

A bond's **duration** is a measure of its sensitivity to interest rate changes. It can be calculated as:

$$\text{Duration} = \sum_t \frac{PV(C_t)}{P} \times t$$

where C_t is the cash flow on date t, $PV(C_t)$ is its present value (evaluated at the bond's yield to maturity), and $P = \sum_t PV(C_t)$ is the total present value of the cash flows, which is equal to the bond's current value. Therefore, the duration weights each maturity t by the percentage contribution of its cash flow to the total present value, $PV(C_t)/P$.

If r, the APR used to discount a stream of cash flows, increases to $r + \varepsilon$, where ε is a small change, then the present value of the cash flows changes by approximately by:

$$\text{Percent change in value} \approx -\text{Duration} \times \frac{\varepsilon}{1 + r/k}$$

where k is the number of compounding periods.

A firm's market capitalization is determined by the difference in the market value of its assets and its liabilities. If changes in interest rates affect these values, they will affect the firm's equity value. A firm's sensitivity to interest rates can be measured by computing the duration of its balance sheet. When the durations of a firm's assets and liabilities are significantly different, the firm has a **duration mismatch**.

To fully protect its equity from an overall increase or decrease in the level of interest rates, a firm needs an equity duration of zero. A portfolio with a zero duration is called a **duration-neutral portfolio** or an **immunized portfolio**, which means that for small interest rate fluctuations, the value of equity should remain unchanged.

Interest rate swaps can be used to modify a firm's interest rate risk exposure without buying or selling assets. An **interest rate swap** is a contract entered into with a bank, in which the firm and the bank agree to exchange the coupons from two different types of loans. In a standard "fixed-for-floating interest rate swap" one party agrees to pay coupons based on a fixed interest rate in exchange for receiving floating rate coupons.

Selected Concepts and Key Terms

Currency Forward Contract

A contract that sets the exchange rate in advance that is usually written between a firm and a bank. In most settings the bank will enter into a second forward contract with offsetting risk to eliminate its risk.

Duration

Duration is a measure of an asset's sensitivity to interest rate changes; it can be calculated as:

$$\text{Duration} = \sum_t \frac{PV(C_t)}{P} \times t.$$

Duration Mismatch

When the durations of a firm's assets and liabilities are significantly different.

Duration-Neutral Portfolio, Immunized Portfolio

A portfolio with a duration of zero such that, for small interest rate fluctuations, the value of portfolio remains unchanged.

Forward Exchange Rate

The exchange rate set in a forward contract. By entering into a currency forward contract, a firm can lock in an exchange rate in advance and reduce or eliminate its exposure to fluctuations in a currency's value.

Futures Contract

An agreement to trade an asset on some future date at a price that is locked in today. Futures contracts are traded anonymously on an exchange at a publicly observed market price and are generally very liquid. Both the buyer and the seller can get out of the contract at any time by selling it to a third party at the current market price.

Interest Rate Swap

A contract entered into with a bank, much like a forward contract, in which the firm and the bank agree to exchange the coupons from two different types of loans. In a standard "fixed-for-floating interest rate swap" one party agrees to pay coupons based on a fixed interest rate in exchange for receiving floating rate coupons.

Natural Hedge

A condition in which an exposure to a risk is offset or partly offset by an opposite exposure to that risk factor or that can be passed on to on as a cost increase to its customers or revenue decreases to its suppliers.

Concept Check Questions and Answers

30.1.1. How can insurance add value to a firm?

The value of insurance comes from reducing the cost of market imperfections to the firm. Insurance may be beneficial to a firm because of its impact on bankruptcy and financial distress costs, issuance costs, taxes, debt capacity, and risk assessment.

30.1.2. Identify the costs of insurance that arise due to market imperfections.

The cost of insurance includes administrative and overhead costs, adverse selection, and moral hazard.

30.2.1. Discuss risk management strategies that firms use to hedge commodity price risk.

Firms use several risk management strategies to hedge commodity price risk.
1. Firms can make real investments in assets with offsetting risk using techniques such as vertical integration and storage.
2. Firms can enter long-term contracts with suppliers or customers to achieve price stability.
3. Firms can hedge risk by trading commodity futures contracts.

30.2.2. What are the potential risks associated with hedging using futures contracts?

Basis risk is the risk that arises because the value of a futures contract is not perfectly correlated with the firm's exposure.

30.3.1. How can firms hedge exchange rate risk?

Firms can hedge exchange rate risk in financial markets using currency forward contracts to lock in an exchange rate in advance, and currency option contracts to protect against an exchange rate moving beyond a certain level.

30.3.2. Why may a firm prefer to hedge exchange rate risk with options rather than forward contracts?

A firm prefers options to forward contracts when there is a chance that the transaction it hedges will not take place. In this case, a forward contract requires the firm to make an exchange at an unfavorable rate for the currency it does not need, whereas an option allows the firm to walk way from the exchange.

30.4.1. How do we calculate the duration of a portfolio?

The duration of a portfolio is the value-weighted average duration of each security in the portfolio.

30.4.2. How do firms manage interest rate risk?

Firms manage interest rate risk by buying or selling assets to make their equity duration neutral.

Examples with Step-by-Step Solutions

Solving Problems

Problems may require an understanding of how forward contracts can be used to eliminate exchange rate risk. You should also understand how to calculate the duration of a bond and understand the relation between duration and expected changes in value. Problems may also require the determination of an actuarially fair insurance premium, the pricing of currency options, and the process used in an interest rate swap.

Examples

1. On the first day of 2004, Espresso Parts Northwest (EPNW) ordered 2 million euros worth of Mazzer espresso grinders from the Italian manufacturer, Mazzer Luigi S.r.l. The payment in euros was due when the grinders were delivered in one year. The exchange rate at the beginning of the year was $1.05 per euro. On the last day of 2004, the exchange rate was $1.24 per euro.

   [A]   What was the actual cost in dollars for EPNW when the payment was due?

   [B]   If the price was set in dollars at the current exchange rate, how much would Mazzer receive in euros when the payment was due?

   [C]   At the beginning of 2004, banks were offering one-year currency forward contracts with a forward exchange rate of $1.03 per euro. Suppose that, when EPNW placed the order with Mazzer, it simultaneously hedged by entering into a forward contract to purchase 2 million euros at the forward exchange rate. What payment would EPNW be required to make when the payment was due?

   [D]   Should EPNW use the forward contract?

Step 1. Determine the cost in dollars of the unhedged euro payment.

With the price set at 2 million euros, EPNW had to pay:

($1.24/euro) × (2 million euros) = $2.48 million.

Step 2. Determine the value in euros to Mazzer of the unhedged dollar payment.

If the price had been set in dollars, EPNW would have paid:

($1.05/euro)/(2 million euros) = $2.1 million.

which would have been worth only $2.1 million/($1.24/euro) = 1.694 million euros to Mazzer.

Whether the price was set in euros or dollars, one of the parties would have suffered a substantial loss.

Step 3. Determine the value of the hedged payment to Mazzer.

Even though the exchange rate rose to $1.24 per euro at the end of the year making the euro more expensive, EPNW would obtain the 2 million euros using the forward contract at the forward exchange rate of $1.03 per euro.

Thus EPNW must pay:

2 million euros × $1.03/euro = $2.06 million in December 2003.

EPNW would pay this amount to the bank in exchange for 2 million euros, which are then paid to Mazzer.

Step 4. Determine if the forward contract is a good idea for EPNW.

This forward contract would have been a good deal for EPNW because without the hedge, it would have had to exchange dollars for euros at the prevailing rate of $1.24 per euro raising its cost to $2.48 million. However, the exchange rate could have moved the other way. If the exchange rate had fallen to $0.90 per euro, the forward contract still commits EPNW to pay $1.03 per euro.

So, the forward contract locks in the exchange rate and eliminates the risk, but it could turn out to be a good or bad deal depending on the change in the exchange rate. In addition, hedging may reduce the probability of financial distress and allow the managers to focus on running the firm without worrying about changes in the exchange rate.

2. **Your firm has the following bonds outstanding. All of the bonds have $1,000 face values; the coupon-paying bonds were issued yesterday at par, while the zero-coupon bond was issued yesterday at $713.**
   [A] **What is the duration of a 5-year bond with 8% annual coupons?**
   [B] **What is the duration of a 5-year bond with a 16% annual coupon rate?**
   [C] **What is the duration of a 5-year, zero-coupon bond?**
   [D] **Based on the bonds' durations, if the required return on each bond rose by 3%, approximately how much would the value of each bond change?**

Step 1. Determine the duration of the 8% coupon-paying bond.

You need to use the equation: duration = $\sum_t \dfrac{PV(C_t)}{P} \times t$.

Since the bond is selling at par, the yield to maturity is the same as the coupon rate and so the coupons should be discounted at 8% to find PV(C_t) each period.

Period (t)	C_t	PV(C_t)	PV(C_t)/P	PV(C_t)/P×t
1	80	74.07	7.41%	0.074
2	80	68.59	6.86%	0.137
3	80	63.51	6.35%	0.191
4	80	58.80	5.88%	0.235
5	1,080	735.03	73.50%	3.675

$$\text{Duration} = \sum_t \frac{PV(C_t)}{P} \times t = 4.31 \text{ years}$$

Step 2. Determine the duration of the 16% coupon-paying bond.

Since the bond is selling at par, the coupons should be discounted at the 16% to find PV(C_t) each period.

Period (t)	C_t	PV(C_t)	PV(C_t)/P	PV(C_t)/P×t
1	160	137.93	13.79%	0.138
2	160	118.91	11.89%	0.238
3	160	102.51	10.25%	0.308
4	160	88.37	8.84%	0.354
5	1,160	552.29	55.23%	2.76

$$\text{Duration} = \sum_t \frac{PV(C_t)}{P} \times t = 3.80 \text{ years.}$$

Step 3. Determine the duration of the zero-coupon bond.

For a zero-coupon bond, the yield to maturity is:

$$\$713 = \frac{\$1,000}{(1+r)^5} \Rightarrow r = 7\%.$$

There is only a single cash flow, and PV(C_t) = P, so:

$$\text{Duration} = \sum_t \frac{PV(C_t)}{P} \times t = \sum_t \frac{\$713}{\$713} \times 5 = 5 \text{ years}$$

Step 4. Determine the expected price changes if rates increase by 3%.

Using the fact that percent change in value $\approx -\text{Duration} \times \dfrac{\varepsilon}{1+r/k}$

For the 8% coupon bond:

$$\text{percent change in value} \approx -\text{Duration} \times \frac{\varepsilon}{1+r/k} = -4.31 \times \frac{0.03}{1.08} = -12.6\%$$

For the 16% coupon bond:

$$\text{percent change in value} \approx -\text{Duration} \times \frac{\varepsilon}{1+r/k} = -3.80 \times \frac{0.03}{1.16} = -9.8\%$$

For the 8% coupon bond:

$$\text{percent change in value} \approx -\text{Duration} \times \frac{\varepsilon}{1+r/k} = -5.0 \times \frac{0.03}{1.07} = -14.0\%$$

3. Your Savings and Loan has the following balance sheet in millions of dollars:

Assets		Liabilities	
Cash Reserves	50	Checking and Savings	100
Mortgages	900	Certificates of Deposit	100
Other Loans	50	Long-Term Financing	700
Total Assets	1,000	Total Liabilities	900
		Owner's Equity	100
		Total Liabilities and Equity	1,000

The duration of the mortgages is 20 years, and the other loans have a duration of 4 years. The cash reserves and the checking and savings accounts have a zero duration. The certificates of deposit have a duration of one year and the long-term financing has a 15-year duration.

[A] What is the duration of the S&L's equity?
[B] If interest rates fall from 6% to 5%, estimate the approximate change in the value of the S&L's equity.
[C] Suppose that before a change in interest rates, you manage risk by buying 30-year Treasury STRIPS. How many should the firm buy or sell to eliminate the interest rate risk?

Step 1. Determine how to calculate the duration of the equity.

The equity duration can be calculated as follows

$$D_{A+L} = \frac{A}{A+L}D_A + \frac{L}{A+L}D_L \text{ and Equity = Assets} - \text{Liabilities, so}$$

$$D_E = D_{A-L} = \frac{A}{A-L}D_A - \frac{L}{A-L}D_L$$

Step 2. Calculate the duration of the equity.

$$\text{Asset Duration} = \frac{50}{1,000}(0 \text{ years}) + \frac{900}{1,000}(20 \text{ years}) + \frac{50}{1,000}(4 \text{ years}) = 18.2 \text{ years}$$

$$\text{Liability Duration} = \frac{100}{900}(0 \text{ years}) + \frac{100}{900}(1 \text{ year}) + \frac{700}{900}(15 \text{ years}) = 11.8 \text{ years}$$

$$\text{Equity Duration} = \frac{A}{A-L}D_A - \frac{L}{A-L}D_L = \frac{1,000}{100}18.2 - \frac{900}{100}11.8 = 75.8$$

Step 3. Determine the expected change in equity value if interest rates fall from 6% to 5%.

$$\text{Percent change in value} \approx -\text{Duration} \times \frac{\varepsilon}{1+r/k} = -75.8 \times \frac{0.01}{1.06} = -72\%$$

If interest rates drop by 1%, you would expect the value of the S&L's equity to drop by about 72% to $28 million from $100 million.

Step 4. Determine how many 30-year Treasury STRIPS the firm should buy or sell to eliminate the interest rate risk.

You would like to increase the duration of the assets, so you should buy long-term bonds. Because 30-year STRIPS are zero-coupon bonds they have a 30-year duration. Using Eq. 30.10:

$$\text{Amount to Exchange} = \frac{\Delta \text{ in Portfolio Duration} \times \text{Portfolio Value}}{\Delta \text{ in Asset duration}}$$

$$= \frac{\overbrace{(75.6)}^{\text{change in equity duration}} \times \overbrace{100}^{\text{equity value}}}{\underbrace{30}_{\text{duration of STRIPS (vs. cash)}}} = 252.$$

Thus, you would need to buy $252 million worth of 30-year STRIPS.

Questions and Problems

1. Suppose the current exchange rate is $1.20/euro. The interest rate in the United States is 5%, the interest rate in the United Kingdom is 4.0%, and the volatility of the $/euro exchange rate is 10%. Use the Black-Scholes formula to determine the price of a six-month European call option on the British pound with a strike price of $1.20/euro.

2. Carnival Cruise Lines operates 79 cruise ships around the world. They are looking to insure a new ship for the next year for its replacement cost of $100 million. Suppose the likelihood of such a loss is 0.5%, the risk-free interest rate is 5%, and the expected return on the market is 12%. If the risk has a beta of zero, what is the actuarially fair insurance premium? What is the premium if the beta is –0.5?

3. A coffee roaster will need 10,000 pounds of coffee beans in one year. The current market price of green coffee beans is $2 per pound. At this price, the firm expects earnings before interest and taxes of $100,000 next year.
   [A]   What will the firm's EBIT be if the price of coffee beans rises to $3 per pound?
   [B]   What will EBIT be if the firm enters into a supply contract for coffee beans for a fixed price of $2.10 per ton?

4. What other methods, besides the long-term contract, could the coffee roaster in problem 3 use to reduce risk?

5. Your firm needs to raise $50 million in debt financing. You can borrow short term at a spread of 150 basis points over LIBOR. Alternatively, you can issue ten-year, fixed-rate bonds at a spread of 2.50% over ten-year Treasuries, which currently yield 8%. Current ten-year interest rate swaps are quoted at LIBOR versus the 7% fixed rate. Management believes that the firm's credit rating is likely to improve in the next two years. How can the managers use an interest rate swap to reduce interest rate risk and still maintain the flexibility to take advantage of any improvement in their credit quality?

Solutions to Questions and Problems

1. The inputs are S = spot exchange rate = 1.20, K = strike price = 1.20, T = 0.5, $r_\$$ = 5%, $r_\pounds$ = 4.0%, σ = volatility = 10%. From Eq. 30.3,

$F_T = S(1 + r_\$)^T / (1 + r_\pounds)^T = 1.20(1.05)^{0.5} / (1.04)^{0.5} = \$1.15/\text{euro}$

Therefore, from Eq. 30.5

$$d_1 = \frac{\ln[F_T / K)]}{\sigma\sqrt{T}} + \frac{\sigma\sqrt{T}}{2} = \frac{\ln(1.15 / 1.20)}{0.10\sqrt{0.5}} + \frac{0.10\sqrt{0.5}}{2} = -0.60 + 0.04 = -0.56,$$

and $d_2 = -0.56 - 0.10\sqrt{0.5} = -0.63$

Using the NORMSDIST function in Excel:

$N(d_1)$: = NORMSDIST(-0.56) = 0.29

$N(d_2)$: = NORMSDIST(-0.63) = 0.26

From Eq. 30.4,

C = (1.20 / (1.04)$^{0.5}$) × (0.29) – (1.20 / (1.05)$^{0.5}$) × (0.26) = $0.34 – .30

Thus, the call option price is $0.04/euro.

2. The expected loss is:

Pr(Loss) × E[Payment in the event of a loss] = 0.005 × $100 million = $500,000.

When the beta is 0 then r_L, the appropriate cost of capital for the risk of the loss, is the risk free rate of 5%.

Thus, the actuarially fair premium is:

$$\text{Insurance Premium} = \frac{\text{Pr(Loss)} \times E[\text{Payment in the event of a loss}]}{1 + r_L} = \frac{\$500,000}{1.05} = \$476,191.$$

When the beta is –0.5 then r_L is:

$r_L = r_f + \beta_i^{Mkt}(E[R_{Mkt}] - r_f)$ = 5% + –0.5(12% – 5%) = 1.5%.

Thus, the actuarially fair premium is:

$$\text{Insurance Premium} = \frac{\text{Pr(Loss)} \times E[\text{Payment in the event of a loss}]}{1 + r_L} = \frac{\$500,000}{1.015} = \$492,611.$$

3. [A] If the price of cocoa beans increases to $3 per ton, the firm's costs will increase by 10,000 × $1 = $10,000. All else equal, EBIT will decline to $90,000.

   [B] If the firm enters into the supply contract the firm's costs will increase by 10,000 × $0.10 = $1,000. All else equal, EBIT will decline to $99,000.

4. It can use vertical integration by purchasing a coffee bean farm, it can buy more today and store the beans for the year, or it can and hedge risk by trading commodity futures contracts.

5. They can borrow the $50 million short term paying LIBOR + 1.5% and then enter a $50 million notional swap to receive LIBOR and pay a 7% fixed rate.

   The effective borrowing rate is (LIBOR + 1.5%) – LIBOR + 7% = 8.5%.

   This is better than borrowing long-term which would have cost 8% + 2.5% = 10.5%.

CHAPTER 31

International Corporate Finance

Chapter Synopsis

31.1 Internationally Integrated Capital Markets

Two countries' capital markets are **internationally integrated** when an investor in either country can exchange either currency in any amount at the spot rate or forward rate and is free to purchase or sell any security in any amount in either country at their current market prices.

Consider a risky foreign asset in an internationally integrated market that is expected to pay the foreign currency cash flow C_{FC} in one period. In a competitive market, the price of this asset in a foreign market is the present value of this cash flow using r_{FC} the cost of capital of a local investor:

$$PV = \frac{C_{FC}}{(1 + r_{FC})}$$

A U.S. investor who wants to purchase this asset in dollars will have to pay:

$$S \times \frac{C_{FC}}{(1 + r_{FC})}$$

where S is current spot exchange rate in dollars into the foreign currency.

To value this cash flow, assume that the U.S. investor contracts today to convert the expected cash flow in one period at the forward rate, F, quoted as dollars per foreign currency. The present value of this expected cash flow is:

$$\frac{F \times C_{FC}}{(1 + r_{\$})}$$

where $r_{\$}$ is the appropriate cost of capital from the standpoint of a U.S. investor.

By the Law of One Price, this value must be equal to what the U.S. investor paid for the security:

$$S \times \frac{C_{FC}}{(1 + r_{FC})} = \frac{F \times C_{FC}}{(1 + r_\$)} \Rightarrow F = \frac{(1 + r_\$)}{(1 + r_{FC})} \times S$$

which is called covered interest parity.

31.2 Valuation of Foreign Currency Cash Flows

In an internationally integrated capital market, two equivalent methods are available for calculating the NPV of a foreign project.

1. You can calculate the NPV in the foreign country and convert it to the local currency at the spot rate, or

2. You can convert the cash flows of the foreign project into the local currency and then calculate the NPV of these cash flows.

When using the second method, the foreign cost of capital in terms of the domestic cost of capital and interest rates is:

$$r_{FC} = \frac{1 + r_{FC}}{1 + r_\$}\left(1 + r_\$\right) - 1$$

31.3 Valuation and International Taxation

Determining the corporate tax rate on foreign income is complicated because corporate income taxes must be paid to two national governments: the host government and the home government. If the foreign project is a separately incorporated subsidiary of the parent, the amount of taxes a firm pays generally depends on the amount of profits **repatriated** and brought back to the home country.

U.S. tax policy requires U.S. corporations to pay taxes on their foreign income at the same rate as profits earned in the United States. However, a full tax credit is given for foreign taxes paid up to the amount of the U.S. tax liability. If the foreign tax rate exceeds the U.S. tax rate, companies must pay this higher rate on foreign earnings.

Under U.S. tax law, multinational corporations may use any excess tax credits generated in high-tax foreign countries to offset their net U.S. tax liabilities on earnings in low-tax foreign countries. Thus, if the U.S. tax rate exceeds the combined tax rate on all foreign income, it is valid to assume that the firm pays the same tax rate on all income no matter where it is earned. Otherwise, the firm must pay a higher tax rate on its foreign income.

When the foreign tax rate is less than the U.S. tax rate, deferring the repatriation lowers the overall tax burden in much the same way as deferring capital gains lowers the tax burden imposed by the capital gains tax.

31.4 Internationally Segmented Capital Markets

Segmented capital markets occur when all investors do not have equal access to financial securities in different capital markets.

In some cases, a country's risk-free securities are internationally integrated but markets for a specific firm's securities are not. Firms may face differential access to markets if there is any kind of asymmetry with respect to information about them. Using a currency swap, a firm can borrow in the market where it has the best access to capital, and then "swap" the coupon and principal payments to whichever currency it would prefer to make its payments in. Thus, swaps allow firms to mitigate their exchange rate risk exposure between assets and liabilities, while still making investments and raising funds in the most attractive locales.

When capital markets are internationally segmented, the important implication is that one country or currency has a higher cost of capital than another country or currency when the two are compared in the same currency. If the return difference results from a market friction such as capital controls, corporations can exploit this friction by setting up projects in the high-return country/currency and raising capital in the low-return country/currency.

31.5 Capital Budgeting with Exchange Risk

Many firms use imported inputs in their production processes or export some of their output to foreign countries. These scenarios alter the nature of a project's foreign exchange risk and, in turn, change the valuation of the foreign currency cash flows.

Whenever a project has cash flows that depend on the values of multiple currencies, the most convenient approach is to separate the cash flows according to the currency they depend on. To correctly value such projects, the foreign and domestic cash flows should be valued separately.

Selected Concepts and Key Terms

Currency Swaps

An arrangement in which the holder receives coupons in one currency and pays coupons and the final face value denominated in a different currency. Using a currency swap, a firm can borrow in the market where it has the best access to capital, and then "swap" the coupon and principal payments to whichever currency it would prefer to make payments in. Thus, swaps allow firms to mitigate their exchange rate risk exposure between assets and liabilities, while still making investments and raising funds in the most attractive locales.

Internationally Integrated Capital Market

International markets in which any investor can exchange any currency in any amount at the spot rate or forward rates and is free to purchase or sell any security in any amount in any country at their current market prices.

Repatriated Profits

Firm profits that are brought back to the home country from a foreign country.

Segmented Capital Markets

International markets in which all investors do not have equal access to financial securities. In some cases, a country's risk-free securities are internationally integrated but markets for a specific firm's securities are not.

Concept Check Questions and Answers

31.1.1. What assumptions are necessary for internationally integrated capital markets?

We make the following assumptions: any investor can exchange either currency in any amount at the spot rate or forward rate and is free to purchase or sell any security in any amount in either country at their current market prices.

31.1.2. What implication do internationally integrated capital markets have for the value of the same asset in different countries?

The condition for internationally integrated capital markets is that the value of a foreign investment does not depend on the currency (home or foreign) we use in the analysis.

31.2.1. Explain two methods we use to calculate the NPV of a foreign project.

We can calculate the NPV of a foreign project using two different methods. We can calculate the NPV in the foreign country and convert it to local currency at the spot rate. Alternatively, we can convert the cash flows of the foreign project into local currency and then calculate the NPV of these cash flows.

31.2.2. When do these two methods give the same NPV of the foreign project?

The two methods give the same NPV of a foreign project when markets are internationally integrated and uncertainty in spot exchange rates are uncorrelated with the foreign currency cash flows.

31.3.1. What tax rate should we use to value a foreign project?

Because a U.S. corporation pays the higher of the foreign or domestic tax rate on its foreign project, we should use the higher of these two rates to value a foreign project.

31.3.2. How can a U.S. firm lower its taxes on foreign projects?

A U.S. firm can lower its taxes by having foreign projects in other countries that can be pooled with the new project or by deferring the repatriation of earnings.

31.4.1. What is the main implication for international corporate finance of a segmented financial market?

The implication for international corporate finance of a segmented financial market is that one country or currency has a higher rate of return than another, when compared in the same currency.

31.4.2. What are the reasons for segmentation of the capital markets?

Some of the reasons for market segmentation are:
1. A country's risk-free securities are internationally integrated but markets for specific firm's securities are not;
2. Some countries impose capital control or foreign exchange controls that create barriers to international capital flows.

31.5.1. What conditions cause the cash flows of a foreign project to be affected by exchange rate risk?

To correctly value projects that have inputs and outputs in different currencies, the foreign and domestic cash flows should be valued separately.

31.5.2. How do we make adjustments when a project has inputs and outputs in different currencies?

When a project has inputs and outputs in different currencies, the foreign denominated cash flows are likely to be correlated with changes in spot rates.

Examples with Step-by-Step Solutions

Solving Problems

Problems using the ideas in this chapter may require valuing foreign currency cash flows and an understanding of forward exchange rates—with internationally integrated capital markets, the forward rate given by covered interest parity; with internationally segmented capital markets, the forward rate may be different. You should also be able to determine the NPV of a foreign project. Finally, problems may involve determining the tax effects of repatriating international earnings.

Examples

1. The spot yen-dollar exchange rate is ¥110/$ and the one-year forward rate is ¥106.8571/$. The appropriate dollar cost of capital is $r_\$ = 5\%$ and the appropriate yen cost of capital for is $r = 2\%$.

   [A] What is the present value of a ¥20 million cash flow to a Japanese corporation in one year? What is the dollar equivalent of this amount?

   [B] What is the present value of a ¥20 million cash flow for a U.S. corporation who first converts the ¥20 million into dollars and then applies the dollar discount rate?

Step 1. Find the present value of the yen cash flow to a Japanese corporation.

This can be found by discounting the yen cash flow at the yen cost of capital:

$$PV = \frac{¥20 \text{ million}}{1.02} = ¥19,607,843.$$

Step 2. Find the dollar equivalent.

Using the current spot rate, S = ¥110/$:

$$\text{Dollar equivalent} = S \times \frac{C_{FC}}{(1+r_{FC})} = \frac{\$1}{¥110} \times ¥19,607,843 = \$178,253.$$

Step 3. Find the present value of a ¥20 million cash flow for a U.S. corporation who first converts the ¥20 million into dollars and then applies the dollar discount rate.

First, using the forward rate:

$$\text{Dollar equivalent} = \frac{¥20 \text{ million}}{106.8571} = \$187,166.$$

Then, using the dollar cost of capital:

$$PV = \frac{\$187,166}{1.05} = 178,253.$$

Because the U.S. and Japanese capital markets are internationally integrated,

$$F = \frac{(1 + r_{¥})}{(1 + r_{\$})} \times S = \frac{(1.02)}{(1.05)} \times 110 = 106.8571$$

and both methods produce the same result.

2. Your U.S. firm is considering a new project in Spain with expected free cash flows in euros of:

Year	Free cash Flow in millions of €
0	−100
1	20
2	70
3	40

The spot exchange rate is $1.26 per euro, the risk-free interest rate in dollars is 5% and the risk-free interest rate on euros is 7%. The dollar WACC for these cash flows is 10%. What is the dollar present value of the project?

Step 1. To utilize the home currency approach, first calculate the forward rates:

$$F_1 = (\$1.26/€)\frac{(1.05)}{(1.07)} = \$1.2364/€$$

$$F_2 = (\$1.26/€)\frac{(1.05)^2}{(1.07)^2} = \$1.2133/€$$

$$F_3 = (\$1.26/€)\frac{(1.05)^3}{(1.07)^3} = \$1.1907/€$$

Step 2. Next, convert euro cash flows into dollars:

Year	Euro Cash Flow	Exchange Rate	Dollar Cash Flow
0	−100	1.2600	−126
1	20	1.2364	24.728
2	70	1.2133	84.931
3	40	1.1907	47.628

Step 3. Finally, the net present value can be calculated:

$$\text{NPV} = -126 + \frac{24.728}{1.10} + \frac{84.931}{1.10^2} + \frac{47.628}{1.10^3} = \$2.45 \text{ million}$$

Step 4. Note that the foreign currency approach can be used. The euro cost of capital can be calculated using the International Fisher Effect as:

$$R_{FC} = \frac{(1 + r_{FC})}{(1 + r_{\$})} \times (1 + R_{\$}) - 1 = \frac{(1.07)}{(1.05)} \times 1.10 = 12.1\%$$

Step 5. The NPV in the foreign currency can be determined as:

$$NPV = -100 + \frac{20}{1.121} + \frac{70}{1.121^2} + \frac{40}{1.121^3} = 1.94 \text{ million euros}$$

Converted back to dollars at the spot rate, the NPV is 1.94(1.26)=$2.44 million.

Thus both methods provide the same result (the difference is due to rounding).

3. **Starbucks, a U.S. company, is considering vertically integrating by acquiring La Marzocco S.r.l., an espresso machine manufacturer in Italy. The acquisition is expected to increase Starbucks' free cash flows by 50 million euros the first year. The free cash flow is expected to grow at a rate of 4% per year from then on. The acquisition would cost $1 billion euros and the current exchange rate of $1.25 per euro. Starbucks believes that the appropriate after-tax euro WACC is 10% and that its after-tax dollar WACC for this expansion is 8%. Assume that the markets for risk-free securities are integrated and that the yield curve in both countries is flat. U.S. risk-free interest rates are 5%, and euro risk-free interest rates are 7%.**
   [A]   **What is the value of La Marzocco to Starbucks in terms of euro cash flows?**
   [B]   **What is the value of La Marzocco to Starbucks in terms of dollar cash flows?**
   [C]   **Which valuation method is better? What should they do?**

Step 1. Calculate the value of the deal in euros.

First, determine the cash flows:

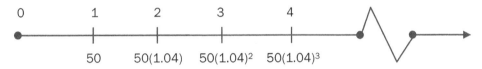

Next, determine the value of the future expected cash flows, which are a growing perpetuity:

$$\text{Value} = \frac{50}{0.10 - 0.04} = 833 \text{ million euros}$$

So, the NPV is –1 billion + 833 million = –167 million euros.

The NPV converted to dollars at the spot rate is:

$$-167 \text{ million euros} \times \frac{\$1.25}{1 \text{ euro}} = -\$209 \text{ million}$$

Step 2. Convert the cash flows to dollars using i-year forward rates.

From the relation in chapter 30:

$$\underbrace{F_T}_{\substack{\$ \text{ in } T \text{ years} \\ \text{€ in } T \text{ years}}} = \underbrace{S}_{\substack{\$ \text{ today} \\ \text{€ today}}} \times \underbrace{\frac{\left(1 + r_\$\right)^T}{\left(1 + r_\text{€}\right)^T}}_{\substack{\$ \text{ in } T \text{ years}/\$ \text{ today} \\ \text{€ in } T \text{ years}/\text{€ today}}}$$

$$F_T = 1.25 \times \left(\frac{1.05}{1.07}\right)^T = 1.25 \times 0.9813^T = 1.2266 \times 0.9813^{T-1}$$

Thus, the dollar expected cash flows are:

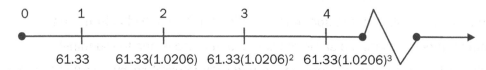

$$C_\epsilon^T \times F_T = 50(1.04)^{T-1} \times \left(1.2266 \times 0.9813^{T-1}\right) = 61.33 \times 1.0206^{T-1}$$

0	1	2	3	4	
	61.33	61.33(1.0206)	61.33(1.0206)²	61.33(1.0206)³	

So the dollar cash flows are expected to grow at 2.06% per year.

Step 3. Calculate the NPV in dollar cash flows.

First, find the present value of the future cash flows:

$$\text{Value} = \frac{61.33}{0.08 - 0.0206} = \$1.032 \text{ billion}$$

The up front investment is:

$$1 \text{ billion euros} \times \frac{\$1.25}{1 \text{ euro}} = \$1.25 \text{ billion}$$

So, the NPV is –$1.250 billion + $1.032 million = –$218 million.

Step 4. Make a conclusion.

Note that the dollar NPV calculated with dollar cash flows is a bit lower than the euro cash flow NPV, but they are pretty close.

Which NPV more accurately represents the benefits of the expansion?

Both methods have potential sources of estimation error. To compute the dollar expected cash flows by converting the euro expected cash flows at the forward rate, the implicit assumption that spot rates and the project cash flows are uncorrelated. The difference might simply reflect that this assumption failed to hold. Another possibility is that the difference reflects estimation error in the respective WACC estimates.

In any case, the NPV is negative, and the forecasts do not suggest that it is a good deal for Starbucks.

Questions and Problems

1. Your company is considering an investment in Japan. Your dollar cost of equity is 10%, and you are trying to determine the comparable cost of equity in Japanese yen for a project with free cash flows that are uncorrelated with spot exchange rates. The risk-free interest rate in the United States is 6%, and the risk-free interest rate in Japanese yen is 2%. You believe that, in this case, capital markets are internationally integrated. What is the yen cost of equity?

2. Intel has a subsidiary in China. This year, the subsidiary reported and repatriated earnings before interest and taxes (EBIT) of 1 billion Chinese yuan. The current fixed exchange rate is $7.896 per yuan. The Chinese tax rate on this activity is 33%. U.S. tax law requires Intel to pay taxes on the Chinese earnings at the same rate as profits earned in the United States, which is currently 35%. However, the United States gives a full tax credit for foreign taxes

$$\frac{100{,}000 \text{ peso}}{\left(\dfrac{2{,}323 \text{ pesos}}{\$1}\right)} \times \frac{\$1.04 \text{ in one year}}{\$1 \text{ today}} \times \frac{2{,}477 \text{ pesos}}{\$1 \text{ in one year}} = 110{,}895 \text{ pesos in one year}$$

for an effective peso risk-free rate of 10.895%.